JOHN BAILEY'S FI

WHER
FISH
IN BRITAIN & IRELAND

FLY FISHING · COARSE FISHING · SEA FISHING

John Bailey

SB

Published by Silverdale Books, an imprint of Bookmart Ltd in 2003

Bookmart Ltd,
Desford Road, Enderby,
Leicester LE19 4AD

ISBN 1 85605 798 4

Edited and designed by Design Revolution Limited,
Queens Park Villa, 30 West Drive, Brighton BN2 0QW
Project Editor: Ian Whitelaw
Design: Gülen Shevki, Lindsey Johns, Andrew Easton
Concept Designer: Andrew Easton
Editor: Julie Whitaker

Index by Indexing Specialists,
202 Church Road, Hove BN3 2DJ

Publishing Manager: Jo Hemmings
Senior Editor: Kate Michell
Assistant Editor: Rose Hudson
Production Controller: Joan Woodroffe

Reproduction by Pica Digital Pte Ltd, Singapore
Printed and bound in Malaysia by Times Offset (M) Sdn Bhd

Contents

Contents

Contents

Introduction

This book has several objectives. It may well find its home in the glove compartment of your car, waiting to be taken out when you find yourself in an unfamiliar part of the British Isles with some time for fishing. You'll be able to look up the particular area and pick the right water, and hopefully you'll have a great day. You should do, because all these locations have been hand-picked, and each one is a favourite of mine or of a friend whose word I trust implicitly.

It could be that you are taking up fishing as a relative newcomer and you just want a few pointers to good, accessible waters in your own area. Once again, I'm pretty sure you'll find an ideal place – somewhere to fit your level of expertise perfectly. Even for the experienced angler who knows his or her home area well, I hope that this book may reveal some new venues and some good sport.

I'm particularly pleased that this book brings together fly, coarse and sea fishing, because it's my firm belief that the boundaries between these branches of the sport are melting away, and helping this process is another of this book's objectives. If you are inspired to experiment beyond your chosen area, then that goal will have been achieved. More and more coarse and sea anglers are picking up a fly rod, either for game fish or for their own chosen quarry, be it pike, roach, mackerel or sea bass, and the sport it provides is terrific. Dyed-in-the-wool fly anglers are now targeting saltwater species, too, and many are discovering the delights of fishing with bait or a lure. Fishing is fishing, and the more kinds you can enjoy, the better.

Tackle and Techniques

As well as details of specific locations, I've included as many practical hints and tips as possible. Sometimes, on a strange water particularly, you just need that slightest of nudges in the right direction. You might be doing nearly everything right, but it's the last few steps that turn potential into actual bites. What's more, a few tips breed confidence, and without confidence you just won't catch. I don't know why that should be, but it's true.

For the Fly Fisher

The great thing about fly fishing is its simplicity. A rod, a reel, a few flies, polarising glasses, Wellingtons and you're off. You can pop your outfit in the car boot and travel to any point of the compass, knowing that if you find yourself near a water with a few hours on your hands, then you're ready to go. Two hours or eight hours, it doesn't really make a lot of difference. Unlike coarse fishing, you don't need to prepare bait, feed up a swim or anything like that... no, once the fly is on the tippet and in the water, you stand a good chance of a fish, and that can be within two minutes of leaving the car-park.

Whatever particular branch of fly fishing you're into, hopefully there will be plenty for you here. I've covered all parts of the country and all types of fishing, from commercial ponds outside London to deserted moorland lochs. You'll find waters for salmon, sea trout, wild brown trout, stocked rainbows, grayling and even the odd mullet and bass. So, whether you're urban or rural, north or south, still water or river, there will be an entry that makes the nerves tingle!

For the Coarse Angler

Here I've tried to include all types of waters – wild, difficult, challenging ones, as well as the new breed of commercial fisheries: generally small waters that are heavily stocked and have great facilities. They may not set quite as much of a problem as the big, natural lakes and rivers, but you've still got to winkle the fish out, and that isn't always easy.

As a coarse angler, you may well get to know a particular stretch of water like the back of your hand, and you are in a prime position to act as a guardian of the waterways. If you spot a problem with wildlife, contact one or more of these agencies: the RSPCA on 08705 555999; the Wildlife Hospital Trust on 01844 292292; or the National Swan Sanctuary on 01784 431667.

Keep your eyes open for any signs of fish dying inexplicably or other signs of pollution. If you sense there is something wrong with the water you are fishing, phone the Environment Agency Hotline on 0800 807060. The work of the Environment Agency is augmented by the Anglers' Conservation Association, which fights vigorously against water pollution. All serious anglers should become members, so phone for details on 01189 714770.

For the Sea Angler

During my research I spoke to innumerable sea anglers from every part of the United Kingdom. There were some laments for times past, when stocks of some fish, cod especially, were far better than they are now, but on the whole there is a healthy optimism, and certainly great praise for the wealth and variety of fishing that there is to be enjoyed around our spectacular coastline.

One interesting side-effect of global warming appears to be a wider variety of fish visiting our shores. In this book, for example, you'll read about the possibilities of tuna off the Irish coast, and I have recently heard rumours of sailfish off the Lincolnshire coast and a barracuda caught in an offshore net. Who knows, a bonefish could be taking your fly in a shallow Devonshire cove next summer!

Our native fish also seem to be on the increase. Bass are a good example – not only are numbers apparently increasing in their well-known hotspots, but they are also appearing in good numbers along stretches of coast that scarcely had a bass run at all in the past. Sea trout also appear to be making some sort of recovery after a worrying absence in many areas, and mullet once again appear to be visiting our shores in ever-increasing numbers during the summer. All in all, this is a very good time for the sea angler to be trying out new marks and new species.

Good Luck

In these pages, you'll find some of my favourite fishing waters, venues I love to go to and enjoy. I doubt whether I'm passing on anything that the local expert won't know, but I hope I'm offering signposts to the thousands of anglers who like to travel and face fresh challenges. Hopefully, this book will enhance your fishing and, who knows, perhaps one day soon we'll meet up, share some angling tales, and you can put me onto the right fly, bait or lure for the day. Tight lines.

MAP OF BRITAIN & IRELAND

WHERE TO FLY FISH

Fly-Fishing Sites in the South West

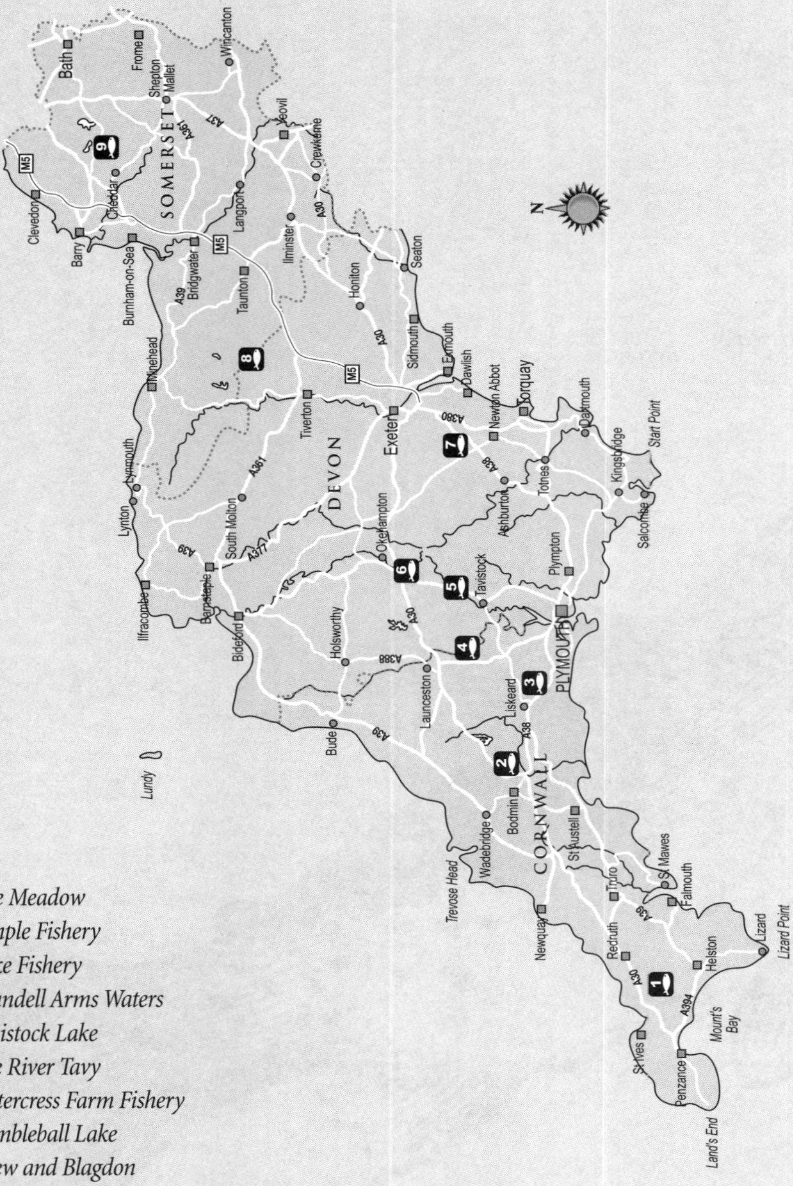

1. Tree Meadow
2. Temple Fishery
3. Bake Fishery
4. Arundell Arms Waters
5. Tavistock Lake
6. The River Tavy
7. Watercress Farm Fishery
8. Wimbleball Lake
9. Chew and Blagdon

The South West

The rivers of the West Country are unique. There are over sixty of them in the three counties of Somerset, Devon and Cornwall, running down from the great uplands of Exmoor, Dartmoor and Bodmin – wild unspoilt rivers that the French would call "primitif". All of them hold abundant brown trout, and many have big runs of salmon and sea trout. This is a part of England where kingfishers and buzzards still fly, where you can fish all day and see no-one, where the rivers are still clean and full of life and sparkle.

ANNE VOSS BARK, OWNER OF THE ARUNDELL ARMS AND REVERED FLY FISHER

Anne is quite right. There is something uniquely special about fly fishing in the West Country on rivers that dance along, simply singing out to you, 'Fish me, fish me, please'. It sometimes seems that every valley is gushing with water, generally crystal clear, and frequently full of fish. Perhaps the sea trout runs – 'peal' as they call them in these parts – aren't quite what they once were, but there are still fish aplenty, and in surroundings that you'll never forget.

But there's more. Anybody who has fished Chew, Blagdon or the heart-stoppingly beautiful Wimbleball can tell you that. Wimbleball is probably my personal favourite, nestling in the most beautiful countryside. And still more. The West Country is fortunate in having some top-class commercial fisheries; the standard, in my view, is probably higher than in any other part of the country. So there really is something here for everybody. What's more, if you fancy it and you're up to it, there's even fly fishing around the coast for the king of the inshore waters, the bass.

The South West is a holiday paradise. It offers everything for the whole family. There are beautiful beaches and rugged coves. You can visit quaint villages or thriving market towns. You can explore the moors, walk the coastal paths or visit the old properties and exciting gardens open to the general public. But, above all, don't forget to bring that fishing rod!

Tree Meadow – Cornwall

I'll never forget my first – and, it has to be said, only – visit to Tree Meadow. The water is just beautiful, the fish are spectacular and the fishing itself is so thrilling, it's an expedition I'll never forget. Tree Meadow is a stunning place, surrounded by woods and fields, and you're so far south-west that you really can believe you're in another world. Certainly, it's a world that grips you totally since the fish are big, the water is clear and the whole experience is utterly fascinating. Tree Meadow comprises the larger Willow Lake and the smaller Sedge Lake, and they're both fabulously rich in natural food stocks – one of the things that accounts for both the browns and the rainbows being in such excellent condition.

There are some very large fish around, and double-figure rainbows are not rare by any stretch of the imagination, so don't consider using leaders less than five pounds in weight. This is very much a stalking water, so don't forget your peaked cap and your Polaroids and all the usual imitative patterns. Dry fly often works – try hawthorn, black gnat, sedges, daddies and so on. Buzzers, too, work very well indeed, and if you don't see fish moving on the surface, damsels, corixa, shrimps and beetles will all catch their fair share of fish. Nowhere are the lakes much over twelve to fifteen feet in depth, so the chances are that a floating line is pretty much the only thing you'll need all day

Catch and Release

Catch and release is rightfully a growing trend. However, there is no point in putting back a fish that is condemned to die a slow, lingering death because of bad handling. To avoid harming a fish, follow these rules:

- *Always fish with barbless hooks for easy release.*
- *Try to avoid taking a fish from the water at all if you possibly can. Unhook it in the margins.*
- *Never touch a fish with dry hands.*
- *Play a fish quickly and firmly – though not ruthlessly – so it is not exhausted in the battle.*
- *Never use unnecessarily light leaders as this simply prolongs the fight and increases the chance of a break-off.*
- *Always carry forceps with you for quick and easy unhooking.*
- *Hold the fish upright, into a current if possible, until it is strong enough to swim away. A fish that sinks to the bottom on its back will drown.*
- *If a fish is deep hooked and appears to be bleeding, in all probability it's best to kill it as quickly and cleanly as possible.*

long, though at times, in very hot weather, it does pay to put on a long leader and get down deep.

You're pretty well assured of a lovely day's fishing at Tree Meadow in beautiful surroundings, and a very warm and generous welcome.

Season – open all year.
Tickets – write to Tree Meadow, Deveral Road, Fraddam, Hayle, Cornwall. On Willow Lake, a day ticket costs £35 for four fish and £21 for two fish. You can practise catch and release on Sedge Lake for a £20 day ticket or an evening ticket of £15.
Records – rainbows 17lb 8oz and browns 10lb 7oz.
Directions – leave the A30 for Hayle and drive through the town until you come to a mini-roundabout before a viaduct. Take the first left off this roundabout onto the B3302. You will reach Fraddam village. Take the next left, signposted Deveral Road. Tree Meadow Fishery is about a mile on the right.
Accommodation – phone the Tourist Information Centre at St Ives on 01736 796297 for information on accommodation in the area.

Temple Fishery – Cornwall

Temple Fishery is beautifully situated, especially Mallard Lake. This lake is an old china clay pit, which has matured totally and now blends seamlessly into the landscape of Bodmin Moor. There are now actually two lakes in the fishery. Mallard has an area of almost three acres and is up to forty feet deep with a twenty-five foot average. Teal Lake is larger, at four and a half acres, but shallower. The deepest holes there are fifteen feet, with an average of eight feet.

Both waters are very well cared for indeed, but the abundant vegetation really does foster a feeling of privacy, that the waters are your very own. The waters are largely spring-fed but this doesn't stop them having a slightly peaty tinge to them – remember that they are dug into the bowels of the moor itself. They're both rich lakes and this probably explains why the owner, Julian Jones, recommends damsel nymphs and especially buzzers, of which the lakes have big hatches. Also, over the last couple of years, mayfly have been seen in increasing numbers and there's every chance of a really significant hatch in the near future.

Obviously, the two different lakes can demand different approaches – especially on really bright, hot days when the fish have the ability to get down really deep in Mallard Lake. It's then that a fast-sinking line really comes into its own with perhaps a larger fly such as the Montana or a Woolly Bugger. The best strategy is to retrieve very slowly and to give the fish plenty of time to see what's going on. One last tip – Bodmin is no stranger to gusty winds, and this often produces a build-up of terrestrials. At the right times of the year, daddy patterns work exceedingly well.

SEASON – open all year.

TICKETS – phone Julian on 01208 821730 for prior booking or write to Temple Trout Fishery, Temple Road, Bodmin, Cornwall. There are two different price structures. On Teal Lake, a five-fish limit costs £12. This is because the stocked fish are smaller than on Mallard – averaging just a pound or so. On Mallard, a five-fish limit costs £20.50 and the stocked fish average one and a half to two pounds with some very big fish present.

DIRECTIONS – if you're travelling west across Bodmin Moor on the A30, Temple Fishery is about four miles past the Jamaica Inn on the left side of the road. It is very well signposted.

ACCOMMODATION – Bodmin is close by and both the north and south Cornish coasts are easily accessible. Phone the Tourist Information Centre in Bodmin on 01208 76616 for further details.

BAKE FISHERY – CORNWALL

Right down in Cornwall you'll find the excellently run Bake Fishery, which has three trout lakes set in lovely, rolling countryside. In all, there are about eight acres of water to be fished, but the great thing is that under nearly all conditions you'll find fish on or near the surface, so chances are that all you'll need is a floating line, a selection of dry flies (black gnats and grey dusters are favourites), some buzzers, emergers, goldheads and nymphs. Yes, this is exciting hands-on fishing. The rainbows themselves are exciting, too: the hallmarks of a Bake fish are a full set of fins and a rainbow that really powers off. My own advice is to purchase one of the 'rover' tickets, as this allows you to move around freely, swappng from one lake to another and really exploring everything the fishery has to offer.

There is some catch and release allowed – something I'm personally very much in favour of. It allows fish to grow on and mature and also to develop a cunning that makes them a very serious challenge to the angler indeed. You're just beginning to think that the fish in front of you have seen it all before when suddenly your buzzer is taken, your line zaps a couple of inches forwards and you're playing a fish that really and truly does have you with your heart in your mouth. The fishing here really is excellent, and Bake is highly recommended.

SEASON – open all year.

TICKETS – contact Tony Lister on 01752 849027 at Bake Fishing Lakes, Trerulefoot, Nr. Saltash, Cornwall, PL12 5BL. There is a whole range of ticket prices but, as an example, a five-fish limit costs £25 and a four-fish limit £22. You can also go catch and release for £10 per day.

RECORDS – the rainbow record is nearly 12lb 8oz and the brown record is just into double figures.

FACILITIES – tackle hire is available, along with some tuition. There are toilets on site and disabled facilities.

Directions – a few miles before Liskeard on the A38 take the Bake exit on the Trerulefoot roundabout. Take the first right, then the first left and after about a quarter of a mile you will find the fishery entrance on the right-hand side .

Accommodation – the coastal towns of Fowey and Looe are close, as is the county town of Plymouth. Phone the Tourist Information Centre in Plymouth on 01752 304849 for details.

Arundell Arms Waters – Devon

If you're touring the South West you really owe it to yourself to pop into the Arundell Arms for a couple of days – or more if you've got the time and the money. The reason is simple: you just won't find better, more beautiful, more superbly managed river fishing anywhere in the country. I can honestly say that the few days that I've spent at the Arundell Arms over the years have remained highlights in my fishing life – every single solitary one of them. I don't know if it's the countryside, the rivers or the friendly, helpful efficiency of the hotel's ghillies, but I've never left without aching to return.

The charm of the Arundell rivers is that they're wild. The Lyd, the Wolf, the Carey and the tiny Thrushel rise on Dartmoor and bring all the wildness of that bleak area down into the valleys with them. These are flashing, chattering rivers. Shallow and clear, often overgrown – they offer a huge challenge, and the hours simply melt by. The trout aren't generally large, but they're as wild as leopards and on light gear – which is obligatory – they fight like leopards, too.

All these rivers join their more serious parent, the Tamar, within a mile of the hotel and this is where the serious salmon fishing begins. The average weight is around ten pounds but twenty-pounders are caught.

We haven't even looked at the sea trout fishing yet, which can be excellent on the Tamar, Lyd and Thrushel. In fact, my first real sea trout fishing took place on the Lyd. A mild, high summer evening. A moon masked by light cloud. A pool full of fish. A large artificial skating the surface near the tail. A rise. A tug. A screaming reel and a memory that lives on brightly through the passing of twenty years.

Season – the trout fishing opens on 15th March and closes on 30th September. Sea trout fishing opens on 3rd March – even though fish don't really arrive until June – and closes on 30th September. Salmon fishing opens on 1st March – although mid April is the earliest fish can arrive in normal conditions – and closes on 14th October. The very best brown trout fishing is in May, June and September. Sea trout fishing is at its best in July and August and the salmon fishing builds up to a crescendo, peaking in September and October.

Rules – the hotel operates a system of beat rotation. In order to preserve wild stocks, the hotel asks that no more than one salmon, four sea trout and four brown trout are kept during any twenty-four hour period. (Perhaps even that bag limit is too generous.) Barbless hooks are encouraged for safe return of fish.

Tickets and accommodation – these are all available from the Arundell Arms, Lifton, Devon PL16 0AA, which can be reached on 01566 784666.
Directions – Lifton can be found just off the A30 between Okehampton and Launceston. The Arundell Arms is on the High Street of this very pretty, now by-passed, village. The fishing is all within easy access.

Tavistock Lake – Devon

Tavistock Lake is another of these wonderfully run, sublimely attractive commercial fisheries that have developed over the past few years. It consists of three lakes – Kingfisher Lake and Heron Lake, which are stocked more routinely, and Osprey Lake, which contains some really outsized fish and offers that much more of a challenge. The size of the rainbows in the two former lakes averages around the two-pound mark, whereas in Osprey things kick-off at three pounds and above... going all the way up to the fishery record of thirty pounds – a one-time rainbow record a few years ago.

But it's not necessarily the size of the fish that makes the reputation of a fishery, and Tavistock is beloved by the regulars for far more than pounds and ounces. The lakes are pretty, the stocking levels are good, the atmosphere is warm and generous and the fishing is absolutely all you'd want from any water. The lakes are rich – there are even nice mayfly hatches – and respond to imitative patterns. You can, of course. take fish on lures, but look first of all to nymphs, buzzers and dry flies.

Osprey is considered the hardest lake of all and it does offer a real challenge in its moody, fascinating way. But that's the delight of fishing, isn't it? And believe me, once banked, those rainbows are worth every minute of effort. So if it's a well-tended, verdant, fascinating venue you're looking for, Tavistock is definitely for you.

Season – open all year.
Tickets – contact Abigail Underhill at Tavistock Lake, Parkwood Road, Tavistock, Devon, PL19 9JW on 01822 615441. For Osprey Lake, a five-fish limit costs £40 and a two-fish limit, £19. There is a range of ticket prices in between. For Kingfisher and Heron Lakes, the five-fish limit costs £20.50.
Records – brown 9lb 9oz and rainbow 30lb 12oz.
Facilities – there is an on-site pub serving good meals. Tea and coffee are dispensed free. There is a tackle shop, stocking virtually all you may need, and a lodge. The farm shop sells trout if you can't catch any!
Directions – from Tavistock, head north on the A386 along the edge of Dartmoor towards Okehampton. About a mile past the grounds of Kelly College, you will find the fishery on your left. The car park is opposite.
Accommodation – there is holiday accommodation on site or phone the Tourist Information Centre in Tavistock on 01822 612938.

Sea Trout Rivers of the South West

Where do you start to describe the sea trout delights of this part of the world, given that there are at least fifty rivers worthy of mention in Devon, Cornwall and Somerset? And I suppose before I go any further I ought to point out that salmon and brown trout are present in many of these rivers as well. But it's the sea trout that make these rivers so special, especially in this day and age when rivers elsewhere in Britain are frequently experiencing failing runs. Of course, down in the South West there are inevitably problems – many of them brought about, no doubt, by the emphatic change in this country's climatic patterns. Whereas we once talked about spring-, summer- and autumn-run fish, it's much more difficult nowadays to draw the distinctions... global warming, call it what you will, has changed the old patterns of behaviour.

Nonetheless, providing these south-west rivers get some rain early in the year, there are still runs of fish,and these are often plentiful. Many of the school sea trout are only in the one-and-a-half- to two-and-a-half-pound mark, but some of the rivers – for example the Tavy – experience vast numbers of fish in the five- to six-pound region, as well as fish that run into double figures, each and every year.

Sea trout tend to rest up in deeper pools during the day and then move up river during the hours of darkness, and the moving fish are generally the ones that can be caught. For this reason, most sea trout fishing takes place after dusk, but do make sure you spy out the land before getting onto the river. It's no fun stumbling around in the darkness wondering where the hell you are!

A longish rod between ten and eleven feet is about right – it just gives you that little bit more control over a hard-fighting fish, and it also means you barely have to cast when you want to put out a short line. And short lines are best. Don't be too over-ambitious casting in the dark, especially on a river that might be relatively new to you. Instead, keep it short and tight, and move as gently and as quietly as you possibly can. Favoured patterns include the Alexandra, the Bloody Butcher, the Teal Blue and Silver, Medicine and Peter Ross. I like using muddlers when fish are moving freely on the surface. Larger, traditional dry flies can appeal during these periods, too, often when there's a full moon and/or thundery weather when the barometer is high.

A couple of last tips: even if the days have been warm, the nights can be cool. Thermal underwear helps to keep the night chill away and a flask of tea provides inner warmth and a stimulating break. Make sure you take insect repellent – midges can be maddening on still nights. Don't forget a small torch – necessary for tying knots and selecting flies – and it's never a bad idea to paint the rim of your landing net white. This makes it much easier to see in the dark and it's a tip that's saved many an angler a last-ditch, struggling, six-pound sea trout!

But where exactly should you fish? The region's excellent rivers include the Dart, the Fowey, the Lyn, the Plym, the Tamar, the Tavy and the Torridge. That's not to say there aren't others but they'll do for starters and, anyway, has anyone fished the lot?

SEASON – The season for migratory trout does vary to some degree. Most of the rivers open in either March or April but the general closing date is 30th September. Check local restrictions when making enquiries.

TICKETS – Many of the waters are tightly controlled and access can be limited. However, contact South-west Water Leisure Services for detailed advice. Permits for the Tavy, the Walkham and Plym can be obtained from Barkells, 15 Duke Street, Tavistock PL19 0BA. Contact Two Bridges Hotel, just outside Princetown, on 01822 890581 for tickets for the Dart. The Prince Hall Hotel in Princetown, on 01822 890403, also offers tickets for the Dart, as does the Forest Inn, Hexworthy, PL20 6SD, which can be reached on 01364 631211. The Ensly House Hotel at Milton Abbot, Devon PL19 0PQ has permits on the Tamar. For the Taw, try the Rising Sun Hotel at Umberleigh, on 01769 560447, and the Fox and Hounds Hotel at Eggsford, Devon.

Sea Trout In The Daytime

Sea trout fishing is traditionally carried out at night but increasingly anglers are looking for sport during the daytime. And by using the right tactics, they are finding it! Here's how:

- *Move very, very cautiously. Daytime sea trout are particularly fidgety and prone to alarm.*
- *It's important to target your fish by finding them first and not casting haphazardly. Unnecessary casts will only spook the shoal.*
- *You'll find that even large sea trout are willing to come up to take a fly from the surface. But the flies must be small. Try something on a size 14 or 16. Cast well upstream and give the fish plenty of time to see it.*
- *If you can't get the fish to come up, then don't hesitate to get a fly down to where they're lying. Go for something with a bit of vim and vigour about it. Try a big Goldhead or even a Montana. What you're looking for is something that makes a bit of a plop and goes down very fast indeed.*
- *Try casting directly into the shoal or immediately in front of a specific fish and watch the fly go down.*
- *You'll either get an immediate take… or it will be a disaster and the entire shoal will take fright. If this is the case, don't carry on scaring the fish. You've got to think of those anglers who are out on the bank after dusk, and they don't want to come across heavily spooked trout.*
- *That's the mystery of sea trout – sometimes they'll take during the day and sometimes they won't. They know their own mind and there's little we can do to change it.*

Accommodation – There is a wide variety of bed and breakfast, self-catering and hotel accommodation in this bustling tourist area. Contact the Dartmoor Tourist Association at the Dutchy Building, Tavistock Road, Princetown, Plymouth, Devon PL20 6QF, on 01822 890567. Contact the Tourist Information Centre in Plymouth, on 01752 304849, for more general advice on accommodation in the area.

Watercress Farm Fishery – Devon

Watercress Farm boasts three lakes, all now very well matured, with one of them going back nearly fifty years. The lakes are all spring-fed, which helps explain their crystal-clear qualities. The water is very rich indeed, with abundant weed growth and a big range of insect life. Depths range from around four feet to fourteen on average, but there are plenty of deeper holes that the fish look to in bright, warm weather. The largest lake, Ash, runs down to thirty feet, whereas the central lake, Oak, has extensive margins only a couple of feet deep or so and running down to fifteen feet. This allows for a great range of insect life. Alder, the most recent lake, has depths to about ten feet.

The lakes are also surrounded by abundant tree growth, so there are plenty of terrestrials blown off into the water – hence the popularity of the Flying Ant and the Black Fly for those liking to fish on the top.

Watercress sees big hatches of buzzers through the year, and many of the locals fish little else. However, damsel nymphs and Montanas all catch a good number of fish. The basic rule at Watercress is to fish tight and inconspicuously, always remembering that if you can see the fish, there's a good chance that they can see you.

Watercress does not stand still, and at present one of the lakes is extensively stocked with brown trout, brook trout and tiger trout to provide welcome alternatives to the ubiquitous rainbow. This lake does have a closed season – from October through to March – but the other lakes are open all year round. Most stocked fish come out at around two pounds in weight but a sixteen-and-a-half-pound trout has recently been caught, with innumerable ten-pound plus fish.

Season – the fishery is open the year round.
Tickets – phone 01626 852168 for prior booking or write to Watercress Farm Fishery, Kerswells Chudleigh, Newton Abbot, Devon. A five-fish limit costs £20, a four-fish limit £17, a three-fish limit £14 and a two-fish limit £11.
Directions – leave the M5 onto the A38 Exeter to Plymouth road. Leave the A38 onto the B3344 road and the lane that goes past Watercress Farm is between the Highwayman's Haunt and the entrance to the caravan park. It's well signposted.
Accommodation – there is a caravan park next to the fishery – Holman's Wood – but the major centres of Torquay and Paignton are close at hand. Phone the Tourist Information Centre in Torquay on 0906 680 1268 for further details of various kinds of accommodation.

The Reservoirs of Somerset

True, Blagdon, Chew and Wimbleball are all geographically closely sited, but they each have their own unique characters. What they do share is fascinating fishing for well-conditioned fish in dramatic countryside. They're all very good-sized waters – Chew comes in at twelve hundred acres, Blagdon almost four hundred and fifty acres and Wimbleball nearly four hundred... so there's plenty of bank and boat fishing to explore. There is prolific fly life on all three reservoirs and that, combined with very good stocking levels, gives you every chance of a good day's fishing.

Obviously, all the usual techniques work on these three reservoirs, but what is not so often tried is dry fly fishing, a real winner in the summer months and right into the early autumn. Indeed, from the end of April, providing the weather is warm, dry flies begin to work with a vengeance. Look out for wind and scum lanes, because both of these hold food and the trout will never be far away nor, even more importantly, far from the surface in these areas.

Remember when you're fishing dry flies to cast them accurately, speedily and with a good presentation. Look very carefully at the route that the rising trout is taking and try to present your fly a couple of feet or so in front of where you guess its nose is likely to be. Never cast directly at the ring of the last rise, because the fish will have moved on and you'll be casting behind it.

An overcast, warm day with a light wind is pefect weather for fishing. If it's overcast but windy, simply step up the size of the flies on your leader. In flat calms, don't cast too often because all you'll do is disturb the water. Wait till you see a fish move and then cast to it in one gentle, unhurried movement. Other tips? When a trout takes your fly, delay for a split second and then strike, even though you won't feel a pull on the hand. Always degrease your leader with a mixture of Fuller's Earth and washing-up liquid so that it sinks beneath the surface.

Remember, too, to grease your dry fly with a floatant – spray it or rub it onto your finger first and then apply to the fly. And as for choosing the right fly, well, there are endless possible patterns, so it really pays to take the advice of the bailiffs on the water. If I had to choose a favourite for much of the year, it would have to be the simple Black Gnat. If you're getting refusals, it could be that your fly is too big – going down a couple of sizes might do the trick.

So, just a few tips for really exciting fishing on three of the most lovely reservoirs that you'll come across in the South West – or anywhere else, come to that.

Season – in essence, you're allowed to fish from April through to November, but there are various restrictions on taking brown trout. On Chew, for example, boat fishing ends on 29th October and bank fishing on 26th November. Fishing is until sunset or one hour afterwards on all three reservoirs.

Tickets – Chew and Blagdon are controlled by Bristol Water PLC, Recreations

Department, Woodford Lodge, Chew Stoke, Bristol BS18 8XH. You can contact them on 01275 332339. Permits are available in advance, from the lodges or from ticket machines. For fishing on Wimbleball Lake, phone Lance Nicholson, High Street, Dulverton, Somerset, on 01398 323409. There is a whole range of ticket prices. For example, on Chew a boat day permit is £55 for two rods. This includes boat hire, fishing tickets and a total of 16 fish.

FACILITIES – All three reservoirs have lodges, well-maintained boats, weighing stations and so on. But you should also be aware that on each there are areas out of bounds to fishermen. These are all important nature reserves and it's essential, for the reputation of angling, to observe the 'no go' areas.

DIRECTIONS – Both Chew and Blagdon are situated to the south west of Bristol, just off the A368, midway between Bath and Weston-Super-Mare. They are well signposted, and there are plenty of car parks. Wimbleball is situated to the east of Dulverton and the south of Brompton Regis. It is best reached from the B3190, which runs from Brampton northwards towards Watchet.

ACCOMMODATION – The local Tourist Information Centres will give details on various kinds of accommodation available in the area. Phone the Bristol office on 0117 926 0767 or Tiverton on 01884 255827.

HIGHLY RECOMMENDED FISHERIES

- *Bellbrook Valley Trout Fishery, Nr. Exbridge, Devon. Call 01398 351292. Beautiful string of peaceful, scenic lakes, liberally stocked with doubles.*
- *Blakewell Fishery. Can be contacted on 01271 344533. Good morning and evening buzzer water.*
- *Tavistock Trout Fishery, Devon. Phone 01822 615441. A really big fish lake. Fish to twenty pounds plus.*
- *Rose Park Trout Fishery, Cornwall. Phone 01566 86278 for details. Some nice fish. Pleasant surroundings and a warm welcome.*
- *Siblyback Reservoir. Details on 01579 342366. An attractive reservoir, fished very well from a boat.*
- *Quantock Fishery, Somerset. Phone 01823 451367. An excellent mix of varieties – rainbows, browns and tigers.*
- *Hawkridge Reservoir, Somerset. Details can be obtained on 01278 671840. A beautiful water.*
- *Clatworthy Reservoir. An established water offering a really good challenge.*

Fly-Fishing Sites in the South

1. *Avon Springs Fishery*
2. *The Rivers Test and Itchen*
3. *Moorhen Trout Fishery*
4. *Avington Trout Fisheries*
5. *Rooksbury Mill*
6. *Felix Farm*
7. *Vicarage Spinney Trout Fishery*

"To the chalk-stream fisherman, June is the best month of all, for who would not, if he could, choose a windless day in June? It is a month of the meadow flowers, and though the different shades of green are less marked and emerging into their summer sameness, the yellow iris makes the banks a garden, the wild rose stars the hedges and the guelder rose hangs its green-coloured lamps over the carriers."

J. W. HILLS, *A SUMMER ON THE TEST*, 1924

THE SOUTH

The southern counties and trout fishing are quite synonymous, and rivers such as the Test and Itchen have a fundamental place at the heart of the sport for game fishermen around the world. These southern rivers were, in many ways, the cradle of fly fishing. It was here that modern dry fly fishing and nymphing were brought to fruition.

There's something about the water quality – not just the rivers – of these southern counties. Perhaps it's because the water so often runs from chalk and is crystal clear and immensely fertile. As a result, the fish grow big and are habitually cunning, and anglers for generations have been able to see just where they've been going wrong.

When the world thinks of southern England, it's the rivers that spring to mind, but this does not mean to say that there aren't some fabulous still-water fisheries. If anything, these lakes are even clearer than the rivers, and the fish can be every bit as difficult to deceive. At certain fisheries – such as Avington – the angler has the best of both worlds and can move from still water to river as his heart desires. In fact, the southern counties are places where every valley has a twinkling stream and where every fly fisherman goes home fulfilled.

The South offers an intriguing mix of enormous, artificially-bred rainbow trout and some immaculate wild fish. For example, you will find rivers where wild browns still spawn naturally. A short distance away, there may be a lake that has just been stocked with rainbows of double figures. It's important for the angler to realise that both extremes of the sport offer a great deal. This is a broad church indeed.

Avon Springs Fishery – Wiltshire

Avon Springs really shows what commercial fisheries can aspire to. There are two lakes here, one of five acres and one of three acres, in conjunction with four miles of the upper Avon. And what fishing we're talking about. The water is crystal clear, very prolific, with good weed growth. And the fish are sensational. As I write, the average – yes, the average – size of the rainbows is just over six pounds. The browns are not far behind, and there are double-figure fish of both species to be caught. In fact, limit bags of thirty pounds plus are going out every week.

In part, this is down to the stocking policy, but the fish do extraordinarily well in the water and many of them over-winter to become perfect specimens. Naturally enough, damsels work very well, especially when stalking, but most years there is an excellent mayfly hatch, along with prolific hawthorn, so there's the opportunity for really thrilling surface fishing too.

The river also deserves mention because it's really classic here. There's a very good head of wild-bred brown trout, many of them very good fish indeed. And the grayling really get your mouth watering. The average size is something between a pound and a pound and a half, but plenty of fish of two to two and a half pounds plus are taken.

Season – open all year.
Tickets – contact Avon Springs Fishery, Recreation Road, Durrington, Salisbury, Wiltshire, SP4 8EZ. Full-day tickets (four-fish limit) £33. Half-day tickets £25 (three-fish limit) and an evening ticket £17 (two-fish limit). There is no catch and release. Grayling fishing is allowed on the river throughout the winter on a £30 a day sporting ticket. Everything must go back. Details on 01980 653557.
Directions – following the A303 from Exeter to London, turn left at Amesbury along the A345. You will come to a roundabout with the Stonehenge pub opposite. Turn right and follow this road until you get to Rangers Garage on the left. Turn left and Recreation Road is the third on the right with the lakes well signposted.
Accommodation – details of various kinds of accommodation in the Salisbury area can be obtained from the Tourist Information Centre on 01722 334956.

The Southern Rivers

Okay, just conceivably, these are not what they once were and, yes, abstraction and long-term, insidious pollution have had some undesirable effects on these rivers, but the chalk rivers of the south are still a fly-fisher's paradise: the Upper Avon and its tributaries; the Wylye and the Nadder; the Itchen; the Test; the Kennet. These are just a few. Crystal clear, running over chalk, gravel and sand. Prolific weed growth. Abundant fly life. Large, perfectly-formed, cunning fish. Trout fishing at its best.

The fisheries here have a history. These are the streams of Halford, Skues, Sawyer and Dermot Wilson. These are the places where dry fly and nymphing were both brought to their present state of the art. These are the rivers where entomology really first made its big impact on fly fishing. It's on these rivers that some of the very best books on fly fishing ever have been written – witness *Where the Bright Waters Meet* and *A Summer on the Test*.

Highlights... the mayfly season, those two weeks around the end of May and the beginning of June when the valleys are a cascade of golden-glowing insects. Spirals and spirals of mayflies turning the air into a shifting fog. Mayflies falling so thick that cars have to be driven with windscreen wipers turned on high. Rivers coated in the dead insects and trout fat as pigs from the fortnight's feast.

Highlights... men like Ron Holloway, river keepers with a lifetime's experience. Men of passion, men with a commitment to keeping these rivers as pristine as God intended them. Listen to Ron as he tells you how he tends his river and you'll feel there isn't a single grain of gravel he hasn't examined, polished and returned to best effect. Brown trout are his passion, wild brown trout, fish that can still breed freely in a river where they know their fry and fingerlings will be protected.

Highlights... an evening rise, countryside so beautiful you think your heart will break. Watching great browns hanging suspended in water as clear as air. Watching your upstream nymph disappear in a flash of white mouth. And, even if you can't get on some of the most hallowed stretches in the summer, there's a chance for you when it comes to winter grayling.

Grayling aren't always welcome visitors on these streams, not even now in the 21st century, but mostly they're tolerated. And what grayling they are... two pounders are common, three pounders are there to be caught, and in huge numbers.

I remember very well a late January afternoon on the Lambourne when I took my first two-pound grayling on the fly from a little weir pool on a carrier. Twenty minutes later I'd taken three. Two pounds two ounces, two pounds five ounces and two pounds seven ounces. Then there was the walk home, through the frost-crackling wood where the pheasants called and up the high street of the sleepy little rural village to my homely bed and breakfast.

The joys of the southern rivers are infinite. Of course, access is as jealously guarded as the keys to the crown jewels, but it can be done. For a price – not always exorbitant – you can find yourself a day in paradise.

SEASONS – I'm not really going to comment on the seasons for the chalk streams simply because so many fisheries have their own rules and regulations. This is especially true when it comes to the grayling.

TICKETS – Roxton Bailey Robinson, High Street, Hungerford, RG17 0NF is a good starting point for beats on the Test. Phone 01488 683222 for details. It's also worth contacting the Estate Office, Broadlands, Romsey, SO51 9ZE. Call them on 01794 518885. Contact also Roy

Gumbrell on 01264 810833 at The Greyhound Inn, Stockbridge, Hampshire. Call Fishing Breaks Ltd., who also control fishing on the Test, Avon, Itchen and Dever, on 020 7359 8818. Alternatively, write to them at 16 Bickerton Road, London N19 5JR. Perhaps the most important address of all is that excellent tackle shop, The Rod Box, London Road, King's Worthy, Winchester. This excellent shop – where everyone seems to be a mine of information and enthusiastic help – controls several beats on the Itchen, Test, Bourne and Whitewater. Phone 01962 883600 for more details.

ACCOMMODATION – the Tourist Information Centres in Winchester, on 01962 840500, and Southampton, on 023 8022 1106, will be able to give details of accommodation available in the area, from bed and breakfasts to luxury hotels.

MOORHEN TROUT FISHERY – HAMPSHIRE

Despite my liking for catch and release, it can be a problem for fishery owners, especially when the fish are very large. This proved the case at Moorhen. Going back just a handful of years, it was a renowned big fish water, but the problem was that sometimes the big fish just weren't handled well – understandable, I

BUILDING UP KNOWLEDGE

- *You can't really do much better than get out on the bankside with an acknowledged expert. It doesn't matter how much you read, you can't beat the hands-on approach. There are a good number of instructors around the country, but some that I have personal knowledge of and can highly recommend are: Simon Gawsworth, who can be contacted on 0118 930 3860 at Sportfish, Reading; the salmon maestro Arthur Oglesby, on 01423 883565; Leslie Crawford up in the far north of Scotland (01807 811470); and Bill Price, a casting guru who can be contacted at Sportfish in Winforton on 01544 327111. Charles Jardine, the noted fly caster, entomologist and artist, gives occasional courses at the Caer Beris Manor Hotel. Phone 01982 552601 for details.*
- *Game anglers are also fortunate in the quality of magazines on their newsagents shelves. Trout Fisherman is long established and really does point any trout angler in the right direction. Trout and Salmon has been highly respected for many years now and offers a very good overview of the game fishing scene. Total Fly Fishing looks like being an important newcomer.*
- *Try to get to the fairs. The Chatsworth Fly Fishing Fair and the CLA Game Fair offer excellent opportunities to meet skilled fly fishermen and to benefit from casting clinics. The Fisherman's Village at the Game Fair is really worth a visit.*

suppose, in the excitement of the moment – and they were returned only to sink and die. Not good for the fish and also not good for the fishery – and very bad for finances. As a result, Moorhen has reverted to a neater and more manageable type of fishery.

What makes Moorhen so appealing is its stunning appearance. The water isn't large – about two and a half acres – but its setting is really superb. Go there on a pleasant, bright day and I swear you won't be disappointed. The welcome, too, is very warm, and the lodge is well laid out and functional.

Today, Moorhen operates with stocked fish – in beautiful condition – of between one and a half and two pounds, with a number of fish in the five- to six-pound bracket to be caught. Floating lines are generally all that is needed, and buzzers, dries and other imitative patterns do the business. Barbless hooks are, by the way, obligatory – a wise rule indeed.

SEASON – open all year.
TICKETS – the Fishery Manager, Moorhen Lake, Warnford, Nr. Southampton, Hampshire. Phone 01730 829460 for details. Day tickets are £26 for four fish, £21 for three fish and £15 for two fish. No catch and release.
DIRECTIONS – leave the M27 at junction 10 and take the A32 towards Alton. The entrance to the fishery lies right on the road on the left hand side just out of the village of Warnford.
ACCOMMODATION – the Tourist Information Centre in Southampton, on 023 8022 1106, can supply information on various kinds of accommodation in the area.

AVINGTON TROUT FISHERIES – HAMPSHIRE

Avington was opened for trout fishing way back in 1967, so it is, in many ways, one of the forerunners of all commercial trout fisheries. It's certainly amongst the most famous for it's extraordinary stocking policies... huge and perfectly-formed rainbows are very much the order of the day here. Avington is made up of two lakes – one of two acres and one of four acres – and they are both fed by the River Itchen that runs nearby. Indeed, the fishery includes half a mile of Itchen carrier, although this is seldom stocked. Avington is a beautiful, secluded place ringed by trees, the margins dotted with yellow flag. You really are in a glorious little piece of Hampshire countryside at Avington.

The rainbows are reared from fingerlings on site and that policy, combined with brilliant water quality, makes for these fascinating and exceptionally fine rainbows. Mind you, even though stocking is generous and sight fishing is always possible, the fishing is far from easy. A four fish limit really has to be striven for.

A gold-headed damsel nymph is always a good starter – as it is anywhere. Avington fish also come up for buzzers and small white and black lures. However, if you're really going to fish Avington like an expert, think very hard about heavily leaded bugs and nymphs that you can drop in front of a fish knowing they will get to the required depth quickly. That's one of the secrets of stalking – you've got to put your fly at the right level. Of course, there's a lot more to it, and in the first place you've got to see your fish! Always try to get as high as possible to see down into the water – perhaps step up on a bench, making full use of trees behind you to blot out your silhouette. Always wear Polaroids, and a broad-peaked cap helps cut down the light. Move carefully, scanning the water as you go.

Look around weed beds, particularly, and for the fish under the trees at Avington. You'll find a lot of fish in the margins, too. Once you've spotted one that you'd like to target, get down low and watch it carefully as you build up a picture of its patrol route. Once you have this image in your mind, you can drop the fly just ahead of its imminent arrival. That way you won't spook the fish so much.

Look for fish close in if you're new to this, because accurate casting is everything. If you're going to cast twenty yards or more, you'll need quite a bit of skill and experience to get the fly right on the rainbow's nose.

Obviously, you want to go as light as you possibly can, but remember that some of these Avington fish reach twenty pounds, and if there's a lot of weed about... Try, wherever possible, once a fish is hooked, to play it off the reel. It's very common to play trout by the hand but this leaves loops of line all over the place. It's all too easy to step on it just as a big fish makes another surge for freedom. Also, keep using side strain, as this keeps knocking the fish off balance and tires it out more quickly. Yes, stalking is great fun and is the way to catch the biggest fish at Avington, but you've got to choose the right day: bright light and gentle winds are ideal for seeing down into the crystal depths. But, most importantly, remember your manners. Don't encroach on anybody else's fishing space – not even if you're following a big fish that you think has your name on it. Remember that everybody's paid for their ticket and everyone deserves respect. It's all too easy to think that stalking is somehow a superior sport reserved for the gods... it isn't. It's just a very satisfying way of reaching your limit bag.

SEASON – open all year, seven days a week. The fishery is open from 8.00am until dusk.

TICKETS – contact the Fishery Trout Manager on 019627 79312 at Avington Trout Fishery, Avington, Winchester, Hants SO21 1BZ. A day ticket is £50 for four fish. An afternoon ticket £30 for two fish. There is no catch and release.

DIRECTIONS – leave the M3 at junction 9 and turn onto the A31 towards Farnham. The road down to Avington and Itchen Abbas is on the left.

ACCOMMODATION – contact the Tourist Information Centre in Winchester on 01962 840500 for details of accommodation available in the area.

Rooksbury Mill – Hampshire

Rooksbury has built up a great reputation over the years as a fabulous, big-fish water in tremendous surroundings and offering a really warm welcome. There are two lakes – six acres and three acres – with maximum depths going down to twelve or fourteen feet. The lakes are crystal clear and spring-fed: the effect of the springs is to push the fish up towards the surface layers, and even in winter you'll find them most active in the top three feet of water.

For this reason, all you'll ever need at Rooksbury is a floating line and long leader. A couple of years back, a survey was taken of all the catch returns, and the top three flies proved to be damsel imitations, Green Montanas and gold-ribbed Hare's Ears, with Sawyer nymphs coming in fourth. Nick Carbury, who controls the water, stresses that a slow, careful retrieve is probably the best way to lure these fine fish, which average between four and five pounds in weight.

There's also a stretch of the Anton controlled by the fishery. This beautiful tributary of the Test holds wild browns and a few roaming rainbows. There are also grayling.

Season – the fishery is open virtually all the year round, apart from a few days in early March that are set aside for restocking and general maintenance work. There are also a few days at the start of the season reserved for the season ticket holders. So, if you're thinking of going in the early part of March, it makes sense to ring and enquire.

Tickets – write to Nick Carbury at Rooksbury Mill Trout Fisheries, Andover, Hampshire or phone him on 01264 352921. A day ticket for five fish is £32, a half-day ticket for three fish is £24 and a three-hour evening ticket for two fish is £17.

Directions – come off the A303 Exeter to London Road and take the A343 towards Andover and Newbury. Just before Andover town centre you will come to a garage on the left, at a crossroads. Turn right into Rooksbury Road. Drive to the end of this road where you will find the fishery car park.

Accommodation – the Tourist Information Centre in Andover, on 01264 324320, will be able to supply a list of available accommodation. Alternatively, contact the Winchester Tourist Information Centre on 01962 840500 or the Salisbury Tourist Information Centre on 01722 334956.

Felix Farm – Berkshire

Felix Farm was dug back in the seventies to provide gravel for the nearby M4. It's now a very mature ten-acre lake with a firm following of regular visitors. A lot of the water is surprisingly shallow for an old gravel pit, but there are good areas that dip to twenty feet or so. These are fishable from one of the boats, which must be moored up at well-positioned buoys.

Felix Farm is spring-fed and has a constant water supply, and it is clear enough for heart-stopping stalking techniques to be used. The trout are stocked on a daily basis –

probably averaging around the two-pound mark – but bigger fish go in every week. It's a prolific water: there are buzzer hatches throughout the year, even in winter, along with hawthorns and mayfly, which generally seem to appear in June. Naturally enough, this means that surface fishing with buzzers and dries is one of the most effective methods at Felix. Try the Grey Wolf tied on a size fourteen. Sedge patterns also work well, but don't go too light on your leader strength, because there are some hefty trout about. This is a pretty, well-thought-out fishery that produces a very nice stamp of fish indeed. Try it!

SEASON – open all year including bank holidays, 8.00am to dusk.
TICKETS – contact Martin Suddards on 01189 345527 or write to him at Felix Farm Trout Fishery, Howe Lane, Binfield, Bracknell Berkshire, RG 42 5QL. Day tickets are about £25. It is advisable to phone and make a booking. The fishery only takes about 18 people.
DIRECTIONS – leave the M4 at junction 8/9 and take the A308 for Windsor, then the Bracknell and Ascot road through Hollyport and Touchen End. Take the right hand fork and you will pass the Win Again pub on the Twyford road. After a mile, turn left for Binfield. The entrance to the fishery is opposite the Jolly Farmer pub.
ACCOMMODATION – bed and breakfast is available at Felix Farm. Phone for details. Contact the Tourist Information Centre at Bracknell on 01344 868196 for details of other accommodation in the area.

VICARAGE SPINNEY TROUT FISHERY – BUCKINGHAMSHIRE

I first went to Vicarage Spinney way back after a talk given at a local fly fishing club by Alan Pearson, then boss of the fishery. I was inspired to visit, and Vicarage Spinney lived up to Alan's billing. I caught bigger trout that day than I'd ever seen before, and all from a very attractive water. Alan left, the fishery faded from the limelight and everything went quiet. But, today, the mood has changed and Vicarage Spinney is back amongst the top still-water trout waters of the country. A lot of money and care has gone into bringing Vicarage back to life again; there's a good spirit about the place and the fishing once more is fantastic, with high stocking levels of good-conditioned, good-sized fish.

Vicarage fishes well in both summer and winter. In the summer, the deep holes, down to 30 feet or so, and the spring-fed water combine to keep the fish on the feed. In winter, the amount of coarse fish fry keeps them stimulated. Whatever the season, early and late in the day tend to be the best times at Vicarage. Locals talk about the big buzzer hatches, and certainly buzzers work very well, as, naturally enough, do the ubiquitous damsel flies. Nymphs also take fish, especially if they're fished not too fast.

It can be a good idea to take out one of the boats during the daytime so that you can fish the deeper water. Alternatively, enjoy a good lunch in the very comfortable lodge.

SEASON – open all year.
TICKETS – contact the Fishery Manager on 01908 612227 at the Vicarage Spinney Trout Fishery, Haversham Road, Little Lindford, Milton Keynes, Buckinghamshire, MK19 7EA. Tickets cost from £12.50 to £20 for a three fish limit.
DIRECTIONS – Vicarage Spinney is off the M1 between junctions 14 and 15. Pick up the B526 from Newport Pagnell to Northampton. After two miles, turn left over the motorway towards Little Lindford. The fishery will be clearly signposted from here.
ACCOMMODATION – Milton Keynes Tourist Information Centre on 01908 558300 will be able to provide lists of various kinds of accommodation available in this area.

HIGHLY RECOMMENDED FISHERIES

- *Hazelcopse, Nr. Ridgwick, Surrey. Call 01403 822878 for details. Two attractive lakes offering huge browns, rainbows and still water salmon.*
- *Chiphall Lake, Fareham, Hants. Phone 01329 833295. Crystal stalking water in the Meon valley. Big rainbows.*
- *Leominstead Trout Fishery, Lyndhurst, Hants. Phone 02380 282610 for information. Very pretty, well-stocked water.*
- *Frensham Trout Fishery, Surrey. Phone 01252 794321. A great autumn water.*
- *Albury. Call 01483 202323 for details. Super water. Tremendous fishing. Highly recommended.*
- *Coltsford Mill, Surrey. Phone 01883 715666 for details. Excellent facilities and some very big fish.*
- *John O'Gaunts. Phone 01794 388130. A tremendous water with high average weight. Highly recommended.*
- *Dever Springs, Hampshire. Details can be obtained on 01264 720592. The original huge-fish water. An amazing experience. Do it at least once!*
- *Meon Springs, Hampshire. Contact on 01730 823249. Great visibility, great stock of fish and great welcome.*

FLY-FISHING SITES IN THE SOUTH EAST

1. Chalk Springs Trout Fishery
2. Bewl Water
3. Halliford Mere
4. Syon Park Fishery
5. Walthamstow Reservoir
6. Cottington Lakes
7. Rib Valley Fishery
8. Norton Fishery
9. Brickhouse Farm
10. Hanningfield Reservoir
11. Clavering Lake

The South East

*And, next, I shall tell you, that it is observed…
that there is no better Salmon than in England; and
that though some of our northern counties have as fat,
and as large, as the river Thames, yet none are
of so excellent a taste…
There are also, in divers rivers, especially that relate to,
or be near to the sea, as Winchester, or the Thames about
Windsor, a little Trout called a Samlet, or Skegger Trout,
in both which places I have caught twenty or forty at a
standing, that will bite as fast and as freely as Minnows:
these be by some taken to be young Salmons.*

IZAAK WALTON, *THE COMPLEAT ANGLER*, 1653

Any reader of Izaak Walton's *Complete Angler* will know that back in the seventeenth century a fisherman could find his heart's content within strolling distance of Charing Cross. These, of course, were the days when apprentices revolted against the monotony of their daily fare of salmon, and when any number of small streams ran in and around the capital, all of them holding trout.

Things were to change dramatically, however, and by the 1850s, Walton wouldn't have known the rivers and streams that he once so happily fished. The rapid population increase – and more importantly, its sewage – just about destroyed the Londoner's Thames, and for the next century, the situation got little better. Now, however, for a man in London with a fly rod the prospects are nowhere near as bleak as they once were. All right, a twenty-first-century Walton might well not be able to find as many wild fish – or indeed any – but there will nonetheless be places to delight his heart.

The growth of commercial trout fisheries over the last twenty years has been a phenomenon, and there can have been few places around Britain to have profited so profoundly as London. Now a Londoner can hop on the tube and fish a delightful day at Syon Park or take a bus out to Walthamstow and enjoy himself on the trout-filled reservoirs there.

Chalk Springs Trout Fishery – Sussex

I've only actually fished Chalk Springs once, but it was a day of pleasure that I could never forget. Okay, the weather was warm and sunny, which always helps, but there's far more that sticks in the mind. In short, Chalk Springs offers something for everybody. The four lakes there cater for the inexperienced fisherman as well as the man who wants a real challenge. I had my kicks stalking a fish of around four pounds in gin-clear water over luxuriant weed growth for about an hour with four or five different sort of flies... and I failed.

No matter, there were all manner of other very attractive looking fish for me to go for. Finally, I succeeded with a rainbow of about two and three quarter pounds that fought magnificently and looked even better. And some trout that I watched in the adjoining lake looked well into the twelve-pound region.

Obviously fish will come to the lure at Chalk Springs, but I really think that small, imitative patterns are all that's really needed. And you won't need a sinking line – you won't find water anywhere deeper than ten to fifteen feet – though a long leader is sometimes a good idea to get really down deep to fish that are sulking in the heat of the day. The fishery is run on the most friendly of bases and you're really made to feel a very welcome guest indeed. In short, a glorious place to while away a splendid day.

Season – Chalk Springs is open all year including Bank Holidays, but do book in advance. The lakes are quite small and a limited number of tickets are issued. The fishery opens at 8.30am and closes at dusk.

Tickets – apply to Darren Smith at Chalk Springs Trout Fishery, Park Bottom, Arundel, West Sussex, BN18 0AA or phone 01903 883742. Adult day-ticket prices start from around £36 but there are cheaper alternatives. There are concessions for juniors and senior citizens.

Records – brown trout 13lb 7oz, rainbow trout 18lb, tiger trout 14lb 2oz and blue trout 13lb 12oz.

Directions – if you take the A27 from Worthing and Brighton to Arundel and then bypass the town, you will cross the river and come to a roundabout. Continue along the A27, signposted Chichester. After a short distance, you will see the lodge on the right-hand side and signs to Chalk Springs. If you reach the hospital, you have gone too far.

Accommodation – lists of accommodation available in Arundel and the surrounding area can be obtained from the Tourist Information Centre in Arundel on 01903 882268.

Bewl Water – Kent

Bewl Water is the largest inland water in the south-east of England. Its seventeen miles of bankside can be intimidating for visiting anglers , or at least until you get to know it. This is rather a shame because, in actual fact, Bewl is both outstandingly beautiful and very generously stocked. Indeed, Bewl is much more intimate than its size might suggest, and this is down to the many bays

that divide the water up and give it an exceptional character. What's more, at Bewl you can always find somewhere to get out of the wind and the chances are that you'll probably have a little cove pretty much to yourself. And what lovely names the bays have... Goose Creek, Tinkers' Marsh, The Nose... there's enough magic and mystery there for anyone!

Bewl is a working reservoir, so it can be subject to a significant draw down during hot summer months when water is in short supply, and it's then, in July and August, that weed growth can be something of a problem, especially for bank anglers. If you're thinking of visiting Bewl during this period, a boat may prove to be a worthwhile investment. Mind you, if you're happier on the bank, don't worry too much – the trout will come into the fertile shallows and they'll feed there throughout the day, especially if there hasn't been much disturbance. If you can get on the water early and stay out until last knockings, then you're very likely to find the best of the bankside sport.

All forms of fly fishing can score at Bewl. Lure stripping – especially with a muddler minnow on calm days – will have an impact. Nymphing, though, is favourite. Also, try dry flies, especially in high summer towards dusk when buzzers also come into their own. It pays to keep on the move to some degree. Some anglers do tend to be too static and if you move around a bit you're much more likely to come across a group of fish that probably haven't been attempted for a day or two.

Local knowledge is always essential, no matter how big the fishery, and here at Bewl the staff really do know their stuff. Indeed, if it's a little instruction that you think your fly fishing could do with, Bewl is the perfect place. It has deservedly gained an enviable reputation for its excellent one-day courses. There is a beginners' course, a junior fly-fishing course and a very useful problem-solving course, which is designed for those who have some experience and wish to improve their casting.

Bewl has a lot more to offer and it's the perfect place for a family day out, so the fisherman need not feel guilty. For example, the passenger boat Frances Mary offers an cruise around the reservoir for a very modest charge. There are walks, picnic areas, woodland playgrounds and so on. And it's all in a designated 'Area of Outstanding Natural Beauty', so you're likely to see a wealth of birdlife and even a fox or wild deer. Given that Bewl stocks annually with over fifty thousand trout and produces double-figure browns and rainbows, you couldn't wish for a better fly fishing venue.

SEASON – Bewl opens on 21st March and closes around 17th November. Bank fishing takes place from sunrise to one hour after sunset. Boat fishing begins at 9.00am and finishes at 10.00pm or one hour after sunset, whichever is earlier.

TICKETS – these are available from the Fishing Lodge, Bewl Water, Lamberhurst, Kent TN3 8JH. There is a scale of charges but a basic day ticket that gives an eight-fish limit bag costs between £14 and £15. Motor boats are available for around £20 a day and rowing boats for around £12. Phone 01892 890352 for the entire list of charges. Though the fishing fleet runs to about fifty boats in its entirety, prior booking is still recommended.

→ **Directions** – access to the fishing lodge is via the A21 London to Hastings road and Bewl Bridge Lane. Then follow the signs on site.

Accommodation – the Tourist Information Office in Tunbridge Wells will provide information on accommodation in the area. Phone 01892 515675 for details.

Halliford Mere – Middlesex

Halliford is a really useful water for Londoners and for visitors to the capital. The major reason for this is its very enlightened policy towards fishing. Halliford is now virtually totally catch and release, although you can take fish from one lake at a cost of £2 per head. But, for the rest, the fish go back and it's a system that works. According to Bill Berwick, the owner, it's also a popular system: 'Okay, we've lost a few die-hards by changing our policy, but we've picked up far more people than we've lost. Most people, it seems, are fed up with killing things and just seeing them go to waste in deep freezers. It's all right if you definitely want a fish to eat – and we cater for that – but it's a lot more rewarding generally to see a fish swim away free'. I suppose the worry for most fishery owners is how effectively catch and release operates in the summer when water temperatures can climb over eighteen degrees. Bill counters this by pointing out that the fish at this time of the year are much, much more difficult to catch anyway and, I suppose, Halliford Mere, being spring-fed, keeps temperatures to a reasonable level.

But to the fishing... The spring water of Halliford Mere is a major factor in the fabulous fishing. There are about fourteen acres available at Halliford, an original large lake split up into four smaller ones. They're all crystal clear and abound with natural insect life. Damsels, buzzers, shrimps, beetles, corixa... you name it and Halliford Mere will hold it. There are few great depths at Halliford – twenty feet or so is the extreme in one of the lakes, while the other three rarely dip much below ten or twelve feet. This means that virtually all the regulars use floating lines with longish leaders and that's all you're likely to need, especially as the vast majority of Halliford fish come from the surface.

Yes, it's pretty well all imitative stuff at Halliford. Buzzers, naturally, score highly but there's great dry fly fishing, especially with a variety of sedges. Things change to some degree when the water cools down – from about the middle of October through to March. It's then that lure fishing comes into its own, especially as the trout are increasingly feeding on the coarse fish fry. However, damsel nymphs, inevitably, continue to work, especially fished deeper down.

Winter or summer, it's possible to sight fish for individual trout at Halliford. The fish range between two and eighteen pounds so there are some very interesting fish to target... not that they'll be easy. Remember that most of the fish have been caught at least once or twice in the past and trout certainly do learn from their mistakes.

Season – open all year apart from Christmas Day.
Tickets – contact Bill Berwick at Halliford Mere Fishery, Chertsey Road, Shepperton, Middlesex on 01932 253553. Catch and release tickets are available at a blanket price of £18.50, and these allow you to fish from 8.00am right through to dusk. There is one lake where fish can be taken for £2 per head.
Directions – heading south on the M25 towards Gatwick, take junction 11 signposted for Chertsey. Follow the signs for Shepperton and cross over the Thames towards the town. Cross the mini-roundabout and half a mile further on, turn right to Church Square. The entrance will be found shortly on the left.
Accommodation – the Tourist Information Centre in Kingston-upon-Thames on 020 8547 5592 will be able to advise on accommodation in the area.

Syon Park Fishery – Middlesex

I've only fished Syon Park once and that was a revelation. I'd actually been to the big house, interviewing the retired ex-butler there – a charming man who showed me round the beautiful house and grounds. The interview went so well that I found myself with a few hours on my hands, and as I'd got fly tackle in the boot and there was a sparkling lake seconds from the car park, I didn't need much persuading! The whole estate of Syon is a surprise: you somehow don't expect to find such serenity and beauty so close to the M25 and Heathrow.

Apparently, this very long, thin lake was dug to Capability Brown's plans some two hundred years ago. Like many other estate lakes, it was allowed to silt and decay until a few years back, when the diggers were brought in. Now, it's a sparkling fishery and its shape almost gives you the impression that you're fishing a river. In fact, it is stream-fed: the Duke of Northumberland's River runs in at the far end and out near the car park. This has the benefit of keeping the water cool in the summer and warming it in the winter. Perhaps this is the reason that fish seem to move whatever the weather or season. In fact, you are unlikely to go to Syon at any time and be disappointed.

Wading is correctly banned here, to help the banksides grow up as wild and natural as possible. This has the added bonus of pulling the fish in close, and you'll often see big, big fish cruising a rod length out. In fact, it's the ideal place to do a bit of stalking. I found it paid me to take my time, study the water and not rush into the fishing. The locals also reckon that you can get away fishing quite light, and if you use leaders of six pounds or over, you're actually cutting back on your chances. Of course, if you are going down to four pounds or so, it does mean that you need a light enough rod to cope – especially when you think that the fish are big. The trout, all rainbows, are stocked at two pounds, but there are plenty of doubles and I saw a couple of fish that I'd put at fourteen or fifteen.

All the usual flies work well – damsels, buzzers, daddies, muddler minnows – and if you haven't got what you need in your own fly box, you'll find plenty on offer in the bailiff's own collection. And don't be worried about asking for advice – it will be very freely given. A floating line is probably all you're really going to need since Syon has no real depth. There is one area that goes down to about twelve feet, but most of the rest is around five or six.

All in all, a very attractive, characterful fishery set in lovely surroundings, and just a stone's throw from the capital.

Season – open all year apart from 25th and 26th December. The fishery opens at 8.00am and ends at dusk.

Tickets – contact Syon Park Fishery, Syon Park, Brentford, Middlesex, TW8 8JF on 020 8568 6354 or 0956 378138 (mobile). Andrew Allen is the more than helpful manager. There's a whole range of ticket prices but they begin at £26 for the full day.

Directions – take the A315 west from the Chiswick roundabout on the North Circular at the start of the M4. You will see the sign at the pedestrian entrance for Syon Park – it gives directions for the car entrance lower down. Turn left at the traffic lights on Twickenham Road and drive into the car park. The fishery is near to the well-signposted Butterfly House. Or you can visit by tube – the nearest station is Gunnersbury Park on the District Line.

Accommodation – the Tourist Information Centre in Twickenham on 020 8891 7272 will supply details of accommodation in this area.

Walthamstow and Hanningfield Reservoirs – London and Essex

It would be quite wrong not to mention these very important reservoirs for the game angler in the South East. They are both very significant in their own ways. Walthamstow Reservoirs 4 and 5, just a few miles from the centre of London, are both available on day ticket and offer huge opportunities for the visitor and local alike. Of course, you're not going to revel in the countryside or feel a million miles from civilisation at Walthamstow. No, these are concrete bowls in the heart of our capital city, but they are full of fish. Lure fishing is generally the most practised of the arts, but the fish will come up to buzzers and dry flies, too, at certain times of the year.

Hanningfield at Chelmsford in Essex is, once again, close to the capital, but its six hundred acres of water are much more attractive than Walthamstow's and, vitally, have set a whole new stamp for rainbow trout fishing. Hanningfield's rainbows are simply stunning. They are the crème-de-la-crème, the rainbows that every other fishery strives to emulate. Fishing at Hanningfield is all about big rainbows. You rarely get one beneath two pounds and they're caught all the way up to twenty pounds and more – the fishery record stands at twenty-four pounds and one ounce. Not that the brown trout are slouches either, and they, too, are in stupendous condition – especially when they edge towards that double-figure mark.

SEASON – Walthamstow closes between March and June. Hanningfield closes on 31st October and reopens on 27th March.

TICKETS – for Walthamstow, phone Thames Water on 020 8808 1527. For Hanningfield, contact Brian Joslin or Tracey Maclellan at Hanningfield Trout Fishery, Gifford's Lane, South Hanningfield, Chelmsford, Essex, CM3 8HX. Day tickets at Hanningfield start at £11. At Walthamstow they are £6, with concessionary tickets at £4.

DIRECTIONS – Walthamstow reservoirs can be found just off the A10 going north. Turn right onto the A503 and the reservoirs are alongside the road. Hanningfield lies to the west of the A130. Travelling north towards Chelmsford, look for signposts to South Hanningfield on the left-hand side. The reservoir is well signposted. As it lies only a few miles from Brentwood and the M25, it is still well within range of the tourist visiting London.

ACCOMMODATION – for Hanningfield, contact the Tourist Information Centre in Chelmsford on 01245 283400, or Brentwood on 01277 200300. The centre in Waltham Abbey will be able to help with accommodation in the area around Walthamstow reservoirs. Phone them on 01992 652295.

COTTINGTON LAKES – KENT

I felt that I should include Cottington even though most of the complex is now given up to coarse fishing. The reason for this is that Pepper Lake, the trout fishing lake, is crystal clear, with a beautiful stock of over-wintered fish, for Cottington is catch and release. I have a real penchant for this type of fishery. How many of us have been sickened by the sight of a freezer full of starched white bodies, I wonder? Another reason for its inclusion is that Cottington really stretches the imagination... the fish are very worldly wise, there's lots of natural food, and the catch and release policy increases the challenge factor.

Not that they're impossible. There are no great depths at Cottington and weed can be a problem, so you're probably looking to fish surface or just sub-surface. Buzzers, daddies, nymphs of all sorts work their various wonders. All in all, this is a very pretty, well-matured little lake that deserves support.

SEASON – open all year.

TICKETS – Cottington Lakes, Sholden, Nr. Deal, Kent. Phone 01304 380691 for details. Prices vary according to the length of time spent fishing and the number of fish taken. For example, £24 will buy you a whole day on the water and you can take three fish before fishing catch and release. There are rainbows and browns to double figures or thereabouts, and the fish are in excellent condition.

DIRECTIONS – take the A258 from Deal towards Sandwich and the lake complex will be well signposted once you reach the village of Sholden.

ACCOMMODATION – the Information Centre in Deal on 01304 369576 can give advice on accommodation in the surrounding area.

Rib Valley Fishery – Hertfordshire

This delightful, very thoughtfully-run fishery is in actual fact made up of two lakes. Rib Valley, the original water, spreads to around twelve acres whilst the newer, smaller Millennium Lake covers about four. Both are spectacular waters, but the Millennium really catches the eye. It's so stunningly crystal clear that you wonder how you're ever going to get a trout out of it.

Indeed, in bright, clear conditions fish can be challenging, even though stocking levels are kept pretty high. The management suggests fishing with comparatively small flies and keeping on the move. Also, keep an eye open for fish circuiting the lake, often close in and frequently feeding hard. A nymph fished in front of them can produce the goods. But, be warned, you'll get many a rejection and it's probably better to fish whatever fly you've got on very slowly indeed.

It's tempting to go down on leader diameter when conditions seem to make life impossible, but be wary. There are some very big fish in both Rib Valley and Millennium and they fight spectacularly well. In fact, most locals advise against going beneath six or seven pound breaking strain.

As far as flies go, all the usual suspects feature at Rib Valley. Take a few lures with you – not really the purest way but sometimes necessary to stir the aggression of a rainbow. Make sure you've got teams of buzzers and be prepared to fish nymphs pretty well static close to the bottom. Above all, take the advice of the management and the regulars because they really do know what they're talking about and they'll go out of their way to make sure you get a bend in your rod.

According to conditions, there's an enlightened approach to catch and release at Rib Valley, where it is encouraged providing water temperatures remain reasonably low. Catch and release is a thorny issue on many still waters and there remain some anglers staunchly against it. In the Millennium Lake, it's so clear that you can actually see that it works: many fish are caught repeatedly, showing that the fish can go back and live on without any ill-effect – providing they're treated well and unhooked carefully.

There are some cracking fish at Rib Valley – the lake record stands at over eighteen pounds – but you'll find plenty of fish in the four- to eight-pound category and above... very good-looking specimens that fight tremendously well. The little River Rib winds its way around the fishery and only helps encourage the natural feel of the entire place. Naturally enough, you can't help feeling a pang for the past when you see this tiny watercourse and you remember how rivers such as the Rib, the Bean and the Minram were, not so long ago, glorious trout streams in their own right. Abstraction has tragically seen them off, of course, and it's to the credit of the new breed of fishery managers that we now have still waters to take their place.

Season – open all year round.

Tickets – contact Richard Vigus at Westmill Farm, Ware, Herts on 01920 469290. Booking is important for the Millennium Lake. There is a whole range of price structures, the most expensive being £50 a day on Millennium Lake for a four-fish bag. However, Rib Valley is less expensive at £26 for four fish. There is a whole scale of charges for lower bag limits, half-day fishing, catch and release and so on. Boat hire is available on Rib Valley.

Directions – the fishery lies off the A602 Ware/Stevenage road, half a mile from the A10 roundabout. You'll find it signposted on the left when you head north. There's a rough track past a garden centre into the valley, and you'll find the two lakes and lodge at the bottom of the hill.

Accommodation – the Tourist Information Centre in Hertford on 01992 584322 can advise on the various kinds of accommodation in the area.

Norton Fishery – Essex

Norton is another of these small fisheries that have sprung up in the Greater London area, providing a welcome amount of sport for resident Londoners and visitors alike.

Norton isn't a particularly old water but it's settled down nicely and is maturing well. The bank side is beginning to look mature and the water certainly is in tiptop order. There are casting platforms around the lake, which don't add to a natural look but they are practical and well built and, combined with the really warm welcome you receive at Norton, make you feel that you're being looked after very well.

There's plenty of weed in the water and, if the sun is high, you get some pretty spectacular views through Polaroid glasses – especially some of the very big fish that inhabit the lake. If you latch onto one of the over-wintered rainbows, for example, you're really in for a treat. Norton is a water that's crying out for surface fishing – buzzers, sedges, mayflies, hoppers, daddies and so on – but there are times when a slow sinking line with a damsel fly, for example, worked back just above the weed, will work wonders. Try something like this when the light is very bright and the fish are sulking. Careful catch and release is allowed, which I'm all for because it makes a challenge on a crystal clear water such as Norton all the more intriguing.

Season – open all year.

Tickets – apply to Bert Norton or Jason Brown at Norton Fishery, Stapleford Tawny, Abridge, Essex on 01708 688445. Prices start at £30 a day with a whole range of prices beneath that for shorter durations. Boats are also available.

Records – stocking is with very good-sized rainbows indeed and the present record is 18lb plus.

Directions – leave the M11 at junction 6 and take the A113 to Abridge. Turn left over the River Roding onto the B172, which is signposted Theydon Bois. Take the first right to Abridge golf course and eventually you will come to the fishery on your right.

Accommodation – the Tourist Information Centre in Brentwood on 01277 200300 will be able to give advice on accommodation in the area.

Brickhouse Farm – Essex

Brickhouse is representative of the brave attempts to bring fly fishing right into the heart of the South East. Brickhouse is very close indeed to the M25 but it's in a truly rural location that gives it a real feel of serenity and charm. This is only a relatively small water but it's intimate and does have a very fishy feel to it. Moreover, the fish do come from the renowned Hanningfield's stock, so they're beautiful and really do put a bend in the rod.

The water is well stocked and you probably won't need to resort to anything particularly fancy to catch the fish. A floating line will probably do. If you want to go deeper, simply increase the length of your leader. A gold head nymph, Pheasant Tail or any one of the buzzer tribe will probably do for starters.

All in all, a pleasant little trout fishery with improving facilities.

Season – open all year round.

Tickets – contact Dennis Bean, Brickhouse Farm, Doddinghurst Road, Brentwood, Essex CM15 0SG on 07713 952999. There is a scale of ticket charges, rising to £20. Catch and release is available for members, and membership is reasonably priced.

Directions – Brickhouse is just north of Brentwood. Leave the M25 at junction 28 and head along the A1023 towards Brentwood town centre. Take the A128 to Chipping Ongar. Turn right into Doddinghurst Road, which you'll find just before the Robin Hood pub. Drive under the A12 towards Doddinghurst, past a leisure centre. After about a mile, you will see the fishery well signposted. You'll find it down a track, past the farm.

Accommodation – information about various kinds of accommodation can be obtained from the Tourist Information Centre in Brentwood. Phone 01277 200300 for details.

Clavering Lake – Essex

Clavering offers two lakes hidden away deep in the heart of rural Essex. The M11 might roar close by, but you won't hear it... only horses' hooves trotting down the lane behind. There are two lakes at Clavering – one of around four acres, going down to about twelve feet at its deepest, and another of around two acres offering depths to some fourteen feet. The lakes are set in very pleasant surroundings and hold splendidly-conditioned fish in gin-clear water.

There's an adventurous stocking policy at Clavering, with fish well in excess of double figures going in on a frequent basis. Look out for the excellent rainbows, browns, brookies and tigers. The average size of fish going in is well over two pounds, so you won't be disappointed when it comes to the size of the fish.

One of the things that makes Clavering really out of the ordinary is the quality of the winter fly fishing. Really good sport can be enjoyed on the top throughout the winter months, and daddies, for example, work well throughout the year. In fact, the only time that Clavering fish can prove difficult is during very hot summer periods, when they tend to get a bit sluggish. You can still take them off the surface if you show a little patience – they come very well to all manner of buzzers. Failing that, perhaps put on an intermediate line and work a nymph very slowly down deep.

Season – open all year.
Tickets – here is a quite complicated system of charges – £25 allows you to fish for the day, take four fish and operate catch and release; £15 allows you simply to fish catch and release. Please note that fish over three pounds are not to be taken.
Directions – take the B1038, which runs from Newport to Buntingford. Follow the road into Clavering and on a sharp left-hand bend you will see the Cricketers pub on the right. Turn right next to the pub, then take the first left. Follow the road for a mile until you see a green sign with the name 'Greenhall' on it. Turn right and continue until you see the lake. Purchase the tickets from the farmhouse, which is past the lake on the left.
Accommodation – details about various kinds of accommodation can be obtained from the Tourist Information Centre in Saffron Walden on 01799 510444.

Highly Recommended Fisheries

- *Felix Farm, Bracknell, Berks. Ten-acre fishery. Very well stocked with some big fish. Spring-fed. Highly recommended.*
- *Woodchurch Trout Fishery, near Ashford, Kent. Phone 01233 860253 for details. Pleasant fishery with good-sized rainbows.*
- *Tenterden Trout Waters, Tenterden, Kent. Contact on 01580 763201. A lot of surface activity with good-sized fish.*
- *Yew Tree Trout Fishery, Rotherfield, East Sussex. Call for information on 01892 662982. Fishes well to dry flies and small buzzers on floating line. Pleasant fishery.*
- *Duncton Mill, Petworth, West Sussex. Call 01798 342048 for more information. Three lakes. Feeling of space. Nice fishery.*

Fly-Fishing Sites in East Anglia

1. *Grafham Water*
2. *Northbank Trout Fishery*
3. *Larkwood Trout Fishery*
4. *Cross Green Fly Fishery*
5. *Whinburgh Trout Lakes*
6. *The River Wensum*
7. *Bure Valley Lakes*

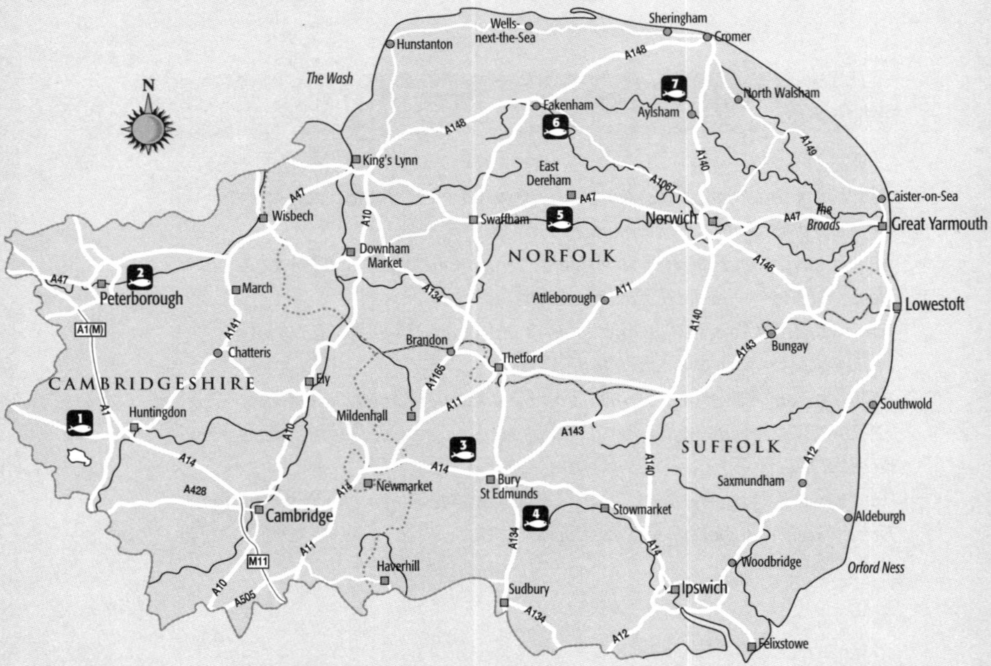

"East Anglia is a bit underrated, I guess, when it comes to game fishing. Everybody seems to think solely of the coarse fishing in the region, which I agree is very good indeed. But there is water for the trout man and some of it's of high quality and relatively obtainable. Of course, we East Anglians do have Grafham Water, which is still one of the best reservoirs anywhere. And there are a number of really first-class commercial trout fisheries that have stood the test of time and gone from strength to strength. In Norfolk, especially, there are also some first rate little trout streams. The problem for the visitor is that access is closely guarded. You do have the Wensum, though, in central Norfolk, which gives you a really good idea of what things are like. A real chalk stream this one is. And then, finally, you've got the unexpected. The North Norfolk coast, for example, is absolutely ideal for fly fishing for bass. It's generally sandy but with gently shelving gravel banks and the fish come in really close. My preference is for a floating line and a big streamer-type fly that resembles a sand eel. Providing you can get a fly out a bit of a way you've always got a chance. Watch out for small fish breaking the surface or gulls coming down for a feeding spree and you can be sure bass are somewhere close at hand. And who knows, you might also pick up one or two of the sea trout that also visit the area. All exciting stuff."

JOE REED, NATIONAL TRUST WARDEN OF THE NORTH NORFOLK COAST

And Joe is right, East Anglia offers a huge amount to the visitor and some of it you wouldn't suspect. A couple of the streams – the Nar and Wensum in particular – have stretches that are available to Salmon and Trout Association members. Phone 0207 2835838 for membership details. So, in conclusion, when you're planning a family holiday with a trout rod also in mind, don't discount East Anglia: you could be surprised.

Grafham Water – Cambridgeshire

Grafham Water is really one of the jewels of East Anglia – a historic trout water that continues to produce quite staggering catches of rainbows. In fact, 1999 was officially Grafham's best season ever – and that's saying something – with sixty percent of the trout caught weighing two pounds or more and a fishery record of eleven pounds twelve ounces.

In part, Grafham has always produced such excellent quality fish because of the high numbers of roach and bream fry that are spawned every season. These small fish allow the rainbows to pile on weight very quickly indeed, and the browns – some of them really huge fish – benefit particularly.

Grafham has a fleet of fifty boats – well-designed and very stable – and records seem to suggest that catches are higher afloat than from the bank. For those visitors who are a little unsure about boat fishing, courses are available from one of the experts who run the fishery lodge.

Grafham has always been a very appealing place to fish: lovely scenery, very high-quality rainbows and browns, and free-rising fish. Black and green flies have often seemed to do very well at Grafham, certainly for the very big fish taken over the last

On the Riverbank

- *If you see numbers of fish dying or in distress you are probably witnessing a pollution incident. It's your responsibility to phone the Environment Agency (EA)emergency hotline on 0800 807060 immediately. This number is free and is available twenty-four hours a day anywhere in England and Wales.*
- *The faster you act, the more likely it is that the incident can be controlled and dealt with. Contact club officials, too.*
- *When reporting incidents, ensure you give clear, concise details of what you have seen and good directions to the actual location of the incident.*
- *Take water samples if you can. Any samples taken at the time can provide the vital evidence needed to assist the EA in bringing a successful prosecution.*
- *If you have a camera with you, its useful to take photographs of what you are witnessing. This may also help in the prosecution process.*
- *Enjoy the countryside and respect its life and work.*
- *Fasten all gates.*
- *Keep to public footpaths across farmland.*
- *Take your litter home.*
- *Help to keep all water clean.*
- *Protect wildlife, plants and trees.*

few years. So, bearing that in mind, try a Viva or even a Green Pea. These work well on floating lines, sometimes with a long leader if conditions are still and bright. Don't overlook buzzer fishing for much of the year – you'd be surprised just how many big fish fall to these tiny flies in the surface film.

Season – Grafham opens on 1st April and runs through to 31st December.
Tickets – phone the fishery's lodge on 01480 810531 to book either a bank or boat permit. A day ticket costs £16 with an eight-fish limit and a morning or late afternoon ticket is £10 with a four-fish limit. A two-man boat costs £20 a day and £12 for the evening.
Records – brown trout 19lbs 12oz and rainbow trout 13lbs 13oz.
Rules – do ensure that you obtain a fishery map before setting out. There is no fishing close to the bird hides or around the nature reserve.
Directions – Grafham Water can be accessed from the A14 to Grafham village or from the A1 to Buckden. The various access points are well signposted.
Accommodation – the Tourist Information Centre in Cambridge on 01223 322640 can supply details of various kinds of accommodation in the area.

Northbank Trout Fishery – Cambridgeshire

Northbank really is a superb trout fishery – pretty, remote and beautifully cared for. It is one of those places that give you a huge amount of faith in the commercial trout fishery. It's a comparatively large water at around sixteen acres or so, with a large island that also increases the amount of bank space available. In fact, given the two together, there's well over a mile of fishing on offer. It's not a particularly deep water, with holes going to around sixteen feet or so, but this hardly matters – especially as the water is so clear and the dry fly works so well.

This is a point emphasised by one of the bailiffs, Clyde Anthony: 'Northbank is an absolutely superb dry-fly fishery, partly because it's so crystal clear. We open in March and I go dry fly from the word go. I use small flies early season and then get bigger as conditions dictate. All the usual patterns work – Black and Peacock Spider, for example, or gold-ribbed Hare's Ear. Later on in the summer you can't beat a Daddy's. Fish the water carefully and slowly and don't be in too much of a hurry to keep taking your line out. It's the same when the fish are fry feeding towards the back end. All manner of Victors and Butchers work well, but once again, don't drag them back at ninety miles an hour. Think about what you're doing and how to make them realistic. If you want a bit of guidance, I'm always willing to advise'.

That's the hallmark of this attractive, friendly fishery: you never really feel you're on your own at Northbank – there's always somebody willing to help out. A really great fishery in a lost, lonely part of the world.

Season – Northbank is open from 6th March to 24th October, and the lake opens from 7.00am and closes at dusk.

Tickets – contact the owner John Cutteridge at Northbank Trout Fishery, Northbank, Thorney, Peterborough, Cambridgeshire, PE6 0RP or phone him on 01733 203998. Tickets for four hours cost £7, allowing you to take one fish and then move on to catch and release. For two fish taken, you pay £10. An all-day ticket with one fish taken is £9, with two fish £12 and with four fish taken £18. Catch and release is available thereafter.

Records – the lake is stocked with both browns and rainbows from one and a quarter pounds upwards but with plenty of far bigger fish. The lake record is 15lbs 2oz with many fish of 5lbs and above.

Directions – take the A47 towards Peterborough turning down the B1040 signposted to Whittlesey. In three and a half to four miles, you will come to the Dog in Doublet Bridge with lock gates over the River Nene. Turn right at the bridge along the road following the Nene. You will see signs to the fishery on the right-hand side.

Accommodation – try Wisteria House, Church Lane, Peterborough, PE6 7DT on 01733 252272 or contact the Tourist Information Centre in Peterborough on 01733 452336.

Larkwood Trout Fishery – Suffolk

Larkwood Fishery, created just over fifteen years ago, goes from strength to strength. There are two lakes at Larkwood – Glebe Lake and West Stow – both about three acres and featuring shallows and depths down to about twenty feet. Both waters are very pretty and totally matured, surrounded by trees and good reed growth. Providing the weather does not become too warm, both lakes remain clear and there is a profusion of natural life. Look out for alder fly larva, pea mussels, shrimps, snails, beetle larva of all kinds, corixa and damsel fly nymphs. It's on a diet as rich and varied as this that both the rainbow and brown trout grow on very quickly to become superb fish.

The fishery is run by that expert angler, Ian McGregor, a most entertaining Scot who offers an outstandingly warm welcome. Ian stocks with fish of about a pound and a quarter to a pound and a half minimum. However, there are plenty of fish much bigger than that into the seven- to eight-pound bracket and even above. Ian also takes care to stock every other day so there's a constant top up of fresh fish, and sport is very rarely dull. 'Virtually all my regulars here use nothing but a floating line', says Ian.

'Depending on the depth they want to get a fly down to, they simply alter the length of the leader. If the fish are down deep, then they'll use a long leader and obviously if they're up on the surface you can go that bit shorter. And you don't need many different fly patterns here. Providing you've got some damsels, Hare's Ears, some Pheasant Tails and Cats Whiskers then you should really do okay, I guess.'

Larkwood is open all the year round and fishes particularly well in the winter when it's still possible to take fish – very well-mended rainbows indeed – on nymphs as well as lures. Larkwood is highly recommended, especially in an area where there isn't a huge amount of competition – not that that means Ian is going to relax his standards.

SEASON – open all year round.
TICKETS – contact Ian McGregor on 01284 728612 at Larkwood Fishery, West Stow, Bury St Edmunds, Suffolk. Permits cost £15 for four fish and £9 for two fish. It is possible to practise catch and release after you've taken your limit.
DIRECTIONS – from Bury St Edmunds, take the A1101 towards Mildenhall. Turn right at the West Stow signpost and follow this road down past the country park. The fishery is one mile further along the road, situated on the right.
ACCOMMODATION – phone the local Tourist Information Centre in Bury St Edmunds on 01284 764667 for advice on various kinds of accommodation in the area.

CROSS GREEN FLY FISHERY – SUFFOLK

Cross Green has been up and running for twelve years now but it's only in the past few years that its owner, Mr Steward, has opened to the public on anything like a full-scale basis. Cross Green is a friendly, quiet sort of place, set in the most beautiful of surroundings with the most friendly of welcomes. Just the sort of venue you want if you fancy a bit of a challenge but something comparatively low-key .

There are about four and a half acres of water at Cross Green, divided into four lakes – two large ones and two slightly smaller. The lakes are spring-fed and this gives them a remarkable clarity – something that even the introduced carp haven't managed to destroy. These fish have come on in leaps and bounds but are regularly netted so that they don't adversely affect water quality.

This isn't a big fish water, or at least that's not its purpose. As Mr Steward says: 'I don't really encourage bounty hunters here. What I like is people who come and appreciate the peace and quiet. That's what they tell me, that they find peace here, and I think that's what fishing should be'.

Hear, hear to that! Mind you, the fish are more than worth catching. Cross Green holds both browns and rainbows averaging around two pounds in weight with occasional double-figure fish landed – not bad for a small trout fishery!

Cross Green is highly attractive: the trees around it were planted many years ago and are now reaching maturity. There's also plenty of wildlife and some very interesting duck species. It's a characterful sort of water all round – the office here is made from an old steam plough van that dates back to the 1930s! There is a good-sized car park and flush toilets.

All the normal methods and flies work here. 'Daddies are very popular in the late summer', says Mr Steward. 'Buzzers work throughout the year and Goldhead Nymphs and Montanas seem popular. In fact, I don't think there's anything here that doesn't really work... providing the fisherman knows how to fish them!' So if you're looking for a gentle, relaxing experience with some beautifully conditioned fish in a serene setting, you can't do better than Cross Green.

Season – open year round from dawn to dusk.

Tickets – contact Mr K.B. Steward on 01284 828820 at Cross Green Fly Fishery, Cross Green Farm, Cockfield, Bury St Edmunds, Suffolk IP30 0LG. Day-ticket prices are £16. For this you can catch eight fish, take two and release six. Half-day prices are £10. You can catch four fish and release three.

Directions – from Bury St Edmunds, take the A134 south. In four or five miles, turn left onto the A1141, signposted to Lavenham. The fishery is situated three hundred yards down this road on the left.

Accommodation – top of the market accommodation includes the Swan Hotel at Lavenham. Phone for details on 0870 400 8116. Alternatively, try the Angel Hotel at Bury St Edmunds on 01284 714000. There is also the highly recommended Kiln Farm Guesthouse in Bury St Edmunds on 0135 9242604. Alternatively, contact the Tourist Information Centre in Bury St Edmunds on 01284 764667 for details of further accommodation.

Your Responsibilities

Fishing shouldn't take place in a vacuum. As an angler it is important that you support the bodies that fight for the sport that you love. These organisations cannot operate without the help of fishermen... and very frequently pathetically small numbers join the most worthwhile of organisations.

- *The Atlantic Salmon Trust, on 01796 473439, fights tooth and nail for the welfare of salmon both in home waters and in the high the seas.*
- *The Salmon and Trout Association not only provides good local fishing for members but also works very hard indeed to ensure stable habitats. You can contact the Association on 020 7283 5838.*
- *The Wild Trout Society not only publishes an excellent magazine for its members but also promotes the wild brown trout fishing of this country. The address is 92-104 Carnwarth Road, London SW6 3HW.*
- *The Grayling Society fights directly for one of our most beautiful freshwater fish that is frequently under pressure. To join, contact Mike Tebbs, Ayott Lodge, 38 The Crescent, Belmont, Sutton, Surrey SM2 6BJ.*
- *The Anglers Conservation Association has been fighting polluters for over half a century. Its list of court successes is extraordinary. Join this if you join nothing else, by contacting the Association on 0118 971 4770.*

Whinburgh Trout Lakes – Norfolk

There really are some idyllic commercial trout fisheries available now all over the country, and Whinburgh, deep in the heart of Norfolk, is one of the nicest. Whinburgh comprises two lakes joined in the middle and set in beautiful, mature, landscaped grounds. There's easy access for wheelchairs, along with a brew-up shed. Wives and friends who aren't fishing are more than welcome... providing they're well-behaved, says owner Mr Potter!

Whinburgh is a fertile, sheltered water holding both browns and rainbows, generally between one and ten pounds in weight. The water lends itself to dry fly fishing, as it only averages six feet deep and the water is frequently very clear indeed.

Overall, Whinburgh is a very lovely, very friendly place to fish, and the trout, which are in excellent condition, offer a satisfying challenge without ever appearing too diabolically difficult! Highly recommended.

Season – Whinburgh is open all year round and there is a competition once a month.

Tickets – phone Mr Potter on 01362 850201 for up-to-the-minute ticket information. At the time of writing, day tickets are £12.50 for nine hours on a catch and release basis. Half-day tickets (five hours) cost £7.50. Concessions are made for anglers aged 65 plus on Tuesday, Wednesday and Thursday. Phone for details.

Records – the biggest rainbow has clocked in at over 13lb and double-figure browns have been seen, even if not landed.

Rules – Whinburgh is based on catch and release so barbless hooks are mandatory. It is permitted to kill rainbows and these cost £1.75 per pound to take.

Directions – Whinburgh is situated on the B1135 between Dereham and Wymondham. Phone Mr Potter for exact details.

Accommodation – there are a number of bed and breakfast guesthouses in the area and the Tourist Information Centre in Dereham will be able to supply details. Phone them on 01362 698992.

The River Wensum – Norfolk

The Wensum up until fifty years ago was an unsung delight. It runs over chalk, is largely spring-fed and for many centuries in its life was at least the equivalent of many of the Hampshire streams. Then agriculture took over. The river was, tragically, dredged. The water table fell, the glistening gravel rapids became clogged with silt, and fish stocks – especially of trout and grayling – began to plummet.

However, all is not lost. The Environment Agency has really ploughed ahead and instituted sweeping changes along the river system. Fakenham Angling Club is also a very progressive body and, wherever possible, has devoted itself to bettering the trout fishing. So, today, the upper River Wensum is absolutely worth anybody's visit.

Fakenham Angling Club controls some two to three miles of top quality river trout fishing in the vicinity of Fakenham itself. Here you can wander, almost always alone, through lovely farmland and fish a gin-clear river. In places it's deep. There are pools. There are dancing shallows. You'll come across dace, perhaps roach, and you'll see the odd pike sauntering away. It's that type of mixed river but, believe me, the brown trout fishing can be quite excellent. I say brown trout because Fakenham, in their wisdom, only stock browns and will have no truck with rainbows. So, you see, the spirit of the old Wensum is being kept alive nicely.

Stalk your fish very carefully. The water is so clear, as I've said, and these fish become very wild indeed. Actually, it's quite possible that some of them truly are wild, because a certain amount of natural breeding does still take place today. Nymphs of all sorts work well – especially leaded ones in the deeper water, which runs over luxuriant weed beds. There is something of a mayfly hatch and, for the dry fly fisherman, there are rises most evenings during warmer periods.

So, okay, this might not be quite the style of trout fishing that you'd find on some of the Hampshire streams but it's not far behind and, for £5 a day, I don't think you'd find much better anywhere.

Season – 1st April to 30th October, though the best of the fishing is from later in the spring to the early autumn.
Tickets – Fakenham Angling Club sells tickets from Dave's Fishing Tackle, Miller's Walk, Fakenham. Phone 01328 862543 for details. It pays to phone in advance because a limited number of day tickets are issued. Also, note that there are no day tickets issued for Sundays.
Directions – The Wensum rises just to the west of Fakenham and flows south east, more or less parallel to the A1067 to Norwich.
Accommodation – why not try Sculthorpe Mill, close to Fakenham, on 01328 856161 right at the head of the fishing itself? This is a delightfully converted old water mill that provides excellent accommodation and food.

Bure Valley Lakes – Norfolk

Bure Valley Fisheries offers some wonderfully secluded trout fishing in a fold of North Norfolk countryside well away from maddening civilisation. Moreover, the fishery is run with huge intelligence by Mike Smith, its owner. Catch and release on the fifteen-acre lake is encouraged, although rainbows can be taken at a cost of £1.80 a pound. Interestingly, Mike says that at least eighty percent of fish are returned. This means that he does not have to rely overly on stocked fish, and the condition and wariness of the resident rainbows continually increases. In fact, regulars say there is not a still-water trout fishery to touch it in the whole of East Anglia.

There is more to come, as the name of the fishery implies. The upper River Bure winds alongside the lake and is an absolute delight to fish for those who appreciate the charm of small, wild brown trout. These fish are not particularly large – six to eight ounces is the norm – but what they lack in size they make up for in cunning, beauty and fighting ability on light tackle. The river really is a delight and a challenge to fish. It abounds with features and this is really creepy-crawly stuff to flick your fly into miniature pools and riffles.

Most excitingly of all, the infant Bure has a startlingly rich mayfly hatch that takes place in very late May and early June. The mayflies tend to dribble off through most of the daylight hours, which gives the trout fisherman a real chance of some spectacular sport. All browns must be returned at once and the fishing is available over six generously laid-out beats.

Season – the lake is open all the year round and the river fishing begins on April 1st and ends on the last day of October.

Tickets – the trout lakes cost £12.50 for a full day, £10 for six hours and £7.50 for an evening ticket. The river costs £12.50 per day, per beat. All fishing is catch and release, though rainbows can be taken for £1.80 per pound.

Records – 9lb exactly for a wild brown trout and 12lb 6oz for rainbows. As the lake is stocked with fish to fifteen pounds plus, this record must surely be smashed shortly.

Directions – Take the A140 from Norwich to Aylsham, then the B1354 to Saxthorpe. The fishery is on the right-hand side, four miles out of Aylsham. You will find it down a mile long cart track.

Accommodation – contact the Tourist Information Centre in Cromer on 01263 512497 or at North Walsham on 01263 721070. They will advise on local accommodation.

Highly Recommended Fisheries

- *Earith Lakes, Cambridgeshire. Call 01487 740301 for further information. Really big fish in lovely condition. Highly recommended.*
- *Narborough Trout Farm, Nr. King's Lynn, Norfolk, phone 01760 338005. Four lakes and a stream. Very long established fishery with an historic big fish reputation.*

Fly-Fishing Sites in the Midlands

1. Arnfield Reservoir
2. Ladybower Reservoir
3. Claybridge Trout Lakes
4. The Derbyshire Rivers
5. Yeaveley Trout Fishery
6. Gailey Trout Fishery
7. Loynton Hall
8. Packington Fisheries
9. Ravensthorpe
10. Eyebrook
11. Rutland Water
12. Pitsford Water
13. Draycote Water
14. Salford Trout Lakes
15. Farmoor Trout Fishery

'You know John, these Midland reservoirs came at just the right time for me in many ways. I'd started out as a coarse fisherman and done very well with pike and tench and all the usual species, but I was looking for a new challenge. Then, suddenly, all these extraordinary venues burst upon the fishing scene, and as a young man I realised I could be in at the beginnings of it all. Exciting stuff. Everybody was learning. New rods, new reels, new flies and new methods.'

BOB CHURCH, ENGLAND FLY-FISHING INTERNATIONAL (IN AN INTERVIEW IN 1988)

The Midlands, especially Northamptonshire, will always be remembered as the home of British reservoir trout fishing techniques. This side of the sport really took off in the 1960s: greater affluence, increasing car transport and improving tackle standards all meant that game angling began to look attractive to men and women who had previously only fished coarse. The large reservoirs scattered around the Midlands, created to supply domestic and industrial needs, cried out to be stocked, and the results were frequently spectacular. Grafham in Cambridgeshire really lead the way. When the fishing was opened here, the trout that had been stocked were found to have put on weight dramatically. Traditional fly-fishing gear was rendered useless. The same at Rutland, Eyebrook, Draycote and a host of other waters.

In response to the demands of these big reservoirs and savage trout, new rods, reels and techniques were developed by such legendary masters of the Northamptonshire reservoir school as Dick Shrive, Arthur Cove and Bob Church. The reservoirs of the Midlands are now a vital part of the game-fishing scene. Thanks to men like Church, you can now enjoy these fisheries with tackle and techniques that have been honed to perfection over the last forty years or so. These are great waters and the fish that swim in them can be really stunning. Ticket prices are generally very reasonable and at every reservoir you will find very helpful fishery staff who go out of their way to make sure that your visit is as enjoyable and fruitful as possible.

Arnfield Reservoir – Cheshire

Arnfield is close to the village of Tintwistle on the edge of the Peak District moorland. I've got a particular affection for the reservoirs of this area because it was here that I first learnt to fly fish as a child. Then, the reservoirs seemed huge places to me, almost intelligible, full of trout that boggled my imagination. I remember one vividly: it was a cold night in April, and all I knew about in those days was dry fly fishing. I put out a small blue fly – I couldn't for the life of me tell you its name – and it was taken the instant it settled on the water's surface. I played that fish until my knees shook with both cold and excitement. Then, right at the end, as I was scrabbling for the net, the leader parted. A few days later I was back at the reservoir and the bailiff called to see me. A big trout had been found dead by the dam with my fly in its scissors. Six pounds five ounces. A brown. I was devastated.

I wasn't doing everything wrong. Arnfield Reservoir – a forty-acre, Victorian construction – is one of the best top waters in this part of the country. All manner of dry flies and buzzers work very well indeed. And that includes the cold months too. Mind you, it does go down to about fifty feet in places, so there are times, in the heat of the summer and the very depths of winter, when a sinking line and team of deep-working nymphs is probably what is needed. There's a fleet of well-equipped boats on the fishery, so it's possible to fish almost loch-style when a breeze gets up.

At the time of writing, Arnfield is about to undergo complete renovation because of a quite serious leak. The feeling is that it will soon be back in action and very probably, if this is possible, the fishery will be vastly improved as a result.

As it is, stocking is very generous indeed, at around two hundred pounds per acre, with some very big fish going in. In fact, there are quite a few monsters of over twenty pounds in the water. As a general rule, the fish are around two pounds, along with some natural browns, some of them growing nicely to four pounds plus. These, particularly, can be picked up down deep. Mind you, to fish deep at Arnfield is generally missing the point: it's not often that you get a comparatively large, exposed water like this that fishes so well to surface methods. Try it and you'll be delighted.

Season – the fishery is closed for a month, generally in February. It's a good idea to phone before making a journey around this time of year.

Tickets – contact Arnfield Fly Fishery, Tintwistle, via Hyde, Cheshire SK14 7HP on 0780 3038776. A four-hour, two-fish limit, ticket costs £12, a six-hour, three-fish limit, is £16 and an eight-hour, four-fish limit, is £18. There is catch and release once the limits have been reached. There is also a very progressive, sixteen-hour flexi-ticket. This allows four fish to be taken and the hours can be used any time during the course of a week. Obviously a real boon for holidaying anglers. Please note that barbless or de-barbed hooks must be used.

Directions – pick up the M67 heading east. At the end of the motorway, take the A628 towards Barnsley. After two miles, just beyond the village of Tintwistle, there is a Northwest

Water Treatment plant to your right. Opposite this, on the left, is a narrow lane leading to Arnfield Fishery.

Accommodation – the Tourist Information Centre in Glossop on 01457 863223 can provide details of various kinds of accommodation in this area.

Ladybower Reservoir – Derbyshire

I caught my very first trout on a fly at lovely Ladybower reservoir many, many years ago, and for that reason alone I retain huge affection for the water. But it's always a joy to go back to Ladybower, perched high in the Peak District National Park, enjoying stunning views over an amazingly mountainous landscape. Ladybower is wild, lonesome fishing and you'd hardly believe you're a mere dozen or so miles west of Sheffield when you're out there, either on the water or enjoying the thirteen miles of virtually untrodden bankside.

The stocking policies are very generous indeed, and each year over thirty-five thousand mixed browns and rainbows are stocked – including browns to over four pounds and rainbows to ten pounds plus. And these are wonderful fish, nearly all of them raised very carefully at the fishery itself under expert care.

Hiring a boat probably gives you the best chance of a bumper bag of fish but Ladybower is about more than this. I prefer to travel light and walk as many miles of the bank as I feel up to during the day. Imitative patterns can succeed at Ladybower, but most of the locals tend to go for more traditional reservoir flies like the Ace of Spades, the Orange Chenille and Viva. There are times, however, especially later on in the summer, when fish will come to the surface quite avidly and dry fly fishing can pay dividends both early and late. One bonus with such a large water is that much of the marginal path is largely untrodden during the day and even big fish will come in very close indeed. So take your time, stalk carefully and you could be in for quite a surprise.

Season – Ladybower opens on 6th March and closes on 13th October.

Tickets – tickets are available from the Fishery Office, Ladybower Reservoir, Ashopton Road, Bamford, Derbyshire S33 0AZ on 01433 651254. Day tickets cost £10.90 for the full day and £7.70 for an afternoon/evening ticket. A seven-day ticket for £42 is also available, ideal for visitors. Boats, with or without electric outboards, are also bookable through the Fishery Office. Tuition is also available with prior booking through the Fishery Office.

Records – rainbow trout 17lb 4oz, brown trout 11lb 7oz.

Directions – the reservoir is well-signposted off the A6013, ten miles west of Sheffield.

Accommodation – Bamford, a short distance from the reservoir, boasts several good hotels – try the Ladybower Inn on 01433 651241, the Yorkshire Bridge Inn on 01433 651361, the Marquis of Granby on 01433 651206 and the Rising Sun on 01433 651323. The Tourist Information Centre in Sheffield on 0114 221 1900 will also be able to advise on further accommodation.

Reservoir Tips (The Midlands)

Reservoirs can appear very daunting on first view, especially if you've been used to a small, commercial-type fishery. However, the benefits of reservoir fishing are immense.

- *Location is obviously a key. Don't get too entrenched, rather keep on the move until you contact fish. Remember rainbows especially are shoal fish and where you get one take, you're likely to get more.*
- *Binoculars aren't a bad idea to spot surface activity up or down the bank. Look for rising fish, fry feeding fish and fish feeding just sub-surface.*
- *Where it's permitted, it's tempting to wade out from the bank a little way to get nearer to fish rising just beyond your casting capabilities. Remember, however, that all you're likely to do is push the fish even further away from the bank, and so little is achieved. You also run the risk of scaring fish that are willing to feed close in.*
- *If your casting is a problem to you, the chances are you need to either learn or brush up on your double haul techniques. You'll find that casting clinics are available at some of the big Midland reservoirs or, alternatively, you could get yourself down to the Sportfish fly fishing school at Reading. Phone 0118 9303860 for more details.*
- *Don't be afraid to experiment. If, for example, you've been a lure fisherman all your life, by all means start out with this technique but don't be afraid to switch over to nymphs, buzzers or even dry flies if you think they'd serve you better. And you'll be amazed how quickly you pick up the new techniques.*
- *A boat can work wonders on large waters. Always wear buoyancy aids and, if you're a little unsure about taking to the waves, go out a few times with somebody experienced. That way your confidence will build up and you'll begin to appreciate the advantages boat fishing can give you.*
- *Reservoir experts often take a whole team of sinkers but, for a kick off, I'd suggest to you an intermediate line with a sink rate of between one and a half inches per second and two and a half inches per second. This way you can count your lies down and get a rough idea of the depths your flies are fishing at.*
- *If you've been used to lure fishing, don't forget that you can fish nymphs, buzzers, very, very slowly. Indeed, fishing them static is more and more common. Of course they're not totally immobile because there'll always be some drift but we are talking about techniques that work the flies in the gentlest of ways.*
- *Above all, don't be afraid to ask advice of other anglers and, especially, the fishery staff. Almost invariably these will prove to be hugely helpful and very generous with their time and advice.*

CLAYBRIDGE TROUT LAKES – LINCOLNSHIRE

I make mention of Claybridge Trout Lakes not because they pose a huge challenge to the most obsessive of fly fishermen but because they offer a very nice option in an area not overly rich with trout fisheries. The water is about four acres and nestles in an attractive setting. Stocking is very generous, with fish of between a pound and going well into doubles, with the occasional twenty also being released! The high level of stocking means that most methods work and this makes it an ideal water for the family or for an angler trying to build up his or her confidence.

SEASON – open all year.
TICKETS – contact Claybridge Trout Lakes, Bullington, Wragby, Market Rasen, Lincolnshire LN8 5NN on 01673 857014. A £3 day ticket allows you to catch and keep fish at £1.45 per pound weight. There is also a very generous £6 catch and release ticket.
DIRECTIONS – take the A158 from Lincoln to Horncastle and you will find Wragby between the two towns. The fishery is well signposted on the main road.
ACCOMMODATION – you can try the White Swan Hotel, 29 Queen Street, Market Rasen, LN8 3EN on 01673 843356. Advice on other accommodation can be supplied by the Tourist Information Centre in Lincoln on 01522 873256.

THE DERBYSHIRE JEWELS – THE RIVERS DERWENT, WYE AND DOVE

These three rivers, although surrounded by some of the biggest industrial centres of the north, offer some of the most superb fly fishing in the entire country. Mind you, because these waters are so prolific and beautiful and because they are so close to large urban areas, the pressure on them is great, and day tickets are not easy to come across. However, for the visitor, there are opportunities and they are very well worth pursuing indeed. For me, personally, the Derwent is at its best at Baslow along the Chatsworth fishery, which is available to residents of the Cavendish Hotel. There are several miles of beautiful water here and the trout fishing can be just extraordinary. Perhaps even more special is the grayling fishing, especially in the Christmas holiday period when there is a festive spirit in the hotel and the nearby market towns. Fly fishing can be wonderful, but bait fishing is also allowed and some of the very best water is found directly in front of the hall itself, just a little upriver of the imposing bridge.

The Wye is equally prolific and ticket availability exists on the Haddon Hall estate, close to Bakewell. The fishing here can be second to none, and the river is fascinating to read – a snake of meanders, deep pools and enticing ripples. Once again, grayling are present and can grow very large indeed, but it's probably the wild-bred rainbows that excite the most. Yes, wild-bred... these stunning fish are like miniature steelheads and have looks and battling qualities you'll remember the rest of your days.

Now we come to what is perhaps the jewel in the crown, the River Dove, the enchanting stream made famous in *The Complete Angler* by Izaak Walton and his collaborator, Cotton. Trout and grayling waters don't come any more beautiful than this, and the pinnacle of northern fly fishing can be seen in Dovedale itself. Just the walk itself is breathtaking. Of course, it is a walker's paradise, but if you can get out early or late you can almost sense the presence of Walton at your shoulder.

Once again, the trout fishing is quite, quite superb and on a summer evening, fishing the dry fly, you'd think you were in paradise. Imagine this: small, characterful, crystal-clear river, winding between dramatic hills, overhung with forest. But, again, once the frosts begin to bite and the leaves fall, the grayling come into their own – and what grayling these are. Two-pounders are not uncommon and threes exist, lurking in the deep, mysterious pools.

SEASON – generally, the waters are available for trout from the beginning of April until early October but it is as well to check on local restrictions. Grayling fishing on most of the waters continues throughout the winter, closing on 14th March.

TICKETS – the head river keeper on the Haddon Estate, Mr Ross, is of great help both for tickets on the Derwent and the Wye. Contact him on 01629 636255. Two-day tickets for the Derwent are also available from the Peacock Hotel, Rowsley, on 01629 733518, both to residents and non-residents. The other possibility on the Derwent is the Cavendish water. Phone the Cavendish Hotel on 01246 582311 for full details. You have to be resident at the hotel, which is not cheap, but, believe me, the experience is one that lasts. As for the Wye, Mr Ross will give full information. The Dove can be fished by guests of the Izaak Walton Hotel, Yeaveley Estate, Nr. Ashbourne. Phone 01335 350555 for information. There is also a small trout lake available – perfect for beginners. The tackle shop, Foster's of Ashbourne Ltd., Compton Bridge, Ashbourne DE6 1BX is also a fund of information and publishes a local guide to day-ticket waters.

DIRECTIONS – it is best to apply to the various ticket sources for directions to these waters. Be careful not to stray over beat boundaries. Try also Stephen Moores on 01629 640159 for day tickets on the Monsal Dale Fishery.

ACCOMMODATION – the hotels mentioned are all excellent. There is also a good deal of bed and breakfast accommodation in this popular holiday area. Contact Mr & Mrs Beltney, Congreave Farm, Congreave, Stanton in the Peak, Derbyshire DE4 2NF. The Tourist Information Centres at Ashbourne, on 01335 343666, and Bakewell, on 01629 813227, will also be able to give advice about accommodation.

Yeaveley Trout Fishery – Derbyshire

I've included Yeaveley for several reasons. Although it is only a small water, it does provide something of an antidote to the larger reservoirs found all around the Midlands. At times it's just nice to go intimate. Secondly, I've frequently been happy to use Yeaveley in the autumn and winter when I've initially wanted to fish for grayling in the surrounding rivers but found them totally out of condition and in flood. A day spent on Yeaveley has been a very happy substitute. And thirdly, and certainly not least, Yeaveley is a really spectacularly attractive and challenging little fishery in its own right.

It's only around one and a quarter acres or so but is now around ten years old and has matured magnificently. There are good levels of cover that allow for successful stalking (if you're good enough) on a water that is always crystal clear. Two springs account for this and also help to promote a very active fly life on the water.

Depths aren't great – around fifteen feet maximum – so it's quite possible to fish the year round with a floating line or, at most, an intermediate. Yeaveley is a spectacular dry fly water; on the phone with the owner recently I was told that a fourteen-pound rainbow had actually come off the surface, and that was in late October. Buzzers tend to work well the year round, especially very small ones on a size sixteen or even an eighteen. In fact, stay small whatever flies you decide to use.

And go barbless. Yeaveley operates a very progressive ticket system. You can take your first three fish and then operate on catch and release thereafter, to what is considered a sportsman-like limit. That's around about ten fish or so in the eyes of the fishery owner, and who would quibble at that? Quite sensibly, too, he suggests not taking fish of over three and a half pounds.

You're afforded a very warm welcome at Yeaveley. There's a welcoming cabin, a pub close by, and tuition can also be arranged. And, with the sight of ten-pound-plus rainbows cruising in the clear water at my feet, I don't find it too hard to give up on my grayling fishing for the day!

Season – open all year apart from Christmas Day.

Tickets – contact Yeaveley Estate and Trout Fishery, Yeaveley, Nr. Ashbourne, Derbyshire, on 01335 330247. Tickets cost £17 per day. The first three fish are taken, and catch and release thereafter. Barbless hooks please.

Directions – take the A515 south from Ashbourne for about two miles. You'll find the village of Yeaveley signposted on the left. Follow the road into the village and you will see the Horseshoe pub on the right. This is next to the driveway to the fishery, which is well signposted.

Accommodation – the Tourist Information Centre in Ashbourne, on 01335 343666, will be able to supply information on various kinds of accommodation in the area. Ashbourne has a wealth of hotels and bed and breakfast accommodation.

Gailey Trout Fishery – Staffordshire

Gailey is well worth a look for many reasons. Firstly, it is situated just off the M6 and couldn't be easier to find. Secondly, at thirty-eight acres it gives a nice impression of space and variety. You never really feel crowded on the water, especially if you book one of the reasonably-priced boats and get out behind one of the islands.

Gailey is also renowned as a top water, and throughout most of the year dry flies and buzzers on a floating line are pretty much all you will need. Mind you, as autumn develops, the bigger trout, particularly, begin to fry feed with a vengeance. The water is kept very well stocked and if you don't succeed down at the deeper dam end where the water is around seventeen feet, you can try stalking the fish up in the shallows where you'll find three feet or less. Stocking policies are not only generous but fish sizes, too, are impressive. The smallest fish that you will come across are around a pound and a half but there is a generous quota of double-figure fish. There are browns, rainbows, spectacular tigers and a few brook trout.

I ought to make mention of the pike fishing. From the first Sunday in November you might well be sharing the water with some keen predator men. Mind you, although we're talking about big pike here with many going over twenty-five and even thirty pounds, they don't really interfere with the trout fishing at all. Fish of this size simply take one big fish every week or so and then lie pretty well dormant. There was a problem with jack pike but the management have sorted this out. Research over the last fifteen or twenty years has proved that providing you keep the big pike in the water, the jacks will have a very hard time of it and trout fishing will benefit. Out of interest, the pike fishing costs £7.50 a day and £1 is retained, put in a kitty and paid out at the end of the season to the angler with the biggest recorded specimen!

A very attractive, very well-stocked fishery and highly recommended.

Season – open throughout the year. The fishery opens at 8.00am and closes at dusk.

Tickets – contact Gailey Trout Fishery, Gailey Lea Lane, Gailey, Stafford ST1P 5PT, or phone 01785 715848 for details. £25 allows a seven-fish limit with catch and release thereafter. A half-day ticket costs £15, with a four-fish limit and catch and release afterwards. There is also a very enlightened junior special ticket that costs £8 and allows one fish to be taken and catch and release after that.

Directions – on the M6, take junction 12 and the A5 towards Cannock. Take the first turning on the left and you will come to the fishery entrance. This is a cul-de-sac with a canal at the end so you can't go far wrong!

Accommodation – the Tourist Information Centre in Stafford, on 01785 610619, can give advice on suitable accommodation in the area.

Loynton Hall – Staffordshire

Loynton Hall has deservedly built up a tremendous reputation in this part of the country. There are three lakes, all set in stunning countryside and all very well stocked. The water goes down to forty feet in places and can colour up after heavy rain. All this means that floating lines can and do work, but don't neglect to bring along a sinker – especially in the summer when the water is warmer and the fish can go down deep.

The rainbows are stunning... they're put in at a minimum of two pounds, but – and this is the exciting thing – they do go up to thirty pounds with lots of twenties. In fact, regular visitors can easily get a dozen or more doubles during the course of a season. There are also some very good browns as well, but please note that all browns caught must be released.

There aren't really any specific tips for Loynton Hall – the fishery owners say that most of the locals do best by keeping on the move, and it's best to experiment freely with flies, depths, retrieves and so on until a winning formula for the day is found. What's made quite clear is that this is not a stocky-bashing water by any stretch of the imagination. Loynton really is a place to take seriously. Mind you, the welcome is very warm indeed and it's such a beautiful place with big fish that the whole package is very difficult to resist.

Season – open all year round. The fishery opens at 8.00am Saturday and Sunday and 9.00am through the course of the week. It's quite an early closing fishery and shuts down at 8.00pm, even in the summer.

Tickets – contact Steve Masters at Loynton Hall Trout Fishery, Nr. Woodseaves, Staffordshire on 01785 284261. A five-fish day ticket is £30, a four-fish day ticket £25, a three-fish, eight-hour ticket £20 and a two-fish, six-hour ticket £15. You can take your quota and then move on to catch and release, but do this very carefully indeed. There are also five sporting tickets each day priced at £10 for six hours or all day for £15. Note, there is no catch and release on the lodge lake, nearest the lodge.

Directions – you'll find Loynton Hall north of Telbury on the A519, between Newport and Eccleshall. Loynton Hall is very well signposted in the little village of Woodseaves.

Accommodation – contact the Tourist Information Centre in Stafford, on 01785 619619, for details of accommodation in this area.

Packington Fisheries – Warwickshire

No wonder Packington is so massively popular amongst Midland anglers, situated as it is between Birmingham and Coventry and yet in its own placid, countryside setting. Packington has built up a tremendous reputation over the years as a place offering a wide variety of sport over three day-ticket lakes, all generously stocked with high quality, good-sized fish.

There are three lakes at Packington open to the day-ticket fisherman. Broadwater and Cocks Close are both into the teens of acres. Cocks Close is almost invariably very clear, whereas Broadwater does colour up after rain. There is also six-acre Burnetiron, the smallest of the three waters but the one open for catch and release methods.

Damsel fly patterns are probably the most reliable, year-round fish catchers at Packington, but the water fishes very well for nymphs and buzzers throughout the warmer months, epoxy buzzers being particularly recommended. As the water cools, lures such as Appetisers and Cat's Whiskers come into their own, but don't be tempted to fish them too quickly .

Packington is within the hurly-burly of the Midlands but you really wouldn't know it and so if you do find yourself in the area and you fancy catching beautifully conditioned trout from one and a half to ten pounds or more, give this enchanting fishery a few hours of your time.

SEASON – open all the year apart from Christmas Day, Boxing Day and New Year's Day.
TICKETS – contact Packington Fisheries, Broadwater, Maxstoke Lane, Meriden, Nr. Coventry CV7 7HR on 01676 522754. Day-ticket prices vary. You can pay a flat £9 and £3 a fish taken thereafter. Alternatively, go for a £13 ticket that entitles you to two fish or, at the top of the scale, a £23 ticket that allows you eight fish. There is catch and release on the one lake, Burnetiron, at £7.
DIRECTIONS – take the A45 from Coventry towards Birmingham. You will find Packington Fisheries just before the M42 on the right-hand side. Turn down Shepherds Lane right next to the Forest of Arden Hotel.
ACCOMMODATION – the Forest of Arden is highly recommended. For further information contact the Tourist Information Centre in Coventry on 02476 227264.

RAVENSTHORPE – NORTHAMPTONSHIRE

Ravensthorpe is a comparatively small reservoir, set in rolling middle-English countryside. There are many exciting things about Ravensthorpe. One of them is the catch and release policy that allows anglers to carry on fishing way beyond their two fish bag limit. Above all, Ravensthorpe's other claim to fame is float tubing – the unique form of fishing in which you climb into something that looks like a cross between a frogman's outfit and a rubber tyre. It really is the way to get close to your fish and all the necessary equipment is available for hire at £10 a day or £6 for half a day, including tuition.

Less adventurous fishermen might also try one of the fleet of boats with an electric outboard – a really excellent tool for gliding you in close to rising fish. This really is a lovely, friendly, smaller water where the visiting angler is instantly welcomed and made to feel at home. Lovely fish and a lovely setting – who could ask for more?

SEASON – 26th February to 31st December.

TICKETS – these are £14 per day (£12 for concessionary tickets). There are no half day tickets. Boats start at £11 a day for a single occupant. Phone 01604 781350 and speak to the Senior Warden at the Pitsford Lodge for full details.

RECORDS – brown trout 8lb 6oz, rainbow trout 12lb 6oz.

DIRECTIONS – Ravensthorpe is situated very close to the M1/M6 junction and is well signposted.

ACCOMMODATION – information about suitable accommodation can be obtained from the Tourist Information Centre in Northampton on 01604 622677.

EYEBROOK – LEICESTERSHIRE

Reservoirs can have character, be beautiful and possess a charming individuality. This is what Eyebrook proves. Perhaps it's something to do with its age: it's an old, mature reservoir and has offered fly fishing for just on sixty years. Perhaps it's something to do with its coziness. Eyebrook is 'only' four hundred acres, and this makes it manageable, even to a newcomer. There are still five miles of very good bank fishing available and all of them are easily accessible by quiet, picturesque country lanes.

This is a lovely water, nestling amongst the rolling hills of the Welland valley. It's a little like a lowland loch and you only have to half close your eyes to feel the remoteness. This setting makes it important as a Site of Special Scientific Interest, and as a focus of local wildlife groups. Anglers, please remember this aspect when you're fishing and take special care not to leave litter or nylon.

Fishing at Eyebrook is nearly always productive. That's partly because there is a lot of good, top-water action from trout that are both high in quality and numbers. For example, in the 2000 season, the fishery was stocked with over twenty-five thousand trout and many of those were five pounds plus.

My own personal favourite at Eyebrook is to get afloat: naturally, a boat gives you advantages of access, especially when, like Eyebrook itself, the boats are modern and well-maintained. The feeling of loneliness that Eyebrook induces is also enhanced when you're out on your own on the water.

Lures tend to work well early season when the waters are cold, but as conditions warm, nymphs and buzzers begin to take over. Although depths are frequently over twenty feet, a floating line is generally sufficient once that chill goes off the reservoir. Late season sport can be excellent with daddies and shrimp and corixa imitations. Remember, Eyebrook is a fertile reservoir and the well-conditioned trout are used to a natural larder. All in all, highly recommended.

SEASON – The reservoir is open between 30th March and 29th October.

TICKETS – these are available at the reservoir. Contact the Fishing Lodge, Eyebrook

Reservoir, Great Eastern Road, Caldecott, Leicestershire on 01536 770264. There is a range of ticket prices but, in essence, a day ticket costs around £13.50 and an evening one £9. Rowing boats cost £10 and motorboats £16. There are fifteen motorboats and ten rowing boats.

→ **DIRECTIONS** – You will find Eyebrook off the A47 between Leicester and Peterborough. At Uppingham, take the A6003 south to Caldecott. Then follow the AA signs to the reservoir.

+ **EXTRA INFORMATION** – Eyebrook sports an excellent modern fishing lodge with disabled facilities. There is also a specialist mobile tackle shop at the reservoir each weekend and there are always flies and leaders on sale at the lodge.

ACCOMMODATION – the Tourist Information Centre in Leicester on 0116 299 8888 will be able to advise on suitable accommodation.

RUTLAND WATER – LEICESTERSHIRE

Rutland Water offers three thousand, one hundred acres of some of Europe's best trout fishing. Set in lovely rolling countryside, a day at Rutland is always a pleasure both for the rawest novice and the most experienced international match angler. On a water as large as Rutland, it makes real sense to get local knowledge, and the fishery staff here really are welcoming and experienced. Nigel Savage, Nathan Clayton and the rest of the Rutland team are enthusiasts who fish the water themselves regularly. As they like to say, they know their fishing, they understand their water better than anyone – and they have years of experience in helping others to enjoy their sport.

Just a word about Rutland in the autumn and early winter. More and more anglers are finding that, brilliant though the summer sport is, as the year begins to wane the quality of the fish themselves becomes outstanding.

Many of the very big fish are caught on fry imitations – not surprising, considering the millions of coarse fish fingerlings that inhabit the water. However, by the late summer, insect hatches are extravagant and dry flies and buzzer fishing in the surface film can produce some excellent fishing. For example, the best brown of all in 1999 – 11lb 10 oz – was caught off the bank using a floating line and a small black buzzer!

There's a great deal of sensitivity in the rules and regulations at Rutland, and boat and bank anglers can opt for catch and release. This was introduced for anglers who want to continue fishing beyond any bag limit, but also for those who simply want to practise their technique and those who just don't like the idea of killing their fish.

Facilities at Rutland are now excellent, with a fully-equipped tackle shop offering everything the angler might need. There is a large and well-maintained fleet of sixty-five powered boats, and the fishing lodge is the place to glean information and reasonably-priced food and drink. Another great idea is the introduction of a special low-priced one fish permit for beginners who can also hire tackle inexpensively from the lodge. Courses are run, and individual tuition is available for anglers of all standards. So, if on holiday, you can really make this a family day out.

SEASON – the fishery opens between 1st April and 31st December.

TICKETS – for bookings, contact Rutland Water Fishery Lodge, Rutland Water South Shore, Normanton Car Park, Edith Weston, Oakham, Rutland LE15 8HD, or phone the fishery lodge on 01780 686441 for their scale of charges. For example, a standard day ticket costs £16. The tackle shop can be contacted on 01780 686443. There is also a twenty-four-hour weather line on 09063 610206.

RECORDS – 14lb 12oz and 13lb 8oz for brown trout and rainbow respectively.

RULES – do obey fishery rules and avoid nature reserves and bird watching centres.

DIRECTIONS – Rutland Water is found very close to the town of Uppingham on the A47 from Leicester. It is well-signposted.

ACCOMMODATION – try the White Hart, Uppingham, on 01572 822229. Or phone Rutland Water Angling Breaks on 01572 723004 quoting booking reference ANG 1901. Try also The Exeter Arms, Barrowden, Rutland, on 01572 747247; The Old Rectory, Belton, Nr. Uppingham, on 01572 717279; or The Horse and Jockey, Manton, on 01572 737335. For a B & B, contact Little Hoo Bed and Breakfast on 01780 460293. Try also the Tourist Information Centre in Leicester on 0116 299 8888.

PITSFORD WATER – NORTHAMPTONSHIRE

Pitsford lies in lovely, wooded countryside next to the Brixworth Country Park. Being so close to Northampton, its situation attracts nature lovers and anglers alike, so always remember that you are an ambassador for our sport. Indeed, co-operation is very much the name of the game at Pitsford, and the lovely new lodge that blends in so well with its surroundings is a centre for both anglers and nature reserve wardens who work for the peace and future of the fishery.

Pitsford is all about education and the environment. There is a schoolroom in the lodge where techniques can be brushed up on. To encourage newcomers, the management also offers cheaper day and boat tickets. So, in theory, you and your family can learn to fish and then go out onto the water and put what you have learnt into practice – and all for a very modest charge. This, surely, is very much the caring face of fishing in the future. Naturally enough, there is also a catch and release policy, and the water is also made available for pike fishing on certain weekends of the year.

Everyone, therefore is catered for, and, as an angler, please be aware that some parts of the fishery are out of bounds at certain times of the year. This is done very much for the good of the wildlife, and it doesn't do the fish any harm either to have some sort of sanctuary.

There is a range of tickets available, so please enquire when booking. Pitsford is also now open well into December, so it's worthwhile just having a quick thought about some tips for late autumn and the really cold months. You will find that there will be fly hatches, especially after Indian summers, on most reservoirs until the frosts become really cruel. For this reason you can still fish a floating line and a team of buzzers. But remember to fish them slowly, ideally in a crosswind, so that they swing around gently in an arc. You'll find that fish are quite happy to come into the shallows at this time of the year, especially early and late in the day, and, as the fishing is visual, you won't have any problems detecting takes.

It's tempting to think that you'll need a sinking line to get down deep for coldwater fish, but this certainly isn't always the case and floaters or intermediates are generally all you'll need. Remember that you'll probably have to work your flies more slowly than you do in the summer and for this reason a floater with a long leader gives you perfect control. You'll find that fish are still roaming quite freely, although their pace will probably have slowed down. It's only after a very hard frost that the fish won't be near the surface and you'll probably have to count your intermediate line down.

Don't discount the first few hours of the afternoon in the winter. The water is probably at its warmest between noon and about 3.00pm, especially if there's any sun. The fish are very likely to respond. And you may not find any great advantage in going out in a boat once the weather really cools down. Remember that winter fishing is all about that slow retrieve I've talked about, and this is frequently more easily achieved from the bank. Don't bother fishing into the teeth of an icy wind. Wrap up well in warm, watertight clothing, and break the day up with two or three visits back to the lodge for coffee and a chat. If the fishing is a little difficult, it's amazing how confidence rises after a few minutes' fishing talk.

SEASON – 17th March to 31st December.

TICKETS – Pitsford Water, Pitsford Lodge, Brixworth Road, Holcot NN6 9SJ. Bookings can be made on 01604 781350.

DIRECTIONS – take the A508 north from Northampton towards Market Harborough. Pitsford Reservoir is on the right-hand side in a few miles. It will be signed along with the Brixworth Country Park.

ACCOMMODATION – the Tourist Information Centre in Northampton, on 01604 622677, will be able to supply details of accommodation in the area.

DRAYCOTE WATER – WARWICKSHIRE

As fishery manager Keith Causer explains, Draycote has been an excellent buzzer water for the last two or three years. For large parts of the season, buzzers on floating lines have been all that any angler has needed to take the excellently conditioned browns and rainbows from Draycote

Draycote is a big reservoir and, at six hundred acres, it often attracts quite a breeze. If you are fishing a team of buzzers, it can be difficult to get a line out, especially with a long leader and with the wind blowing directly into your face. Remember that if you are having trouble trying to straighten your leader, try to cast 'under the wind' as they say. If you're fishing a long leader, make sure your heaviest fly, perhaps a damsel fly nymph or something similar, is on the point. This will help turn the whole team over nicely. Also, remember that casting a long leader involves having more line out than the length of the leader itself. Unless you do this, you just can't get casting. If you want to fish very close into the bank, therefore, what you're going to have to do is simply stand further back from the water to get everything in action. As an added bonus... the fish are less likely to see you.

The average weight at Draycote tends to be around two pounds for both browns and rainbows, but the fish grow on excellently – in the 2000 season, browns to over thirteen pounds were taken and rainbows just a little lighter.

Season – open April to October inclusive. The fishery opens at 7.30am and closes one hour after dusk.

Tickets – contact Draycote Water, Kites Hardwick, Rugby, Warwickshire, CV23 8AB, on 01788 812018. A £15 day ticket allows you to take eight fish and a £10.50 ticket after 3.00pm allows you to take five fish. You are allowed to catch and release fish until you've actually killed your limit, then you must cease fishing. There are twenty-five motorboats available at £20.50 per day. Three people are allowed in the boat, but only two may fish because of safety reasons. Rowing boats are £12 a day.

Directions – Draycote is found off the A426 south of Rugby. Cross the M45 and you will see it signposted shortly after on the right.

Accommodation – try Judy Slater, The Orchards, Kites Hardwick, Rugby, Warwickshire, on 01926 812621. The Tourist Information Centre in Rugby, on 01788 534970, will be able to advise on other suitable accommodation.

Salford Trout Lakes – Oxfordshire

Salford was a water unknown to me until a recent fishing trip to Wales when it was highly recommended by one of my companions. Salford's reputation isn't particularly built on massive rainbows and as my companion said, 'You won't find the fishmongers there!' No, Salford is more about quiet serenity, fascinating fishing and beautiful surroundings. Two lovely lakes make up the fishery, both with islands, and neither particularly deep – ten feet is around about the maximum. That means that floating lines and buzzers are a pretty good way to start. Mind you, dry flies and damsels all work too. That's the pleasurable part about Salford – imitative patterns are just all the rage!

A good fish at Salford is three or four pounds and the fishery record, a rainbow, is only about eight pounds. But does that matter? This is a guidebook, not one on angling ethics, but perhaps we've become a little too obsessed with size over the last twenty-five years or so. Perhaps size is just a macho thing or something to do with the trophy mentality. You won't need any of that at Salford – just an appreciation of beautiful waters and a very genuine, warm welcome and atmosphere.

SEASON – Salford Trout Lakes are closed from the end of October to early March. Phone for exact dates.

TICKETS – contact Mrs E. Colston at Salford Trout Lakes, Rectory Farm, Salford, Chipping Norton, Oxfordshire, OX7 5YZ. Tickets cost £20 for four fish. A half-day ticket costs £14 and entitles you to two fish.

DIRECTIONS – from Chipping Norton, north-west of Oxford, take the A44 Evesham road. After a mile, take the right-hand road to Salford. At the T-junction, turn right, then left. Follow this road for about half a mile and you will see a farm track signposted Rectory Farm and Trout Lakes on the left.

ACCOMMODATION – details of accommodation can be obtained from the Tourist Information Centres in Chipping Norton on 01608 644379 and Oxford on 01865 726871. There are also bed and breakfast facilities at Rectory Farm itself. Also, contact South Coombe Lodge Guesthouse, The Bungalow, Chipping Norton, Oxfordshire, on 01608 643068. Or, Swan Lodge, Oxford Road, Chipping Norton, Oxfordshire, on 01608 678736.

FARMOOR TROUT FISHERY – OXFORDSHIRE

Farmoor, at around about two hundred and forty acres, has long been a stamping ground for Oxfordshire trout fishermen. Although it's pretty much a concrete bowl, the stocking levels are high and the challenge is great. And, reputedly, Farmoor trout fight like tigers.

From the bank, play around with buzzers and nymphs, especially in the warmer months. Strike indicators are firm favourites with the locals and these mean that the most delicate takes can be seen and struck at. The other advantage of a strike indicator is that you can set your flies to work at a predetermined depth, and this can be very useful on days when they're being very picky.

When the water is high, you'll find that the trout will come in close, in just three to five feet of water, but if the water level is lower, you'll probably find them further out and deeper down. A standard leader between ten and fifteen feet in length is enough for most conditions, but if you're not getting takes, then a twenty-foot leader can make all the difference. The whole point is to fish sensitively and thoughtfully and keep experimenting with flies, depths and retrieves until you begin to pick up fish. In the winter, the Booby seems to take over, especially as there's deep water close in. Fish the fly very slowly with a figure of eight retrieve, or even let it hang static.

Farmoor operates a catch and kill policy when fishing from the bank – it's simply that too many trout were landed, allowed to bounce on the stones and then were returned in a dying condition. This is a particular shame when you think that the browns and rainbows are only stocked at one to two pounds in Farmoor but quickly grow on to double-figure size. Fine fish like this have to be respected. Catch and release is possible from a boat providing sporting ethics are upheld. Barbless hooks, nymphs and imitative flies and, if possible, unhooking in the water all help to preserve stocks.

SEASON – Farmoor opens in mid March and runs until the end of January. The fishery opens at 10.30am and closes at dusk.

TICKETS – contact Farmoor Trout Fishery, Cumnor Road, Farmoor, Oxford OX2 9NS on 01865 863033. From the bank, an eight-fish limit costs £16 and a four-fish limit £13. There is a two fish evening ticket that covers the last three hours of the day for £7.50. A motorboat costs £8 for one person and £10 for two people. Ordinary ticket prices apply on top. From the boat, you can also buy a one-man sporting ticket for £20 or a two-man sporting ticket for £25. All fish are returned.

DIRECTIONS – from Oxford, take the A40 towards Cheltenham. In three miles or so, turn left onto the B4044. Cross the toll bridge, which costs five pence! In Farmoor village, turn right onto the B017. in three quarters of a mile you will find the reservoir on the right-hand side. Look out for the brown sign.

ACCOMMODATION – contact the Tourist Information Centre in Oxford, on 01865 726871, who can supply information on various kinds of accommodation available in the area.

HIGHLY RECOMMENDED FISHERIES

- *Santhill Trout Fishery, Bourton-on-the-Water, Gloucestershire. Phone 01451 810291. Beautiful twenty-six-acre lake. Very rich. Imitative patterns work well. Closed January and February.*
- *Elinor Trout Fishery, Nr. Aldwincle, Northants. For details, phone 01832 720786. Fifty-acre gravel pit. Well matured. Big rainbows and browns. Good challenge.*
- *Churchill Fishery, Mursley, Bucks. Pretty, well-stocked lake. Nice lodge. Feeling of exclusivity.*

FLY-FISHING SITES IN WALES

1. *Anglesey*
2. *The River Dee*
3. *Gwernan Lake*
4. *Tal-y-Llyn Fisheries*
5. *The River Irfon*
6. *The Rivers Nevern & Teifi*
7. *White House Mill Fishery*
8. *The River Towy*
9. *Maesgwyn*
10. *Glyncorrwg Ponds*
11. *Ravensnest*
12. *The River Usk*

"When I first came to Wales, like everybody else I'd heard of the famous sea trout rivers like the Teifi or the Conway, and knew there were some really excellent brown trout lakes like Bala and Vyrnwy. I also knew that the Wye had been the foremost salmon river in England or Wales, and that the Usk wasn't far behind it. But it was only after I'd lived here for a few years that I began to appreciate what tremendous potential for the game fisherman is hidden under the surface. The point about Wales is that for every famous game fishery, there are twenty forgotten or undiscovered ones. For example, you'll find mountain streams and hidden hill lakes full of wild browns. Or, you can find small west coast spate rivers that can produce unexpectedly large sea trout. Even salmon. There are pools everywhere tucked into mountainsides where you can enjoy excellent rainbow trout fishing, and in the all but unknown tributaries of the Wye you'll find some of the best grayling fishing anywhere in Europe. There are so many grayling in central Wales of such a large size with no-one fishing for them that I almost feel I'm king of my own private paradise."

PETER SMITH, WRITER, HOTELIER AND ADVISOR TO THE WELSH TOURIST BOARD

And Peter even missed out chub, dace and pike from some of the crystal rivers, and even bass and mullet from many of the estuaries... all well within the scope of the fly fisherman. You can drive east to west or north to south, criss-crossing Wales however you like, and I honestly doubt if you'll go ten miles without finding your own little fly-fishing paradise.

Much of the water is controlled by local clubs and it's often possible to pick up a season's membership for a very low fee, especially considering the standard of the fishing on offer. Alternatively, hotels also control many lengths of river and you can nearly always find somebody to point you in the right direction.

Fly Fishing on Anglesey

This lovely island offers some extraordinarily fine and unexpected fly fishing to the visitor. Moreover, the whole pace of life here – especially away from the coast – is easy, ambling and you can wind down to the flow of nature in the way that every successful game angler should.

Game fishing on the island is dominated by three waters – Llyn Alaw, Llyn Cefni and Llyn Coron – all three of which are beautiful, well-stocked and available to the visiting angler. Llyn Alaw is the largest of the waters, covering nearly eight hundred acres, and is in the centre of north Anglesey. It's a shallow, fertile water and lies among rolling, open pasture land. The surroundings are lovely, though a brisk wind can make fly casting difficult at times. Still, the lake has many bays and headlands that offer possible fishing opportunities whichever direction the wind blows in. The reservoir is also a haven for wildlife, and supports a variety of breeding birds throughout the summer. You will find common terns at the eastern shallow end of the reservoir, which, sensibly, has been designated a nature reserve.

Llyn Cefni is a quarter the size of Alaw and again is found in central Anglesey. The water is fringed by conifer plantations, although areas have been felled to give more light and a greater feeling of space. There are two interconnected lakes divided by a disused railway line and, marvellously, there is still a large population of naturally spawning brown trout.

Llyn Coron is a shallow, rich seventy-acre lake lying at the inland end of the Aberffraw dune system and this gives it a really unique character. Llyn Coron supports

A Few Words to the Wise

Just a few advisory words about fishing in Wales:

- *Do be careful with the beats on some of these Welsh rivers and streams as they're not always very clearly marked and you can unwittingly end up poaching – an embarrassing situation that you need to avoid.*
- *Also, rather like Scotland, the weather in the wilder parts of Wales can change dramatically. Even on an apparently warm, summer morning it pays to stick a waterproof in your bag if you're going to be out for any length of time.*
- *Take special care on the bigger lakes and reservoirs as a wind can easily spring up out of seemingly nowhere.*
- *A final word of warning: if you're thinking of pursuing those upper Wye grayling that Peter talks about, then avoid the annual Royal Welsh Show that's based in Builth Wells… you'll find the roads a nightmare and accommodation impossible to come by.*

a good stock of brown trout and, excitingly, some sea trout have also been caught in the lake after running up the River Ffraw during the summer months. In short, these waters really provide a huge resource for the visiting fly fisherman and between them, offer something for everyone.

Llyn Alaw

Season – rainbow trout run from 16th March to 26th October and brown trout from 20th March to 17th October.

Tickets and rules – permits are available from the Llyn Alaw visitors' centre, which can be contacted by phone or fax on 01407 730762. Six fish are allowed per permit. Note that spinning and worm fishing is also allowed on this reservoir so you might not be alone! Day tickets cost £10.50 and evening tickets £8.50. Four-week tickets cost £55. Boats are also available, but it pays to book in advance.

Directions – travel along the A5 until you come to a signpost directing you to turn right towards Llanerchymedd/Trefor. Travel along this road until you reach a crossroads. Turn left and take the next right. Follow the brown signs until you reach the end of the road. Turn right, then take another right at the next brown sign.

Llyn Cefni

Season – you can fish from 20th March to 17th October for all trout, both browns and rainbows. A thousand brown trout are stocked at the start of the season and rainbows are put in as the season progresses.

Records – The record catch is 7lb for a brown trout and 6lb for a rainbow.

Tickets and rules – tickets can be bought from Tackle and Guns Shop, Menai Bridge, or Pete Rowe Jewellers, Llangefni. You can also direct enquiries to the Honorary Secretary, G. R. Williams, Tyn Lon, Pentre Perw, Gaerwen, Anglesey. There is a bag limit of six fish per permit and the size limit is ten inches. Day tickets are £10, weekly tickets are £33.

Directions – take the A5 express way along Anglesey to Llangefni. Then take the B5109 towards Bodffordd. After about two miles turn right, signposted Welsh Water Cefni Treatment Works.

Llyn Coron

Season – 20th March to 30th September.

Permits and rules – permits are actually issued on the lake itself but for more information phone either 01407 840253 or the Bailiff, Cliff Girling, on 01407 810801. Day tickets cost £6 and evening tickets £5. Boats are an extra £25. The catch limit is six fish per day and four fish for an evening permit, which takes effect after 4.00pm.

Directions – follow the A5 onto the island and through the village of Gaerwen. Go past two right turnings signposted Llangefni, take the next left, signposted Aberffraw. Turn left towards Llangadwaladr, and follow signs over the bridge. Before the village of Aberffrad and the bridge, take a right turn. Follow the track to the lakes.

WELSH GRAYLING

Wales offers an intriguing mix of all manner of fishing types. There are large reservoirs, enchanting sea trout rivers, beautifully run stocked commercial fisheries and major, internationally famous rivers such as the Usk with, at times, important runs of salmon. But there are all sorts of hidden excitements in between, the sort of fishing you'd hardly ever guess at. One of my own personal favourites is the Welsh grayling. Of course, I'm not saying that Welsh grayling are any different to Scottish grayling or English grayling, but there's something about Wales that makes them treasured, as though they're hidden, tucked into folds in the hills.

I have two favourite grayling rivers in Wales so let's start to the north on the Welsh Dee. For me, the grayling really begin around that charming little town of Llangollen. Llangollen Angling Association has twelve miles of bank fishing around the town and it's all accessible and very grayling-rich. Of course there are trout too – some splendid fish running to three pounds or so – but it's the grayling for me that makes the water truly special. Try deep-fished Czech nymphs in some of the major pools or steadier glides. Believe me, there are really big grayling swimming here in the most charming of waters. Every yard cries out to be explored.

Let's move down now to the delightful River Irfon, in mid Wales, centred in the county of Powys. The Irfon is an absolute delight and treks its dancing way through some of the most wonderful, secret Welsh countryside. Once again, there are plenty of trout – beautiful wild browns – and reasonable runs of salmon later in the year, but for me, it's the grayling that win the vote. Like the Dee, there are some very big fish here and there, beautifully proportioned and coloured, probably averaging a pound to a pound and a half. Once again, you will find that they come freely to all manner of nymphs and goldheads – especially fished reasonably deep. There's a real beauty to fishing these waters for their grayling: It's as though it's your secret, as though you're having the time of your life doing something the rest of the world has overlooked.

SEASON – the grayling is classed as a coarse fish and so its closed season is from 14th March to 16th June. However, it's wise to check with the contact numbers that fishing is allowed after the trout season ends in October.

THE DEE

TICKETS – permits are obtainable from Hughes Newsagents, 12 Chapel Street, Llangollen, Denbighshire, LL20 8NN. They can be contacted on 01978 860155.

DIRECTIONS – Llangollen lies on the A5 as you travel west from Chirk, which is on the A5/A483 Oswestry to Wrexham road.

ACCOMMODATION – Llangollen is a bustling holiday town with many bed and breakfasts, guesthouses and hotels. Check out the Royal Hotel on 01978 860202; their bedrooms actually overlook the river.

The Irfon

Tickets and accommodation – up river at Llangammarch Wells, the Lake Country House Hotel LD4 4BS has around five miles of the Irfon and day tickets are sometimes offered to non-residents, although this is a spectacular place to stay. Phone 01591 620202 for details. Down river we come to some splendid water at Builth Wells, where the River Irfon joins its parent, the River Wye. The place to go here is the Caer Beris Manor Hotel, Builth Wells, Powys, LD2 3MP. The hotel has rods on the water running through its own delightful grounds and can also arrange tickets on nearby stretches of the Wye. Phone 01982 552601 for more information. There is also an enchanting stocked rainbow trout water just across from the hotel over the Indiana Jones-type suspension bridge. This is truly delightful fishing and if you find the groups of grayling you are truly in for an excellent day. The contact name here is Peter Smith, an Englishman but a long-term resident in Wales who knows absolutely everything about the fishing hereabouts and is a fund of knowledge and generosity.

Sight Indicators

Sight indicators are a little like floats in coarse fishing, in so far as they aid detection of a take. There are anglers who dislike them and regard them as unethical, but there are just as many who think that in the right place they are totally legitimate, enhance enjoyment and increase sport.

- *Before even considering putting one on the line, always check with the fishery to see whether sight indicators can be used.*
- *Sight indicators are very useful indeed if you're dead drifting a nymph, say, in a stream for a winter grayling or before the wind in a reservoir.*
- *The sight indicator tends to act as a float, so adjust it until the flies beneath it are fishing the depth that you want.*
- *Always make sure that the sight indicator shows up brightly against the water that you're fishing. Reds and yellows are favourite colours.*
- *Don't make the sight indicator too big and heavy for the job.*
- *There are all manner of different sight indicator materials on the market. My own favourites tend to be little balls made out of polystyrene. Experiment until you find the kind of indicator pattern that works for you.*
- *Try different shapes. A marble-shaped indicator provides necessary buoyancy in fast water. If bites are delicate, try a longer, thinner shape.*
- *You don't always have to wait for the sight indicator to go beneath the surface. Strike if it holds up momentarily or moves against the current.*
- *Remember that the sight indicator puts extra weight on your line, so you'll need to punch out your cast a little harder, especially into a wind.*

GWERNAN LAKE – GWYNEDD

Gwernan is a beautiful water set in the shadow of Cader Idris. This eleven-acre water is generally crystal clear with a maximum depth of around fifty feet and numerous deep holes providing shelter for the fish during very hot weather conditions. But there's more for the angler than the fish at Gwernan. With full SSSI status, the lake is patrolled by buzzards and red kites and there's a real feeling of peace and seclusion. Fishing is from any one of the Gwernan Lake Hotel's boats. This allows you to have good access to the fish, close to the lily and reed beds – natural magnets for the fish.

There are plenty of wild browns in the water, and the owners ask you to return these even though they do grow to around four pounds in weight. Most of the rainbows are stocked between one and a half and two pounds but they grow on very rapidly to six or seven pounds, and they fight extraordinarily well in this crystal-clear water. There is no doubt that this is a water where small imitative patterns are very successful. It's a perfect place for those that like to fish near the surface with dry flies and buzzers. If you're going down deeper, try spider, shrimp and nymph patterns.

In short, Gwernan is a perfect place to fish in seclusion with astonishing scenery and wildlife all around.

SEASON – the water is open all year round apart from Christmas Day.

TICKETS – phone Gwernan Lake Hotel on 01341 422488 or write to the hotel at Cader Road, Dolgellau, Gwynedd. £17.50 entitles you to a boat and a four-fish limit. An evening boat costs £10.

DIRECTIONS – from Dolgellau, take the Cader road south-west from the town. Take a left turn to the hotel just before a Shell garage on the right-hand side. Follow this road up towards Cader Idris itself. The lake and the hotel are on the right, approximately two miles from the centre of the town.

ACCOMMODATION – the Gwernan Lake Hotel itself offers very comfortable and reasonably priced accommodation. Bed and breakfast starts at £22.50 per head. There is also extensive bed and breakfast, guesthouse and hotel accommodation in Dolgellau itself. Contact the Tourist Information Centre in Dolgellau on 01341 422888 for further information. The Wales Tourist Board, Brunel House, 2 Fitzalan Road, Cardiff CF24 0UY can also offer advice.

TAL-Y-LLYN FISHERIES – GWYNEDD

Tal-y-Llyn Lake is set in spectacular mountain scenery beneath the southern slopes of Cader Idris on the head waters of the Afon Dysynni. It's a shallow but very productive lake, just over two hundred acres in extent, and provides some of the finest brown trout fishing in Wales. Later on in the season, there is also a run of sea trout and salmon up the river and these can provide excellent and unexpected sport.

It's generally considered that April to June is the best period for brown trout when dapping and fly fishing can both present a very rewarding challenge. Throughout most of the season, however, Tal-y-Llyn has a famous hatch of olives, and imitative fly patterns are highly recommended.

This is a very beautiful water and the fishing is of the highest standard, so it is quite popular. Advance booking is advisable, especially for the boats, which are fully equipped with petrol engines and lifejackets. There's also a fishery shop that stocks a whole range of tackle.

SEASON – 1st April to 17th October. The fishery is open from 9.00am until dusk.
TICKETS – a full-day charge is £15 and a part-day, £10. Boat hire (with engine) is £18 for the full day. For enquiries, phone the fishery office on 01654 782282.
RULES – artificial fly only from the bank or from a drifting boat. Natural fly may be used when dapping. No fishing when anchored up. Trolling, spinning and bait fishing are prohibited. No brown trout must be taken less than twelve inches, measured from the tip of the nose to the fork of the tail, and no more than four in a single day. Catch and release, using barbless hooks, is increasingly appreciated. All anglers must submit a return of catch, including a nil return, to the fishery office.
DIRECTIONS – Tal-y-lLyn is well-served by a number of primary roads including the A470 Cardiff to Llandudno road, the A487 from south-west Wales, the A494 to Chester and Merseyside and the A458 to Shrewsbury, connecting with the M54 and M6 for easy access, especially for the Midlands. The lake itself lies on the B4405, west of the A487 between Dolgellau and Machynlleth.
ACCOMMODATION – anglers really cannot do better than stay at the Tynycornel Hotel This old and picturesque hotel is right on the shores of the lake and is geared up for the needs of the fishermen. The hotel also has its own boats. For more details, phone 01654 782282 or send a fax on 01654 782679.
ADDITIONAL FISHING – Tal-y-Llyn Fisheries also control the fishing on Llyn Bugeilyn, a moorland lake set high up in the hills. This very beautiful water provides excellent small, wild brown trout fishing with no additional stocking. It's wisely considered important to maintain the wild nature of this extraordinary little fishery. Phone the fishery for details.

PEMBROKESHIRE RIVERS

Pembrokeshire is such a wonderful county that it's not surprising that its four major rivers are so appealing. These are the eastern Cleddau, the western Cleddau, the Nevern and the Lower Teifi – all of them mixed game fisheries running through stunning countryside. The first three are comparatively small, intimate rivers where a certain amount of stalking and careful casting is called for. They are principally sea and brown trout waters with only the occasional salmon showing. The Teifi can be a fine salmon river when it's on song and,

its devotees would argue, it's the best mixed game fish river in either England or Wales. However, the quality of the sea trout fishing in all the rivers can be high and ten-pound fish are far from uncommon. And you'd be surprised at the quality of the brown trout fishing as well.

All four are spate rivers and fine down quickly after rain. In fact, a good flush out generally leads to an influx of fish. But get a move on – after only a few hours the rivers run crystal clear again, winding their way through bleached beaches of gravel. If the water is low, search out the deep pools, especially the undercut banks, and it's there that you'll find salmon and the bigger sea trout lurking.

The fining down period for salmon is the real taking time, especially later on in the season when more and more fish are progressing up to their spawning grounds. Traditionally, night-time will see the sea trout anglers abroad, searching their way through the darkness, listening for the sound of moving fish, plopping after insects or forcing their way up the shallows. Mind you, more anglers are experimenting with sea trout fishing during the daytime, perhaps using smaller flies on lighter leaders. Certainly, enough are caught during the hours of daylight to justify further experiments. The other bonus of daytime fishing is that the beauty of this lovely countryside – so much of it wooded – can really be absorbed. Fish are important but, let's remember, they're not everything and it's possible to enjoy the fishing in Pembrokeshire whatever the final tally.

Season – the best time for sea trout is from late May to early September, and for salmon from August until October. The brown trout season runs from 1st April until 31st October.

Tickets – the River Nevern is largely private but Nevern Angling Association controls six miles of some of the best fishing. Day tickets are very reasonably priced at £10 and available from the Trewern Arms, Nevern; The Reel Thing, Lower Market, Cardigan; and from Castaways, Cardigan. Enquiries can be addressed to Mrs Nika Pritchard on 01239 820671. The Nevern Angling Association also owns a stretch of the Teifi – see above for ticket details – and the Teifi Trout Association has control of twenty miles of water between Cardigan and Newcastle Emlyn. This includes the famous Cenarth Falls stretch, which is extraordinarily scenic and prolific. Day tickets at £20 are available from The Reel Thing in Cardigan; Cenarth Falls Holiday Park; The Salmon Leap Inn, Cenarth; and the Afon Teifi Caravan Park in Pentrecagal. For the eastern Cleddau, tickets can be obtained from T. and P.J. Murphy on 01437 563604. For the western Cleddau, contact County Sports, 3 Old Bridge, Haverfordwest, who have day tickets available for £10 a day.

Accommodation – Pembrokeshire is a very popular tourist area, and the county's Tourist Board offers a holiday guide packed with the best accommodation available, from country house hotels to seaside cottage hideaways. Phone the Pembroke Visitors' Centre on 01646 622388 for copies.

White House Mill Fishery – Dyfed

One of the more acclaimed still waters of Wales is definitely White House Mill, and over the years it's built up a reputation for producing some splendidly conditioned fish. The lake is very picturesque indeed, surrounded by unspoilt farmland in the beautiful Marlais valley. It's not a huge water but there's a great deal of variety to its contours, and depths range between four feet in the margins to nineteen feet in the northern corner. But the thing that makes White House Mill so spectacular is the amount of natural food. It has a near-perfect pH of 7.4 and obtains a quarter of a million gallons a day from the nearby River Cwm. All this results in a heavy weed growth that heaves with shrimps, beetles, corixa... you name it.

The fishing here is very civilised and the owners quite rightly like to see anglers using floating lines, nymphs, dry flies. In short, go imitative and not flash. The fish deserve this: they over-winter beautifully and you're always in with a chance of a stunning fish or two – both rainbow and brown. True, in this crystal, fertile water the fish are not easy – especially as the owners allow a certain amount of catch and release for the regulars. So, you could say, some of the biggest fish have seen it all before. In all, White House Mill is a really marvellous experience, big fish in a superb water and you can't ask for more than that.

Season – open all year.

Tickets – for permits, phone 01834 831304. Or write to White House Mill, Lampeter Velfry, Whitland, Pembrokeshire. Tickets cost £10 and this allows you on the water and to catch two fish. Thereafter, you pay £5 per fish. You pay for the fish at the end of the day.

Facilities – tackle hire is available in the very pleasant lodge. There are some platforms and a couple of anglers' shelters.

Directions – the village of Whitland is halfway between Carmarthen and Haverfordwest on the A140. Turn south in the village by the fish and chip shop and cross the railway. Take a right turn shortly after this and follow the road for the best part of two miles as it gets narrower and narrower. The sign for the fishery is on the right.

Accommodation – there is a self-catering cottage on site but the owners will give addresses of local bed and breakfasts. Wales Tourist Board on 029 2049 9909 is also able to advise on accommodation. Or write to them at Brunel House, 2 Fitzalan Road, Cardiff CF24 0UY. A brochure giving details of accommodation and other information about Pembrokeshire is available by phoning 08705 103103.

The River Towy

If there is a national fish of Wales, then it's certainly the sea trout, and one of the most fertile of all the principality's rivers is the Towy with its main tributary the Cothi. The source of the seventy-five mile long Towy is in the

Cambrian Mountains of mid-Wales and it has long been recognised as the best sea trout fishery in Britain, possibly in all of western Europe. Certainly, at its best, it can provide shattering sport. Runs have declined in recent years, in common with most waters, but it's still an outstanding fishery, and individual specimens of eight pounds and over are caught most months. These are really fast growing fish and the largest ones enter the river in March and April, with the sizes gradually declining through the summer. Mind you, the numbers of three- to six-pound fish running the river at this time can be phenomenal. Fresh-run sea trout continue to enter the river during September, but many of the fish that have come up earlier are turning gravid and should be left alone.

The Towy valley is a magical place, and to wander its banks as the ducks are coming in is a wonderful experience, especially when the fish are on the move and you can hear them powering through the pools and even scuttering up the rapids. All the traditional flies and methods will work here, but for added excitement try a big moth pattern, skating it back under the far bank branches.

While most people will still want to fish the water at night, there can be times when fishing small flies in the day can also be productive. Try a quite heavily weighted nymph and cast it to fish that you can see: you tend to find that they'll either vacate the area immediately or you'll get an instant take. It can be exciting stuff.

One important tip... do not come to a new river at dusk and expect to be able to fish it competently. Instead, spend the day walking the length of river you intend to visit and get to know all its peculiarities, depths, possible snags and so on. It's a different world after dark and you can easily be caught out.

The Towy is true sea-trouting experience and one that is widely available for the visiting angler. You might have caught many a rainbow trout from a reservoir or stocked pond in the past, but to call yourself a true fly fisherman, you need to tangle with a Welsh sea trout at some time or another in your life!

SEASON – 2nd April to 7th October.

TICKETS – day and weekly permits are available from a wide variety of sources. Try the Carmarthen Amateur Anglers' Association. Weekly permits vary between £45 and £55. The Carmarthen and District Angling Association offers day tickets at £20. Phone Towy Sports, 9 King Street, Llandeilo on 01558 822637; Tight Lines, 72 Wind Street, Ammanford on 01269 595858; or Fishfinder, King Street, Carmarthen on 01267 220226. The Cross Hands and District Angling Association has several blocks of fishing on the Towy. Once again, phone Towy Sports or Fishfinder for details. Towy Sports can also advise on the limited numbers of weekly and day permits for the Llandeilo Angling Association water, which is in high demand.

DIRECTIONS – The A40 from Llandovery, through Llandeilo to Carmarthen follows the course of the River Towy, which can be reached from the northwest via Builth Wells along the A483, from Abergavenny via the A40, or from Swansea via the M4 and A48.

Accommodation – Capel Dewi Uchaf Country House, on 01267 290799 or e-mail uchaffarm@aol.com, is highly recommended and has a riverside setting. Try Golden Grove Arms, Llanarthhne on 01558 668551 – just yards from some of the best sea trout fishing in Wales. Or, contact Llanerchindda Farm, Llandovery, Carmarthenshire SA20 0NB on 01550 750274 or e-mail nick@cambrianway.com; a lovely setting, very good accommodation and local ghillies available. Edwinsford Fishery and Cottages offer over four miles of double-bank fishing on the Cothi; contact Jonathan Heron, Edwinsford Farmhouse, Talley, Llandeilo, SA19 7BX on 01558 685848 (telephone), 01558 685849 (fax), email herons@edwinsfordestate.co.uk (www.edwinsfordestate.co.uk).

Maesgwyn – Glamorgan

Maesgwyn, just north of Swansea, used to be famous for holding the Welsh rainbow trout record of just over twenty-five pounds. But times have changed somewhat, and the fishery now concentrates on quality rather than size alone. It's a policy that's paid off because Maesgwyn rainbows really are magnificent, silver, bullet-like fish that fight crazily to the end. One very positive aspect to Maesgwyn is the spread of waters available.

There are four pools catering for the beginner up to the expert. In fact, the gin-clear water of the top pool is enough to set a challenge to anyone. So, father can fish the Top Pool for some of the most difficult trout that you'll find anywhere in Wales, whilst his beginner son or daughter can have a bash worm fishing on one of the bottom pools and take away six fish for a £10 ticket. Something here for everyone.

Measgwyn is also set in beautiful countryside and if you're very lucky you might well see that icon of all Welsh birds, the kite, hovering overhead. Very well worth a visit.

Season – open all year.

Tickets – phone Paul Coleman on 01792 846488 or write to Maesgwyn Fishery, Rhydypandy Road, Morriston, Swansea. Ticket prices are from £30 on the top lake for four fish down to the worming pond at £10 for six fish.

Facilities – Maesgwyn offers a shop, café, toilets and tackle for hire.

Directions – from junction 46 of the M4, follow signs for Morriston Hospital. Just as you get to the hospital, turn left into Rhydypandy Road. The fishery is a hundred yards on your left after you've past the pub.

Accommodation – Swansea has a whole range of hotels, guesthouses and bed and breakfast accommodation. The Black Mountains are close by and it's possible to find more rural accommodation here. The Wales Tourist Board are able to advise on various kinds of accommodation. Contact them at Brunel House, 2 Fitzalan Road, Cardiff CF24 0UY, or phone 029 2049 9909.

Glyncorrwg Ponds – Glamorgan

This is yet another Welsh jewel, hidden in a small isolated valley of the River Corrwg, a tributary of the Afan, and set amidst the 9,000-acre Afan Forest Park. The development of Glyncorrwg began over a decade ago, when the Countryside Commission donated half a million pounds to create the three pools. The trout fishing lake is a gem, not large at a couple of acres, but with depths reaching fifteen feet – sufficient to keep the fish cool in the summer and to give shelter in the winter. The lake is stream-fed and is generally crystal clear, which allows for good sight fishing.

There are both browns and rainbows in the water. The browns average perhaps little more than a pound and a half, but there are always stocks of fish to five pounds or more. The rainbows go in at around two pounds but grow on well and have been caught well into double figures.

In warmish weather, the fish are always willing to take from the surface but it's also an idea to take along a slow-sinking line and some heavier nymphs if you want to get amongst those big browns that tend to keep low down in the water. Don't be in too much of a hurry to move either: it's interesting that a brown will often take a fly after it's been drawn over its head a number of times. In short, this is an interesting water in a stunning location.

Season – open all year.

Tickets – phone the manager on 01639 851900 for bookings. Costs are £5 to fish, then £3 for each fish taken, up to a maximum of four.

Directions – leave the M4 on junction 40 and take the A4107 to Cwmafan. When you reach the village of Cymer, take the turning left for Glyncorrwg. The fishery is about one mile along on your left.

Accommodation – Wales Tourist Board can provide information about various kinds of accommodation. Contact them on 029 2049 9909 or write to Brunel House, 2 Fitzalan Road, Cardiff CF24 0UY.

Ravensnest – Gwent

Ravensnest nestles in the beautiful Wye valley, with Tintern Abbey only a mile away, so you couldn't have a better setting for a fishery. Indeed, it's hard to believe that it's only ten minutes or so from the M4 and the old Severn Bridge. Another beauty of Ravensnest is that it's more like fishing a river than a still water. The two pools that make up the fishery are fed by the Angid stream and so have a constant flow. Perhaps favourite conditions are during the dry spell, since both pools then become gin clear and stalking the very big fish that the waters hold is a distinct possibility. Mind you, when there is a tinge of colour in the water, the fishing is frequently easier.

This is truly a great stalking water with plenty of high banks to give you good views of what is going on. The fish themselves are also of excellent quality and fight magnificently, especially when the water is crystal. Recommended flies are buzzers, black ones in particular, mayflies, damsels, but also take a selection of nymphs

There is plenty of variety amongst the fish as well. You'd expect the rainbows and possibly the browns, but not the blues and the goldies, which can look truly spectacular as they power up and down. All in all, this is a beautifully-run, friendly fishery that sets some fascinating challenges in very beautiful countryside.

Season – Ravensnest is open all year.

Tickets – contact the owner Simon Bridge on 01291 689564 or write to him at Ravensnest, Raglan Road, Tintern, Chepstow, Gwent. Prices for tickets are £17 for a four-fish limit, £10 for a sporting ticket.

Records – the biggest rainbow weighed in at 26lb 3oz.

Facilities – the lodge at Ravensnest is purpose built, with its own toilets. Food and soft drinks are available along with flies and some tackle. Tuition can also be arranged.

Directions – take junction 4 off the M48 and head for Chepstow. At the first roundabout, carry straight on, passing the racecourse. At St Arvans, turn left, signposted Devauden. Carry on until you see a sign for The Cott. Turn left here onto the Tintern road. The fishery is one mile further down on your right.

Accommodation – there is plenty of guesthouse and bed and breakfast accommodation in Chepstow and up the road towards Tintern. Wales Tourist Board, Brunel House, 2 Fitzalan Road, Cardiff CR24 0UY will be able to advise. Contact them on 029 2049 9909.

The River Usk – Powys

The River Usk becomes everyone's favourite river once they've fished it. It rises in the Brecon Beacons and then runs in that wonderful, unspoilt countryside between the Beacons themselves and the Black Mountains, before disgorging out into the Bristol Channel at Newport. Until a few years ago, the Usk seemed to be in trouble, but a renaissance is thankfully taking place. A plan by Newport Borough Council to build a barrage across the estuary has, fortunately, been scotched, and a lot of work is being done by the Environment Agency and the United Usk Fishermen's Association to encourage salmon to return and also to improve the river habitat for all species. If proof is needed that the Usk is once again a flourishing, fertile river, all you need to do is look at the number of dippers, the contented state of the herons and the return of the otters.

Above all, the Usk is, and always has been, famous for its stocks of wild brown trout – fish averaging around ten to twelve ounces, but frequently topping the pound. And what fish they are! I remember, with absolute joy, taking six wild browns from a half-mile length of broken white water one afternoon in 1997, and each one made me draw breath as I looked at it. A little bit of paradise indeed. In the early season, late March and April, try march browns tied on a ten or twelve, olive nymphs on a twelve or a fourteen or small hare's ears. As the summer begins to warm up, evening and blue duns and light olives take over. In the high summer, it's difficult to beat light and dark Sedges, Ginger quills, copper Tups, Badgers and the whole gamut of nymphs.

To get the best out of Usk, you will need to wade the river. Travel gently, though, taking care not to scrunch on the stones as these wildies really are poised for flight. Be careful of your shadow, and beware of a line falling loosely, as the slightest mistake will result in the arrows of fleeing, panicked trout.

Salmon are holding their own on the Usk and nowhere will you find better water than that offered by the Gliffaes Country House Hotel near Crichowell. There are perfect holding pools and there's evidence that the large springers for which the river was once renowned could be poised for a return.

SEASON – the trout opens on 3rd March and closes on 30th September. Salmon fishing also begins on 3rd March but ends on 17th October. For salmon, it is fly fishing only until 16th June and all fish must be returned. After 16th June, spinning is permitted and caught salmon may be kept. The hotel wisely encourages its fishermen to return salmon later in the season nearer spawning time. Big females should always be returned.

TICKETS – tickets at Gliffaes cost £15.50 per day for trout, and the brown trout fishing is top quality. Hotel residents take priority but all fishermen are welcomed. It makes sense, obviously, to phone the hotel to check on availability before travelling. Call free on 0800 146719. The water is split into beats with rods restricted to two on each length.

DIRECTIONS – Crichowell lies northeast of Abergavenny on the A40 Brecon road. Two and a half miles west of Crichowell, Gliffaes is signposted to the left. Follow this road for a mile and you will arrive at the gates of the hotel.

ACCOMMODATION – I've always fished the Usk at Gliffaes and I don't think you could find a better base. At least, you'd be doing yourself a favour to start there, especially as the information you will receive on the two and a half miles of water is absolutely first rate.

TUITION – the hotel offers periodic courses on everything to do with wild river fishing. I mention this because the instructor is the absolutely excellent Bill Price, a man I personally know to be one of the best around. Phone the hotel for details.

Highly Recommended Fisheries

- *Hayricks Lake, Nr. Merthyr Tydfil, Glamorgan. Phone 01443 829262 for details. Well stocked and attractive. Catch and release also.*
- *Gludy Lake, Brecon, Powys. Call 01874 610093 for more information. Truly beautiful water. Great fish. Very secluded. Marvellous lodge and log cabin accommodation. Highly recommended.*
- *Llandegfedd, Pontypool. Contact on 01291 673722. Four hundred and thirty acres. Well stocked. Good fleet of boats. Lovely situation.*
- *Pantyreos, Newport, Gwent. Fourteen-acre reservoir in lovely surroundings. Catch and release. Fighting fit fish.*
- *Plasynant Fishery, Anglesey. Some excellent fish in a nice situation.*
- *Valley Dam Fishery, Denbighshire. Phone for details on 01691 648837. Super quality fish. Good surface fishing.*
- *Llyn Gwyn, Nr. Builth Wells, Powys. Phone 01597 811099. Good stocking levels. Stunning location with awe-inspiring views. Some big fish in this remote lake.*
- *Peterstone Trout Lake, Newport, Gwent. Phone 01633 680905. Generous stocking with good-sized fish, average three pounds and plenty of doubles. Lures work well, but try buzzers as the water warms.*

Fly-Fishing Sites in the North

1. Pennine Fishery
2. Loveclough
3. Raygill Fishery
4. The River Wharfe
5. The River Nidd
6. Lockwood Beck
7. Gyllhead Trout Fishery
8. Esthwaite Water
9. Dubbs Trout Fishery
10. High Newton Trout Fishery
11. The River Eden
12. The River Till
13. Coldingham Loch

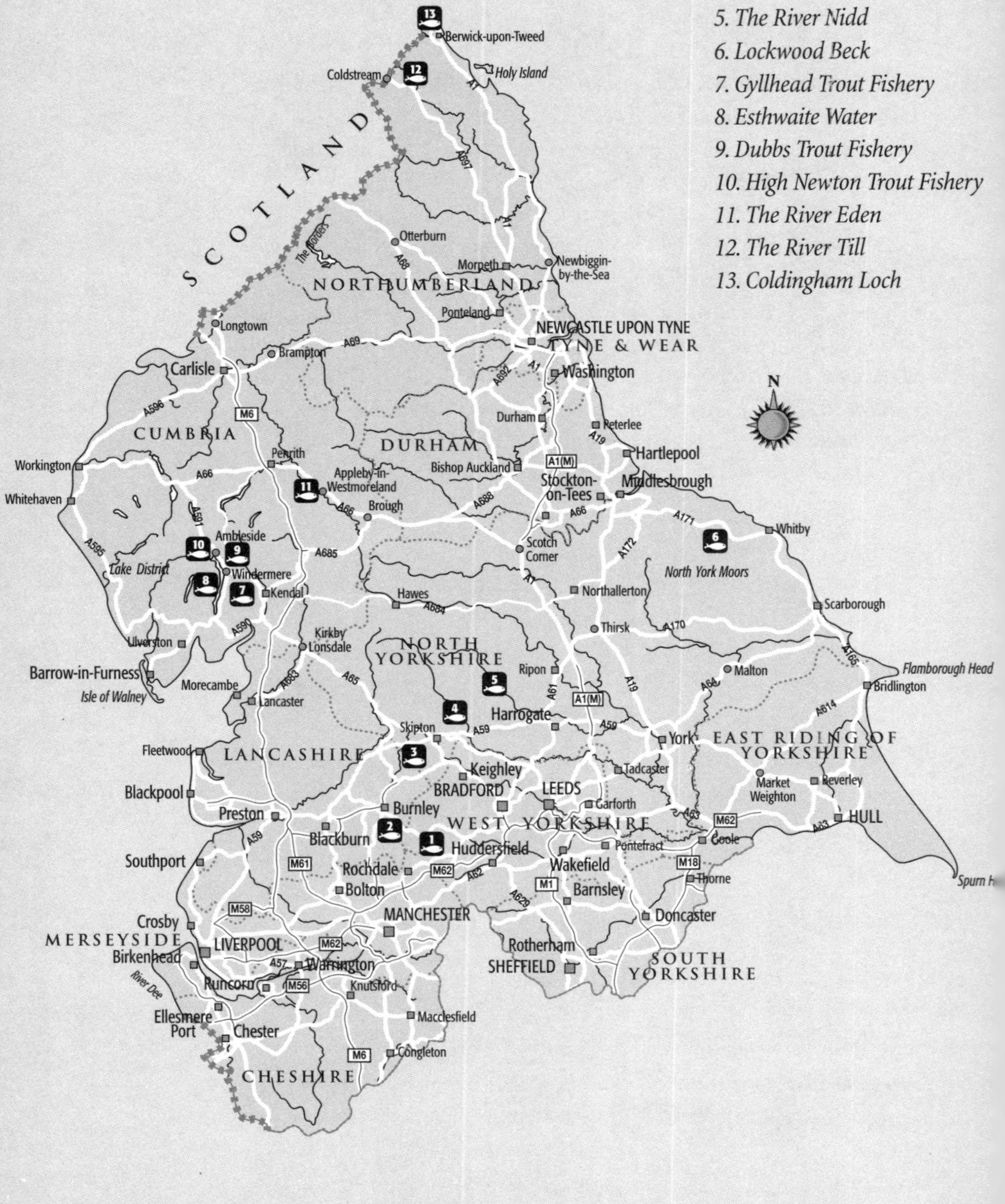

'I've fished the Lakes now for forty years, since I was a boy of seven, and reckon I know a fair bit about them. For me, fly fishing in the Lake District has always been about adventures, long walks, steep climbs to find untouched fish and crystal clear streams, gin-like lakes or tumbling spate rivers. There's so much mystery around – perhaps my favourite place is Wast Water, the deepest and clearest lake in England, overshadowed by Scafell, the country's highest mountain. I also love the variety of fish in the Lake District – superb salmon fishing if you know where to find it, and the sea trout can be an absolute dream. The trout of the tarns are also special, often silver with jet-black spots. If you know where to catch them, you can find char as well – those fabulous, flitting little bird-like fish from the Ice Age.'

ALISTAIR NICHOLSON – FISHING TV PRESENTER AND WRITER

So that's on the west of the area – how about the east? Karen Brunton of the Northumberland Rivers' Project has this to say: 'Northumberland is often ignored in the game fishers lemming-like annual stampede to cross the Scottish border, but its clean rivers, fresh lakes and vast reservoirs are a priceless jewel set in a varied and dramatic landscape. The main waters of the north and south Tyne, Till, Coquet, Aln and Wansbeck host an increasing abundance of salmon and trout on beats that remain accessible and affordable. Some great fishing in some magnificent countryside'.

How on earth do you even begin to describe the wealth of fly fishing that is available in that broad band from Cumbria, through Lancashire and Yorkshire up towards Durham and Northumberland? There's just about everything available, from tiny browns to huge rainbows – there is even a good number of salmon about. And you've got the char of Windermere to boot! Indeed, this is a huge swathe of the British Isles and it encompasses some of our most rugged and unspoilt countryside.

PENNINE FISHERY – LANCASHIRE

Pennine Fishery has built up a really grand reputation in the north-west for many very good reasons. The fish stocked are invariably in really good condition and, moreover, they're big. It's not unusual to see double-figure fish cruising around, and even twenties are in the water. Also, Pennine is a challenging sort of place. Perched up in the moors, the weather is frequently unpredictable and there's often a good chop on the water but that doesn't mean you can get away with heavy gear or stereotyped fishing. No, far from it, Pennine really does demand that you think about what you're doing, assess the ever-changing situation and fish intelligently.

There are two lakes at Pennine, both well stocked and both deep. Try buzzers, on the surface and also down deeper. Dry flies can work, especially in the evening when big fish will come up to the surface. Lures are worth a spin, especially if you see a big fish feeding in close. What you are unlikely to get at Pennine are grab-and-smash-type takes. The fish are wary and, for example, it's often a good idea to have a sight indicator on your leader if you're fishing small nymphs or buzzers down deep. You often just won't pick up takes otherwise.

Pennine is a beautiful, peaceful place to fish and there's a very friendly atmosphere about the place. It's built up a tremendous reputation, so it's a good idea to book a ticket before making the journey.

SEASON – Pennine is open all year round.
TICKETS – contact Lee Moran at Pennine Fishery, Caldebrook Road, Littleborough, Nr. Rochdale, Lancs on 01706 378325. An eight-hour, three-fish ticket costs £19.95. A four-hour, two-fish ticket is £13.80. An eight-hour sporting ticket costs £12. A four-hour sporting ticket £9.
RECORDS – at present the rainbow record is 29lb 7oz, the brown trout record 15lb 8oz and golden trout 14lb 8oz.
DIRECTIONS – from Rochdale, take the A58 to Littleborough. Before reaching the town centre, take the White Lees road and continue until it becomes Caldebrook Road. The fishery is a mile further on and very easily seen.
ACCOMMODATION – contact the Tourist Information Centre in Rochdale on 01706 356592 for details of various kinds of accommodation in the area.

LOVECLOUGH – LANCASHIRE

Loveclough is a dramatic water indeed, perched high amidst the moorland of the Rossendale valley. The water is only about three acres but somehow its spacious surroundings give it a more ample, totally uncramped feel – it's probably got something to do with the fabulous views over the curlew-haunted countryside. But let's get to the fishing, which can be stunning. Although the water is quite deep, dropping to twenty-three feet from a ledge

at fourteen feet, most anglers still like to fish on or near the surface. Indeed, Loveclough is very much a dry fly man's paradise and you can pick fish up on buzzers even in the winter. There might be times in the heat of the summer months when a sinking line can get you down to skulking fish, but even then most of the regulars would rather use a long leader and a heavy nymph to search deeper water.

The water is generally very clear indeed, and only occasionally colours up a little after very heavy rain, which clouds the feeder stream. For the rest, the springs tend to maintain a remarkable clarity, which makes fish spotting possible. There's generally a breeze at this sort of altitude and Loveclough is open to the elements. However, a slight chop is perfect for the dry-fly man. In a brisk wind, my advice is to stay clear of a three fly team and fish one or, at the most, two flies until you're really practised in the art. In fact, my own preference has always been for just the one. Cast across the wind and let your fly drift naturally, covering as much water as you possibly can, and you'll find that very frequently this method picks out the canniest of the fish. Remember that a fish that has seen a lot before will often want to study a fly before making up its mind.

Loveclough is stocked with fish in the one-and-a-half- to two-pound bracket, and what glorious specimens they are, both rainbows and browns. By the way, the management team requests that you return the latter. There are also big numbers of

Fluorocarbon

Fluorocarbon leaders are now all the rage. But what is fluorocarbon? Basically, it's a chemical fusion of fluoride and carbon, which makes for a stiff and abrasion-resistant material.

- *A major advantage of fluorocarbon is that it has a refractive index so close to that of water that it is nearly invisible under the surface. In clear venues, this can be a huge step forward.*
- *A further advantage is that fluorocarbons sink very quickly. This is very useful when trying to get small flies like buzzers and nymphs down to the depths. Ordinary monofilament is much more slow sinking.*
- *Be careful with fluorocarbons if you're using dry flies. They can sink under the weight.*
- *Take care with your knots. An ordinary half-blood knot will work, but you must tie it carefully. Don't attempt to attach fluorocarbon to nylon.*
- *There are now many different fluorocarbons on the market. Take your time and try to trial test as many as possible. Once you've settled on the one for you, stick with it and build up your confidence.*

fish in the eight- to eleven-pound bracket, with rainbows of fourteen to fifteen pounds caught and seen. Now imagine one of those sipping in your Black Gnat as dusk begins to creep across the moorland!

SEASON – Loveclough is open all year apart from Christmas Day and New Year's Day.
TICKETS – contact Mrs G. Dumbill, Loveclough Fishery, Commercial Street, Loveclough, Rossendale, Lancashire on 01706 212541. A four-fish, eight-hour ticket costs £17, a two-fish, five-hour ticket costs £11 and a one-fish, three-hour ticket is £7. Catch and release is also available at £1.75 per hour.
DIRECTIONS – the village of Loveclough is situated on the A682 between Rawtenstall and Burnley. If you're travelling northwards, Commercial Street is on the left-hand side of the main road and the fishery is clearly signposted.
ACCOMMODATION – information about a variety of accommodation can be obtained from the Tourist Information Centre in Accrington on 01254 872595.

RAYGILL FISHERY – YORKSHIRE

Raygill is an extraordinary place, as far as the trout fisherman is concerned. It is made up of two lakes – one comparatively small at just over an acre and the second one at eight and a half acres. This is sunk deep into a disused limestone quarry with vertical cliffs around its perimeter – a truly dramatic setting for a very peaceful and very intelligently-run fishery.

Realising that the days of the big bag merchants are pretty much now on the wane, a sporting ticket has been introduced at Raygill, which is all the rage. Most fish are returned and this has increased the size of the fish and the challenge of the water.

Everything about Raygill is on a big scale – the deep water so close in shore, the clarity, and the shadows of the huge fish you can see crisscrossing beneath you. It's an exciting place to fish without any doubt. Mind you, even despite the depths, the fish are very easy to tempt to the surface and some of the biggest of the boys fall to well-fished buzzers. But remember that many of the fish have been caught and released and everything has to be fished intelligently if it's going to be successful. Once again, there's no magic fly – it's a matter of how it's fished.

Of course, you can put on a fast-sinking line and really try to plumb the depths. On hot days especially, this approach can reap its rewards, but you don't always have to go deep at Raygill. Daddies, for example, work very well later on in the summer and in the early autumn. There are also a good number of roach and bream fry appearing, and any fly patterns take their share of fish, so don't forget your Zonkers and Muddlers.

Not content with one experiment, the management has set about another! A good number of big pike have been purposefully introduced on the smaller trout lake. It's an interesting idea, the concept being that these big fish – all of them big doubles – actually profit from any dying or failing rainbows. The idea seems to have been a success so far – the pike have grown on quickly and the quality of the rainbows has increased substantially. Pike fishing now is very popular amongst some of the locals and only recently a pike of thirty pounds and four ounces was taken on a six-inch fry pattern fly! Quite an achievement.

Season – open all year. Fishing is from 8.30am to dusk.
Tickets – write to the Fishery Manager, Raygill Fishery, 1 Raygill Cottage, Lothersdale, Skipton, North Yorkshire or contact him on 01535 632500. Sporting tickets cost £2 per hour or £12 for the full day. All fish are returned. Any fish can be taken at a cost of £1.75 per pound. Big fish are increasingly popular for a Christmas treat.
Records – the fish grow on very quickly at Raygill and the rainbow record is 21lb 8oz with many double figure fish. The browns are stocked at about ten inches or so but they grow quickly to 5lb plus.
Directions – from the end of the M65 eastbound, take the A6068 and then turn left for Lothersdale. Go down the steep hill to the village. At the bottom, take the turning for the caravan site. The fishery is then four hundred yards along on the left. From Skipton, take the A629 and turn right on the outskirts of the town onto the Carleton Road, signposted Carleton and Lothersdale. Once you enter Lothersdale, keep the pub on the right and drive through the village. At the bend in the road, take the left turning for the caravan site.
Accommodation – the Tourist Information Centre in Skipton on 01756 792809 will be able to supply information on various kinds of accommodation available.

The River Wharfe – Yorkshire

Of all the Dales rivers, the Wharfe is perhaps the most beloved and the most typical of this alternatively rugged and lush Yorkshire countryside. The Wharfe itself rises on Cam Fell and flows sixty miles south-east to join the Ouse. There are coarse fish in its lower reaches but it's the trout fishing higher up that is really exceptional.

Probably the easiest and certainly the most dramatic opportunities for the visiting angler exist at Bolton Abbey, the famous estate of the Duke of Devonshire. The River Wharfe flows through the centre of the estate and offers spectacular fishing. It flows over limestone and the excellent quality of the water is reflected in the abundance of fly life and the exceptional condition of the brown trout. Bolton Abbey is a wondrous place to fish. Dippers, sandpipers, kingfishers, sand martins, warblers, swifts and swallows all make fishing there in the summer an unforgettable experience.

Mind you, the fishing isn't always easy – the frequently low, crystal-clear water sees to that. Also, it has to be said that Bolton Abbey is visited by many non-anglers and the trout do get wary of the shadows cast over them. However, the river bailiff – certainly the one I met – proved to be exceptionally helpful. As a good standard, he recommended the Grey Duster as the outstanding dry fly pretty well season round.

Going sub-surface, he suggested that the pheasant-tailed nymph was hard to beat. Mind you, he also had a leaning towards the partridge in orange, partridge in yellow and the treacle Parkin.

There are beats of this river that you just cannot afford to miss. Fish around at the Strid early in the morning before the sightseers arrive. There is something primeval about the spectacular point where the Wharfe surges through its narrow gorge. Best of all, though, move down to the Priory around sunset and pick up a fish or two as the shafts of light trace their shadows on the ancient brickwork. Yes, Bolton Abbey is an exhilarating place to catch a trout or a grayling.

Season – trout fishing runs from the 1st April to 30th September. Trout and grayling combined run from 16th June to 30th September. Grayling tickets only are available from 1st October to 22nd December.

Tickets – these are available for fishing the estate waters – around four and a half miles along both banks – from the Estate Office Monday to Friday from 9.00am to 10.00am and

A Handful of Tips

It's often a good idea to keep on the move if you're bank fishing, rather than stay in one spot. The trout in the area will get spooked if you over-fish them.

- *A change of fly is always a good idea after you've fished in the same place for a while. If you've been fishing white, try black. If you've been fishing big, try small. Anything that is different can trigger a response.*
- *If you see fish swirling on the surface but you're not getting any takes to a dry fly, it could be that the fish are taking insects just beneath the surface, emerging before hatching. In this case, try a team of buzzers fished just a few inches beneath the surface.*
- *Try fishing into the wind. Casting is more difficult, but fish will be concentrated in the downwind areas and the chances are most anglers will have tended to avoid them.*
- *Only put on a finer leader if you're absolutely sure that's the only way to get a take. There's not much point hooking that fish only to lose it.*
- *Don't panic. The temptation is to try to cast further and farther and probably get into more tangles. Instead, take a rest, sit down and think things out. If somebody else is catching, then take time to watch and, if need be, ask a couple of polite questions.*
- *Remember that learning is all-important. It's not as though you need to catch those fish to live, so enjoyment should be the name of the game.*

9.30am to 10.30am on Saturday and Sunday. Phone 01756 710227 for further details. The adult day ticket is £15 and the junior day ticket is £8.

Rules – fishing is permitted between 9.00am to one hour after sunset. A beat will be allocated to you, which you must adhere to until 3.00pm after which you can fish any stretch of the river beneath the aqueduct as far as Kex Beck. The fishery is very tightly managed for the good of these excellently-conditioned trout. Please note that you can only use a barbless hook – a £75 fine for transgressors! No hooks must be used larger than a size twelve, which rules out lures and reservoir flies. Also, for the good of the fishery, all returns must be completed even if no fish have been taken.

Directions – As you head east from Skipton towards Harrogate along the A59, turn left onto the B6160 and Bolton Abbey is less than a mile north.

Accommodation – there is a wealth of bed and breakfast accommodation in the area. Particularly recommended is Bondcroft Farm on 01756 793371. Alternatives include Heskith Farm Cottage on 01756 710541 (just three quarters of a mile from the Priory itself), The Manor House on 01756 730226, Langerton Farm on 01756 730260 and Holmhouse Farm on 01756 720661. The Devonshire Arms Country House Hotel is situated right on the river itself and offers superb food and accommodation. Highly recommended. Phone 01756 710441 for information.

The River Nidd – Yorkshire

The Nidd is a lovely Yorkshire river that holds coarse fish lower down its reaches but offers spectacular trout and grayling fishing nearer to its source. Perhaps the easiest access to wonderful water for the visitor is offered by Nidderdale Angling Club who control about eleven miles of the mid river. And what wonderful water it is – full of charm and character, often overhung by trees as it winds through lush meadowland. Deep pools, twists and turns, dancing shallows – everything is here for the fly fisherman.

I enjoyed an enchanting May day just beneath Pately Bridge a couple of years back. My companion and I did not see another angler even though it was Sunday and the weather was fine. But we did see fish. Five grayling to around about a pound and as many trout – including a stunner of a pound and a half – made the day. Most were caught on nymphs, as you might expect early in the season, but two fish fell to a Grey Duster and the biggest grayling rose to sip in a Green Wells.

The day was also made complete for me by watching a number of brook lampreys digging their nests ready for spawning. In fact, in one place, the gravels were alive with these tiny eel-like creatures just four or five inches long.

When I have fished and found other anglers, I've been overwhelmed with the warm welcome and generous advice: that's the way of things up in Yorkshire. The term 'the brotherhood of the angle' still holds fast here and if you've got a question you know it will be answered directly.

TICKETS – Nidderdale Angling Club issue day tickets for £8 per person at the Post Offices in the villages of Lofthouse, Pately Bridge, Glasshouses and Summerbridge. Anglers must obtain tickets before fishing.

RULES – although the club owns most of the water on both banks, do consult maps and make sure that you do not trespass on the occasional private beats. Take great care with gates as there are frequently livestock grazing the riverbanks. For the same reasons, take even greater care with any discarded nylon, bags or other rubbish.

DIRECTIONS – Pateley Bridge lies between Ripon and Skipton on the B6265.

ACCOMMODATION – the Tourist Information Centre in Ripon on 01765 604625 will be able to supply information about various kinds of accommodation available in the area.

LOCKWOOD BECK – YORKSHIRE

I really enjoyed my day on Lockwood Beck a couple of years ago for several reasons. Firstly, the sixty-four-acre water is stunningly beautiful, set high on the moors with panoramic views all round. Secondly, I enjoyed the warmth of the welcome and the advice freely passed on to me by the regulars. And then, inevitably, there was the fishing. Lockwood browns and rainbows are big, beautifully finned and fight magnificently... as well as setting a really serious challenge.

Lockwood is an old reservoir, Victorian I think, but that doesn't really matter. What is important is that it is now leased from Northumbria Water and, because it is no longer used for water supply, the levels remain constant. It's got a really spacious feel to it and, because the boats are propelled by oars or your own electric engine, there's a real serenity. The management here is truly far thinking. Firstly, the quality of the fish, as I've said, is outstanding. You really won't find nicer rainbows anywhere. Secondly, you've got the added bonus that the water produces its own natural wild brown stock and these fish are quite spectacular, sometimes running to seven or eight pounds or even more. The rumour is that there's even the odd double in there. The reason? Well, there are lots of perch fry, huge stocks of minnows and stone loach and Lockwood anyway is very rich in insect life. All in all, a perfect combination.

Fishing is pretty well year round. You can catch fish on buzzers even in winter and, when the weather's mild, on dry fly. Daphnia can be a slight problem in the summer – good for fish growth obviously but the very devil if you're trying to entice a fish to take a small nymph.

You'll get lots of advice when you arrive at Lockwood, and everybody has their own solution. Catches do seem to be divided reasonably equally between bank and boat fishermen but I personally enjoy fishing the boat. The big key, as always, is not to over extend yourself for a fish thirty yards away, but simply sit tight and fish neat and close so you don't disturb those that are within easy casting range. Let yourself drift and you'll soon come close to feeding fish. At times, you look round at Lockwood and see fish everywhere. Mind you, it might look easy but it very rarely is! So, look for top of the water sport with small flies in the summer but don't forget muddlers, Cats Whiskers and so on if you're looking for the odd big wild brown. But they can, and do, come on virtually anything. I'm told that Christmas time is particularly good, though quite why that should be nobody seems to know.

Season – there is generally a two-week closed season about the beginning of March whilst the water is rested and restocked. All stocked fish are over two pounds in weight.
Tickets – contact Lockwood Fishery, Nr. Guisborough, North Yorkshire on 01287 660501. There are several ticket structures but basically £17 will buy you a four-fish ticket, with catch and release included. An evening ticket costs £11, and for this you can take two fish and release others. From November or thereabouts, a different price structure kicks in with cheaper fishing as stocking ceases, but there are always plenty of fish in the water. In the summer, fishing begins at 8.00am. And at the end of October at 10.00am.

Extending the Use of Buzzers

More and more these days buzzers are an integral part of the fly-fishing scene, especially on still waters. Traditionally buzzers have been fished either in the surface film or just inches beneath it, but it is possible to fish buzzers on quick-sink lines – very effective, especially in the winter. Remember that trout can, and will, take buzzers on the drop as they sink, during the retrieve, on the lift or even as you hang the flies in front of the boat.

- *Firstly, let your flies drop for as long as possible before pulling them back. Use slender flies dressed on heavyweight hooks.*
- *Keep in touch with your flies as they are sinking through the water – it's important if you're going to feel that take.*
- *Try different retrieve rates as you're bringing the flies back to the boat or the bank. It's a good idea sometimes to let them simply hang static for a moment to try and trick a trout that's been following.*
- *Remember takes can be very gentle. Always look where the line enters the water and strike if you see a slight tightening. Occasionally, also, your rod tip might just twitch.*
- *Don't get disillusioned if you don't pick up fish instantly. Deep water buzzer work can sometimes be slow but then is enlivened by frenetic activity. This is triggered by a deep water buzzer hatch.*
- *Never fish automatically. Try to animate your flies as much as possible, vary the retrieve and always, always concentrate so you can pick up that very delicate take.*

Records – rainbows of around 15lb have been recorded, and browns over 12lb.

Directions – from Guisborough, just south-west of Middlesborough, take the A171 towards Whitby. After about five miles, you will see the reservoir on the right – it is well signposted.

Accommodation – there is a variety of accommodation available in nearby Whitby and Scarborough. Contact the Tourist Information Offices in these two towns on 01947 602674 (Whitby) and 01723 3733333 (Scarborough) for further details. There is also good bed and breakfast accommodation in the small villages on the North Yorkshire moors.

Gyllhead Trout Fishery – Cumbria

Gyllhead is a beautifully matured reservoir in the hills to the south-east of Lake Windermere. It's a place that offers fabulous views of the south lakeland mountains, especially during the summer evening. The reservoir is long and thin, winding along a steep valley for most of its eleven acres. Virtually all the shoreline is fishable and several small streams feed the reservoir, the fresh water frequently attracting fish in close. The deepest water is down by the dam, at around seventeen feet or so, and it gradually tapers towards the shallows of three feet or less at the far end. At least two thirds of the reservoir is, however, ten feet or more in depth. There are a few browns present in the water that are naturally sustaining, so if you do catch one of these the WADAA, who control the water expertly, plead with you to return them. You will mostly catch rainbows and the average size of stock is around a pound and a half, though there are a number of bigger fish, several in excess of five or six pounds.

There are plenty of fish-holding features, but it makes sense on a water such as Gyllhead to keep on the move. Try one area, fish it intently and then move on until fish are contacted. Most of the regulars tend to fish a floating line, with a long or short leader depending on where in the water they're expecting to find fish. In the cold weather, fish will certainly be found in the deeper water, but during the summer they move into the bays and shallows where you'll often find them feeding on buzzers and dry flies. In very hot weather, the fish will once again be in the deeps, often close to the springs that offer cool, oxygenated water. It's at times like this that a very fast-sinking line can work wonders, especially if you're using a fly that has to be worked quickly.

As for flies, try Vivas and Black Chenille very early in the season, but don't forget buzzer hatches will be occurring by late March and certainly into April. By May, lake olives will be seen, and as the summer progresses trout will begin to fry feed and chase daddy longlegs. But, once again, remember that buzzers work pretty well throughout the entire season. And anyway, it's not the fly, as they say, it's the driver.

Gyllhead, with its steep banks, is well sheltered from the winds that frequently pound the Lakes, so it's a good water to go to if conditions are stormy. In fact, come to that, it's a good water to visit anytime, simply to bask in the peace and serenity.

Season – starts on 15th March and finishes on 31st December.

Tickets – Gyllhead Reservoir is controlled by the Windermere and Ambleside Angling Association. A two-fish day ticket costs £10 and catch and release is then allowed, providing that it is carried out sensitively.

Directions – to find the fishery, take the A592 from Windermere towards Bowness. Turn first right into the small lane signposted Cartmel Fell Road. The trout fishery is on the right-hand side of the road after half a mile. Car parking is available on the left, half way along the reservoir.

Accommodation – phone the Tourist Information Centre in Windermere on 015394 46499 or in Ambleside on 015394 32582 for details of the plentiful accommodation.

Esthwaite Water – Cumbria

Esthwaite is one of Cumbria's most beautiful waters, situated just to the west of Windermere in the most magnificent rolling, tree-rich countryside. It's a large lake – nearly three hundred acres – split into the north and the south basins. The north basin is fly only, whereas any method goes in the south. It's a very prolific water indeed, with huge hatches of buzzer and caddis fly. Damsel fly and corixa also feature large. The trout average something between a pound and a pound and a half, but on their rich diet, they soon grow on to become beautiful, silvery fish – often large in size. The fishery record is twelve pounds, and there are probably rainbows lurking that could smash that. And, to add a bit of spice, there are also some wild brown trout, which grow large. Again, the record is nine pounds and eight ounces for the water, but who knows?

You don't have to take a boat out on Esthwaite but it probably helps if you want to explore everything the water has to offer. In the same way, it's wise to hedge your bets when it comes to the fishing.

On cold, windy days, or alternatively hot, still ones, you might well find the fish down deep and that a sinking line is necessary. But, for the most part, a floating line will probably do, along with a team of buzzers. Remember, as I've already said, this is a very buzzer-rich water indeed. A final tip – don't work your buzzers too quickly at all on Esthwaite. Indeed, in a mild breeze, simply let them drift, giving them the odd tweak now and again.

Season – open all year.

Tickets – contact David Coleman at Esthwaite Water Trout Fishery, The Boathouse, Hawkshead, Cumbria on 01539 436541. Day-ticket prices are £16m, with a six fish-limit A boat for two costs £23 per day, with reduced boat charges from November to February inclusive. The boats are powered by electric engines.

Facilities – lodge with tackle shop, toilets and plenty of coffee!

Records – rainbow trout 16lb, brown trout 9lb 8oz.

Directions – from the M6 leave at junction 36 and follow the A590 to the Newby Bridge roundabout. Stay on the A590 towards Barrow. Turn right at the signpost for Lakeside and Hawkshead, passing through Lakeside. Continue for about seven miles and the fishery is well-signposted on the right.

Accommodation – the Tourist Information Centre in Windermere can provide details of a variety of accommodation in the area. Phone for details on 015394 46499.

Dubbs Trout Fishery – Cumbria

Dubbs is one of my absolute favourite still-water trout fisheries in the north. It's way up in the hills, seven hundred and fifty feet above sea level, and it offers superb views. It is well off the beaten track and can be difficult to find – it's a good job that day permits have a detailed location map on the rear!

Dubbs is not a water for the fainthearted. It's gin-clear and, being very highly alkaline, has a rich and varied aquatic life. This means that there's a great deal of natural food and the trout, which are stocked on a fortnightly basis, don't always respond to the fly easily. They will come to the surface if there is a plentiful hatch but often you won't see them because they've got food enough down deep. Mind you, when they are on the top, Dubbs' trout are really scintillating. You can sometimes get a buzzer hatch or a summer evening rise to caenis, and you'll find top water sport beyond compare. Equally, spring and autumn olives and summer sedges can give rise to periods of frantic activity and small black flies can be relied upon to bring fish up on any overcast day.

Still, you've got to consider nymphs if you're going to experience action throughout the day. Most of the bank sees you casting into water around ten feet deep, so this can be tackled on a floating line with leaders anything up to twenty or twenty-five feet. A slow sinking line can be used off the dam, however. You can get away with one or two quite heavily leaded nymphs as Dubbs does remain remarkably weed free throughout the summer and seldom presents problems to a deep-fished fly. The Pheasant Tail is always a good Dubbs' standby but a Hare's Ear is probably as good an all round bet as any. As for buzzers, on my limited visits I've found black and olive colours to be as good as anything. Locals tell you that the wind has a big effect on Dubbs – not surprising, as it's a relatively open water at altitude – and if the wind is from the east, just don't bother!

Season – starts on 15th March and finishes on 31st December.

Tickets – Dubbs is controlled by the Windermere and Ambleside Angling Association. Permits are available from the Service Station at Ings on the A591 and also from the Tourist Information Centres in Windermere and Ambleside (see below).

Records – the average size of fished stocked is a 1lb 8oz, but frequent fish of 8lb plus are introduced.

Directions – from the Ing Service Station on the A591, head towards Windermere and take the second turning on the right. Travel along this road for about a mile, ignoring the first small road on the right, to High Borrans. Dubbs road is about a quarter of a mile further, on the right, and is nothing more than a rough stone track. The fishery is about half a mile up the track. There is a car park near the dam.

Accommodation – the local Tourist Information Centres in Windermere on 015394 46499 and Ambleside on 015394 32582 will be able to recommend accommodation.

High Newton Trout Fishery – Cumbria

High Newton is about eleven acres in extent, once again set in stunning scenery overlooking Morecambe Bay. It is stocked on a two weekly basis, with rainbows averaging nearly two pounds, along with some bigger fish approaching ten pounds. There's also an excellent population of wild brown trout, which go to a decent size. As is common with all WADAA waters, there is a two-fish limit, but catch and release, using barbless hooks is encouraged thereafter. The large tagged fish, by the way, must be released: they are simply put in to give added zest to what's already very good fishing indeed.

Because of its altitude and lack of shelter, High Newton can be bleak early in the season when lures and weighted nymphs hold sway. Sport really begins in mid to late April when the daytime buzzer hatches begin. These peak in May and continue for much of the rest of the year, so always go prepared to fish Black or Suspender buzzers, especially into a slight ripple. Hawthorn fly are about from early May, and Beetles and other terrestrials keep the fish surface feeding right through the early summer. From mid June onwards, most surface activity is either early or late – especially in hot spells. Then, buzzers and caenis can be prolific, with sedges hatching from mid July. Be careful of hot, still days in summer when the fish go dour and deep, but if you go on a mild, ripply sort of day, you'll probably get rises throughout. September and early October are cracking months at Newton and, providing the weather is reasonably kind, you'll see fish rising right into November.

Although High Newton is a stocked fishery, it's still better to treat it as you would a moorland tarn and keep on the move. Okay, you'll sometimes find groups of fish but, as a general rule, the rainbows keep mobile and have to be tracked down. Equally, though, lures do take their fair share, smaller imitative patterns are generally far more effective. Accurate casting is a must: target rising fish and you'll keep picking them up day long. And, finally, don't High Newton rainbows fight!

Season – open from the 15th March to 31st December inclusive.

Tickets – these can be bought in advance from the Tourist Information Centres at Windermere on 015394 46499 and Ambleside on 015394 32582. They can also be purchased from Newby Bridge Motors at Newby Bridge on the A592.

➡ **DIRECTIONS** – to find the fishery, head towards High Newton on the A592 from Windermere. After a mile, you will pass a caravan site on the left-hand side of the road. The turn-off to High Newton is a small, concealed road about two hundred yards further, on the left. If you've passed the farm shop, then you've missed the turning. The reservoir is up the fell road, through two gates, which you must close. Parking is on the right, a hundred and fifty yards after the second gate.

ACCOMMODATION – details of a variety of accommodation can be obtained from the local Tourist Information Centre. Telephone numbers as above.

THE RIVERS EDEN AND TILL

Two of my most beloved northern rivers are frequently overlooked – the Eden in the west and the Till, a tributary of Tweed, in the east. I've classified them together as they're both much the same sort of size, both hold salmon, sea trout, brown trout and grayling and, above all, both possess an intimate, and charming character. Rivers mean different things to different people, quite obviously, but a small river, for me anyway, speaks straight to the soul. Especially in surroundings as delightful as you'll find in the valleys of these two rivers.

Fishing on the Till is not always easily come by but when I've chanced upon it, I've had some quite glorious sport, with sea trout especially, the occasional salmon and magnificent grayling. It's one of the delights of the Tweed area that the 'lady of the stream' is so frequently overlooked. For grayling fishing on the Till, I favour a team of nymphs – two, or at the most three – fished close to the bottom under a tiny strike indicator. Takes are often minute, perhaps just a holding up of the line or a quick jab downwards. Strike at once and you can easily find a fish of two pounds in weight on the end. Look for grayling in deep, pacy runs, perhaps where gravel or a sandbar dips down into deeper water. Keep everything tight and close and don't try to cast long distances. All that you'll do that way is to lose control.

There are good grayling on the Eden as well, but perhaps the real beauty of this river are the wild browns that average something in the region of twelve ounces or so, but can grow to magnificent fish of three or four pounds or even more. Some of the most dramatic fly fishing I've had in my entire life has been on the Eden, as the summer shadows stretch over the pools and dusk falls in this beautiful part of the world. At times, it's as though the river, which has appeared barren during the day, literally boils with fish. Big fish. Fish cartwheeling out of the water. And, from time to time, there's the tremendous roar of a salmon stimulated by the cooling air. Magnificent memories, and, if you can, you should make a point of investigating both of these marvellous waters.

Tickets – my own favourite area of the Eden is centred on Appleby-in-Westmoreland, Cumbria. The Tufton Arms on 01768 351593 can arrange fishing and is situated very close to the river. The management is heavily into fishing as well. Try also the Sandford Arms on 01768 351121, which has private fly fishing for guests on over five miles of double bank water. For the Till, try Brian Thompson, River Keeper, Redscar Cottage, Milfield, Wooler, Northumberland NE71 6JQ on 01668 216223. Or the Estate Office, Ford, Berwick-on-Tweed, on 01890 820224. The Tilmouth Park Hotel, Cornhill-on-Tweed, TD12 4UU can also provide fishing on the Till with its junction on the Tweed. The hotel also offers tremendous salmon fishing for residents. Phone 01890 882255 for details. Prices for both rivers depend on the season and the target fish. Obviously salmon fishing costs more than trout and grayling.
Directions – you will find Appleby on the A66 between Penrith and Barnard Castle. The Till runs into the River Tweed close to Cornhill.
Accommodation – for various kinds of accommodation to be found in the area contact the Tourist Information Centres in Penrith on 01768 867466 or Barnard Castle on 01833 690909. For the River Till area, call the Centre at Coldstream on 01890 882607.

Coldingham Loch – Northumberland

Coldingham Loch, perched right on the cliffs between Eyemouth and Dunbar, is a jewel of a place. It's twenty-two acres in extent – giving around a mile of bankside fishing – so there's always room to get away and enjoy seclusion. Let's deal with its setting first: you can hear, see and smell the ocean from the banks of Coldingham. It's a mixture of barren upland and fertile, seductive woodland. Set in a small country estate called Westloch, you can sense it's an ancient place. The estate provides an ideal centre for naturalists, walkers and for those who simply want to relax and enjoy unspoilt country surroundings. There are also prehistoric hill forts and settlements of archaeological interest in the vicinity.

The loch itself is similarly fascinating. It's deep, generally crystal clear and burgeoning with fertility. Perhaps rare in a loch so far north, annual and frequent weed cutting needs to take place. The owner of the loch, Dr Wise, stresses that this very high water quality makes for some special fishing. In the first place – browns and rainbows – are nearly always in absolutely first-class condition. Great care goes into the stocking policies – generally fish of one and a half to two pounds – and they grow on well in such a friendly environment. In fact, over-wintered rainbows of three and four pounds are commonplace, as are brown trout ranging anything up to six pounds. The fish also fight spectacularly hard: their condition, their almost inevitably perfect fins and the deep, clear water obviously all prove to be stimulating.

The clear, fertile waters of Coldingham Loch also produce fish that are generally only to be caught on imitative patterns. Okay, some small reservoir lures do take fish, but the general Coldingham visitor prefers to fish more cunningly than that.

Throughout the season, buzzers work extraordinarily well – especially towards evening on a warm, muggy day perhaps. All patterns seem to work but it's best to have a good selection with you. Dry flies, too, prove popular. Daddy longleg patterns, sedge patterns, dry hoppers and even caenis imitations throughout June.

In April and May, sunshine leads to an explosion of terrestrial patterns and an eternally rising stock of fish. However, as the heat of the summer progresses, both browns and especially rainbows tend to go deeper. It's now that a floating line with a very long leader and small, weighted nymphs really come into their own. (This is how I personally have been successful at Coldingham – often with leaders in excess of twenty feet in length.) Dr Wise also advises the use of a silver Invictor as a dropper on a two-fly leader. It pays to work the nymph, perhaps a goldhead or something similar, as slowly as possible, keeping an eagle eye open for a very quick jabbing take.

Coldingham, perched so close to the sea, is very much ruled by weather conditions. Strong, cold north-easterlies are not particularly good, nor are bright, calm days in the height of the summer. Ideal is the day with light winds and overcast skies, but even then Coldingham won't offer up its fish easily. Be warned: those of you accustomed to easy put and take stew ponds will find this most beautiful water a tad of a challenge. It's probably fair to say that you need six or seven visits before you can confidently begin to say that you're getting the hang of this charming, characterful loch.

Dr Wise's top tips: it pays to keep on the move and to try different areas until fish can be located. Even on a small water, the trout can be localised and it pays to search until they're found. The other bonus with Coldingham is that Dr Wise is on hand each and every day to impart his expert and deep knowledge of the water.

Season – the brown trout season runs from 15th March to 6th October, whilst the rainbow trout season runs from 15th March to 31st October.

Tickets – these are bought in advance from Dr E. J. Wise on 01890 771270. A day ticket with a four-fish limit costs £17 and an evening ticket with a three-fish limit is £14. Boat charges are £4 and £3 respectively, extra per fishing rod. It's important to note that day tickets are by advance booking only as numbers are strictly regulated.

Rules – single hooks only, no larger than a size 10. These must be barbless or de-barbed if you intend to return fish to the water. There is a twelve-inch minimum takeable size limit and all undersized fish should be returned very carefully. High standards of behaviour are expected at Coldingham as it is a wildlife reserve.

Directions – taking the A1 north from Berwick-upon-Tweed, turn off onto the A1107 signposted for Eyemouth. Follow the road through Eyemouth and you will come to Coldingham village. Staying on the A1107, leave the village going north towards Edinburgh and turn right immediately at the school, heading towards the coast. This road is not signposted. It is a narrow single-track lane, a no-through road with passing places. This will bring you to Westloch House, the estate and the loch itself. You are asked to drive slowly and carefully along the Westloch road.

Accommodation – there is much bed and breakfast and guesthouse accommodation in the area but why not stay on the estate itself in one of the delightful lodges, cottages or chalets? These offer self-catering accommodation of the very highest standard and, for the fisherman, they provide the added bonus of being on the water itself.

Highly Recommended Fisheries

- *Tewit Fields, Nr. Carnforth, Lancs. Phone 01524 730331 for details. Seven acres. Good-conditioned, well-sized fish.*
- *Watendlath Tarn, Cumbria. One of Britain's most gorgeous waters. Stunning browns. Highly recommended.*
- *Wykeham Trout Lake, Scarborough, North Yorkshire. Three lakes, all with different levels of challenge. Interesting fishing.*
- *Kielder Reservoir, Northumberland. Phone 01434 240398 for more details. Two thousand seven hundred acres. Heavily stocked. Stunning surroundings.*
- *Langley Dam, Northumberland. Call 01434 688846 for details. An attractive fishery. Fishing closes in November.*

Fly-Fishing Sites in Scotland

1. Rosslynlee Fishery
2. The Isle of Bute
3. Carron Valley Reservoir
4. Loch Leven
5. Lindores Loch
6. Loch Awe
7. Lochs Laidon, Ericht & Rannoch
8. The River Tummel
9. Lintrathen Loch
10. The River Dee
11. The River Garry
12. Upper River Garry System
13. South Uist
14. The River Spey
15. Stoneyfield Lochs
16. The River Cassley
17. The Rivers Inver & Kirkaig and Loch Assynt
18. Scourie Hill Lochs
19. Tongue Hill Lochs
20. The Shetland Trout Lochs

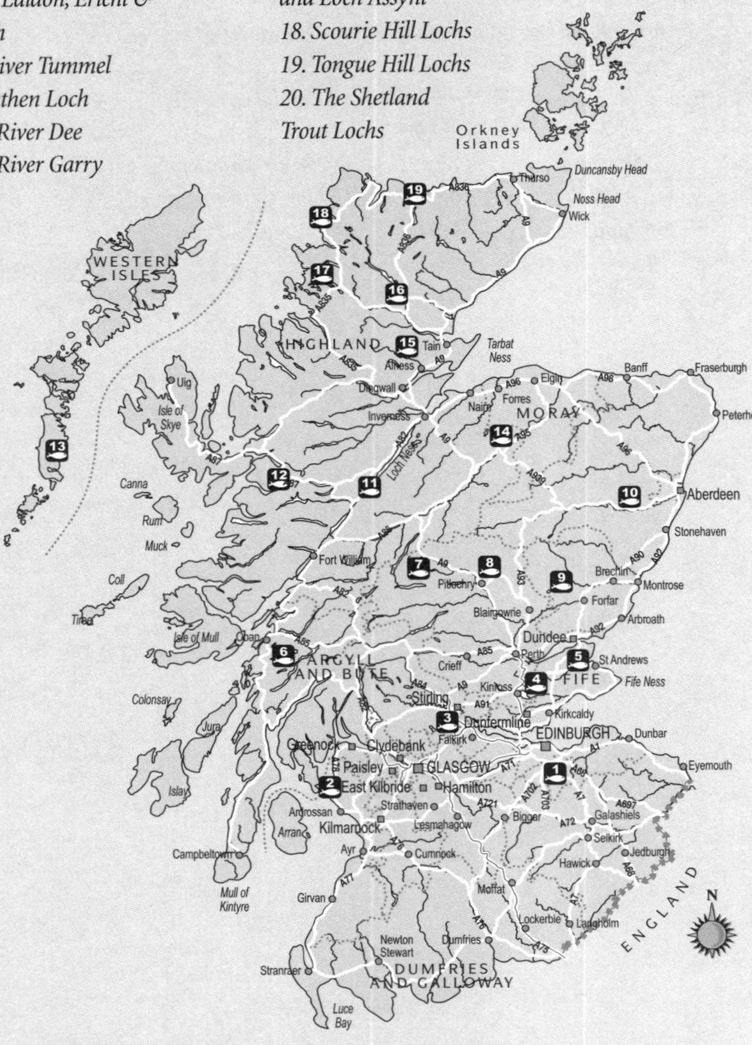

"You have tramped the glen and climbed the hill, the sun is hot on your back and the air is heather sweet. Warm from the exertion, you sight at last the loch of your dreams glittering temptingly between the rolling crest. At the water's edge, you pause to drink in the tranquil beauty of it all before the splash of a trout stirs you into action. Fish are cruising the margins in search of their prey and if you cast later, the first trout of the day snatches your Pennel. As you slip it back, its golden flanks wink at you signalling better to come. Right now, this is paradise and there is no finer place to be."

LESLIE CRAWFORD, RENOWNED HILL LOCH GUIDE AND AUTHOR

Leslie highlights just one aspect of what Scotland has to offer the fly fisherman but there is much, much more. North of the border, there is just about everything that a fly rod was built for: mighty salmon rivers and wee trout-rich burns; pocket handkerchief lochans, and lochs the size of inland seas; immaculately-run commercial fisheries and lakes so wild they've never seen a line before. Salmon, grilse, ferox trout, brown trout, sea trout, rainbow trout, grayling and char. The mountainous valleys of the west and the rolling plains of the east, invariably beautiful, peaceful and unspoiled. Indeed, for anyone to say they know everything about Scottish fly fishing would be a nonsense – there's just too much for any lifetime to take in. I hope in this brief guide to Scottish waters that I have given you some indication of what you can expect to find in the most glorious of settings.

Just a very quick mention of char here. They are present in virtually all the deep lochs and are generally unfished. They do, however, come to the surface on warm, summer evenings and can be spotted dimpling around the margins in shallower areas of these lakes. Very small dry flies or nymphs can pick up these beautiful fish. On some lochs where there are fish cages – Loch Garry, for example – some of the char have grown very big indeed on pellets and can be contacted on spinners and plugs. These fish can be in excess of five pounds.

Rosslynlee Fishery

Rosslynlee is an enchanting, intimate trout fishery in its own right but especially important because it is so close to Edinburgh, lying just twenty-five miles due south from the city centre. It's a beautiful water, nestling quietly amongst arable land, with stunning views of the Pentland hills stretching out to the west and the Moorfoot range to the south. In fact, a more enticing gateway to the Scottish borders could barely be imagined.

Rosslynlee is a water for all manner of fishing: at just on seven acres, it's not too large to be daunting for beginners and yet still offers a sizeable challenge for the more experienced game fishermen. Given its lush, rural surroundings, Rosslynlee is also large enough to provide peace and serenity for those who want more than just a hooped rod.

High summer can be a problem on many of these smaller fisheries with stale, warm water and over-abundant weed growth, but not here. Rosslynlee is spring-fed and this maintains water level and clarity whilst also helping to keep temperatures stable throughout the year. Perhaps this explains why the feeding in the lochan is so prolific with midge, caddis, snails, daphnia, olives and fry all present in abundance. This obviously makes for a water ideal for the imitative approach and, not surprisingly, buzzer and dry-fly fishing are both particularly popular during the warmer months. Lure fishing – always favoured by beginners is, however, successful year round and especially so through the colder winter period.

Gilbert Scott, the owner of the fishery, prides himself on the quality of the fish he stocks. These average at least two pounds in weight, with much bigger ones also introduced. But best of all – these are fully finned fish in prime condition. Apart from rainbow trout, which make up the majority of the stocks, there are also brown trout along with some golden and blue trout – always a welcome addition to the basket.

So, if you are holidaying in the borders or making your way up to the city of Edinburgh, this is the perfect stop-over for a few hours of peace and quiet in magnificent surroundings.

Season – Rosslynlee is open all the year round. Tuition is offered by Gilbert Scott, a former Scottish international fly fisherman.

Tickets – contact Gilbert Scott, the owner, at Rosslynlee Trout Fishery, New Biggin Hill, Penicuik, Midlothian, Scotland or phone him on 01968 679606. Tickets cost £17.50 for a full day and a four-fish limit. Half-day and evening tickets are £14.50, with three-fish limits. You can continue to catch and release trout after securing your limit providing you are using small flies only.

Directions – you will find Rosslynlee just south-west of Edinburgh near Penicuik. It's on the A6094 between Howgate and Rosewell. The fishery is well-signposted.

Accommodation – there is accommodation available on site, but phone in plenty of time to assure a booking.

The Isle of Bute

I love the Isle of Bute simply because it feels like the Highlands and yet it's so easily accessible from the city of Glasgow. In fact, just an hour or so after leaving the M8 you can feel yourself entering into another world. And that's what it's like fishing two remarkable waters on the island – Loch Fad and Loch Quien. These are very different types of water even though they are so close together. Fad gives more of an impression of a highland water, a bit more rugged, somewhat more steeply-sided. Quien, on the other hand, is more low-lying and gives the impression of greater fertility. Both, however, offer great and exciting challenges.

Fad is the deeper loch and although it can be approached from the bank, it is probably better tackled by boat – and there is a fleet of thirty on the water. Typical loch-style tactics work well on this long, thin loch, which is a mile and three quarters long and a hundred and seventy-five acres in extent. Never be afraid to ask for the most up-to-the-minute information at the bailiff's hut, where you will meet with the friendliest advice imaginable.

Dealing with Ghillies

You're up in Scotland for the first time, you've forked out for a top beat and you are to meet the hoary old ghilly down by the salmon hut at ten. Help!

- *Don't be intimidated. It's very easy to almost feel that you have no right to be on the river. Remember you're paying him to help.*
- *On the other hand, don't be patronising and overbearing. Remember it's important to build up a good relationship.*
- *It's only sense to confess your weaknesses from the outset. If you try to hide anything or pretend you're an expert, he'll pretty soon see through you.*
- *Ask for help with your weak areas, whatever they are. A good ghilly will always advise and teach conscientiously.*
- *Always do what your ghilly advises – at least for the first few days until you have ideas of your own. Remember that he is going to know that stretch of the river a thousand times better than you can ever do.*
- *Don't blame the ghilly for your own mistakes. If you miss or lose a fish, be brave enough to admit your fault.*
- *Remember that there's nothing like a pint or two back in the bar in the evening to build up rapport. A bit of bonding gets the best out of the day to come.*
- *Remember that salmon fishing is an unpredictable pastime. Don't blame your ghilly if the fishing is hard or there are very few fish in the river.*

Quien is somehow a quieter water, very beautiful, but the fish are easily spooked. There are only four boats on this ninety-acre loch and all without outboards – something that speaks for itself. In fact, you can approach Quien quite happily from the bank. Near the boathouse, for example, there are large areas of water only two to four feet deep and stalking fish here becomes a distinct possibility. Naturally, lures do work but this is very definitely a nymph man's water as well. The fish benefit from a rich larder, so shrimp, beetle and corixa patterns are all favourites as well.

In short, these beautiful lochs offer a typical highland far-away trouting experience and yet lie only an hour or so from the hurly-burly of Glasgow itself.

SEASON – Quien, a wild and stocked brown trout water, is open from 15th March to 16th October. This water is strictly fly fishing only. Loch Fad, offering both rainbows and browns, is open for fly fishing from 1st March to 17th December and for bait fishing and spinning from 15th March to 6th October. Note that bait and lure fishermen can only operate from the bank.

TICKETS – these are available from Loch Fad Fisheries Limited, Loch Fad, Isle of Bute PA20 9PA. Phone them on 01700 504871. Ticket prices for Loch Quien are £8 a day and for Loch Fad, £14 a day. It's advisable to book boats. These cost £11 a day on a weekday and £13 for the weekend. Tackle is available from the bailiff's hut and fly-fishing rods are for hire, which can be handy if you are visiting in the middle of a business trip, for example.

DIRECTIONS – the mainland ferry terminal at Wemyss Bay on the Clyde coast is easily reached from Glasgow along the M8, turning on to the A73 at Greenock. From Wemyss Bay, the crossing to Rothesay takes a mere thirty minutes by ferry, which operates on a frequent daily service. The waters are around about a mile from the town centre of Rothesay. They are well-signposted along the A845. It is worth noticing that a taxi will also take you to the water for a modest fare. It's worth phoning the fishery to book in advance.

ACCOMMODATION – Rothesay, itself has a huge number of hotels, guesthouses and bed and breakfast possibilities. Contact the Isle of Bute Tourist Information Centre on 01700 502151 for up-to-the-minute advice on vacancies in your price bracket.

CARRON VALLEY RESERVOIR

Carron Valley Reservoir is situated in the Strathclyde hills near Denny in the east of Scotland. It's a lovely place to fish – one thousand acres of water ringed by wooded hills and spectacular views in every direction. It's a wild, rugged water and the sense of isolation is probably increased by the fact that bank fishing is not allowed. All you'll see during the course of the day is an abundance of wildlife and a few boats dotted here and there, but never with a sense of overcrowding.

The brown trout fishing is quite excellent and though the fish average just under a pound, several between four and six pounds are taken each year.

Although it's a large water, Carron Valley responds very well to buzzers of various sizes as well as more typical flies such as the Gold Butcher or the Bibio. Try also the Black Pennel, the Soldier Palmer or even dry flies when the water warms up.

Have no fear, there are plenty of fish. There is an outstanding stock of wild browns but the Carron Valley staff also stock around four thousand trout per season, usually introduced on a fortnightly basis. The staff, you'll find, are extremely helpful, pointing you in all the right directions.

Season – boat fishing only, April to September.
Tickets – contact Russel Peyton on 01786 458827 for boat availability. Ticket prices vary from £9 up to £22 depending on concessions. The boats take two rods and outboard hire is £8. Fish limit is six pounds per rod.
Facilities – toilets, fishing lodge, disabled facilites, car parking, outboard hire and lifejackets. There are sixteen boats on the water, four at eighteen feet and twelve at fifteen feet. Lifejackets are supplied, which must be worn.
Directions – Carron Valley Reservoir is situated in the Carron Valley by Denny FK6 RJL. It is well-signposted.

Loch Leven – Perth and Kinross

Loch Leven has probably had more words written about it than any other trout water in Britain, certainly in Scotland. For decades now its special strain of brown trout has been revered and much transported to other waters. There's something special about Leven: it's very large – three thousand five hundred acres – feels remote and yet is uniquely accessible. In fact, it's just north of the great cities of Scotland, hardly a stone's throw off the M90 and yet, when you're out there in your boat you're in another world.

I can't pretend that I've ever done any better than moderately well on Leven: it's a water that really does respond to local knowledge and experience but, having said that, I've never ever regretted a single moment spent on its waters. I'm sure it will get you like that: there's something totally magical about it and even if you only have a moderate bag compared with the experts, I can guarantee you'll still have the time of your life.

Leven is a fascinating water of varying depths, bottom contours and dotted by islands. What's more you can fish late – anything up to 11.30pm in the evening at the peak of the summer – and that gives it a truly magical feel. Potter back to the pier in the half-light with the fish still rising around you, and you'll know you've been a part of something very special.

Both the browns and the splendidly fighting rainbows respond to the notorious moods of Leven, so it pays to ring the changes during the course of the day. Of course, during good weather, it's most exciting to fish buzzers and dry flies on the surface and really see the action, but there are times that you'll have to use sinking lines to get deeper to the fish. The answer is to be adaptable and, if you are, you'll really make the most of this spell-binding water.

Season – 20th March to 6th October.
Tickets – these are available from the pier in Kinross, on the water itself. Day permits cost £30 for a boat with a maximum of three rods. Evening permits vary between £24 and £30, again for three rods. There is no bag limit on browns over ten inches and you're allowed to take twelve rainbows.
Facilities – there is a café, toilets, telephones and tackle hire.
Directions – take the M90 north and turn off at junction 6. The water is well-signposted.
Accommodation – the Roxburghe Guesthouse, 126, High Street, Kinross KY13 7DA is very convenient for the water. Phone 015778 629498 for details.

Lindores Loch – Fife

This is a lovely Scottish water of around ninety-five acres, averaging around eight feet in depth. It is a fertile water and the fact that the loch is so shallow encourages fish to take from the surface. In fact, buzzer patterns are particularly recommended, especially once the water begins to warm up. Most of the fish are rainbows, but they are in excellent condition and average two pounds or above. By the way, there are also stocks of excellent perch sometimes topping three pounds.

This is a particularly beautiful water and fishes very well on warm, still evenings. Also watch out for such rarities as the occasional passing osprey.

But, whatever, remember to pack those buzzers, particularly in olive, claret and black. Nymphs, however, are also taken in this water, along with traditionals such as an Invicta Wickham's.

Season – March to the end of November.
Tickets – contact Andy Mitchell on 01337 810488 or write to him at The Fishing Hut, Lindores Loch, By Newburgh, Fife KY14 6JB. A two-man boat costs £32. Ten fish allowed per boat. A three-man boat costs £36, with fifteen fish allowed per boat. For a single angler, subject to availability, £16 with a five-fish limit. Catch and release is allowed after the limit is taken on de-barbed hooks.
Records – 8lb 4oz rainbow, 5lb 8oz brown.
Facilities – Toilets. Lodge with seating, cooker, free tea and coffee, sale of fly patterns, tuition, electric outboard hire.
Directions – from Edinburgh, come north on the M90, turning right at junction 8 and taking the A91 Cupar–St. Andrews road. Turn left onto the B937, signposted Newburgh. The loch is two miles along this road on the left-hand side.

LOCH AWE – ARGYLL

I'm going to talk unreservedly now about one of my great passions – ferox fishing. The ferox is the mighty, Scottish predatorial trout, and it has been a great favourite with anglers for well over a century now, ever since the trolling style of fishing, pioneered by Victorian sportsmen. There are those that say that trolling is boring but I cannot agree with them. It's exhilarating to be out on a grand day in a beautiful loch such as Awe, with its spectacular views. Take binoculars with you and you will be sure to see some magnificent bird life, and perhaps even some deer as they come to drink at the water's edge as the dusk pulls in.

And what fish these ferox are. You won't find anything like them anywhere else in the world – big, bold, brilliantly coloured. Of course, trolling is a specialised art but there are books on the subject, and perhaps you've already done some anyway. Certainly, my advice if you're heading to Scotland is to stick in a spinning rod and some lures and you'll be halfway there.

Awe is justly famous for its huge ferox – fish of over twenty-five pounds certainly exist in this mysterious loch. But there are also other fine trout to be taken on fly as well. Mostly the 'normal' trout weigh around half a pound or so but there are better fish of at least double that weight to be taken on the fly.

Just a word or two about safety: always wear a lifejacket, always take oars, make sure you have a reliable engine and plenty of fuel. Let people know your course and estimated time of return, and don't go out in stormy weather or if there's a bad weather forecast. In short, never take any risks whatsoever. A ferox is a mighty prize indeed but not one worth dying for!

My favourite months are March to early June and then again in September but there are times when high summer can prove very productive.

SEASON – the annual close season for trout extends from 7th October to 14th March, both days included.

TICKETS – the Loch Awe Improvement Association sells season, weekly and daily tickets and these can be found in hotels, Post Offices and tackle shops throughout Scotland. They can also be obtained from from D. Wilson, Ardbrecknish House, Dalmally, PA33 1AQ. Boats and permits can also be bought from the Taycreggan Hotel, Kilchrenan, by Taynuilt, Argyle PA35 1HQ on 01866 833211, the Cuil-na-sithe Hotel on 01866 833234 and the Sonachan Hotel, Port Sonachan, by Dalmally, Argyle PA33 1BN on 01866 833240. Also contact Mr. N. D. Clark, 11 Dalavich, by Taynuilt on 01866 844209.

DIRECTIONS – take the A82 to Tyndrum and from there the A85 on to Dalmally at the head of the loch.

ACCOMMODATION – any of the hotels named above. The Taycreggan Hotel has my personal recommendation. It is situated right on the loch side with its own jetty and fishing fleet. An excellent experience.

Lochs Laidon, Ericht and Rannoch – Invernesshire

There is a remarkable cluster of lochs, just to the west of Pitlochry, set in some of the most dramatic of Scottish scenery. Between them, Ericht, Rannoch and Laidon have produced extraordinary numbers of both ferox trout and normal brown trout over the past few years. These are very wild places to fish indeed, and not for the timid, but the rewards can be excellent. So beautiful is the scenery that even a fish-less day is no hardship. Trolling is practised on all three lochs but it's also possible to catch excellent trout on traditional fly tactics, simply drifting with the wind and fishing a team of flies close to the surface.

There are other bonuses. Try, for example, the River Gaur that links Laidon to Rannoch. This is a mesmerising, tumultuous river full of wicked rapids and deep, slow pools. Once again, it's the home of many trout and some earth-shattering ferox. In short, if you fancy something on the wild side, think hard about a journey up to this spellbinding part of Scotland.

Season – the closed season for trout is 7th October to 14th March inclusive.
Tickets – The Loch Rannoch Conservation Association has fishing on Loch Rannoch and the local shops and hotels sell permits. For Loch Ericht, permits are available from the Loch Ericht Hotel, Dalwhinnie, Invernesshire PH14 1AF. Phone 01528 522257 for details. A day permit is £6 and boats are available to hire. For Loch Laidon and the River Gaur, contact the Moor of Rannoch Hotel, Rannoch Station PH17 2QA on 01882 633238. Tickets are £3 per rod or £25 per day with a boat and outboard. The local tackle shop, The Country Store, Kinlochrannoch, Perthshire is also a fund of information.
Directions – for Rannoch and Laidon, take the A9 north of Pitlochry. After eight miles, turn off left on the B847 Kinlochrannoch. Follow the picturesque B846 as far as it goes to Rannoch Station, way out on Rannoch moor. Loch Laidon can be found further to the west. For Dalwhinnie, continue up the A9 turning off left on the A889.
Accommodation – the Moor of Rannoch Hotel, Rannoch Station is one of the most dramatic outposts any angler will ever come across. The Ericht Hotel also has a fine feroxing reputation! See above for details.

The River Tummel – Perthshire

The River Tummel in and around Pitlochry offers some wonderful rough-water trout and grayling fishing. Most of the beats are controlled by the Pitlochry Angling Club, which affords some tremendous opportunities for visiting anglers. Brown trout fishing opens on 15th March and is fly only to 30th June. Bait from then onwards , until the trout fishing finishes on 6th October. However, grayling fishing specifically opens on 7th October and continues until 14th March. So, you see, fishing is pretty well all year round.

Trout fishing is probably at its best in the late spring and summer with some tremendous hatches taking place in the early evening. Moreover, the trout are browns and in beautiful condition.

Perhaps it's for the grayling fishing, though, that many people will make the effort to travel so far north. These really are grayling as God originally made them! There are some very big fish indeed, and two pounders aren't at all unusual. These are deep, heavily-shouldered fish with brilliant deep blue colouring. They can be taken on both fly and bait and look for the deeper streamier runs. It also pays to keep moving, keep searching different lies until a group of grayling is contacted. Fun can then be fast and furious, but use barbless hooks so they can be slipped back with ease.

Season – trout and grayling fishing 15th March to 6th October; grayling fishing 7th October to 14th March.

Tickets – £4 per day and £12 per week for both trout and grayling. Tickets are available from the excellent Mitchells' tackle shop of Pitlochry. Phone 01796 472613 for the latest information. Tickets can also be obtained from Pitlochry Tourist Information Centre on 01796 472215. For season tickets, apply to the club secretary on 01796 472484.

Directions – the fishing is generally through Pitlochry town and on the outskirts. It is wise to visit Mitchells' tackle shop and look closely at the map for the proper beats.

Accommodation – Pitlochry offers a wealth of bed and breakfasts, guesthouses and hotels. The Pitlochry Tourist Information Centre on 01796 472215 can provide you with phone numbers.

Lintrathen Loch – Angus

This is a really stunning water, not that far north of Dundee, but still a great place to get away from it all. The lovely thing about Lintrathen is that we are talking about immaculately conditioned brown trout, many of them wild but with stocks judiciously topped up with quality fish. Fishing is by boat and because of the loch's size, you can easily get away from company if you fancy fishing on your own. A lot of the water is ringed by rhododendron bushes and the roots and overhanging branches attract a good number of fish. Also, look around the rocky shorelines and the dam for bigger fish.

Most Lintrathen browns average around twelve ounces to a pound and a half but two pound plus fish are quite common, with a very few going to double figures. But it's not size that attracts anglers back again and again to this charming water: it's the views, the quality of the fishing and the feeling of spaciousness.

Top wet flies are the Bibio, the Black Pennel and Black Spider. Try a Black Hoppers and Black Buzzers for evening rises. A last tip, stick to the margins of this water where the majority of the natural food is to be found. This is a working reservoir with very deep, comparatively sterile water out in the middle.

Season – first weekend in April to first Sunday in October.

Tickets – Boats are £32 and this includes the outboard motor along with fuel. There's a fifteen-fish boat limit. Please phone Mr. Yule for prior booking (see below).

Contact – Jack Yule on 01575 560327 or 01575 573816. Lintrathen Angling Club, The Boathouse Lodge, Lintrathen Reservoir, by Alyth.

Records – the heaviest recorded brown weighed 11lb 4oz, but 3lb is considered an excellent fish.

Facilities – there are toilets and an anglers' shelter along with weighing facilities but don't expect smart clubhouses, refreshments and so on. It's not that kind of fishery.

Directions – Lintrathen lies to the north of the A926 Alyth–Kirriemuir road. Turn off the A926 onto the B954, signposted Glenisla. You pass a couple of golf courses and then turn right, following this road past the Reekie Lin – which is a series of waterfalls – past the turn off for Backwater Reservoir until you come to the Lintrathen Anglers' car park.

The River Dee – Aberdeenshire

The River Dee is another of Scotland's classic salmon rivers and justifiably so. Indeed, for many anglers, the Dee is the epitome of a fly river with endless pools just built for the job. Most of my time on the Dee has been in the Spring when fly fishing has been something of a chore. But on one notable occasion I had a week in the summer when there were fish around, when the water was low and clear and you could really get in tune with the fish.

It's not particularly hard to catch salmon in perfect conditions, when the river is at a good level and the fish are teeming through. It's much harder when the water is low, clear and warm, and under such conditions an angler really has to fish skilfully to stand a great chance. Try using a floating line and a small black fly. Work your way down the pool methodically, casting twice from each stance then dropping a couple of paces down river before casting again. Put your fly across the river and slightly downstream so it works across in a steady movement. Visualise your fly working some six or eight inches beneath the surface and concentrate hard. If you do get a take, don't necessarily expect a hard tug – sometimes all you'll feel is a tweak or just see a gleam of silver. Yes, the great days on the Dee, or any other salmon river come to that, come when the rain has fallen and there's colour in the water but that doesn't mean to say that you can't have great fun throughout the warmer months too.

Season – early February to 1st November

Tickets – the Dee, as you'd expect, is very difficult to get fishing on. It's beats are highly-prized. However, rods are sometimes available from the Factor, Invercauld Estates Office, Braemar, by Ballater AB3 5TR on 01339 741224. Also try Glen Tanar Estate, Brooks House, Glen Tanar AB34 5EU on 01339 886451. The Banchory Lodge Hotel, Banchory AB31 3HS, also has salmon and trout fishing on the Dee available for five rods. Phone 01330 822625.

→ **Directions** – the Dee runs west from Aberdeen. Banchory and Ballater can both be accessed along the A93. This charming road runs the length of the Dee valley.

Accommodation – there is a wealth of bed and breakfast and guesthouse accommodation in Banchory, Aboyne and Ballater. The Banchory Lodge Hotel is situated right on the river with a glorious pool outside the dining room windows. It is expensive but comes highly, personally recommended.

The River Garry – Invernesshire

You don't have to go too far back into history to read of a time when the Invernesshire Garry was one of Scotland's most famous salmon waters. Since the 1950s, however, the advent of hydro-electric power has damaged runs of fish to some degree. However, the river is still an absolutely enchanting place to fish and still offers very healthy stocks indeed. The river is perhaps at its best from the foot of Loch Garry to the river mouth in Loch Oich. Here you have three and a half miles of spectacular water – a mixture of tumbling falls and open glides all amid the most wondrous Scottish scenery.

Although spinning is permitted, the pools are ideal for fly fishing and, certainly once the temperatures begin to rise, it would be a crime really to do anything else. Big fish come in early and January can often see salmon in excess of twenty-five pounds. The prime weeks are generally considered to be in April and May, but runs of grilse are common later on in the season throughout August and September.

The river is being extremely well looked after – recently the thick rhododendron undergrowth has been cleared somewhat to allow more light on the water and better access for the anglers.

There's also a catch and release policy that plays an important part in the overall fishery management plan. Each party may keep one wild salmon each week fished, but all others should be returned. And here's the exciting part: for each fresh fish returned, you will be given a whole farmed salmon in its place. What a great idea!

Season – 15th January to 14th October

Tickets – the fishing is let by the week and information is obtainable from Garry Fishings, c/o Invergarry Hotel, Invergarry, Invernesshire. Phone 01809 501206 for more information. Prices vary according to the popularity of the week.

Arrangements – fishing is restricted to six rods on any day. Tenants who book an entire week of six rods will have totally exclusive use of all facilities – this includes the spacious fishing cabin with table and chairs, lighting, mains water and sink, microwave oven and conventional cooker with, naturally enough, rod racks. This is situated on the river bank with its own private car park.

→ **Directions** – Invergarry is found on the junction of the A87 and the A82, south of Fort Augustus. Fort Augustus is seven miles away and Fort William twenty-five miles.

ACCOMMODATION – the Invergarry Hotel itself on 01809 501206, is a delightful and convenient place to stay, as is its sister hotel the Glengarry Castle, on 01809 501254, situated on the banks of Loch Oich. Self-catering is available at the Old Mill in the village. Phone Kevin Reed on 01207 545538.

UPPER RIVER GARRY SYSTEM – TOMDOUN

Tomdoun is the centre of it all. This extraordinary Highland lodge dates from the late Victorian period and boasts one of the best views of anywhere in the world. Walk outside the Tomdoun, now a cosy fisherman's hotel, and all you will see is mountains and water, all available to residents. Brace yourself – you really are in paradise.

So what have you got within a five or six mile radius? Firstly, there is Loch Quoich – a stunning lunar-type loch up in the mountains where you will see deer and snow on the summits virtually every month of the year. Quoich is a ferox trout loch for those who care to troll and for the fly fisher, a wild brown trout water that can produce twenty or more fish a day averaging around ten to twelve ounces. Fish Quoich traditionally on the drift and as the sun begins to set and the wind begins to ease, trout will dimple the surface everywhere. You're in a wonderland.

Dropping down the valley, back towards the hotel, you come to the wonderful Loch Poulary – minute compared with Quoich's eight miles in length and one mile in breadth. Poulary, by comparison, is a mere two hundred acres or so, and much more friendly to those used to smaller waters. In fact, on Poulary – which is equally as stunning as Quoich in its own way – you can probably use a greater variety of methods. Poulary, somehow, is kinder, cosier than Quoich. You can pick up trout on dry fly, buzzer or nymph, as well as traditional wet patterns. And the trout, generally, are bigger. Poulary is more lush and fertile and the browns really grow on a pace. Fish of one to two pounds are not unusual.

As the Garry system falls out of the tail of Poulary, the river really becomes interesting. Pools and rapids proliferate and at times, especially in the later summer, a good number of salmon work their way upstream. This is super salmon fishing, either with spinner or, preferably, with fly – especially when the water is low and clear. And, as ever, the river is surrounded by landscape so beautiful that you simply have to stop and gawp.

You can work your way down river through three or four miles, past the hotel itself sitting proudly on the hillcrest, down to where it enters lovely Loch Inchlaggan – yet another fly fishers' paradise. With an area of around three or four hundred acres, Loch Inchlaggan is shallow apart from the deep central channel. Forty or fifty years ago, the river wound its way through pasture but the dam at Garry raised the waters and Inchlaggan was formed. Like Poulary, Inchlaggan is a warm, fertile sort of water, responsive to all types of fly fishing methods.

And you've got something thrillingly extra in Inchlaggan: we're not just talking about brown trout fishing here – excellent brown trout at that – but also some fabulous Arctic char have begun to make an appearance. Many of these are big fish: expect three, four, or even five pounders! And they can be caught on the fly – honestly! Try brown nymphs, tied on a size eight or ten, fished deep and slow over six to ten feet of water. Don't be in too much of a hurry to move – the char shoals can drift in and out day long. Of course, I'm not guaranteeing that you'll catch one of these super char but to do so, I promise, is a thrill of a lifetime.

Inchlaggan opens out into Loch Garry proper – another famous ferox water. Trout fishing in traditional fashion is also very popular and fish of one to two pounds are frequent. Then, rod weary, it's back to the Tomdoun for a bath, a meal, a bar-side chat and bed. The perfect fisherman's inn, Tomdoun.

Season – the trout fishing runs from 17th March to 6th October. Salmon fishing opens in January and runs until 14th October.

Tickets – Loch Quoich is boat fishing only and the hotel has two boats on it. Loch Poulary is also boat fishing only and boats can be booked from the hotel. Lochs Inchlaggan and Garry are best fished by boat but bankside permits can also be bought for here. Boats cost £30 per day with an engine and £14 each day if you bring your own. Day tickets for the bank are £3. The river itself can only be fished by hotel residents whereas the lochs are open to all comers.

Directions – to find Tomdoun, follow the A82 from Fort William north-west towards Fort Augustus. At Invergarry, turn left on the A87, signposted to Skye. The signs to the Tomdoun Hotel can be found in around four miles, on the left-hand side of the road. The narrow track will take you past Loch Garry to the hotel itself, on the right.

Accommodation – the Tomdoun Hotel can be contacted on 01809 511244.

✕ Other considerations – never go out on the water without a lifejacket, especially on Loch Quoich. Never take more fish than you personally are going to need to eat. The Tomdoun waters are run very carefully with conservation in mind.

South Uist – Hebrides

It's not often that I would think of including a whole island as one single entry, but such is the profusion of fishing in South Uist that I think we can really go for it here! The definitive guide is written by John Kennedy and is called, aptly enough, simply *Seventy Lochs*! South Uist is a haven for the brown trout fly fisherman. There is no other word to use. It can seem that round every bend in the road there is yet another enticing water to fish. I've only been fortunate enough to cast a fly on three or four of them – merely scraping the surface – but those few outings have lived with me even though they took place now some thirteen or so years back.

The great thing about South Uist fishing is the quality of the brown trout. On many, if not most, of the lochs, the browns – all wild and spirited – average at least a pound in weight and that's quite some size for lochs of this nature. Quantity is not the issue, but that still won't stop a reasonably competent fly fisherman getting more than his fair share during a serious day's outing. And what's more, you're almost certain to be on your own. It's like owning your own waters – waters that are either free or ridiculously inexpensive.

As you'd expect on a Western Isle, wind is generally with you. This can help keep midges away and it certainly does help mask a fly line. Flies not to be without include the Soldier Palmer, the Black Penal, Blue Zulu, Peter Ross, Invictor, Grouse and Claret, all the Butcher patterns, the Green French Partridge, the Claret Bumble and the Golden Olive Bumble. At least that's what John Kennedy advises, and who on earth would argue with him? Oh, and as Mr Kennedy says, there's no real need for gossamer-light tippets here. He suggests leaders of six-pounds breaking strain and he could well be about right – don't forget that four- and even five-pound browns are always a very real possibility.

Sea trout have been holding up well on South Uist as well, and later in the year there are good runs of salmon – especially grilse. Sea trout can easily top the six- or seven-pound mark and they come in good numbers. Still, it has to be said that it is the brown trout fishing that makes South Uist so special, the browns that lure dedicated anglers back again and again to the island. That and the island's sublime beauty of course. Its loneliness. Its unspoilt loveliness.

SEASON – brown trout 1st April to 30th September. June is probably seen as the prime month. Sea trout and salmon really begin in July and finish at the end of October.

TICKETS – the fishing rights on most waters in South Uist are owned by the South Uist Estate with the exception of a handful of lochs that are reserved for guests of the estate itself and the Lochboisdale Hotel. The estate has let the fishing rights to the South Uist Angling Club, which issues permits on a daily or weekly basis. These can be obtained from the secretary of the club, from Bornish General Stores in Bornish itself and from Colin Campbell Sports, Balivanich, Benbecula on 01870 602236. Tickets to many lochs are also available from the Lochboisdale Hotel on 01878 700332.

DIRECTIONS – South Uist can be reached by ferry from Oban or Mallaig. Both dock at Lochboisdale. British Airways also run flights to the island. Phone 01870 602310 for details. There is car hire available locally. As for the lochs themselves, it's hard to miss them – especially with Kennedy's guide.

ACCOMMODATION – there is bed and breakfast availability around the island but most serious anglers understandably head for the Lochboisdale Hotel itself (details above). This is the centre of angling activity on the island – as it has been for many, many years. The hotel offers boats, ghillies, and the most up-to-the-minute advice on the best lochs, the best flies and the best methods. A classic Scottish angling hotel and highly recommended.

The River Spey – Invernesshire

The River Spey is one of the classic Scottish salmon rivers, a joy to fish and running through some spectacular Scottish countryside. Of course, in common with all Scottish rivers, stocks have been variable over the past years, but there is every evidence that the situation is on the mend now – perhaps in part because the net fishing ceased at the end of the 1993 season and there is now no commercial netting for salmon within the Spey district.

The Spey is a largely unspoilt river with next to no pollution and it's a water made for fly fishing. In the past, my own favourite time of the year has been late April into early May, although later on in the year runs of grilse can pack the river and make for very exciting sport – especially on a floating line and small fly.

Naturally enough, many beats of the Spey are difficult to get a rod upon but there are some opportunities, and reasonably priced ones at that. Believe me, it's well worth exploration.

Season – the salmon and sea trout season runs from 11th February to 30th September and the brown trout season from 15th March to 30th September. Obviously, the Spey is heavily weather-dependent but all things being equal the best months for salmon appear to be April and May and then August into September towards the end of the season.

Tickets – the Strathspey Angling Improvement Association has seven miles on the Spey and permits are offered to visitors resident in Grantown, Cromdale and surrounding areas. The Seafield Lodge Hotel, Grantown-on-Spey, PH26 3JN, is an excellent base for anglers. Phone 01479 872152 for details of the fishing. It would be wrong not to mention the late Arthur Oglesby and his world-famous course on the Spey, which is based at Grantown – Arthur was one of the most respected instructors in history and a marvellous man to boot. Moving further up river to Aviemore, the Rothiemurchus Highland Estate also offers both salmon and sea trout fishing on four miles of the Spey. The fishing here is by fly only, though spinning is sometimes allowed in high water conditions. For more details phone 01479 810703. The Abernethy Angling Improvement Association also offers fishing on the Spey at a very reasonable cost. The fishing is centred around the Boat of Garten and Aviemore and comprises nearly ten miles of fishing over many named pools. There is water to suit all types of fishing here from both fast runs to deep, slow stretches. The stretches are available to visitors staying locally in the Boat of Garten and Aviemore areas. Tickets can be obtained from Allens, Deshar Road, Boat of Garten, Invernesshire, PH24 3BN, on 01479 831372. and Speyside Sports, 2 Grampian Road, Aviemore, Invernesshire, PH22 1PD, on 01479 810656.

Directions – the area is well-served by both the A9 and the A95.

Accommodation – try the Seafield Lodge Hotel (see abovefor details). For further accommodation apply to the Highlands of Scotland Tourist Board, Peffery House, Strathpeffer, Ross-shire. Phone them on 01870 5143070 for details.

Stoneyfield Lochs – Ross-shire

The Stoneyfield Loch complex consists of two five-acre lochs for fly fishing only and one three-acre loch for both bait and fly. Although this is largely a rainbow-stocked water, I've included it very happily here because it's such a quiet, attractive fishery, ideal for a club competition or for a picturesque family day out. Furthermore, the calibre of the trout is excellent. The fishery stocks on a weekly basis with real quality rainbows ranging from one and a half up to just into double figures. As an added bonus, there are also a number of natural brown trout in the water. Again, these are beautiful fish.

All usual trout fishing methods work, but don't neglect buzzers and dry flies in comparatively calm, warm conditions. Imitative patterns – nymphs in particular – also work well, so don't be blinded by lures.

Overall, this is a lovely place to stop at and enjoy if you're motoring up the east coast. It's a family-run business and the owners pride themselves on giving customers a friendly greeting and a memorable day's fishing.

Season – 1st March to 30th November. Monday to Saturday 9.00am till dusk or 10.00pm whichever is earlier. Sunday 9.00am till 6.00pm.

Tickets – these can be booked from Stonefield Lochs, Newmore, Invergordon, Ross-shire, on 01349 852632, or e-mail stonefieldloch@talk21.com. Tickets cost £7 for two hours, one-fish limit, £11 for four hours, two-fish limit and £18 for eight hours, four-fish limit. Catch and release is possible after the limit has been taken.

Facilities – tackle hire is available and flies are for sale. There is a fishing hut with microwave and tea-making facilities. There is a toilet built with the disabled in mind.

Directions – Stoneyfield is situated just off the A9, three miles north of Alness and three miles from Invergordon. It is well-signposted.

Accommodation – bed and breakfast is available at the Ship Inn Guesthouse, 33 Shore Road, Invergordon, Ross-shire IV18 0ER. Phone 01349 852427 for details. The Highlands of Scotland Tourist Board on 0870 5143070 will be able to recommend further accommodation.

The River Cassley – Rosehall Water – Sutherland

I've only had occasional days on the River Cassley but the Rosehall water will stay with me forever. The Cassley is a short river, just ten or twelve miles long, and is a tributary of the more famous Oykel. However, it's not always possible to get on the really classic salmon rivers and opportunities like the Cassley should be grabbed with both hands. Under the supervision of Hugo Graesser, the fishing is really looking good these days. However, the Cassley offers more than just excellent salmon fishing. This is a truly beautiful, awe-inspiring piece of water that is fished on the fly only. It provides truly challenging fishing with

a wide variety of pools, all set against countryside of outstanding natural beauty. There are waterfalls, gorges and gentle parkland. In fact, the ever-changing backdrop is almost as wonderful as the fishing itself. The fishing is easily accessible by car, so this makes it suitable for older anglers.

There are many salmon rivers in Scotland where it's quite possible to believe that you really are in another magical world, and the Rosehall water is certainly one of these places. It's truly an atmosphere to be savoured and, if you get one of the salmon – as well you might – there's a very big likelihood that it will be covered in sea-lice, always an added bonus.

The management encourages the return of fish and it's gratifying to see that more and more regulars are putting salmon back. We live in a new age that, thankfully, is encouraging the return of these marvellous fish to outstanding rivers like the Cassley.

SEASON – April fishing can be very good and grilse appear around June. If there is a reasonable amount of rain in the late summer and autumn – up till the end of September – many fish are expected to run.

TICKETS – contact Hugo Graesser at Rosehall Sportings to discuss vacant weeks. Prior booking is obviously essential as increasing runs of fish are adding to the Cassley's popularity. Prices vary from £750–£900 for three rods, and the services of an experienced ghilly are included.

RULES – the lower Cassley is run as two beats, each for three rods and rotating daily at 1.00pm. Between the two beats there are twenty-nine named and recognised pools and fish can be caught in most levels of water. Fly fishing only.

DIRECTIONS – the Rosehall water is found thirteen miles west of Bonar Bridge on the A37 Lochinver Road.

ACCOMMODATION – anglers on the river tend to stay at the Achness Hotel situated very close to the river. It's a fine fishing hotel with a friendly atmosphere and good cuisine. Seven double bedrooms with private bathrooms. Phone 01549 441239 for details. The Highlands of Scotland Tourist Board, Peffery House, Strathpeffer, Ross-shire, IV14 9HA, on 0870 5143070 can advise on further accommodation in the area.

THE RIVERS INVER AND KIRKAIG AND LOCH ASSYNT – SUTHERLAND

I've grouped these two beautiful rivers and a stunning loch together as they really do form a unique triumvirate. The Inver drains Assynt into a sea loch on the west coast of Sutherland, whilst the Kirkaig is an equally short river found just three and a half miles south of Loch Inver. Both rivers have good runs of salmon. Loch Assynt is particularly known for its brown trout, especially the fabled ferox. There are also numerous other hill lochs such as Poll, Drumbeg, Culag and Fionn in the area. All these boast excellent wild brown trout fishing.

This really is a very special area indeed, one of outstanding natural beauty. In fact, to walk the valley of the Kirkaig is an experience in itself and if you're lucky to have a salmon rod under your arm, almost heaven! Of course, as is the way of it these days, runs of salmon are unpredictable and these are spate rivers, so good rainfall is frequently necessary. The fish can be quite large considering the size of the rivers, but the fishing itself is fascinating with all manner of challenging pools.

Loch Assynt is wild and wonderful and offers some excellent brown trout fishing, with occasional monsters of ten pounds or more taken on both fly and lure. Once again, to be afloat on Loch Assynt is an experience not to be missed.

I visited the area many times during the eighties and was lucky to catch salmon up to twelve pounds and brown trout up to eight pounds on my visits. But it's not really the fish that I will personally remember, it's more the dramatic scenery and the extraordinary sunsets out across Lochinver harbour. This is a most beautiful part of the fisherman's lovely world.

Season – 16th March to 7th October inclusive.

Tickets – these are not always easily come by but the Inver Lodge Hotel has salmon fishing on three beats of the Inver and further fishing on the Kirkaig. Apply to the Inver Lodge Hotel, Lochinver, IV27 4LU, on 01571 844496. Assynt Angling Club controls twenty-seven hill lochs with excellent brown trout fishing both to the north and east of Lochinver. Tickets are generally between £5 and £6. They are obtainable from the Tourist Office or Simpsons Newsagents, Lochinver. Lochinver Tourist Office also sells tickets for Lochs Poll, Roe, Manse and Tuirk, which still produce sea trout runs. For fishing on Loch Assynt, contact the Inchnadamph Hotel on 01571 822202.

Directions – Lochinver is found off the Ullapool to Scourie road. Pass Inchnadamph and in a few miles, fork left along the shore of Loch Assynt following the A837 to Lochinver. This is stunning countryside.

Accommodation – both the Inver Lodge Hotel and Inchnadamph Hotel are highly recommended and well-geared up for fishermen (see above for details). The Highlands of Scotland Tourist Board, Peffery House, Strathpeffer, Ross-shire, IV14 9HA, on 0870 5143070, will be able to recommend further accommodation.

Scourie Hill Lochs – Highlands

One of the most enchanting times I've ever spent in Scotland was staying at the Scourie Hotel and investigating just a few of the lochs in the hills behind. There is an astonishing profusion of historic waters up here set in extreme remoteness, some at very long distances. The Scourie Hotel itself boasts twenty-five thousand acres of brown trout, sea trout and salmon fishing, along with eighteen boats. However, for the trout, all you need is a good pair of walking boots, strong legs and capacious lungs! It is quite possible that if you're really

adventurous you will find waters that haven't been fished for a season or more, but don't expect the fish to be easy, or necessarily large. What you're looking at here is really challenging – wild brown trout fishing for specimens of unparalleled beauty. It's never a bad idea to take a compass with you: if a mist comes down it can be difficult to find your way down off the hill. And do remember that what started out as a beautiful day can quickly and easily turn into a wild, wet and windy one.

Waters range from the gin-clear to the dark and the peaty, but as there are limestone outcrops in the vicinity you'll find some waters that are very fertile with much bigger fish. Obviously, ask advice, then strike out and do your own thing. All traditional flies work splendidly but don't forget to stick in some imitative patterns: several nymph patterns, buzzers and some sedge patterns can work wonders. The main thing is to be bold and ring the changes. Never forget to work the margins before you try putting out a longer line. If you're the first on the water for weeks, if not months, you'll often find very big fish cruising in the shallow margins, their dorsals clear of the water. Exciting and very beautiful stuff indeed.

SEASON – the trout season runs from 2nd April to 7th October. You will only find wild browns in the Scourie Hill Lochs, some salmon and some sea trout.

TICKETS – phone the Scourie Hotel on 01971 502396 for information on day tickets. These start at around £5. Fishing is free to residents at the hotel. The Scourie Angling Club also has rights on thirty-three lochs north of the village and two lochs south of it. Day tickets cost around £4 and can be bought from Scourie Post Office.

DIRECTIONS – to find Scourie, you can take the A835 and then the A894 from Ullapool. Alternatively, take the A38 from Lairg. Once there, ask for local maps to the widely-flung lochs themselves.

ACCOMMODATION – you really cannot do better than the Scourie Hotel itself. It is geared heavily for anglers and a huge amount of information and advice is available. It's really an excellent fishing experience. Contact the hotel on 01971 502396.

TONGUE HILL LOCHS – HIGHLANDS

Tongue has a marvellous selection of lochs and some are quite easily accessible, especially as the terrain is not as wild as it is at Scourie, for example. Remember that these are popular during the height of the fishing season so it's a good idea, if you value peace and quiet, to take a good old tramp to the least accessible ones. Remember that, even though you're very far north indeed, the sun can be very powerful in such a clear, bright atmosphere. Take plenty of suncream and liquid refreshment – I'm thinking of water and not alcohol! And be warned the midges can be very bad, especially from May through to September on calm, warm days. A head net, as well as lotion, is recommended.

Don't let these things put you off, because the fishing can be quite magnificent. There's a mayfly hatch on a number of the lochs from June right through to early August, and do make a point of visiting Loch Hakel, which is one of the most beautiful lochs in the whole of Scotland.

Mostly, the trout average half a pound or so, but you will come across much bigger fish here and there, especially if you fish imitative patterns. Traditional wet and dry fly are all effective but black, red and brown seem to be the going colours. Once again, just because you're on a remote loch, don't expect the fish to be easy and ring the changes if things aren't working out for you. Also, approach the waters with caution because you will frequently find the fish close in.

There is also salmon fishing in Loch Naver and sea trout fishing in nearby Loch Hope. Both rivers at times have good runs of fish. Prior booking is generally essential.

SEASON – the brown trout fishing runs from 14th March to 7th October. For the salmon and sea trout fishing season, contact the Ben Loyal Hotel (see below)

TICKETS – a phone call to the Ben Loyal Hotel on 01847 611216 will reveal everything you need to know about the area. The hotel is also the headquarters of the Tongue and District Angling Association. Their keeper, Ian MacDonald is available on 01847 756272. Also contact Altnaharra Hotel on 01549 411222 for the salmon fishing on Loch Naver and the sea trout fishing on Loch Hope. Some tickets are given to non-residents.

DIRECTIONS – from Lairg, take the A836 north to Tongue; it is approximately fifty miles. Once in Tongue, rely on local maps.

ACCOMMODATION – the Altnaharra Hotel and Ben Loyal Hotel are both geared up magnificently for fishermen. Ghillies, tackle shops and masses of advice. See above for contact numbers. Both highly recommended. There is also the Tongue Hotel, another favourite for anglers, on 01847 611206.

THE SHETLAND TROUT LOCHS

Of course, it's a long haul to get out to Shetland but once you're there, you'll never regret it, and you'll want to stay forever. I guarantee that there will be tears in your eyes as your ferry pulls away back to the mainland.

The appeal of Shetland is not hard to define: its loneliness, its beauty and lack of modern-day pace make it the perfect holiday destination. Unwind? You totally unravel! And then, of course, you've got the fishing itself, which can be quite wondrous. Okay, the magnificent sea-trout fishing of the past has declined but the brown trout fishing in over three hundred lochs is quite wonderful. And what variety of water you'll find – some are peaty lochans whereas others are alkaline and virtually transparent.

You won't find any mayfly out there but there is good feeding on shrimp, snail, olive and midge. Try any dry patterns, along with nymphs and traditional wet flies, and you'll probably do well. It also pays to listen hard to local knowledge. The Shetland

Anglers Association have worked tirelessly to maintain the lochs on the islands as top-class wild-fishing venues and they publish a really detailed local guide book with immaculate instructions on how to find the hundreds of lochs. You can fish them all for a season ticket of £15! Even the boats are bookable at a weekly cost of £20.

If there is the explorer in you, I can guarantee that Shetland will offer the fly fishing holiday of a lifetime.

Season and tickets – phone Graham Callender, the Honorary President of the Shetland Anglers Association on 01806 503385. He will provide you with all the necessary information on tickets and seasons.

Directions – P&O Scottish Ferries sail to Lerwick from Aberdeen. Phone 01224 572615 for ferry times and bookings. It is advisable to book in advance. The Shetland Islands Council on 01806 244234 also operates local ferry services for the area.

Accommodation – contact Shetland Island Tourism, Market Cross, Lerwick, Shetland ZE1 0LU on 01595 693434 for information on all kinds of accommodation.

Highly Recommended Fisheries

- *Raith Lake, Kirkcaldy. Contact on 01592 646466. Very attractive. Rainbows into double figures, browns, brooks and goldens. Boats.*
- *Kingennie Fishings, Nr. Dundee. Call 01382 350777 for details. A truly beautiful big fish water. An exciting challenge. Highly recommended.*
- *Newton Farm, Nr. Dundee. Phone on 01382 542513. Attractive, shallow, five-acre water. Big fish, top water feeding. Excellent.*
- *Moffatt Fishery, Dumfries and Galloway. Call on 01683 221068. Crystal-clear fishing. Lovely conditioned fish, some brookies. Some interesting fishing.*
- *Springwater Trout Fishery, Nr. Ayr, East Ayrshire. Phone on 01292 560343 for more information. Excellently run, with super fish. Great lodge.*
- *Haylie Fishery, Nr. Largs, North Ayrshire. Contact on 01475 676005. Beautifully scenic. Great view of Clyde estuary. Some big fish.*
- *Lawfield Fishery, Nr. Glasgow. Call on 01505 874182. Great scenery. Very welcoming. Good quality fish. Well patronised by locals – always a good sign.*

Fly-Fishing Sites in Ireland

1. Lough Corrib
2. Lough Mask
3. Lough Carra
4. Lough Arrow
5. Lough Melvin
6. Knockbracken
7. The Sperrins
8. Glenowen
9. Straid Trout Fishery
10. Lough Ennell
11. Aughrim Trout Fishery
12. Ballyvolane House & The River Blackwater
13. Lough Currane

"It's sad but true that when many anglers from across the seas think of Ireland their thoughts concentrate on south of the border. Of course, there is superb fishing there but I urge you to reconsider what the north has to offer. In fact, my own belief is – and I've seen virtually every water in all of the island – that the north can offer every bit as much as the south. We've got some fabulous salmon runs, you can pick up sea trout in all manner of unexpected places and some of our brown trout fishing is beyond compare. What's more, most of it – or at least much of it – is one big, well-kept secret. Everybody knows about the big southern loughs, Mask, Corrib and Conn, but we've got waters that would make any southerner sit up!"

MIKE SHORT, IRISH WRITER, CELEBRITY AND ADVISOR TO THE NORTHERN IRISH TOURIST BOARD

There you have it, Ireland – whether North or South of the border – is a place teeming with opportunities for the game fisherman. There's wild fishing beyond compare but, at the same time, there are the more intimate, commercial fisheries where you can build up your confidence! But then, Ireland is more than just about fishing alone. The countryside – so green, clean and uncluttered. The roads, often so empty you'd think yourself back in the 1930s. Sleepy villages. Welcoming bars, and, inevitably, a pint of Guinness waiting. In fact, most of the business is done in the bars. If you want to know anything, go into the bar, ask around and you will get to hear where there is a boat to hire, a ghillie willing to turn out or when you can expect the next hatch of sedges!

Improvements in ferries and air travel mean that Ireland is ever more accessible. You owe it to yourself to get out there and enjoy game fishing beyond compare.

Lough Corrib – Galway

Corrib, in the west of Ireland, is truly a trout fisherman's paradise. It is over thirty miles long and covers some forty-four thousand acres, liberally scattered with islands and endowed with endless amounts of stunning fish! The lake varies greatly from one area to the next. In lower Corrib, for example, the water is generally quite shallow with depths averaging six to ten feet. The water here is very clear and weedy and there's an abundance of fly life. The northern end of the lake has many shallows too, but also has areas as deep as a hundred and fifty feet. These chasms are also of great interest to the fisherman as they hold brown trout in numbers, including ferox trout, some weighing in excess of fifteen pounds.

Corrib as a whole is a limestone lake and is rich in feeding. Indeed, trout are caught by fly fishermen as early as February, even fishing in the shallows with floating lines and teams of wet flies and nymphs. In March and April, local anglers wait eagerly, however, for the Duck fly. This is a chironamid, black in colour with white wings, and it appears in weedy areas in great numbers. The trout gorge themselves, especially feasting on the pupae. April can also be a good month with good hatches of olives all over the lake. But the real attraction comes when the mayfly appears. From early May, right into June, this magical period sees many visitors on the Corrib as people flock from far and wide. Wet-fly fishing, dapped naturals and dry-fly fishing are all successful. The middle and top half of the lake fish best, particularly around Oughterhard and Greenfields. With a lull in July, August and September can fish well. Sedge patterns and wet flies take a large share of the catches.

Let's have a chat about the ferox... these fish, as I've already said, are usually taken in the northern end of the lake and Inchagoill island is a famous area to work. They feed heavily on roach, small trout and char here. Trolled baits work well in the twenty- to thirty-foot band. Always, however, be careful of bottom contours when trolling. Corrib, like all these western loughs, can throw up reefs and shoals when you least expect them so keep a close look out and never travel too fast over unfamiliar water.

Season – the fly-fishing season opens on Corrib on 15th February and ends on 30th September.

Tickets – The trout fishing is free on Corrib but a salmon licence is required. Many hotels issue licences. Alternatively, contact boatmen. Michael Ryan at River Lodge, Cong, County Mayo, on 00353 9246057, is very knowledgeable, and also rents out boats. Also try Michael Walsh, Ower Guesthouse, Greenfields, Headford, County Galway on 00353 9335446. The tackle shop in Clonbur on 00353 9246197 is also a fund of information.

Directions – Corrib, with its huge size, is really hard to miss. Situated just north of Galway, it is well served by roads both east and west.

Accommodation – phone the Galway Tourist Information Office on 00353 91563081, or contact Basil Shiels at Ardnassillagh Lodge, Oughterhard, Co. Galway, on 091 552550.

LOUGH MASK – GALWAY

Lough Mask is a limestone lake of twenty-two thousand acres. Perch, eels, char, huge pike and some of the very best brown trout fishing in Europe. Possibly one of the best months of my life was spent fishing Lough Mask back in 1991. I admit that at the time I was primarily trolling for ferox trout: up until then, I probably caught about a dozen or so in as many years of trying in Scotland. In that one month, I boated forty ferox trout between five and ten pounds.

Since then, I've been back principally with a fly rod, but the dream has continued. I love Mask anyway. The enchanting west of Ireland. The villages and towns. The people. The lough islands where you can stop and brew a cup of heavenly tasting tea. The mountains in the mists. And the wonderful trout fishing. They say that the mayfly season between mid-May and mid-June cannot be bettered, but I've enjoyed exhilarating days with daddy longlegs and grasshopper patterns way into September. Yes, dapping is a large part of what Mask is about and if you haven't tried it yet I urge you to get out with a boatman and learn this most fascinating and satisfying of skills.

Of course, you can catch Lough Mask trout as you would on any Scottish loch or English reservoir, simply drifting, working teams of wet flies. This is blissful enough but, I repeat, do try the dap if you can.

The beauty of Lough Mask trout deserves a special emphasis. These are absolutely pristine, wild brown trout and, excitingly, they probably average around about the one-and-a-half-pound mark. Certainly four- and five-pound fish are common. And talking about brown trout, let's mention Lough Carra, an offshoot of Mask, a bay almost, but at four thousand acres, a serious water in its own right, shallow and extraordinarily fertile, Lough Carra produces browns that are probably the pick of a very exotic bunch.

Mask, especially as the sun goes down on a gentle-breezed day, is close to magic.

SEASON – early and late fly fishing in March and October can prove difficult and the very best of it really begins in May and runs through to mid-September.

PERMISSION – the fishing on Mask is free but it makes sense to join one of the local angling clubs for an outlay of £5 or so. Ballinrobe, Cong and Tourmakready all have their own associations, and they will help the visitor immensely with all manner of local knowledge and advice. They can also issue maps to show you the best access points.

BOAT HIRE – to get the very best out of Mask, you either need to take your own boat or hire one. Cushlough is a good centre for boat hire, as is the bay of Islands Park and Cahir Pier. On Carra, try Robert's Angling Service on 00353 9243046. Mr R O'Grady of Ballinrobe on 00353 9241142 also has boats for hire.

DIRECTIONS – Lough Mask is situated off the N84, between Castlebar and Ballinrobe.

ACCOMMODATION – all the towns around Mask have numerous small hotels and bed and breakfast facilities. Robert's Angling Service also operates a guesthouse for anglers. Also try Ard Aoidhinn Angling Centre on 00353 9244009 and Derry Park Lodge Angling Centre on 00353 9244081. You will find warm hospitality from everyone in Mask.

Lough Arrow – Bricklieve Mountains – County Sligo

Lough Arrow is unique. The Bricklieve Mountains rise to the west of the lake and as the sun sets, ancient burial mounds are silhouetted in this most lost and wondrous of Irish landscapes. Lough Arrow is one of the unsung Irish heroes – over three thousand acres, spring-fed from under limestone streams. With no population or pollution to ruin its natural balance, it is home to wide-ranging fly hatch. Like many of the western loughs, Arrow is a haven for the mayfly: fish artificials or catch the real mayfly and use them on a blow line. This is when the really big wild browns can be caught and beautiful specimens are landed.

Buzzer fishing in May can be excellent whilst July and August sees two large sedge hatches – the great red sedge and the green Peter sedge. Dense flies often cloud round the boat like a mist. This provides great evening fishing and during the thirty minutes or so of the rise, the water can really look as though it's on the boil. By September, life is beginning to slow down and most of the locals go back on traditional wet flies.

There are many hotspots on this intriguing water. Look for areas around islands and reed beds. During the mayfly season, head for tree-lined areas of the shore. Arrow is famous for its pristine, large browns. Two pounds is average, and threes and fours come out regularly, with the odd five-pounder. But how these fish fight! In the deep, crystal water these browns with majestic tails give any fisherman a time to remember.

Season – trout fishing runs from April to October.
Tickets – you cannot really do better for either tickets or boat hire than contacting Robert Maloney at Arrow Lodge, Kilmactranny, via Boyle, County Sligo, on 00353 7966298.
Directions – Lough Arrow is in the north-west of Southern Ireland, just to the north of Boyle. Approach it on the N4 from the town.
Accommodation – Robert and Stephanie Maloney run the aptly named Arrow Lodge right on the shores of the lough. I cannot recommend this too highly. The Lodge was built for fishermen nearly two centuries ago and rejoices in its current role. It is comfortable, on the waterside and with the most knowledgeable of local ghillies.

Lough Melvin – Leitrim/Donegal

Lough Melvin is a truly wonderful water, straddling the border between North and South, half in Leitrim, half in Donegal. A beautiful water indeed and a famous one for many reasons, in part because of its fish stocks. Lough Melvin has happy memories for me: I was a member of a party fishing there in March 2000 when Fred Buller, the famous fly fisherman and pike historian, caught one of the fabulously rare sonaghan trout for which Melvin is justifiably famous. This was an important moment: Buller had, by catching it, almost completed a full house! Yes, he'd caught all but one of every British freshwater fish species that swims... I believe the missing member is a vendace.

A sonaghan is recognisable by its colour, size, shoaling habits and huge tail. They average between three quarters of a pound and a pound and a quarter and they're dark in colour – a sort of gunmetal silver. That great big tail, quite distinctive, means that they fight frenetically, often with extraordinary leaps into the air. They tend to shoal down deep where they feed on daphnia. Small flies, therefore frequently pick them up and when you get one, you'll generally get others.

Then we come to another Melvin speciality – the gillaroos. Once again, these aren't huge fish, generally between a pound and a pound and a quarter, but what they lack in size is more than compensated for by staggering beauty. These fish are absolutely plastered with the most extraordinary, massive red spots. Catch them mainly in the shallows on dark flies on rough days. Gillaroos are primarily snail feeders and that's what they're looking for in the shallows.

Melvin isn't done yet – brown trout, char, ferox trout, salmon and grilse... a heady combination. The spring time can be slow, but as soon as the weather warms, the lake comes alive. In the early spring, most people are out trolling for salmon that come up the River Drowse. From April, though, the trout fishing really begins to take off. Late June onwards sees the mayfly hatch. As summer progresses, the grilse take over and you can catch those easily dapping with the mayfly. Look for the grilse, especially, around Laureen Bay and Rossinver Bay – two places much favoured by the locals. You can still troll, of course, and hope to pick up one of the ferox: magnificent beasts, though perhaps not quite as large as those that you'll find in Mask and Corrib.

Do you go it alone or do you enjoy the company of one of Ireland's renowned ghillies? Well, I would strongly recommend the latter. Melvin is a big water, does take some knowing and it pays you to look for some short cuts. Moreover, these men are invariably a delight – full of stories and full of tips.

Season – the salmon fishing opens on 1st February and the trout on 1st March. Fishing ends on 30th September.

Tickets – at present there is no limit on the number of day tickets that are available at £10 per rod per day or £25 per rod per season. You can buy tickets from Sean Maguire at Melvin Tackle in Garrison on 028686 58194. Failing that, both the Melvin Bar and the Riverside Bar in Garrison also stock tickets. Sean Maguire can also arrange a boatman. Also contact Thomas Gallagher, Kin Lough, County Leitrim for a boat on 00353 7241208 . He has a huge knowledge of the lough and also controls fishing on the River Drowse.

Directions – Lough Melvin straddles the border a few miles south of Ballyshannon. Garrison is situated on the B52, at the south-eastern end of the water.

Accommodation – there is a huge amount of bed and breakfast and hotel accommodation locally. Mrs Flannagan at Lake View House offers an excellent bed and breakfast. Phone her on 028686 58444. Mr Ferguson, on 013656 58743, offers self-catering accommodation at Devenish Villa Holiday Homes. You can even camp at the Lough Melvin Holiday Centre for £6 a night! Phone 028686 58142 for details.

Knockbracken – County Fermanagh

An interesting adventure this – a small commercial water in an area absolutely riddled with tremendous wild brown trout fishing. How on earth can you ever expect such a place to work? Well, the fact is that it does and the reasons are comparatively easy to see. Even if most of us purists would agree that wild fishing is the thing, it's still an inescapable fact that it can be moody. The big, wild loughs are either on or they're off, and fishing can be very much boom or bust. There are days when all of us just want a bend in our rod and that's where somewhere like Knockbracken fits the bill exactly.

And, as you'd expect in Ireland, Knockbracken is a beautiful venue, expertly tended, too. All fish must be killed, but just a few pounds gets you fishing and if you want to take your fish, you can get them expertly prepared back at the lodge. There is an any-method lake – super if you've got a family with you, of course – but the main lake is fly only, and it is deep and clear. There are plenty of small fish in the margins and you'll often see big rainbows roaring in for the kill. Big, fit fish that fight like dervishes. All the usual techniques work, however. Buzzers do very well, along with dry flies and weighted nymphs and shrimps. In short, it's a great place where you know you can expect some action and that could be just what you need after a few days out on Lough Erne when the heavens have been throwing everything they've got at you!

Season – open all the year.
Tickets - £3.50 for adults, £2.50 for juniors. 70p per fish caught – these must be killed. £1.50 per pound to take away. Contact Knockbracken Trout Lakes, Trillick Road, Ballinamallard, County Fermanagh, Northern Ireland on 02866 388548.
Directions – from Enniskillen, take the A32 north and then turn off on the B46, signposted Ballinamallard and Omagh. Go through Ballinamallard, heading north. The fishery entrance is on the left in about half a mile.
Accommodation – phone Enniskillen Tourist Information on 02866 323110.

The Sperrins – Ulster

I was absolutely knocked out by the Sperrins on a recent visit. This is the name given to an impressive mountain range stretching from Donegal in the west to Lough Neagh in the east, the heart and the hub of Ulster. The four main towns of the region are Cookstown, Magherafelt, Omagh and Strabane. This is an area of outstanding natural beauty and, in many places, as lonely as any other area of Ireland. The three major species are salmon, brown trout and sea trout, although you might also come across the dollaghan, a unique species of Lough Neagh migratory brown trout. These tend to be caught when they run the many tributaries from mid July to the end of October. They can average as much as two pounds and grow to over six pounds abnormally. They travel a long way before spawning, in some ways rather like salmon and sea trout.

The Sperrins offer tremendous salmon opportunities, especially along the Foyle system. The main tributaries running through the Sperrin region from the Foyle are the Mourne, Derg and Strule. These are all fast flowing rocky rivers and salmon begin to enter them from April through to October. Then you've got the Owenkilleu and Glenelly rivers – classic spate rivers that fish very well in the summer and autumn. The Camowen and Owenreagh rivers also provide excellent backend fishing – often for grilse as well.

There are all sorts of surprises: to the north of the region, surrounded by mountains in the most awe-inspiring landscape, you'll find Moor Lough and Lough Ash – two waters both around thirty acres in extent and offering some classic wild brown trout fishing. On and on it goes – the Strule river, the Burn Dennet river... all marvellous waters, all set in stunning, wild countryside. Now that the troubles and the violence are so obviously on the decrease, Northern Ireland is increasingly offering a great deal to the visiting angler. There are tremendous possibilities across this beautiful country, but the Sperrins certainly are a jewel in a very considerable crown.

SEASON – the season in general runs from 1st April to 20th October.
TICKETS – for the salmon fishing on the Foyle rivers, contact the Foyle Fisheries Commission, 8 Victoria Road, Londonderry, BT47 2AB, on 02871 34100. For fishing in the Lough Neagh system, contact the Fisheries Conservation Board, 1 Mahon Road, Portadown, Craigavon, County Armagh, BT62 3EE, on 02838 334666. For Loughs Moor and Ash, contact the Fisheries Conservation Board as above. David Campbell at the Tackle Shop, 28 Main Street, Newtownstewart, on 02881 661543 can provide tickets for the River Mourne, the River Strule and the Glenelly River. Also contact him for the Camowen River, the Drumragh River and the Owenragh River. Chism Fishing Tackle, 25 Old Market Place, Omagh, on 02882 244932, is also a fund of information.
DIRECTIONS – the Omagh Tourist Information Centre, 1 Market Street, Omagh BET78 1EE on 02882 247831 will issue a detailed map of the Sperrins area.
ACCOMMODATION –contact the Omagh Tourist Information Centre as above. Strabane Tourist Information Centre on 02871 883735, Cookstown Tourist Information on 01648 766727 and Magherafelt Tourist Information on 02879 631510 will also give details.

GLENOWEN – LONDONDERRY

Glenowen is a brave project and a very necessary one too for Londonderry, Northern Ireland's second city. If you find yourself here as a resident or traveller, it means you don't have to go far to find some very pleasing fishing indeed. The fishery extends to something like nine or ten acres – a reservoir amidst twenty or so acres of public park situated close to the city's boundary. An unlikely place perhaps, but it is beautifully tended, attractive and gives you the feeling of being way out in the countryside. It's a government funded,

co-operative exercise and one that is obviously working very well indeed. The water is clear, quite deep and the trout are in excellent condition.

You'll find some friendly locals on the water, more than willing to give advice and perhaps lend a fly or two. Above all, what makes this such a heart-warming place is the number of children that come here to learn. We all know that Ireland – north and south – is a wild fish paradise, but the fly-fishing can be difficult if conditions are against you. Hard for a child. Far better to work up his or her enthusiasm on a water like this. An attractive, safe, accessible water where fish aren't impossible to catch.

There are some good fish here – the fishery record is well into double figures – and they come to all manner of flies. In the deep water, however, it's not a bad idea to fish an intermediate line with lures or use a long leader and go for an imitative pattern. The fish will come up to the surface, so have a selection of buzzers and dries with you.

In short, it's great place to stop off if you're visiting. The family can be busy in Londonderry – increasingly a thriving city – while you get a bit of peace and quiet. Or, have just a couple of hours fishing whilst the family roam the very attractive parkland.

SEASON – open all year.
TICKETS – contact Glenowen Fishery, Westway, The Rath, Creggan Estate, Derry City on 02871 371544. A two fish limit plus catch and release is £11. A five-fish limit plus catch and release is £16. Junior tickets cost £6 and allow two fish to be taken.
DIRECTIONS – you need to get onto the west side of the city. Turn left off the Craigavon Bridge and turn right at the next mini-roundabout, which will be signposted for Carmelite Fathers. After about a hundred yards, turn left and go up a steep hill. Take the left at the T-junction by St Peter's School. After about a mile you will come to Creggan Country Park where you will find the fishery signposted. It is well known in the area.
ACCOMMODATION – contact Londonderry Tourist Information on 02871 267284.

STRAID TROUT FISHERY – COUNTY ANTRIM

Straid fishery fulfils a very important function, situated as it is a few miles from Belfast. It's a beautiful water, surrounded by fields and woodland. It's large, too, at twenty-two acres, and well stocked with rainbows. Average depth is between six and a half and seven feet, with occasional pockets going down to twelve. Water visibility is generally very good, it only really colours up after heavy rains.

Straid is popular for a number of reasons. Firstly, the size of the fish averages a healthy two pounds and they fight tremendously well. Secondly, stocking policies achieve just about the right balance. The water isn't too easy but not too difficult either, a perfect challenge for all. The ticket options also appeal greatly. There's a whole range of different prices so that anyone who just wants to come and fish for a couple of hours or so is well catered for. Parents and children will find the ticket to suit them.

All the usual methods work well on the water and the lake has a good sedge hatch with lots of buzzers, midges and olives. So the trout are well fed and used to looking for imitative patterns. Wet flies on an intermediate line are popular – try Green Peter, Silver Invicta or Hare's Ear. Buzzers are particularly effective throughout the summer, fished deep or in the surface film. Imitative patterns – shrimps, beetles and so on – can be fished on a floating line on a long leader, and watch for very careful takes.

SEASON – open all year round.
TICKETS – contact Straid Trout Fishery, Ballymure, Nr. Ballyclare, County Antrim, on 02893 340099. A range of ticket options available: catch and release tickets cost £10, and the two-fish bag limit at £11 is very popular. A five-fish limit costs £16 and junior tickets are also available from as little as £6. Boats are also available at a modest cost and tuition is offered.
DIRECTIONS – take the M2 north from Belfast and turn off at junction 4, signposted Larne. Travel through to the village of Ballymure and take the second right, signposted Straid.
ACCOMMODATION – contact the Belfast Tourist Information Centre on 02890 246609.

LOUGH ENNELL – CO. WESTMEATH

Lough Ennell is a fabulous water and no more than an hour's drive from Dublin itself. It's famous for holding the Irish record trout, way back in 1884, and weighing in at 26lb 2oz. Ennell isn't considered a huge lough by Irish standards – only six or seven miles long! It is a limestone lake and this makes for fabulous water quality. At times visibility is between ten and fifteen feet. Mind you, it hasn't always been as clear as this. The local Lough Ennell Trout Preservation Association has forced down pollution. Their focus has been on the feeder stream, where they've clamped down on the amount of agricultural waste, and sewage in particular, that has flowed into the lough.

It's got to be said immediately that Lough Ennell isn't an easy water. Even experts – and a lot of them come out of Dublin – agree that a brace can be considered a good day. Mind you, you've got to remember that all the browns here are wild and there's no stocking whatsoever. Also, that brace of fish could easily be trout of between three and six pounds in weight. Yes, this is really very special fishing indeed.

The early season can be slow. Then there come huge hatches of Duck fly. Some days fish will feed so heavily that they absolutely gorge themselves. Your own artificial really is little more than a needle in a haystack, a blade of grass in that cow's field. Everything really takes off for the fly fisherman around the second week in May when the mayfly begin to appear. From mid May, therefore, to the end of the month, the fishing on Ennell is on full flow and this is when everyone wants to get afloat. The trout become catchable now, both during the day and in the evenings. Most locals would choose to go for a calm evening, just fishing a spent gnat as the light is beginning to go.

During the day, big dry flies work well – Wulffs, hackled mayflies and the local mosly may. Local lore has it that Pat Cleare ties the best flies for the loughs and his Green Peters really are something else.

After the mayfly come the sedge – Welshman's buttons – those small brown sedge with yellow underbodies. These pull up the big fish, especially in the late evening.

Towards the end of the season, throughout August and September, the lake fishes best on dark, windy days. Try big wet flies then, bumbles and daddies and so on. Look for the shallows around Belvedere House, a rambling mansion close to the shore. Goose Island and Rinn Point are also places to concentrate on.

Ennell is a comparatively safe lake to fish on – especially compared with those monsters in the west. You won't find too many rocks so it's pretty safe to go out on your own, especially in weather that isn't too wild. Go and enjoy.

SEASON – the brown trout season on Ennell runs from 1st March to 12th October.
TICKETS – Lough Ennell is free fishing but please, please join the local Lough Ennell Trout Preservation Association. The Association charges a very modest annual fee and you can rest assured that all your money goes towards the preservation of the water and the promotion of the wild brown trout stocks. It's simply not fair to travel to Ireland, reap the harvest of other people's work and not put anything back in. You can join at any number of outposts in the area.
You will need a boat to fish this water and the recommended contact here is Myles Hope, Lake View, Lynn, Mullingar, County Westmeath, Ireland.
DIRECTIONS – the lough is to the south of Mullingar, on the right-hand side of the N8.
ACCOMMODATION – contact the Irish Tourist Board in Mullingar on 00353 4448650 for information about accommodation in the area.

AUGHRIM TROUT FISHERY – WICKLOW

I think it's essential that I mention this extraordinary fishery, a little way south of Dublin. It's a four-acre lake set within a beautifully designed riverside park. The surroundings are quite gorgeous, but what makes it particularly important is the fact that the water is designed for disabled anglers. Of course, the non-disabled are more than welcome, encouraged even, in the hope that they will help their disabled fishing companions around the lake. Pathways are designed to make sure that wheelchairs can get close to the water and yet are in no danger of capsizing. There's a lovely pavilion, good facilities and an exotic verandah where you can have a drink, a sandwich and look out over the lake.

It's an ideal spot for any family touring the Wicklow area – there's a whole host of things to do and see in this beautiful part of Ireland and the fishing here can be very good indeed. It's all about light line fishing really – go in the summer and you're unlikely to need anything more than a few buzzers and perhaps some Montanas. The fish fight well, are clearly visible and so can be stalked. But above all, it's this added element, knowing that disabled anglers are well catered for on a beautiful water, that really warms the heart. It's good to know that EU funds are from time to time put to really good use. The staff here are very helpful and positive. A tremendous day out.

Season – open all year.
Tickets – contact Angling for All, Aughrim, County Wicklow on 00353 40236552. Prices are very reasonable.
Directions – leave Dublin on the N11 following the coast through Bray and Wicklow as far as Arklow. Turn right onto the R747 to Aughrim. Go through the village, take a left at the traffic lights and the fishery is a short way down on the left. It is well-signposted.
Accommodation – contact Res Ireland on 0800 66866866 for information.

Ballyvolane House – County Cork

I felt it essential to offer Ballyvolane to the angler visiting Ireland with his family. There are two lovely lakes in the grounds of this eighteenth-century mansion, both very well stocked, with rainbows going way above five pounds in weight. The two lakes are kept private, reserved for hotel residents, so you know you won't be fishing shoulder to shoulder.

There are quite a few such waters in Ireland, but there's something special about Ballyvolane. The accommodation is excellent and the beautifully kept gardens have an aviary and a croquet lawn. There's also a little carp fishery planned, ideal for children. It's been voted Ireland's best bed and breakfast by the AA – and the food is superb. Sandwiches can even be served down by the lakeside.

If you want to be a little bit more ambitious, the hotel can arrange fishing on some six miles of the River Blackwater at a very reasonable cost. The house is situated in a wonderful area very close to Cork, in the valley of the River Bride – a tributary of the Blackwater – and a very interesting sea trout river at certain times. You can fly Stansted to Shannon now very cheaply, and this makes venues such as Ballyvolane more than accessible, even for a long weekend. A day on the lakes, an evening after sea trout on the Bride and a day on the Blackwater... a heavenly combination.

Tickets – contact Jeremy and Merrie Green, Ballyvolane House, Castlelyons, County Cork, on 00353 2536349.
Directions – from Cork, take the N8 towards Fermoy. In a few miles you will come to the River Bride. Just before the village of Rathcormack, take the right turning and follow the signs to the house.

Lough Currane – Co. Kerry

This is a magical place, about three miles long, perched down in the south-west of Ireland in County Kerry, next to the delightful town of Waterville. There can't be a more beautiful place in Ireland: it's a magnificent area to take a holiday in. Dingle Bay is just to the north and Bantry Bay a little to the south. Fantastic cliffs, beautiful bathing and countryside to die for. But let's look at the fishing...

If you look back on the Irish specimen fish lists, you will see that Currane dominates when it comes to sea trout. For years, there have been huge, specimen sea trout running into the lough – a water that is free. You've only got to pay boat charges.

During the spring, most people troll for good-sized salmon and very large sea trout. Then, it's all a matter of tobies and rapalas. From May, you can start taking sea trout on the fly and it's brilliant sport. Fish wet flies lough-style – Bumbles, Green Peters, Daddies and so on. You will also pick up the occasional grilse in June and July.

You'll need a boat. These are for hire all around the shoreline, along with local ghillies. This is a very dangerous lake indeed, with many locks, and, being so close to the south-west coast, a storm can blow up at any time. This is a water where it's essential to take a ghilly – for the first day at least. You'd be mad not to. All the ghillies know exactly what they're talking about, but the famous family down here are the O'Sullivans. Like so much of what goes on in Ireland, you'll make contact with one of the clan in any of the local bars. One tip: evening fishing can be especially productive, so try to make sure that you can both be out until last knockings.

Currane is linked to the sea by a tiny river known locally as Butler's Fishery. This is available to those staying at the Butler Arms Hotel. It's private fishing for hotel guests but can be tremendously good, especially when grilse are running. And, finally, if the water is really high, consider Lough Capal, a very small water situated just above Lough Currane itself and linked by streams. When the water is high, the very biggest sea trout run up into this tiny lough. Thrilling stuff.

SEASON – for salmon, 17th January to 13th September; for sea trout, 1st March to 30th September.

TICKETS – free fishing, but you will need a boat. These are widely available.

DIRECTIONS – Currane is just south-west of Waterville, easily seen from the N70 road.

ACCOMMODATION – contact the Tourist Information office at Waterville, on 00353 6694 74646, is open May to mid September.

IRELAND'S COASTLINE

This is really something for the adventurous angler, perhaps the man on holiday looking for something a bit different. You've got to realise that Ireland has a vast number of bays, estuaries, inflowing streams, lagoons... you name it, everything is there for incoming shoals of sea trout, bass and mullet. Of course, I'm not saying that every estuary and river mouth has superb sea trout fishing, but a little exploration often throws up some extraordinary results.

Obviously, you've got to check that fishing is available, but you can normally ask at the nearest bar. The sea trout run best in most parts of Ireland through June, July and August. Try to get out on a rising tide, especially during late evening or dusk. Flies? Well, up in Donegal and Sligo, locals fish Rogan's Gadget as it looks like a sand eel, the basis of the sea trout diet close inshore. Don't fish the flies slowly. Get them going near the surface with a bit of action. Often you'll see a bigger 'v' following your own fly in. Try casting into the current and letting the flow speed the flies' retrieve further. But do experiment. Different retrieve patterns are needed at different times.

Keep on the move until you contact, or at least see, fish. If you see locals congregate, you can be pretty sure that they know a hotspot. You'll get good, honest advice and a warm welcome. They like to see visitors doing something a little out of the ordinary.

I tentatively recommend fly-fishing for mullet. These can be infuriatingly difficult to catch, but there are so many in shallow Irish waters during the summer that they can be a really thrilling alternative. Again, this is very wild fishing and you need to ask the locals for tips. Ideally, you're looking for lagoons where you can wade with security, in water no more than a couple of feet deep. The mullet follow very skinny water, coming in at the beginning of the flow. Often you'll see them working, tails out of the water, muddying the bottom. Wade very carefully until you get to within casting distance and put down as light a line as you can. Obviously, a floating line is all you'll need with any small, dark patterns – any spider imitation should be a good kick-off. Try them on a size fourteen hook initially, but go up or down if necessary. A slow, careful retrieve generally works better, and be prepared for quite a sharp, snaggy take.

Always make sure you are investigating safe areas. Check with locals about tides and potential dangers. Never take risks and always stay absolutely within land reach.

It's wild fishing that Ireland is in essence about. Most of the fishing will be free and most is at its best from May through to September. If you're anywhere near the coast then the chances are that there will be areas to investigate. Good luck.

Highly Recommended Fisheries

- *Delphi Fishery, Leenane, County Galway. Phone 00353 9542211. The magnificent Delphi estate lies in an unspoilt valley in western Connemara. The fishery is a chain of beautiful lakes. There's a good spring run of salmon and grilse arrive in late May, followed by sea trout in late June.*
- *Rathbeggan Lakes, Dublin. Contact on 00353 18240197. Very close to the centre of Dublin. Many facilities, including secure parking. A brave venture.*
- *Springwater Fly Fishery, County Antrim, Northern Ireland. A very promising water. A lot of fish caught on lures.*
- *The Caragh Fishery, County Kerry. Call on 00353 669760102. Offers superb river salmon fishing and excellent lough browns.*
- *The Blackwater, County Waterford. Contact the Blackwater Lodge fishery on 00353 5860235. Recommended accommodation and first-rate fishing.*
- *Lough Sheelin, County Westmeath. One of Ireland's truly great brown trout fishery. Contact Cullens' Fishing Lodge on 00353 4381311.*

Where to Coarse Fish

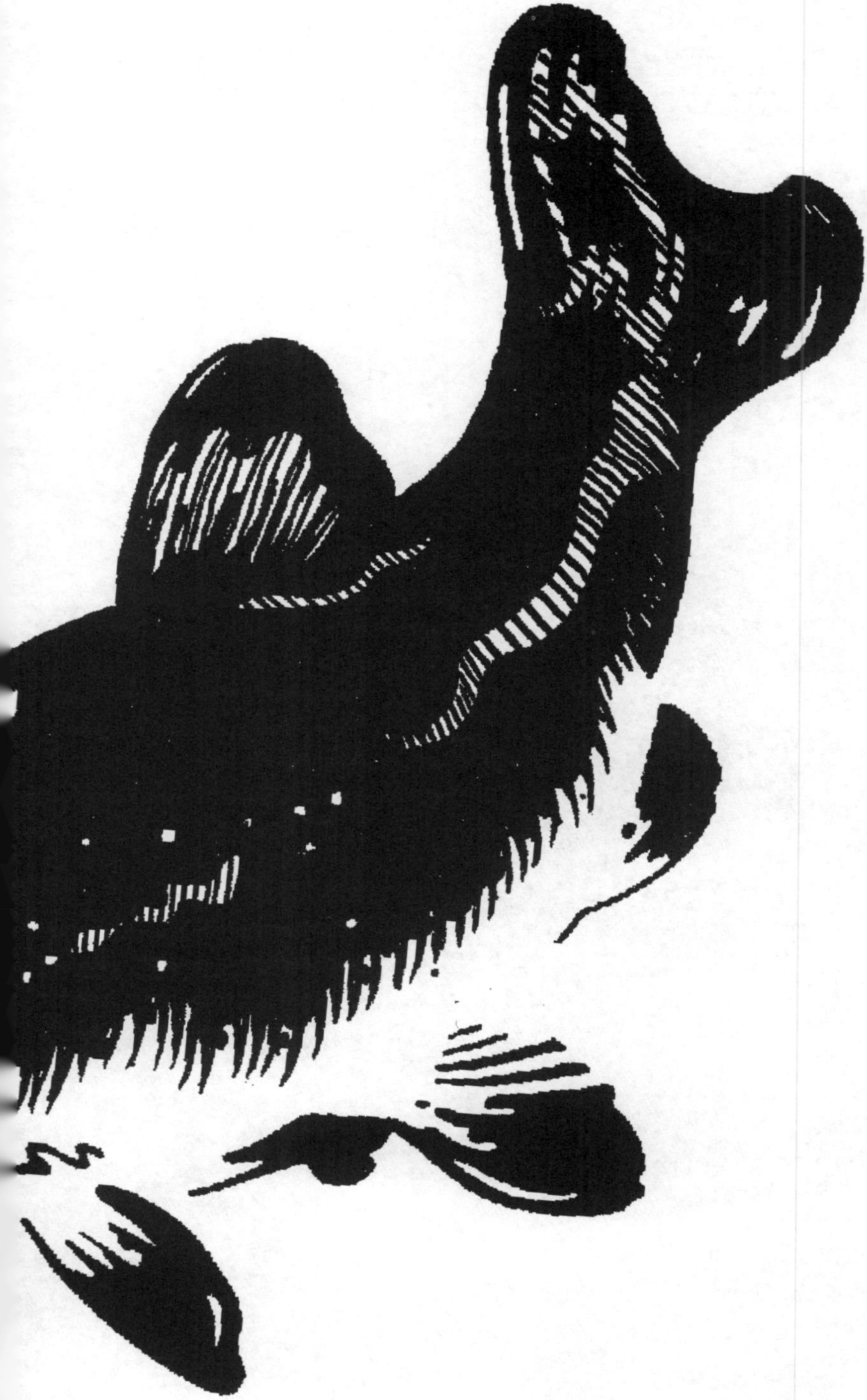

Coarse-Fishing Sites in The South West

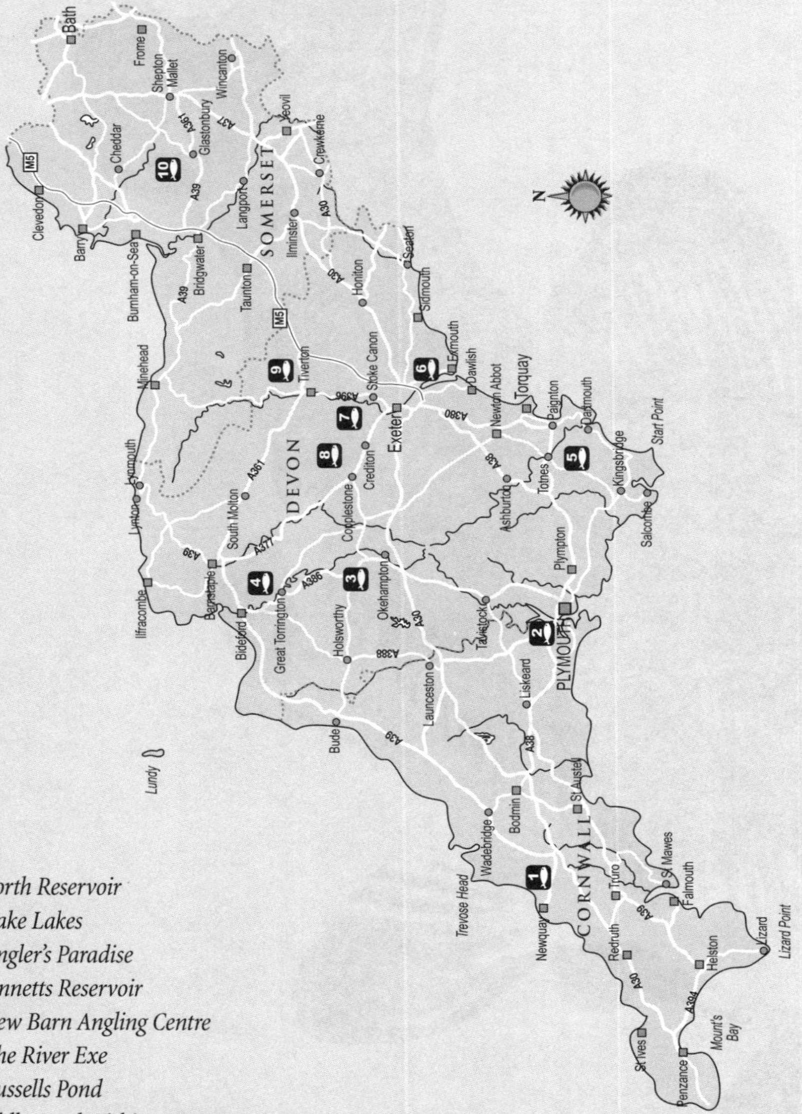

1. *Porth Reservoir*
2. *Bake Lakes*
3. *Angler's Paradise*
4. *Jennetts Reservoir*
5. *New Barn Angling Centre*
6. *The River Exe*
7. *Bussells Pond*
8. *Oldborough Fishing Retreat*
9. *West Pitt Farm*
10. *Viaduct Fishery*

THE SOUTH WEST

‘Water complexes such as Angler’s Paradise show that the South West is clearly determined to force itself on the coarse-fishing map of Britain. For too long, Devon, Cornwall and large parts of Somerset were seen primarily as ground for the game fisherman, with very little opportunity for coarse fishing. Little by little, the balance is being redressed, and whilst the game fishing remains very good, coarse fishers are beginning to sit up and take notice.’

MATT HAYES, ANGLING WRITER AND TELEVISION PRESENTER

All quite true. For generations, game fishermen have travelled to the far South West for the stunning wild brown trout fishing, small stream salmon and excellent sea trout opportunities. Coarse fishing was generally considered very much a junior partner but over the last few years a whole string of very attractive commercial waters has changed the whole complexion of the area. Obviously, tourism is of huge importance to Devon and Cornwall in particular, and the holidaying coarse angler is much too economically important to be overlooked – hence such outstanding fisheries as Angler’s Paradise. However, there are many other waters down there well worth a look. In Cornwall, for example, Boscathnoe reservoir, Bussow reservoir and Porth reservoir are all well worth consideration and hold excellent specimens of all the major species. In Devon, you won’t find nicer fishing anywhere than at Squabmoor reservoir and Jennetts reservoir, both holding carp to well over twenty pounds. But for real beauty, why not try Slapton Ley, a quite wonderful nature reserve just seven miles from Dartmouth? You’ve got to fish the water by boat but the pike and rudd fishing in particular are quite superb.

And if it’s river fishing that you fancy, then there is access to much of the River Exe, which holds good stocks of grayling, dace and chub in its lower reaches. There are also some roach, perch and pike. In fact, the exploring angler on both the Exe and tributaries such as the Creedy and Culm can find some really idyllic spots well out of the way of the maddening crowd.

Porth Reservoir – Cornwall

One of many cracking waters run by South West Water, Porth is a large reservoir at eighty acres, but it still has a very natural feel to it. Above all, this is a big fish venue. The carp are approaching twenty pounds and are growing well. The tench and bream are really very large indeed, with both species approaching ten pounds in weight.

Plenty of small roach, perch and rudd can be caught close in, so it's not simply a water for the specialist. Look, however, for the tench and bream further out and ledger for them with perhaps a cage feeder.

Porth is comparatively open to the wind and don't be afraid of ruffled water. It's always tempting to fish the calm bays, but this isn't always where the fish, especially bream, are found. You'd be surprised at the undertows a wind whips up on an open water like Porth, and bream are looking for food coming towards them in the current. The winds generally tend to be warm, so fishing into them isn't too great a sacrifice.

Season – open all the year round. Night fishing is allowed.

Tickets – these can be obtained from a self-service unit in the car park, but also phone the Newtown Angling Centre on 01736 763721 for further details. Also phone 01837 871565 with general enquiries.

Directions – you'll find the reservoir on the A3059 a couple of miles outside the town of Porth on the right. Follow the brown signposts.

Accommodation – the Tourist Information Centre in Newquay can supply details of a large variety of accommodation on 01637 854020.

Bake Lakes – Cornwall

Bake is a commercial fishery that offers a really good spread of species of all sizes, and caters for all levels of fishing experience. For example, the five-acre specimen lake, Luxor, holds carp just over the twenty-pound mark, bream edging towards double figures and some really good-sized tench. At the other end of the scale, the smaller Treasure Island pond has a really good spread of species up to three or four pounds in weight. So you can fish a float a couple of rod lengths out and end up with roach, bream, carp or tench.

On Luxor, look for the deeper holes, especially close in. Sometimes you'll find drop-offs to twelve feet or more. Conversely, try floating crust early and late for the carp. Maggots, pellets and corn all work well for the tench and bream, but don't over-feed. You will find lots of features – islands, ledges, plateaux and the like – so it pays to do a bit of work with a plummet before actually fishing.

If you're fishing Treasure Island, don't always use very small baits, as there is a large head of gudgeon in the water. Don't forget to take your loaf either: not only is floating crust a good bait, but a knob of flake on a size eight or ten is just right for the tench.

Expect good bags of fish a pound or two in weight. Of all the lakes, Treasure Island, particularly, is generally well coloured, so big bags are possible. However, it's a small water so don't make any unnecessary noise or vibration. Sit well back, bait steadily and build up a going swim.

SEASON – Bake is open year round. There is a ground bait limit of one kilo on Luxor and half a kilo on Treasure Island. Unhooking mats are also essential at Luxor and can be hired. Carp pellets are allowed, but not trout pellets.
TICKETS – tickets range from £6 on Luxor to £3.50 for children on Treasure Island. Tony Lister will give all the details on 01752 849027.
DIRECTIONS – from Plymouth, take the A38 towards Liskeard. Go through Landrake and Tideford and in just over a mile you will come to the Trerulefoot roundabout. Go straight on, head for Bake and turn right at the T-junction. Take the next left towards Hessenford. You will find the fishery entrance approximately a quarter of a mile on the right. It is opposite Bake Farm.
ACCOMMODATION – contact the Tourist Information Centre in Plymouth on 01752 304849 for advice on various kinds of accommodation available in the area.

ANGLER'S PARADISE – DEVON

The designer fishery is now part of the coarse-fishing scene, as it has to be. There simply are not enough 'natural' waters to cater for the huge number of anglers who want to fish. So, the commercial fishery has an increasingly important part to play in the modern fishing scene.

And no designer fishery could conceivably be better planned, more imaginative or more compelling than Angler's Paradise on the fringes of Dartmoor. Zyg Gregorek and his wife Rose created Angler's Paradise on a seventy-acre estate way back in 1985 and since then have set dramatic new standards in the field of commercial fisheries. Zyg has created twelve glorious lakes in this beautiful, rural setting.

And what fish stocks they hold – carp, golden tench, golden orfe, blue orfe, golden rudd, goldfish, catfish, shubunkins, grass carp, koi carp, as well as all the traditional species. Throw in woods full of deer, foxes and badgers, skies teeming with buzzards, barn owls and even kingfisher, and you really start to get the picture. Your angling skills don't matter here; expert or novice, you're bound to find the lakes for your own brand of fishing. There is even a lake where nobody has ever blanked. No, not ever! At the other end of the scale, there are thirty-pound carp to be caught, and record golden tench and orfe.

You stay on site in one of the twenty-plus purpose-built villas. These are beautifully presented and together give the impression of a little Mediterranean village tucked away in the heart of Devon. Add the excellent attractions of this part of the world – the north Cornish coast, the Devon resorts, the old towns of Okehampton and Tavistock –

and you realise that Angler's Paradise offers the perfect family holiday. There's even an African-themed bar where you can all relax in the evening after the heavy job of catching fish is over. As Zyg says, 'So many people rebook before even finishing their present holiday, we know we must be doing something right!'

SEASON – the fishing is year round.
TICKETS AND ACCOMMODATION – contact Zyg or Rose at Angler's Paradise, The Gables, Winsford, Halwill Junction, Devon EX21 5XT, or phone 01409 221559 for their comprehensive list of prices. Lakes and villas do vary in price according to the season and availability. From October to March, there are special winter breaks available – in the warm Devon winters, the carp still feed well.
RULES – the only real rule is to enjoy yourself – at the same time, obviously, taking every precaution over the welfare of these wonderful fish. Zyg will certainly advise on the best way to treat the fish stocks.
DIRECTIONS – at the end of the M5 motorway, take the A30 to Okehampton. At Okehampton junction, take the B3260 to Okehampton and a mile after Okehampton, take the A3079 to Holsworthy and Bude. Take this road for about eleven miles until you reach the Halwill junction. Take the first right-hand turning past the garage, signposted Angler's Eldorado. Go past the Junction Inn and carry on for half a mile until you come across a signpost for Angler's Paradise.

JENNETTS RESERVOIR – DEVON

South West Water controls an intriguing series of reservoirs, generally set in rolling countryside, that are open to the coarse fisherman. All these waters are very well maintained, with nice stocks of fish. Jennetts is the one that I know the best, and it's a lovely water of about eight acres, with depths going down to some thirty feet or so. For a reservoir, it is very natural-looking and set in a beautiful landscape. The fish, too, are splendid – carp to twenty pounds plus, tench averaging three pounds and good roach, bream, rudd, perch and eels.

All the South West Waters hold good stocks of eels and, for those not used to them, they can make an intriguing addition to a holiday bag. Believe me, a big eel is something to be tangled with – and there are some crackers in this part of the world. There are several golden rules when eel fishing, First, make your rig as resistance-free as possible – eels will drop a bait the instant they feel pressure. Next, make sure that you strike immediately you have a run, especially with a small bait, or you will have a deeply hooked eel, which nobody wants. Thirdly, make sure that you can control the eel while you unhook it with forceps. Barbless hooks help considerably in this respect. Eels are not for everyone, admittedly, but if you haven't caught one before, perhaps you'll want to give them a go.

Season – open all year round from 6.30 am until 10.00 pm.
Tickets – on Jennetts these cost £4 a day. Contact the Ranger on 01288 321262 or South West Water Leisure Services on 01837 871565 for details.
Directions – take the A386 out of Bideford towards Great Torrington. After about a mile you will find the reservoir by the side of the road.
Accommodation – contact the Tourist Information Centre in Bideford, on 01437 477676, who will advise on various types of accommodation in the area.

Further South West Water Venues:
Darracott, Nr. Torrington – a three-acre coarse fishery with carp, tench, bream, roach, rudd, perch and eels. Open all year round, twenty-four hours a day.
Melbury Reservoir, Nr. Bideford – twelve acres with carp, bream, roach, perch and eels.
Lower Slade Reservoir – carp tench, bream, roach, rudd, gudgeon and perch,
Trenchford Reservoir, Northeast of Newton Abbott. Big pike.
For details of all these waters contact the Manager at South West Water Leisure Services, Higher Coombe Park, Lewdown, Okehampton EXE20 4QT, or phone. 01837 871565.

New Barn Angling Centre – Devon

New Barn consists of four lakes, one of which is very much for juniors, with huge stocks of roach and perch. Mirror Lake, it's fair to say, is the most popular simply because the carp fishing there is so impressive. There are lots of double-figure fish, and a good number of twenty-pound pluses. It's an interesting fishery to say the least, and the carp can be picked up in a number of ways. Floater fishing works, as does float fishing close in and the more conventional boily approach. They're good-looking fish here, and plenty of them.

Willow and Lily Lakes are both great waters and do tend to be somewhat under-fished. Great for the exploring angler, one who is willing to stalk fish and look for carp feeding in the most unusual of places.

There are three more excellent reasons to go to New Barn. The first of these is the cracking roach fishing on offer. Roach in stillwaters can frequently be a bit of a mixed blessing: they often over breed, lose condition and become pretty stunted. But not here. There are plenty of fish well over the pound. Maggot and casters tend to be favourite baits, and obviously pole fishing does sort out some big bags. But don't neglect the waggler, especially when there's a wind blowing. The second reason to go to New Barn is its stunning situation, set in a verdant valley with tremendous views. This is a lovely bit of the Devonshire countryside and a superb place to just sit and meditate. And third? Well, New Barn is a tremendously welcoming place. There's tuition if you want it, along with all the facilities you could ever need, but without losing the natural feel of the place. In short, it's no wonder that the locals patronise it so regularly. A cracking place.

Season – the fishery is closed from mid November to mid February.

Tickets – day tickets cost £5 for adults and £3 for juniors – phone 01803 553602 .

Directions – take the A385 out of Paignton following the signs to the zoo. You will be on the Totnes road. Pass the zoo and travel straight over the Tweenaways traffic lights, still on the Totnes road. You will travel for two miles. The fishery is on the left just after an 'S' bend.

Accommodation – contact the English Riviera Tourist Board on 0906 680 1268 (premium rate number) for details of accommodation in the whole of this area.

The River Exe – Devon

There isn't a huge amount of wild coarse fishing in the South West, and most of it tends to be centred on the commercial fisheries. The River Exe, however, does offer the occasional opportunity, even though it's better known as a salmon, trout and sea trout river and is naturally rather tightly preserved upstream. However, once you get into the Exeter area itself there are more possibilities, largely because of the excellent Exeter Angling Club.

Trotting For Dace

The River Exe offers some enchanting dace fishing. Okay, dace don't grow huge, but they're a delicate and absorbing fish species. Trotting is the way to catch them. A twelve- or thirteen-foot rod, three-pound main line, two-pound hook length and either centre-pin or fixed-spool reel are ideal.

- *You'll need maggots or casters for bait.*
- *A stick float is ideal, set so that the bait skips its way through the swim, just a couple of inches off the bottom.*
- *Look for reasonably quickly-paced swims between three and six feet in depth, preferably over gravel, sand or clean bottom.*
- *Feed the swim steadily, say ten or fifteen maggots each trot down.*
- *Let the float trot some fifteen or twenty yards before retrieving. Retrieve close in to the bank to avoid disturbing the swim.*
- *If you don't contact dace after thirty to forty minutes, move down the river until you do come across fish. It shouldn't take too long before a dace shoal responds to a steady flow of maggots.*
- *Don't keep dace in keep nets, but release them immediately. This won't unsettle the shoal.*
- *Remember that an eight-ounce dace is a specimen in its own right – so admire it and give it the respect it deserves.*

The Exe here has become a tidal river for much of its length, and has lost the clarity and intimacy of its upper reaches. Still, there are some good fish to be had. Bream are a top species in these tidal reaches, and average a very handy three to five pounds with some fish, apparently, approaching double figures. Location is the problem. With a large tidal range, you tend to find that the shoals look for a reasonable amount of water over their heads and stick to the deeper pools. These are better located at low water, when you can build up a clearer picture of the bottom contours. Make a note and stick with these areas even when the tide is up. Very occasionally, you will see fish roll and that, of course, gives the game away!

Most of my own tidal-river breaming has taken place in Norfolk on the Bure and Thurne, and I've learnt that it is vital to keep bait going in. In fact, because of the depth and speed of the water and the number of fish present, it is difficult to overfeed. Of course, getting your feed in accurately is a problem and this is where a big cage feeder pays dividends. Keep working the area pretty tightly and you should start the fish feeding. Go for a big, obvious bait – a hunk of flake is a good idea, or even a whole lobworm on a size six hook. Obviously, maggots and casters do work, but not nearly as well in extremely coloured water – and there's always a risk of bootlace eels.

The tide is also a consideration. In Norfolk, I always like it when there's been a flow on, but high water can also work as well. It's hard to predict exactly how the fish are going to react and this makes for really challenging, interesting sport. I will add finally that brackish-water bream really fight like the clappers. They're not at all like the manure-sack creatures of the stillwaters. Get a six-pounder with an ebb flow behind it, and you really know you're into a fish.

All the usual species are present, including the occasional big carp and chub. However, one of the most interesting things is the invasion of mullet that takes place during the summer months. These will run the river in huge numbers, but they can be absolutely infuriating to catch. They're feeding all right, often throwing up huge sheets of bubbles – but catching them is another matter!

Sometimes you'll even see them grazing on the bankside grasses and reeds, presumably hoovering off minute insects. Breadflake is probably as good a bait as any to catch them. Throw in handfuls of mash and look for fish swirling amongst the floating pieces. A pinch of breadflake on a size twelve hook fished in mid water can sometimes do the trick – I'm not going to say that it will always work, or even often, because there seem to be no rules in mullet fishing as far as I'm concerned, but it can work. All in all, an interesting place to fish.

Season – check with the controlling club, as the whole question of the closed season is currently under debate.

Tickets – day tickets cost £3 for adults and £1.25 for juniors. Contact Exeter and District Angling Association on 01647 24566.

Directions – take the B3182 out of Exeter towards Exmouth. Turn right at Countess

Wear roundabout, signposted Torquay. This dual carriageway crosses the Exe after half a mile. You will find a car park on the left a little way further on. Park here and walk to the river.

Accommodation – contact the Tourist Information Centre in Exeter on 01392 265700 for details of suitable accommodation.

Bussells Ponds – Devon

I mention these small waters because they're very attractive to fish but, and here's the big thing, they're just four miles from the centre of Exeter, affording a great little fishing adventure for anyone making Exeter their base. And there are some nice surprises, such as the very good-sized bream and tench that you wouldn't expect to get to six pounds plus in waters totalling less than three acres. The carp fishing is the main draw and there are plenty of doubles – I'm not sure about twenties, but time will tell. There are also roach and some quite sizable pike. All in all, a pleasant fishing experience, and only a quarter of an hour or so from the hurly-burly of a major city. A nice idea.

Season – open all year round.

Tickets – these cost £5 – phone 01392 841238.

Directions – take the A396 Tiverton Road out of Exeter for about three miles. You will come to the village of Stoke Canon. Turn right at the church, signposted Poltimore. In about half a mile, turn left opposite the Barton Cross restaurant. The fishery is half a mile down that road on the left.

Accommodation – try Exeter Tourist Information Centre on 01392 265700 for details of suitable accommodation.

Oldborough Fishing Retreat – Devon

I haven't actually fished at Oldborough but I've walked the two waters and found them fascinating. They are not particularly large – both around about the acre, give or take a bit – but they are surrounded by trees, look very natural and, being spring-fed, are very fertile. They're also deep – something that gives an extra dimension to any small stillwater. Fish stocks, too, are good. The carp average double figures and four- and even five-pound tench are the norm. There are some very big perch – don't be surprised by two-pounders – and the roach and rudd are also a good size.

These waters are so intimate that long-range bolt techniques aren't really called for. A fair amount of both waters is also out of bounds and therefore the fish don't get too neurotic and can always go into hiding. Therefore, you've got to use traditional fishing skills to some degree at Oldborough: think about floater fishing or even laying-on under your rod tip. This means that you've got to feed carefully and thoughtfully and gradually get a swim going. All the traditional baits work: if the tench are shy, why not try just half a grain of corn on a size sixteen?

SEASON – open all year.
TICKETS – these must be booked in advance and cost £4 a day, £3 for juniors and senior citizens – phone 01363 877437.
DIRECTIONS – take the A377 north out of Crediton through the village of Copplestone. Turn right at Morchard Road, go up the hill and turn right again at the T-junction. You will find the fishery on the left at the bottom of the hill.
ACCOMMODATION – Holiday chalets on site – phone Oldborough on 01363 877437. For other accommodation, try the Exeter Tourist Information Centre on 01392 265700.

WEST PITT FARM – DEVON

West Pitt Farm is one of the new commercial fisheries that have proved so popular over the past few years, and it really is a beauty. It's the brainchild of owner Rod Crocker, who has developed the four pools into really lovely coarse-fishing waters. Farmyard Pool is, as you'd expect, bordered by the farm buildings themselves, but it has a relaxed atmosphere. In essence, this is an old water, quite shallow, but it holds good stocks of carp, roach and rudd. It's an ideal place to sit and while the day away.

Higher Pool is a newer water, quite small but is nicely mature with good stocks of big bream, tench, roach and some lovely golden orfe. Mallard Pool is quite small – about one and a quarter acres in size – but it holds some beautiful common carp topping the twenty pound mark. Willow Pool is smaller still, but has a very interesting selection of fish species. Tench grow to eight pounds and there are perch and crucian carp over two pounds. There are even a couple of barbel that have found their way in, and now top the three-pound mark.

All in all, West Pitt Farm offers something for everybody. If you want to fish the pole and maggot for small roach and rudd, then you'll catch legions of these all day long. If it's bigger fish that you've set your mind on, there are plenty of specimens available – the perch in particular offer really exciting opportunities. But don't forget those beautiful commons and golden orfe. Lovely waters, lovely landscape and very friendly people all combine to make West Pitt a very desirable fishery.

SEASON – open all year round.
TICKETS – the fishing is free to residents and costs £4.50 for adults. After 5.00 pm, tickets cost £3.50. Contact Rod Crocker on 01884 820296 or fax him on 01884 820818.
DIRECTIONS – West Pitt Farm is only five minutes from junction 27 of the M5 motorway. Take the dual carriageway signed to Barnstaple. After five hundred yards, take the left fork to Sampford Peverell. Almost immediately there is a mini-roundabout where you turn right and

cross over the dual carriageway. Go straight over the next mini-roundabout heading for Holcombe Rogus. Take the next left signed Whitnage – following the green fish signs – and the next right, signed Whitnage, to Pitt crossroads. Turn left, and West Pitt Farm is signed about five hundred yards on the left.

Accommodation – West Pitt Farm offers excellent accommodation on site. Rod Crocker offers a selection of cottages suitable for either individuals, couples or even groups up to nine. There's a modern, indoor, heated swimming pool incorporating a sauna and solarium. Children are catered for with a small but discreet play area. Other facilities include a games room with snooker and table-tennis tables, a grass tennis court, barbecue area and plenty of garden furniture around the lawns and tended grounds in which to relax.

Viaduct Fishery – Somerset

This is an entertaining complex of small waters, deep in the heart of Somerset, with a tremendous stock of fish. This is the appeal. It isn't particularly a specimen water, but the carp fishing on offer is enough for a fantastic family day out. Indeed, the management realise this and offer shared peg facilities for families – a great idea so that everyone can fish together and join in the fun.

The average run of carp is anything between two and seven or eight pounds – not huge, but they're in great condition, fight well and there are bags of them to catch. Try all the normal methods, especially waggler fishing close in for a real thrill. It is obviously a water where the method feeder works particularly well. The method feeder, as you probably know, is a technique that's sweeping the field on many of these small commercial waters.

The concept behind the method feeder is to present a large ball of ground bait with the hook bait tucked right in. When cast into the swim, the carp simply think that you're lobbing in a loose-fed ball of ground bait and they attack it trying to get the food as quickly as possible. The hook bait is therefore mopped up without suspicion. When you're choosing your feeder you'll be faced with an elasticated one or, better, those that feature a hollow tube through which the line runs. These are safer for the fish because they're not actually tied to the main line, which is an advantage in the event of a main line breakage. The fish can simply swim off without towing the feeder behind it. The trick to the method feeder is mixing your ground bait to the right consistency so that it moulds well and doesn't break off the feeder in flight. Experiment a few times until you get it nice and stiff and clingy.

The other tip is to work as much food as you can into that ground bait, so that the offering is as attractive as possible. Perfect additions include hemp seed, casters and sweetcorn. The problem with maggots and worms is that their wriggling can break up the ground bait in flight. Once the feeder settles, the carp will be on it instantly, sucking and pulling. Ignore odd nudges and tugs and wait for the tip to go right round. You're rarely left in any doubt as to when the bait has been taken! This is a highly effective method for the summer, particularly when the carp are really hungry and looking for large amounts of food. It can still work in the winter, but then you should cast out less frequently and give the fish more time.

Back to Viaduct; you'll also contact the odd bream, tench and roach, but perch are the one real specimen species that swims the waters. Now, a big perch is an unpredictable beast. The waters can be full of them one year, and they disappear like magic the next. So when you hear of a water doing the business with perch, it pays to concentrate on it.

SEASON – open all year. Note that barbed hooks and hooks larger than size twelve are banned. There is no night fishing, and several baits, such as nuts, are also prohibited.
TICKETS – available on site for £5 a day and £4 for juniors – phone 01458 74022.
DIRECTIONS – take junction 23 off the M5 and head along the A39 towards Glastonbury. Just before Glastonbury, turn right onto the B3151 and you will come to the village of Somerton. The fishery is well signposted to the north of the town.
ACCOMMODATION – the Tourist Information Centre in Glastonbury, on 01458 832954, or Yeovil, on 01935 471279, can advise on accommodation in their areas.

Highly Recommended Fisheries

- *Coombe Water, Kingsbridge, Devon. A three-lake complex holding good carp, roach and bream. The carp average five to ten pounds, there are some good roach. Tickets cost £5 a day. Phone 01548 852038.*
- *Emerald Pool, Highbridge, Somerset. A really good carp venue with fish around the twenty-pound mark and some very good roach. Popular with matches so check on availability beforehand. Phone Alan Wilkinson on 01278 794707.*
- *Elmfield Farm, Launceston, Cornwall. A really popular venue. Some excellent carp and roach to over two pounds. Superb fish indeed. Good bream, some chub and perch. Phone 01566 781243 for details and directions.*
- *Slapton Ley, Dartmouth, Devon. A beautiful, natural fishery holding pike, rudd, roach, eels and perch. Part of a national nature reserve. Boat fishing only. For tickets contact The Field Centre, Slapton, Kingsbridge, TQ7 2QP, or phone for further information on 01548 580685.*

Coarse-Fishing Sites in The South

1. *The Royalty*
2. *Christchurch Fishing*
3. *The Isle of Wight*
4. *Broadlands Lake*
5. *Kennet and Avon Canal*
6. *The River Kennet*
7. *The River Thames*
8. *Gold Valley Lakes*

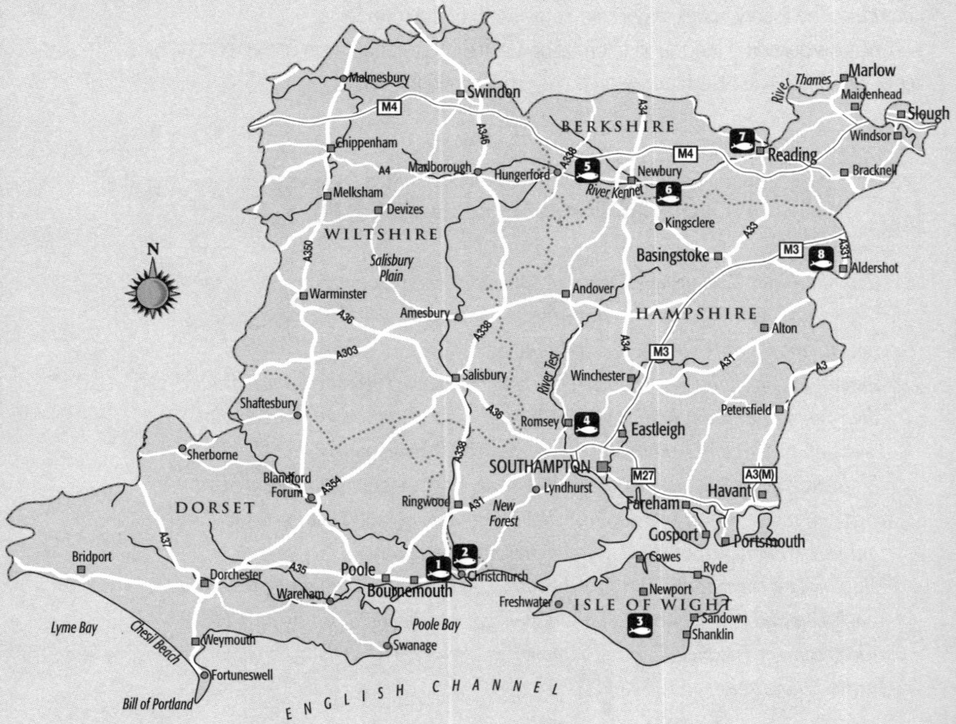

‘Yes, John, I’d really try to get down to the Hampshire Avon if I were you. The Royalty’s the place to begin probably because there’s so much information on it and you can see the fish there. Whoppers. There are definitely chub to over six pounds, and goodness knows how big the barbel go to. Also there are good roach, perch, even some cracking bream. The trend these days seems to be to fish small baits for the barbel, but my advice to you would be to go for a big natural. Try a couple of lobworms or a small dead gudgeon perhaps, and look out for fireworks. It’s really liquid history down on the Royalty you know. There have been so many great anglers, so many amazing captures... a man like you starting out on a big fish career just can’t ignore it.’

A LETTER FROM THE LATE RICHARD WALKER TO THE AUTHOR

As a boy, there was one Mecca that I and my fishing friends all aspired to fish. One day, we told each other, we would fish the Hampshire Avon. The Royalty. The place where Richard Walker, Fred Taylor, Mr Crabtree – heroes real and fictional – all said the biggest coarse fish in England were to be found.

Since those early days, I have fished the Royalty and, though it may not be the river it once was, it’s still exceptional. And that goes for many southern rivers. They have had their problems, but there are still some extraordinary fish to be taken. The Stour, the Kennet, the Avon – even smaller rivers like the Allen – can all still produce leviathans.

As Phil Humm, the well-known Essex fisherman, recently told me; ‘The southern rivers still hold very, very big roach, and in places they are still present in numbers. I remember one particular swim a year or so ago. It was dusk and there were roach – really big roach – just rolling everywhere. Fishing for them wasn’t easy. It never is with roach, but that’s not the point. Those southern rivers can still do it’.

Of course, there are also lovely lakes – Broadlands springs to mind. Large carp, tench, pike – you name it, the southern counties hold them.

The Royalty – Hampshire

For river fishermen, the Hampshire Avon has been their Mecca for decades. And on the Hampshire Avon, no other fishery is as famous as the magnificent Royalty. What a place! It's been glorified ever since the 1930s with strings of extraordinary catches – chub, barbel, roach, pike, perch. For most of the 20th century, the Royalty was the place that all river anglers dreamt of visiting. It became part of angling folklore, back in the 1950s, through Mr Crabtree, who made it appear that every cast would result in a six-pound chub.

Of course, I can't comment on what the Royalty was like in the mid part of the 20th century, as I only came to it properly in the 1980s, when it was still awe-inspiring but definitely difficult. Of course, the Royalty wasn't alone in experiencing hard times. All lowland rivers were having problems. Disastrous river management techniques had had a detrimental impact on rivers throughout all the English counties, and the Avon was not exempt. In fact, much of the upper Hampshire Avon had become even more difficult than the Royalty. The huge roach that once lived there had all but become a distant memory.

The situation today, at the start of the 21st century, looks definitely brighter. The Royalty is once again performing well. Looking back to1998, there were over 140 double-figure barbel caught from the Royalty alone that season, with vast numbers of barbel under three pounds also being caught. Today, those smaller fish are coming through well, and it's possible to see groups of barbel nudging the five-pound mark. These are going to provide great sport for the future.

The Royalty is a strange beast; such is the glamour of its crystal-clear, characterful waters that you tend to forget it's an urban river only five minutes from the centre of Christchurch. Yes, if your concentration wasn't so fixed on the water, you would be aware of traffic, pedestrians and the ugly sounds of civilisation. But as it is, the only world that exists for you is seen through your Polaroids. Such famous swims – the Pipes, Parlour Pool, the Top Weir, Bridge Pool – all places that have settled into angling folklore. In fact, one leading angling paper voted the Royalty as the best day-ticket river fishery in the entire country. We've already discussed the barbel that easily top twelve pounds – didn't Chris Yates stalk a fish in the Parlour Pool for a number of years that he swore was fifteen plus? There are seven-pound chub, perch over two pounds, big bream and carp, and pike weighing over thirty pounds.

Mind you, just because the Royalty is stuffed with big fish, it doesn't mean to say that you're going to catch them. You'll certainly see these whoppers, but that could well be all! So, how about a few tips.

Firstly, don't use line less than eight pounds breaking strain – if you do hook a fish you want to land it. Secondly, master the art of rolling bait. The barbel at the Royalty have become very suspicious of static ones. And thirdly, show a little inventiveness when it does come to baits – don't just use the same old luncheon meat. How about a couple of lobworms or a small dead minnow?

Try baiting a swim up on arrival and then leaving it a couple of hours to see if barbel have moved in and begun feeding. The longer you leave a swim, the greater the confidence of the fish becomes.

Never neglect to wear your Polaroids. Without them, your ability to see into the water is vastly reduced and your chances of success plummet. And travel light. The Royalty is not the place for bivvies, bolt-rigs and bite alarms. A wealth of tackle might increase your confidence initially but it won't help you catch barbel, I promise.

Barbel Basics

Barbel are arguably our most dramatic freshwater fish, and certainly very much the target species of the moment. However, catching these magnificent fish can be a difficult business.

There are two basic approaches to barbel fishing. You can either fish at a known peg and put in a lot of bait, building the swim up, or you can travel light and fish as many swims as possible, hoping to pick fish up as you go. Remember that the best times for barbel fishing are dawn and dusk, just into darkness. But that does not mean that they cannot be caught during the day, even in bright weather.

- *Top baits are maggots, casters, sweetcorn, lobworms, dead minnows, luncheon meat, meatballs and garlic sausage. The important thing to remember is to ally the bait to the right size of hook.*
- *Hemp seed is a great barbel attractor. It certainly gets them feeding, but it can preoccupy them with the tiny seeds and make catching difficult. Use it thoughtfully.*
- *You can either ledger for barbel with a lead or a swim feeder or you can float fish. Float fishing is especially useful when the barbel have been very pressurised and are afraid of static baits.*
- *If you're not attracting bites, never be tempted to scale your tackle down in strength. What's the point of moving to three-pound hook length for it only to be smashed in seconds?*
- *A quiver tip and swim feeder set up is probably the most common method used in barbel fishing today. Don't always expect a huge pull round. Barbel bites can often be a mere flickering of the tip. Watch carefully. A braid hook length can often increase the number of bites.*
- *Never put barbel in a keep net.*
- *Before releasing it, hold the barbel upright against the flow of the river for as long as it takes for its strength to return. Once you begin to feel its muscles flex, you can let it go, safe in the knowledge that it won't turn belly up in the current.*

SEASON – the basic season is June 16th to March 14th. The fishery opens at 7.30am and anglers must leave at sunset. The only exceptions are Bridge Pool and Parlour Pool where 11.00pm is the closing time.

TICKETS – there is a sliding scale of charges depending on the areas to be fished and the time of year. In essence, the cheapest day tickets cost around £8 per day, but these can escalate for the best areas at the best time of the year. For example, you have to book in advance for the Parlour Pool, but this holds three rods at a price of around £50. The best thing is to contact either the Fishery Manager on 01202 591111, the Head Bailiff on 01202 485262 or that legendary tackle shop, Davis Tackle, on 01202 485169 for more details. Remember that tickets must be booked and paid for in advance before you even set up a rod. Also, look very carefully at the rules on your ticket. These can be quite complex, but they do emphasise that no barbel must ever be kept in a keep net.

DIRECTIONS – the main entry to the Royalty is at Avon Buildings, which is just off Bargates in Christchurch. This is very close to the Christchurch by-pass. You will find Davis Tackle shop on the corner. There is a car park at the Avon Building. This is closed at dusk.

ACCOMMODATION – phone the Christchurch Tourist Information Centre on 01202 471780. Anglers speak highly of the Royalty View Guesthouse, 24 Fairfield, Christchurch, Dorset BH23 1QX – 01202 485362. Also recommended are the Grosvenor Lodge on 01202 499008 and the Royalty Inn on 01202 486310.

FISHING THE CHRISTCHURCH AREA

It's not just the Royalty that should attract your attention in this richest of angling areas. There's a lot more besides. In fact, for years, Christchurch has proved a holiday hotspot for coarse anglers and I've made my own pilgrimages there over the years. You can fish the Avon up river – the Winkton and Severals fisheries are particularly prolific.

And, on the Stour, the Avon's sister river, there is the fantastic Throop fishery. In fact, if push comes to shove, I'd almost say that I personally enjoy Throop as much as I do the Royalty. It's arguable that the fish aren't quite as big – but as the barbel run well into double figures, they're big enough for me! And there are lots of them. Moreover, they're just that tad less difficult to catch. Yes, the Throop is a must.

There are also some excellent stillwaters within easy driving distance, and my own favourite is Hatchet Pond. This is hardly a pond, but a lovely expanse of generally shallow water that holds a stunning head of fish – bream, carp and tench especially – set in beautiful surroundings.

There is even more. Why not try Christchurch harbour? This is a super place to fish and, aged ten, it's where I caught my first flounders – on tackle designed for roach, which I would have been pursuing had my parents not booked our annual holiday two weeks out of season! There's a lot more to Christchurch harbour. There are times when the bass come in numbers and the fishing with small spinners is absolutely absorbing.

There are also mullet – and a more rewarding but frustrating fish doesn't swim anywhere in the world. The water in front of you can be black with mullet and you will still not get a bite. At other times, you seem to be hooking one every cast. Try for them with normal roach-type tackle – four- or five-pound line, a float and a size ten hook with a small piece of bread flake as bait. Alternatively, try maggots or a very small redworm. Keep varying the bait until you find something that they like, but remember this preference can change from one day to the next. Fascinating fish in a marvellous part of the coarse angler's world.

Season – generally June 16th to March 14th.
Tickets – permits for all the waters that I have discussed – along with good directions to the venues – can be obtained from Davis Tackle, on 01202 485169. If you are considering a stay of a week or more down in the area, why not try contacting Christchurch Angling Club at 4 Marley Close, New Milton, Hants BH25 5LL for membership? This excellently run club has miles of river on the Stour and Avon. Tickets for Hatchet Pond can also be purchased from the Forestry Commission, Queen's House, Lyndhurst SO43 7NH – 01703 283141. Also contact the Throop Fisheries on 01202 35532. Ringwood and District Anglers' Association also hold some tremendous day ticket venues – Northfield Lakes, for example, cover fifty acres of water. They also have High Town Lake on their ticket, which holds thirty-pound plus common carp. Contact Ringwood Tackle at 5 The Bridges, Ringwood or phone 01425 475155 regarding membership.
Directions – ask when buying tickets for your chosen venue.
Accommodation – the Christchurch Tourist Information Centre on 01202 471780 can supply details of various kinds of accommodation in the area. There is also accommodation on the water at Throop. Apply to the Manager at South Lodge, Holdenhurst Village, Bournemouth, or phone 01202 35532. There is also camping at Hatchet Pond. Contact the Forestry Commission for details.

The Isle of Wight

There is coarse fishing in and around this lovely holiday destination, though it's of the more modest kind and you're not going to rewrite the record books. Nonetheless, that shouldn't put you off: the Isle of Wight has a huge amount to offer for the family holiday and some attractive places to cast a float. There are all the usual species to be found on the island. Most waters hold carp, though a twenty-pounder really would be rated a major success. You'll generally find tench, roach and some bream. The Isle of Wight Freshwater Angling Association, 66 Merrie Gardens, Merrie Gardens Lake, Sandown, Isle of Wight, has plenty of water on its ticket, and a membership enquiry before heading out would be a good idea. The club owns water on the River Yar and some good lake fishing on Gunville Pond and Somerton Reservoir.

Moreton Farm, Bradin offers some top rate coarse fishing on a very prolific, even if small, pool – phone 01983 406132. There's some tremendous fishing for juniors at Jolliffes Farm, Witwell – phone 01983 730783. Gillees Pond has built up something of a reputation, and day tickets cost £2 from Scotties Tackle Shop, 11 Lugley Street, Newport, or 22 Fitzroy Street, Sandown. Don't neglect Bembridge harbour – the bass and mullet fishing can be excellent during the height of summer. Try and get down there either early or late, and make note of the tides as mullet like to come in on the flow.

TICKETS – in general, coarse fishing on the Isle of Wight is very reasonably priced, and all the tackle shops are helpful.

ACCOMMODATION – The Isle of Wight Tourist Board has huge amounts of information on accommodation and will help with fishery details. Phone them on 01983 813818.

FEEDING THE SWIM

Feeding a swim with either ground bait or lose feed is one of the big problems of most coarse fishing scenarios.

- *Do you feed heavily and run the risk of over feeding, or do you feed light knowing you might not be able to hold the fish? As a general rule, it's probably better to under- rather than over-feed. Keep the fish actively looking for bait.*
- *Little and often is generally better than a single mass bait attack. Be careful of putting ground bait over the heads of fish - especially bream - in very shallow water, especially in big balls.*
- *Be careful of putting out too much cereal ground bait during the summer. If it is not eaten it can simply lie and rot on the bottom, souring the swim for days.*
- *As a general rule, feed less in winter, in clear, cold conditions, and more in summer when the water is warm and coloured.*
- *If your swim suddenly goes off, it might not be your feeding that's to blame. A hungry pike may have been attracted by the activity of the show in front of you.*
- *If at all possible, try to buy the large catering cans of sweetcorn. These work out much more economical than smaller tins.*
- *In cold weather, enlarge the holes of a swim feeder with scissors or a shop bought hole enlarger, which will allow sluggish maggots to escape faster.*
- *Before ground baiting in the still water, throw in a little floating bread to check the amount of drift. In even a light wind, enough current can be generated to carry wrongly-positioned ground bait right out of the swim.*
- *When you are catapulting ground bait out, go for a low flow flight path in a wind, as it is less likely to be blown off course.*

Broadlands Lake – Hampshire

The Broadlands Estate has long been a dream for game fishermen, as it straddles the River Test. There are very good chub in this stretch of the river but, sadly for us, it's reserved for the trout and salmon anglers. However, coarse fishing isn't forgotten and there's a glorious lake of almost three acres set in the grounds that offers some tremendous fishing. It's a beautiful water in a very special place and deserves mention.

Fish stocks are immense. For the general angler you can't do better than try the method feeder with maggot on the hook. Failing that, go on the waggler with four-pound line straight through to the hook – about right for the sort of fish that you're likely to hook. Okay, you'll come across a lot of bream in the skimmer class, but almost certainly as the day progresses you'll get better fish of four, five or six pounds. And doubles are always possible. The tench, too, feed well right into the autumn, and then, of course, there are the carp. There's a good head of twenty-pounders in the lake, with many fish in low and mid doubles, but it's the huge numbers of fish in the five- to nine-pound category that provide tremendous sport for the general angler. When that float goes down, you don't know if you're hooking into a two-pound skimmer, a double-figure slab, a five-pound tench or an eleven-pound carp – very appealing fishing.

There's also a stretch of shallow canal alongside the lake that is full of big fish. It's generally a pole and match water, but you can attack it successfully with a waggler.

Season – this runs from 1st March to 7th January.

Tickets – these cost £7 a day and are available from tackle shops in Southampton but it is best to phone the tremendously helpful fishery manager, John Dennis on 07973 523358 to book your ticket in advance. This must be done. John will also advise you on the best way into the estate when he sends you your ticket. He is a fund of information and very welcoming indeed. Do note that there are only twenty-five pegs and these fill up quickly, so do book well in advance. Also, on some Sundays clubs book the whole lake for matches.

Directions – pick up the A36 from junction 2 of the M27. At the first roundabout, take the A3090 north, and Broadlands is on your right shortly before you reach Romsey.

Accommodation – the Tourist Information Centres in Southampton, on 023 8022 1106, and Winchester, on 01962 840500, can give advice on suitable accommodation in the area.

Kennet and Avon Canal – Berkshire

Very different from the river itself, the Kennet and Avon canal still provides some great fishing, especially in the Hungerford area where the Hungerford Angling club controls two tremendous miles. It's the sort of water that appeals to all types of anglers – specimen hunters flock for the big carp that run to over twenty pounds but there are lots of small bream, good roach and very good perch to keep the average angler happy.

Canal carp can be a bit of a conundrum, and my own fish have only come after intensive stalking operations. You'll often find them hanging very close to cover, so do look under bushes, reed beds or moored boats. Again, my own successes have tended to come in the winter, when they're moving very slowly indeed. If you can locate a group of fish and feed very gently and tightly, you'll probably get one or two of them going down during the course of the day – especially in the later afternoon. Casters are good, but also try dyed and flavoured sweetcorn and small redworms.

As for perch on canals, try and get a lot of small fish feeding with light ground bait and a sprinkling of maggots and you'll draw the predators in. Then a small dead bait or lobworm will often be picked up.

Season – the basic season is June 16th to March 14th.

Tickets – these are available in advance from Howard's Pet Shop, Hungerford, on 01488 685314, or Field and Stream, Newbury, on 01635 43186. Day tickets are £3.

Directions – pick up the A338 from junction 14 of the M4. Head towards Hungerford. Once you reach the mini-roundabout, follow the sign for the town centre and pass under the railway bridge. Turn immediately right into Church Street and you'll find the canal.

Accommodation – phone the Tourist Information Centre in Newbury on 01635 30267. They will be able to supply details of accommodation available in the area.

The River Kennet

The River Kennet must appear in any discussion on fishing in the south. The problem for the coarse angler is that it is very difficult to gain access to most stretches. It's a crying shame, but this is a lovely river and it's not surprising that clubs and syndicates have jumped in to claim the best of the water. However, there are one or two opportunities, and the fishing can be a delight.

One of my own personal favourites is Aldermaston Mill in Berkshire, which I've visited several times, seen endless amounts of barbel, and have yet to have anything like a red letter day. Mind you, I realise that's my fault rather than any slur on the river. The key to the Kennet is to fish as differently as possible. If everyone is using ledgered meat, then try free-lining a tiny scrap of pepperami. Only one example, I know, and one that might not work, but I hope you get my point.

It's quite traditional to fish a stick float and caster over hemp close in to snags. This method certainly does hook a lot of fish, but you can have problems getting them out – especially with barbel over six pounds in weight. It's far better, I believe, to bait moderately lavishly close to a known barbel-holding snag and then simply wait. Always resist the temptation to fish at once, but let the barbel build up their confidence. Beware of putting bait in once they're out feeding – this can unsettle them. If you are going to introduce bait, do it well upstream, so that the splash doesn't scare them, and let it drift down to them.

SEASON – open 16th June to 14th March.

TICKETS – from the Old Mill, Aldermaston, RG7 4LB on 01189 712365. Day tickets cost around £8 and directions will be given. It's also worth a quick enquiry to the Wasing Estate to see if any season tickets are still available there. This is a tightly run, beautiful little syndicate and worth taking seriously if you really want to fish the area. Mind you, tickets are like gold dust but try phoning on 01189 714281. Also contact Tony Jenkinson on 01737 643821 regarding day tickets for the river at Bull's Lock and also Calpac associate membership, a steal at £32 and one that opens a whole new window on the river.

ACCOMMODATION – the Reading Tourist Information Centre, on 01189 566226, can advise on various types of accommodation in the area.

THE RIVER THAMES

Naturally enough, it's very difficult to pigeonhole the Thames into any one section of this book, simply because it passes through different counties on its way to the sea. However, the tidal Thames is a very different beast indeed, and away from the capital you've got some beautiful and very under-used fishing to explore. Mind you, exploration is very much the name of the game with much of the Thames.

The Thames is certainly a river with history. For centuries, it's been a major part of our angling heritage and has constantly made the headlines. Big barbel catches in the 19th century. A.E.Hobbs, the brown trout maestro of the early 20th century. Peter Stone's mammoth bream catches in the Oxford area in the 1950s. Strange then that the Thames should have drifted out of popularity for so long.

It's impossible in a book of this size to give a detailed introduction to the Thames – there's just too much of it, with too many permit holders, to make any sense whatsoever, so I'm going to concentrate on two of the most exciting lines of attack.

The first one is to contact Roger Wyndham Barnes, a professional guide on the river who concentrates on the stretch between Reading and Marlow. He's a perfect companion for the day and there is nothing he doesn't know about old Father Thames. A day out with Roger really is a wonderful experience. You'll probably be afloat in his large, comfortable boat, which is generally moored at the Compleat Angler Inn on Marlow weir. Roger will take you for whatever species you want, either in the weirs, on the main river or down in the backwaters. You could spend months, if not years, learning for yourself what Roger will teach you in a single day. Go on, treat yourself.

The other exciting way to tackle the Thames is to buy a permit for the locks and weirs on the river. The Environment Agency sells permits to eighteen Thames sites, including Buscot, Radcot, Sandford, Benson, Bell Weir and so on down the river.

The weirs are marvellous, thrilling places to fish. It's exciting just to get the key and be able to push through the gates marked 'Private'. You truly enter another world on a Thames weir pool.

You'll find virtually every fish swimming in British waters available to you. Barbel, chub, pike, roach, tench, bream, brown trout – you name it, the weir pools have it. Mind you, weir pool fishing isn't always easy. You've got to be able to read the water and fish the muscular currents effectively to get the best out of the experience. Once again, Polaroid glasses are essential: there will be times when you'll see fish in the shallower water and you can work out a plan of attack. Don't be afraid to be bold: big free-lined baits work well. Try two lobworms on a size six hook with perhaps a single SSG shot six inches up the line. Keep close contact with the bait as it trundles along the bottom, and don't allow slack to develop or you could miss that crucial tug.

Try stret-pegging. Sit upstream of the main flow and use a float set three or four feet over depth. In effect, you're ledgering, but the float allows you to lift the weight up every few seconds and let it resettle. It also gives you perfect bite indication and allows you to know exactly where your bait is working.

We're not just talking barbel and chub in this quick water: most of the weir pools have slack areas and here you can find tremendous tench working in the weeds. Early morning is the best time to be out for the tench, and most other species in fact, and that fresh period of the day only enhances the extraordinary beauty of the experience.

If you do take out a weir pool ticket I'm sure you will be inspired to explore more and more of the Thames, building up knowledge as you go. You'll meet river keepers who will give you tips and point you in the right direction. But the great thing about fishing the weirs is that you'll catch fish from the start, and that builds up confidence.

One of the joys of fishing the Thames is the total uncertainty of what you might catch next. Using a lobworm you could pick up a trout, a salmon, a barbel, a chub, a perch, a cracking roach, a huge dace, a tench, a bream, a carp, an eel, a flounder... I think you get the picture. And, what's more, there are some absolute crackers. The late, great Peter Stone caught most of his big fish from this river system and he always felt a thirty-pound river carp was just round the corner for him. Sadly, he didn't quite make it, but that was neither his fault nor this splendid river's. Piking from autumn through the winter can also be excellent.

SEASON – the Thames is currently under the blanket closed season of 14th March to 16th June, but this is under review.

TICKETS – contact Roger Wyndham Barnes at 4 Montreal Terrace, Twyford, Berks RG10 9ND or phone him on 01189 342981. The lock and weir fishing permit, available from the Environment Agency, must be applied for at least ten working days before required use. Write to the Environment Agency, PO Box 214, Reading, RG1 8HQ. Permits cost £21 for adults and £14 for seniors and juniors.

ACCOMMODATION – the Tourist Information Centre can supply details of accommodation in their area. Phone 01189 566226. Roger Wyndham Barnes will also advise on accommodation if you are spending the day with him.

Gold Valley Lakes – Hampshire

These are really beautiful waters – very well managed, surrounded by trees and holding excellent fish stocks. They've become very popular pleasure and match venues over the years and hardly surprisingly: even in cold weather, big bags can be built up. There's pretty well everything here, but ask advice from the fishery manager, who will locate the water most suited to your needs. There are good carp, excellent roach and the crucian fishing can be fantastic.

The carp are the major draw at Gold Valley, and it pays to bait heavily for them. If you skimp on food, then your catch will suffer. Remember that carp, especially in commercial fisheries, can be very greedy fish, so take enough feed with you.

Season – open all year.
Tickets – day tickets cost £10 for one rod and £15 if you're doubling up for the carp. Book them in advance on 01252 336333.
Directions – take the M3. At junction 4, turn onto the A331, heading south. After two miles or so, turn left towards the station. It is also signed Mytchett. When you come to the junction with the A321, turn right. At the next pub, turn right again, go under a low bridge and cross the dual carriageway. You'll find the lake signposted 'Spring Lakes Country Club'.
Accommodation – details of various kinds of accommodation can be obtained from the Tourist Information Centre in Aldershot on 01252 320968.

Highly Recommended Fisheries

- *Longleat, Warminster, Wiltshire. Famous old water in the grounds of a beautiful stately home. Three stream-fed estate lakes hold carp to over thirty pounds, big bream, tench, perch, roach and rudd. A lovely fishery. Phone 01985 844496 for further details.*
- *Todber Manor, Todber, Dorset. Very popular match water. Big bags of carp possible on sweetcorn, maggot, caster and bread. Some quality crucians. Phone 01258 820384.*
- *Golden Pond, Stockbridge, Hampshire. Some excellent roach, good carp fishing and a few exotics – the crucian fantail crosses are particularly spectacular. For more details call 01264 860813.*
- *Hightown Lake, Ringwood, Hampshire. Mature twenty-two acre pit – big carp (over thirty pounds), big pike, bream and tench to seven pounds. Attractive water with some excellent fish. Tickets £7.50 a day. Phone 01425 471466.*

Coarse-Fishing Sites in The South East

1. *Rushmoor Lake*
2. *Bury Hill Fisheries*
3. *Tring Reservoirs*
4. *North Met Pit*
5. *Lake John Fishery*
6. *The River Lea*
7. *The Fennes Fishery*
8. *London's Parks*
9. *Wylands International Angling Centre*

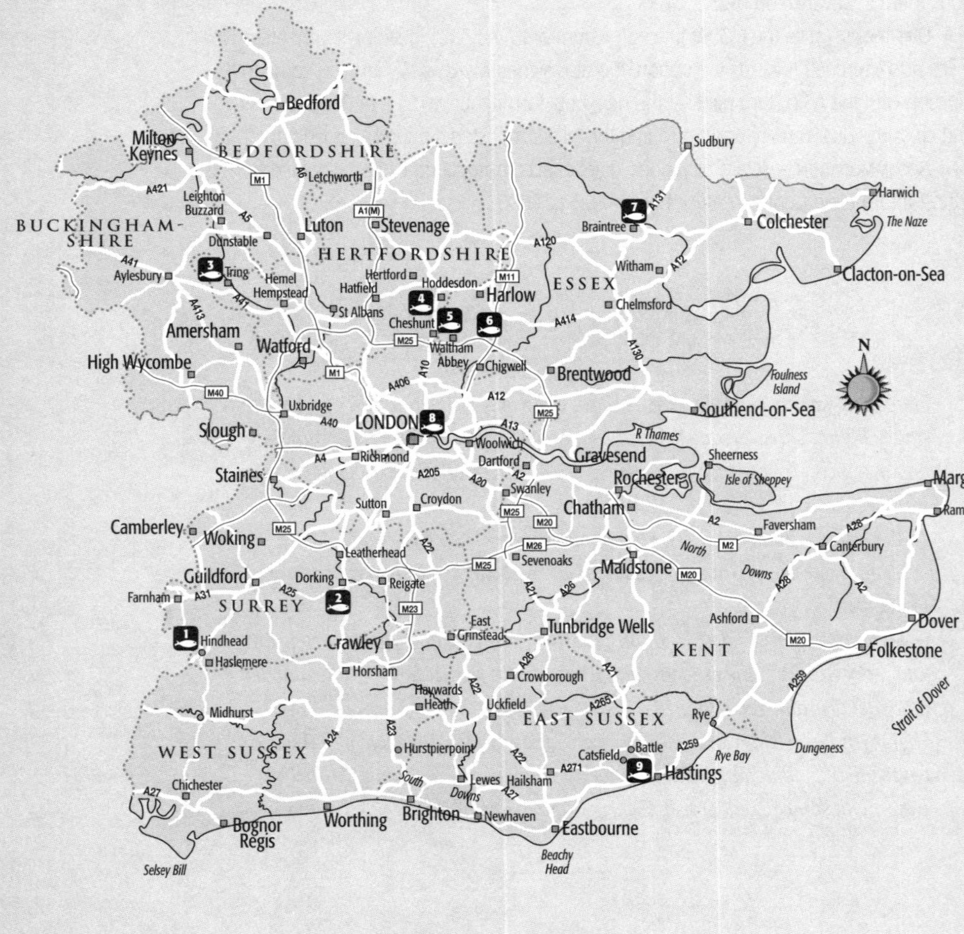

A lot of the fishing hereabouts in the Greater London area might not be of the most attractive sort if it's just rolling valleys and mountains you're into, but believe me, John, there are some real whackers to be caught.

MARTIN LOCKE, BAIT AND TACKLE SPECIALIST AND FAMOUS CARP ANGLER

And Martin was right. I suppose in the main he was talking about the great featureless gravel pits where people like him are quite willing to sit and wait a season out for a single run and to land the fish of their dreams. I haven't really included waters like this in this section – if these are the fish you want, you'll know exactly where to go yourself. Perhaps I haven't talked much about fifty-pound carp waters, but there's still a great deal that is of interest. You can catch barbel to double figures virtually within sight and sound of the M25. Or you can catch double-figure zander down in Surrey, along with huge pike. And how about the massive bream, roach and even catfish up at Tring? The Thames itself is on the way back and needs some investigation. Remember that huge stretches around the city can be fished for free and now hold endless number of species. So, all in all, the lot of the Londoner isn't that bad at all, and if you're here visiting, then you can have the best of both worlds: Europe's most dazzling city together with somewhere to cast a line, often only a tube journey away.

Many of the waters in the south-eastern area are comparatively crowded and noisy, but not all of them by any means. Some of my very best stations ever were spent on Tring Reservoirs – Wilston in particular. These were magical times, and camping in the woods was a true delight. The bream weren't always obliging, but when they moved in, the excitement was intense. Big fish rolling, breaking the water under the moonlight – the bobbins never still as the line is continually brushed by the big, bronzed bodies. And then, a bite... the bobbin screeching to the rod butt, the reel beginning to backwind. A strike. An enormous resistance and then a blow on the rod tip as though a bag of cement has buried it. Great days indeed, in a fabulous setting.

RUSHMOOR LAKE – SURREY

Rushmoor Lake is a beautiful water and absolutely ideal for beginners – the sort of place the family can have a very happy day out. It's a small water of around an acre, generally shallow, but dipping in places down to seven or eight feet. It's set in attractive countryside and the bird life is tremendous. It's mature, well established and it really gives you the feeling of being away from the town. The car park is close by, so you can set out the picnic things as well.

There are carp and bream running to six or eight pounds or so, but most of the fish present are just a few ounces up to a pound. These include tench, chub and crucian carp. There are also golden orfe, koi and all manner of exotics – the sort of species that really bring smiles to young faces. And because there are plenty of fish, the water is clouded and the fishing isn't too difficult. Big fish aren't the order of the day here, so you won't find the bivvies and the bite indicators that mar so many other waters. No, this is a friendly, well-looked-after little water that's ideal for the beginner.

All baits work well, but probably casters and maggots are as good as anything to build up a good mixed bag. Fish them under a float, and remember that no keep nets are allowed and you can only use barbless hooks – two ideal rules for novices.

SEASON – open all year round.
TICKETS – only eight day tickets per day are issued on this small water and they must be bought in advance at the Post Office in Rushmore itself. Contact Dennis Smaile on 01252 793698. The nearby tackle shop, Greyshot Tackle, can also give advice on 01428 606122.
DIRECTIONS – from the A31, turn right at Hindhead traffic lights. After some quarter of a mile, turn right and look for the Pride of Valley pub, which is on the left. The entrance to the lake is about a quarter of a mile past the pub on the right.
ACCOMMODATION – the Tourist Information Centre in Guildford, on 01483 444333, can advise on accommodation in the area.

BURY HILL FISHERIES – SURREY

Bury Hill has long been one of the really revered waters on the big fish circuit, and I remember years ago being in awe of the galaxy of famous anglers that trekked to its banks. Mind you, Bury Hill offers more than big fish alone: it's beautiful, it's friendly, there's plenty of advice on hand and there are fish galore. But let's look at everything in a little bit more detail.

In my early days, Bury Hill consisted of just one large, twelve-and-a-half-acre lake, the water that is now known as Old Bury Hill. This is still a magnificent water, and although it offers seventy or so pegs, there are still plenty of opportunities to get away from any semblance of a crowd. Try booking a punt and getting up into the Jungle– an overgrown area that's inaccessible from the bank. The tench and carp fishing there can be excellent, with big specimens of both species. Eight- and even nine-pound tench are not unknown! Try fishing close to obstructions – reeds, trailing branches and the like – with a float and corn or pellets. Mind you, you've got to use heavy gear because these fish are big, they fight well and the Jungle looks exactly as it sounds.

If you can't get up to the Jungle, don't despair. The Boathouse, which is the deepest part of the lake at around twelve feet, produces some tremendous bags of tench. I also like the Front Bank, where the bottom shallows to only a couple of feet or so. It's quite possible to stalk fish there, and there isn't a more exciting way of fishing.

Old Bury Hill fishes well from spring onwards. You've got everything to go at – bream to ten pounds, tench to nine pounds, crucians to five pounds, good roach, big rudd and perch that can top the three-pound mark. Just think – cast out a big juicy lobworm and you've got every chance of catching a specimen fish of at least six different species. Incredible. Mind you, Old Bury Hill does benefit from a careful approach. Look for your fish, think how you're going to fish and devise a good plan of attack. Why not bait up two patches so that you can look for fish moving in? Try an over-depth waggler and twitch it back along the bottom. Straight sweetcorn is a great bait, but try grains that are flavoured and coloured. Black is one of my own personal favourites. Try natural baits; any sort of worm can bring an instant bite.

From the autumn onwards, Old Bury Hill moves into its predator mode and there is some of the best zander fishing in the country to be found here. And the pike fishing isn't bad either! Stocks of both fish are extensive, and you can expect zander into double figures and pike over twenty pounds if you're lucky.

The zander themselves are a great challenge. Sometimes you can get steaming runs from them, but if there's the slightest hint of resistance, your bait will be dropped like a hot brick, so fish carefully, sensitively and intelligently. The Island is great for zander packs and you can't beat the Jungle for big, roaming pike. If you haven't caught anything throughout the day, don't pack up early because the last couple of hours are particularly good, especially for the zander. And if you're still struggling, try to get your small dead bait as close into the snags as possible – always bearing in mind that you've got a duty to pull the fish out! Don't go light for predators either. Twelve- or even fifteen-pound line is a must.

Ten years or so ago, another couple of lakes were constructed on the site – Bond's Lake and Milton Lake. Bond's is a popular match water, but it's also great for children as it's absolutely packed with smaller fish and it really is the place to get a good number of bites. The carp aren't huge – up to about ten pounds or so – but they fight well and they come along in great shoals.

Milton Lake is something a bit more special. It's got some really first-class crucian carp fishing. And crucians really are one of my own favourite summer species. They're just so enticing. How do you convert those bites into fish hit? It's possible to get a dozen crucian bites and not hook a single one. It's even possible not to know you've even had the bites in the first place. For that reason, set up a float rig as sensitively as you possibly can. It also makes sense to fish close in – especially under any sort of cover. Crucians are very much margin feeders but they don't like to expose themselves to the sun's rays. Bait up carefully for crucians. A little mashed hemp seed drives them crazy. Try a single pink maggot on the hook. A pinch of breadflake is also good.

Bury Hill gives you the whole package – car parks, shops, toilets, cafés, resident bailiffs and even fishing instruction. Highly recommended.

SEASON – Bury Hill is open all year round, apart from Christmas Day.
TICKETS – these are available from Bury Hill Fisheries, Estate Office, Old Bury Hill, Dorking, Surrey RH4 3JU, or phone 01306 88833621. Rods cost £9 for the day with juniors, senior citizens and disabled coming in at £5. There are also evening tickets available. Boats are attractively priced at £5 per person.
DIRECTIONS – Bury Hill Fisheries is just off the A25 Dorking to Guildford road. It is less than a mile from Dorking town centre. Leave the town and you will see the fishery clearly signed on the right. There's a brown tourist sign advertising it.
ACCOMMODATION – the Tourist Information Centre in Guildford, on 01483 444333, will be able to advise on accommodation in the area.

TRING RESERVOIRS

Over the past twenty years or so Tring Reservoirs – that is Wilstone, Startops and Marsworth – have built up a reputation as big fish waters. Indeed, during my time on them, it was big or bust – generally in those days, with limited techniques, tackle and baits, it was bust! Today, you'll still find a lot of long stay anglers who are pursuing the big bream, massive tench, elusive catfish and increasing numbers of carp. There are also very big roach, especially in Startops. These anglers are prepared to sit for virtually a season, fishing hard for potentially mind-blowing rewards.

However, the Tring system is often overlooked by the more casual anglers in favour of the smaller commercial fisheries. This is a great shame. All three reservoirs are very lovely – my own favourites being Wilstone and Marsworth. They're set in lovely countryside with quality fish. Moreover, on Startops especially, if you contact the roach and perch you will be catching fish of a pound or so in succession.

SEASON – open all year round.
TICKETS – contact Bernard Double, the excellent bailiff, on 01442 822379. Day tickets cost under £5 – very reasonable for the stamp of fishing available.
DIRECTIONS – the Tring group of reservoirs is found just north of Tring. Take the A41 west and in a couple of miles turn right onto the B489. The reservoirs will be in a mile or so on the right hand side. The car parks will be signposted.
ACCOMMODATION – the Tourist Information Centres in Aylesbury, on 01296 330559, and Hemel Hempstead, on 01442 234222, can advise on accommodation in the area.

North Met Pit – Hertfordshire

I'm moving a bit off normal territory here to talk about a season ticket water as opposed to a water available to the casual angler. I'm making this exception because North Met Pit, a mature gravel pit controlled by Lee Valley Parks, really is well worth investigating. This whole area is a maze of water, set in unspoilt countryside close to the M25. It's a real jewel.

North Met Pit itself extends to virtually sixty acres and holds some very big fish. The carp can get to forty pounds and average in the mid-twenties. The bream reach double figures, and the tench aren't far behind. There are good perch and roach too.

These big gravel pits take quite a bit of reading, and perhaps they're not waters for the out and out beginner. Most carp fall to traditional tactics – boilies, buzzers and so on. Bait quite heavily, because there are numbers of big fish in the water, but always be prepared to move if you're not getting action. Remember that carp on big waters such as this do tend to follow the wind and it's not unusual to see anglers, gear in wheelbarrows, on the move as the wind swings round in serious fashion.

North Met is an attractive water studded with islands, bays and bars with plateaux. It's a snaggy water too, and can be weedy in summer. In short, it's a water for the tactician, the man who's prepared to put in his research, do his homework and get things absolutely right.

As it's such a big carp venue, the bream, tench and roach tend to be overlooked somewhat, but sport can be really good on swim feeder maggots. Also expect the odd carp to come along as well, falling for a tactic that's different. There are plenty of tench in the water, so you're not really sticking your neck out. You can expect three or four fish a session comfortably, and some of these could well be big ones.

The big pit scene isn't for everyone and it does demand a certain level of expertise, but once you're into it, it's a difficult obsession to let go. The fish are big and they're generally in top condition. North Met Pit does offer a very attractive, comparatively accessible way into the big pit scene. The south east is studded with these waters – Yateley, Darenth and so on – and it's tempting to go in at the very top of the ladder. Don't. Go for a water that's attractive, has a big head of fish and isn't too difficult.

The problem is that if you go for one of the very difficult waters it's not at all unusual to have an entire season there without a single fish to your credit. Even a bite is seen as a triumph. Save this type of ordeal for later.

Season – open all year round.

Tickets – North Met Pit, Cheshunt, Hertfordshire, on 01992 709962. Tickets cost from £75 a season downwards, according to number of rods and concessions.

Directions – take the A10 towards Cheshunt. Turn off into Cheshunt and join the B176. Heading towards the station, access can either be through Windmill Lane or Cadmoor Lane. You'll also find car parks accessible from the B194 at Fishers Green.

Accommodation – call Hertford Tourist Information Centre on 01992 584322 for details.

Lake John Fishery – Essex

This is another water just north of the M25, which is an absolute must for a fishing-mad youngster. In fact, there are two lakes available for fishing here. The lower lake is shallow, can accommodate about twenty anglers and is very heavily stocked. The water holds carp, tench, roach, rudd, bream, perch and chub. There are some good fish, too, with carp just into double figures, bream to five or six pounds, tench to three pounds and roach and rudd nudging the one pound mark. And they're all quality fish, too. One of the nice things about the fishery is that the manager, Colin Bartlett, is always round and about, offering

Long distance Feeder

When you're fishing reservoirs, big pits and large lakes, the long distance feeder is a really useful technique for bream, tench, roach and even carp.

- *Decide on what feeder you are going to use. If it's a closed feeder, you're probably going to be using maggots as both loose feed and hook baits. With an open feeder, you can mix a firm ground bait up and work in all sorts of particle baits such as casters and sweetcorn.*
- *A closed feeder is particularly good in the winter, in clear water when the fish are picky and you're not expecting many bites.*
- *A big, open feeder probably works better in the summer when the water is warm and you're expecting more activity. However, remember, there are no hard and fast rules in fishing.*
- *Decide on your bite indication. You can either use a quiver tip rod, a swing tip or some kind of butt indication. Quiver tipping is big at the moment but butt indication can work better if the fish are very finicky.*
- *If bites are not materialising properly, think about your hook length. Lengthening it – even to four or five feet – can work wonders.*
- *Be accurate with your casting. There is no point casting as far as you can each time if your direction is wayward. You won't build up a baited patch that way. Don't strive for distance until you have accuracy sorted out.*
- *Don't go too light on your main line. Remember that punching out a feeder all day long exerts great strain on your tackle.*
- *There are all manner of complicated feeder rigs in the press at the moment. Choose a simple one to begin with that isn't too complicated to tie up. Don't make life more complex than it needs to be.*
- *Don't keep fish in keep nets unless you really have to, for example, fishing a match. This is especially important in the summer when oxygen levels are low.*

advice and just keeping his eye on the children's safety. This gives the place a friendly feel and makes it an ideal starting ground for kids. Mind you, it isn't too bad for Mum or Dad either!

The top lake is somewhat deeper, going down to around ten feet. Every day, good catches of carp and tench are put together, especially if you fish neatly and tightly, perhaps under a float with sweetcorn or small cubes of meat. Maggots also work well, but the fish aren't stupid and you've got to approach them carefully. The top lake also produces the odd big fish, and you'll see twenty pounders cruising and occasionally caught. All in all, a really well thought out and worthwhile little fishery that offers a great deal of scope for the angler who is climbing the fishing ladder.

SEASON – open all year round.
TICKETS – these cost £4 for half a day and £6 for a full day. Call Colin Bartlett on 0958 938153. Barbed hooks are not allowed and keep nets can only be used in matches (and then they have to be disinfected first). Another nice touch is that boilies too are banned.
DIRECTIONS – from Waltham Abbey, take the A121 eastwards as far as the Crooked Mile roundabout. Take the second exit towards Upshire. Turn left into Galley Hill Road and continue for a mile until you reach Aimes Green. Turn left and follow the road to the fishery.
ACCOMMODATION – contact the Tourist Information Centre in Waltham Abbey, on 01992 652295, who can supply details of accommodation in the area.

THE RIVER LEA

This, of course, is the famous river of Isaak Walton's *Compleat Angler* and even today, hundreds of years down the line, it has some very interesting fishing on offer. The Lea flows through Bedfordshire and Hertfordshire and then along the boundary between Essex and Middlesex before it joins the Thames. It's forty-six miles long and urbanization and the creation of canals have destroyed a great deal of what Walton would have recognised back in the 17th century. Nevertheless, the river still holds good carp, bream and roach – especially where there are canals – and very impressive barbel and chub in those stretches that are still freely flowing. Whilst there are barbel now well up in Hertfordshire, it's probably King's Weir Fishery that most people have heard of and this is the most famous piece of the river today. The fishery combines both the pool and a good few hundred yards down river. It's a cracking place, and even if it's not quite what it once was, you still have to book in advance.

The king of the Lea is Fred Crouch, a true gentleman and an excellent barbel fisherman. It's his opinion that the pool won't produce the same bags as it did in the past, but it's still an inspiring place to fish. Fred's tips are to put in a good amount of loose feed with either a feeder or a bait dropper and, as he says, 'Invite them out of the snags to feed'. Fred's favourite baits for the Lea are maggots, hemp and luncheon meat, but chopped into very tiny cubes indeed so the fish aren't alarmed. After baiting up, Fred likes to leave the swim for an hour, if not two, so the barbel really do move onto the feed and become confident. The problem with fishing immediately is that if they even feel the line, they'll be off, running for sanctuary. So don't rush things. Also don't neglect getting your bait very close in to the side. Remember that barbel love to have the bank at their backs.

A good example of the other side of the Lea is at Enfield Lock in Middlesex. Like much of the river, this lock section is now run by the Lea Angler's Consortium, who have initiated a major stocking programme in recent years. Carp are now the main culprits but big tench are present. The marshes north of the lock are famed for tench, bream, chub and some of the bigger carp. South of the lock, behind the Riffles pub, there are pike – some of them good ones. Pole fishing off the high wall in front of the pub is also popular for perch, roach and so on. Overall, sweetcorn, maggots, worms, hemp, boilies and humble breadflake are the baits that work here.

Two venues on the Lea to tempt you. If the river grabs your affections – and there's no reason why it shouldn't – then you'll want to begin exploring and finding new stretches. Much of it is private but a good deal is available on day ticket.

SEASON – as I write, the closed season on rivers still remains 14th March to 16th June. This writer hopes the closed season is maintained.

TICKETS – for King's Weir Fishery phone 01992 468394 to book day tickets in advance. These are £7 and rules include no wading, no boilies or live baits. It's also compulsory to have unhooking mats with you and remember no barbel – or any species come to that – can be put into keep nets. Day tickets at Enfield Lock cost £3. Call 01279 654434 for details.

DIRECTIONS – King's Weir is situated at Wormley, just north of Waltham Cross. To find Enfield Lock, turn off the A10 into Ordinance Road. Follow this past the level crossing to the main lights and go past the pub. Parking is available on the street next to the canal.

ACCOMMODATION – the Tourist Information Centre in Waltham Abbey, on 01992 652295, hold details of accommodation in the area.

THE FENNES FISHERY – ESSEX

The Fennes is one of the largest coarse fishing complexes in Essex and offers nearly fifteen acres of water, split between three spring-fed lakes. It's an attractive place to fish and the waters were originally excavated from flood meadows and now bear the name of the fields that preceeded them. It's a well thought out fishing complex. There's a shop, café, good car parking and plenty of really sound advice so there's no need whatsoever to feel left out in the cold here. There's one thing about commercial fisheries – they need satisfied customers to succeed and at Fennes you get all the help you and your family, want. But let's look at the lakes.

At around six acres, Ash Grounds is probably the largest lake, and it's also the oldest. It's heavily stocked with all species of carp including ghosts and crucians. And what fish they are. You'll find some really tremendous individual specimens, testimony to the fishery's advanced stocking policy. There are good stocks also of tench, bream, roach and a few rudd. The average carp here aren't that large – fish of around ten pounds are to be expected. The bream run up to nine pounds though, and the best perch is just a shade under four pounds.

Carp

The South East really is the carp man's Mecca. The proliferation of gravel pit fisheries appearing over the last thirty or forty years has meant that there is an endless number of venues now available, and many of the fish in them are very big. Thirty-pounders are now relatively commonplace, whilst forties and even fifties are no longer the stuff of dreams. Mind you, this isn't easy fishing.

- *Read all you can about carp fishing before starting out. There's an extensive literature, so select the right book for your present level.*
- *Try to get as much information on your chosen water as possible. This is not always easy, but you will find some anglers and tackle dealers willing to help.*
- *Don't spend too much money on gear until you're quite sure you like the sport.*
- *Don't go in for very long stay sessions until you're more experienced. Your first days at the waterside ought to be measured in hours rather than days or weeks.*
- *You'll probably start off by using a bolt-rigged boily setup. It makes sense to buy shop-bought baits at first. Don't complicate your fishing by making your own. It's wise to start at a smaller commercial fishery where there are plenty of medium-sized fish. This way, you gain experience of carp behaviour and how they fight. Don't begin at the top rung of the ladder. Chances are you won't get a bite, and if you do hook a fish, it will be too big and powerful for your experience.*
- *Even though I don't recommend very expensive tackle to begin with, you have a duty to the fish to make sure it is sound and won't let you down in a fight.*
- *Remember that once you've landed a carp you really do have to look after it, in part because it is a very expensive item for the fishery owner. Always lay it on an unhooking mat and get it back in the water as quickly as you possibly can, perhaps after an admiring glance and a quick photograph.*
- *Join the Carp Society (01367 253959) and go to their regional meetings. Here you'll find like-minded carp fanatics who are willing to pass on advice.*
- *Don't be intimidated. The carp world initially seems one riddled with secrets and superstars. Take your time and the knowledge will begin to come.*

Ash Grounds is a natural water with islands and plenty of marginal reeds, including reed mace, bulrushes and water lilies. Obviously, all this shelter gives the angler a lot of target areas where he can either use a pole or a running line. But, as ever, make sure that your tackle is up to the job.

All normal baits work – sweetcorn, luncheon meat and maggots – and don't overlook floating baits for the carp. As winter pulls in, most of the fish tend to migrate towards the deeper water close to the car park but it's always worth walking the lake, even in the depths of winter, to see what's working in the shallows.

Hobb's Croft Lake is between three and four acres in extent and has a cracking head of carp, several running to just over the twenty pound mark. There are good heads of bream and tench also approaching seven pounds and, once again, there are good crucians, roach and perch. Most of the lake is shallow – about three feet or so – but there is a deeper section where the depth plummets to eight. This shallow water means that float fishing is generally the favoured line of attack.

Hill and Black Lake is a little way from the main complex and isn't always available, as it's hired out for matches. Mind you, when it isn't, try and get on there, because there really is a very big head of good fish in the water. Particularly interesting are the tench. They grow big and they're very powerful. Never neglect surface fishing in the summer here – it's a brilliant top-bait water.

SEASON – the Fennes is open from 7.30am until sunset, all year round with the exception of Christmas Day and Boxing Day.

TICKETS – apply to the Fennes Fisheries, Fennes Road, Bocking, Braintree, Essex CM7 5LB, on 01376 323285. Day tickets are £6 for adults and £4 for juniors. Evening tickets are available.

DIRECTIONS – heading towards Sudbury along the A131 from Braintree, turn off into Bocking Church Street, you will be directed by the brown Tourist Board signs. The fishery is then signposted half a mile down Fennes Road, which is a right turn by the village hall. Once again, you will see the brown Tourist Board signs. The car park and the two main lakes are on the left four hundred yards down a concrete road.

ACCOMMODATION – contact the Tourist Information Centre in Braintree, on 01376 550066. They can supply details of various kinds of accommodation in the area.

LONDON'S PARKS

There can't be a capital city in the world offering as many park and common pools as London. We tend to overlook how many green spaces there are within the M25 belt, and most of these have fishing available of one sort or another. For example, there are Pen Ponds in Richmond Park, Perch Pond and Hollow Ponds, the Ornamental Water and the Wake Valley Pond all in Epping Forest. We've got the Leg of Mutton Pond, the Rick Pond, Diana Pond, Heron Pond and

the Long Water all in the Royal Parks. There are the free ponds on commons such as Clapham and Tooting, for example, and that's just scraping the surface.

Of course, not all of the ponds offer top-rate fishing but you'd be surprised at the varieties and quality of the fish available. However, you've got to remember that these are very public places and there are periods when it is wise to avoid them. For example, a Bank Holiday Monday is not the best time to be on one of the commons. Night fishing might sound the ideal option but I've had my own scares on the commons in the past and would certainly advise against it – even in permitted places. At the very least, go with a couple of friends.

If I have to give one time when it's best to be out on these waters it must be the very early morning – preferably when the dew is still about. This is when you'll see the London parks and commons at their best anyway and you'll be amazed at the amount of wildlife tripping past, or leaving signs in the dew. This is when the fish are feeding at their best. Even though most of these are not particularly big waters, do take the time to walk round them and don't rush into settling on a swim. If possible, look for feeding fish. Sweetcorn is a good general bait and so too are maggots. Take a loaf with you perhaps, and scatter a few pieces of crust in the margins and you'll be surprised at what will come up: I once had a one-and-three-quarter-pound crucian from Clapham Common on a floating dog biscuit!

The size of that crucian carp shouldn't come as a surprise: there are some pretty hefty fish in these park lakes, far bigger than one would expect. Perch, at least until relatively recently, could grow large, and there are some very big tench about. Even if you don't see carp, that doesn't mean to say that they're not present. It's more likely that they've learned to lie low. There are occasional stray big pike too, and I have an inkling that you could be in for a surprise if you tried a bit of eel fishing. All in all, these are very handy waters and there are some that should be taken seriously.

SEASON – the contact numbers will advise.

TICKETS – for Pen Pond, contact the Park Superintendent on 020 8948 3209. For Perch Pond, Hollow Ponds, the Ornamental Pond and Wake Valley Pond, contact the Superintendent on 020 8532 1010. For the other ponds in the Royal Parks, contact the Garden and Estate Manager on 020 8781 9610.

WYLANDS INTERNATIONAL ANGLING CENTRE – EAST SUSSEX

Wylands is a super place, either for the individual angler or the whole family. There are well over a hundred and fifty acres of rural countryside to be enjoyed – water, woodland and pasture. There are specialist carp lakes and general waters where you can just about catch anything that swims. There's also the county's largest single match lake, which again heaves with fish. Wylands really

is proof that a commercial fishery can settle naturally into the landscape and be of huge benefit to both fishermen and wildlife in general. It's a perfect holiday destination – there's on-site accommodation in self-catering chalets, touring caravans and there's a campsite available if you want to bring your own tent. The snack bar is well stocked and the woodland walks are a treat.

The new Specimen Lake is only about two acres in size but there's a large island and a natural feel to the place. Carp reach well into the twenty pound mark and there are some big rudd and tench. Kell Lake and House Lake also hold big carp. In fact, there are a total of five lakes in the complex where twenty-pounders can be anticipated.

Field Lake is an absolute beauty, only about an acre in size but heavily stocked with small carp and tench – fish averaging between one and three pounds. Exactly the sort of place to bring on a budding juvenile angler or two while father or mother enjoy themselves hugely. And if you want to get very traditional, there's Roses Lakes. There are no carp in here and therefore none of the internal bleeping of optonics that you come to expect on so many waters. In fact, only pole, float and feeder fishing are allowed for the extensive stocks of tench, roach and rudd. A lovely little place – new but settled nicely into the landscape.

These commercial fisheries, as I've said before, really fill a niche and it would be a mistake to think of them as being too easy. These are waters that allow you to enter at any level. Kell Lake, in particular, really does set a challenge to even a skilled carp angler. On the other hand, if you've barely held a rod in your hand before, you're still going to get bites and action.

SEASON – open all year round, twenty-four hours a day.

TICKETS – contact Wylands International Angling Centre, Powdermill Lane, Catsfield, Nr. Battle, East Sussex TN33 0SU, on 01424 893394. Day tickets vary but are on average between £6 and £7 per day with concessions for juniors.

DIRECTIONS – from Battle take the A271 westwards. Two or three miles from the town turn left onto the B2204 to Catsfield. In Catsfield, turn into Powdermill Lane and pass the Burntwood Hotel. Fifty yards further on you come to an open field with a wooden fence. At the end of the field turn into Wylands Farm Drive. It is well signposted.

ACCOMMODATION – you cannot do better, when fishing, than to live on site, and the chalets at Wylands are excellent. Phone for details. Alternatively phone the Tourist Information Centre in Battle on 01424 773721 for details of other accommodation in the area.

Highly Recommended Fisheries

- *Wylands Farm, Battle, Sussex. Four specialist carp lakes and four multi-species lakes – ideal for novice and experienced angler alike. Carp to over twenty pounds, good tench, roach, rudd and bream. Also crucians. Contact Colin Bouner on 01424 893394.*
- *Northlands Park, Felmores, Essex. There are two main lakes here incorporating a conservation area. Plenty of bream in the two- to five-pound bracket. Quiver tip with sweetcorn. Good carp to twenty pounds, roach, tench and big perch. Also some big pike. Tickets £3. Contact Mick Toomer on 01268 282317.*
- *Birds Green Lakes, Fyfield, Essex. A four lake complex beside the river Roding. Good carp fishing, bream to eight pounds and some big tench. One lake holds large carp to thirty pounds plus. Something for everybody. Contact Philip Gadd on 01277 899645.*
- *Jacks Lake, New Barnet, Hertfordshire. Carp to twenty pounds taken on boilies and floaters. Pole fishing for roach, tench, skimmers and crucians. Day tickets £4. Contact Mick Hanley on 020 8364 8009 for further details.*

Coarse-Fishing Sites in East Anglia

1. Earith Lakes
2. Northey Park
3. The Fens
4. Glen Mere Lakes
5. Bure Valley Lakes
6. Blickling Lake
7. Gunton Park Lake
8. Great Witchingham Lakes and River Wensum
9. Woodrising Water Meadows
10. Hickling Broad
11. Fritton Lake
12. Yew Tree Lakes
13. Alton Water
14. Ardleigh Reservoir

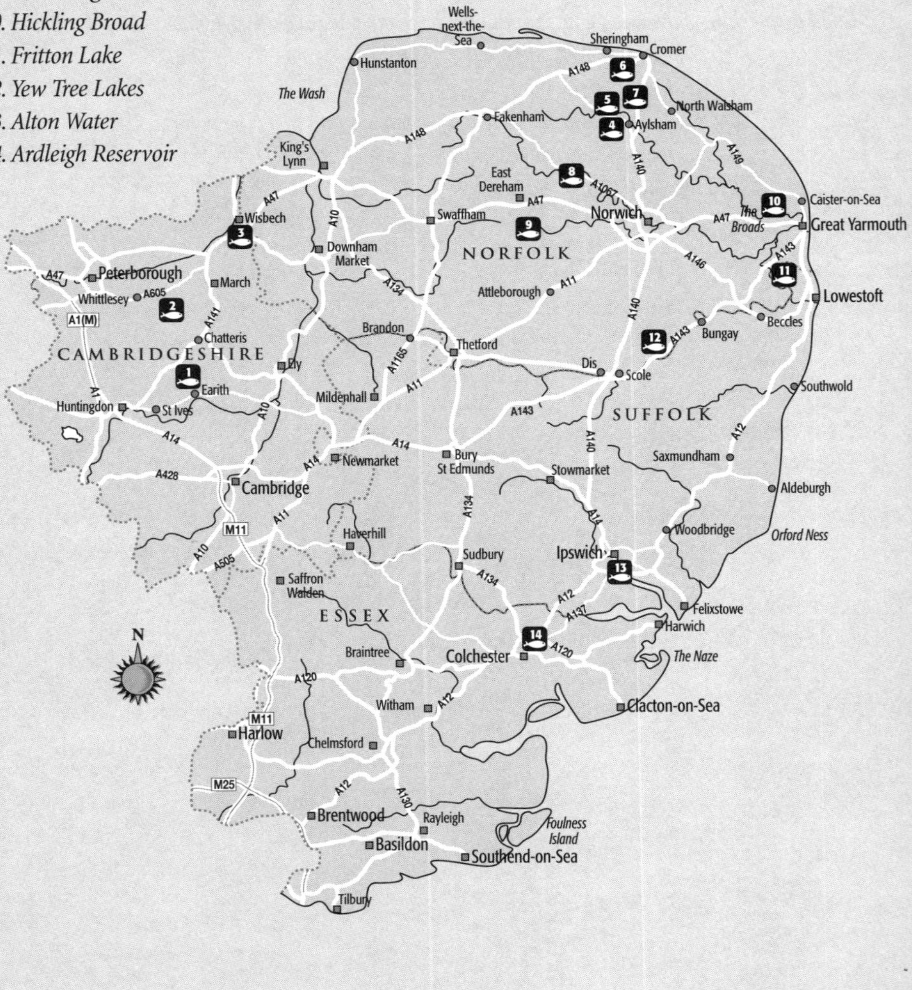

'You ask why I've moved down to Norfolk from Yorkshire, John? Well, here you've got the bloomin' lot. You've got so many different fish species and just look at the sizes they grow to. And some beautiful waters. I'm not saying I didn't have fun up north – and that's where I learnt my trade, I know – but there are few places to compete with what you've got down here in East Anglia.'

DAVE PLUMMER, AUTHOR AND HOLIDAY CONSULTANT, IN CONVERSATION WITH THE AUTHOR

And Dave was, of course, right. I first began to fish in East Anglia when I was a mere five years old and even then I realised how spectacular the fishing was. After all, what does the area not have? You can fish huge, reed-margined, serene broads. Or there are the rivers, some tidal, some fast flowing over chalk bottoms. You can investigate the growing number of gravel pits around the region. And every farm seems to have its own marl pit or pond. And then let's not forget the glory of the estate lakes. In North Norfolk , in particular, there is a string of impressive halls from the west to the east, and each one has its own carefully-sculptured lake. And if that's not enough, you can even take your pike gear, charter a boat from any one of a number of small ports and go a few miles off shore to fish for summer tope. Or, come to that, you can walk the shore line with a simple spinning outfit and catch yourself a bass or two.

And big fish abound. Over the years, the eastern counties have held the pike record, the rudd record, the bream record, and the zander record, and they've come close with both eels and roach.

East Anglia constantly springs surprises, even on those who have known it a lifetime. For example, in the centre of Norwich itself you can occasionally come across a big sea trout fresh up from the coast. Or how about the coastland marshes, frequently flooded but still capable of holding extraordinary tench, rudd, roach and pike?

Dave Plumber is definitely right. We do have the bloomin' lot!

Earith Lakes – Cambridgeshire

We are talking about a commercial fishery here, but one that has matured and holds good fish stocks. There are three lakes available, all on day tickets. They all hold good numbers of very nice carp. Mind you, Earith isn't simply a carp water. One of them, George's Water, although small, holds rudd approaching two pounds, and Pat's Pool, again small, holds tench well over seven pounds. The largest water, Pingree's Pool, holds good fish of many species, and there's even a rumour that there are decent perch about. These three small but charming waters are a delight to fish – there's a multitude of fish-holding features to look for, and bear in mind that the big tench will often cruise the margins. There's nothing more exciting than fishing a float under the rod tip and watching the bubbles fizz to the surface. Alternatively, try a very light feeder on one of the many gravel bars.

All the usual baits work here but tench, in particular, enjoy a little feast of casters. Switch to mini boilies, perhaps, and you also stand a chance of picking up one or two of the very fine carp. You'll enjoy Earith: there's a nice welcoming atmosphere, the surroundings are lovely and the fish really are in the best of condition. Perhaps that's something to do with the rules: you can only use barbless hooks; no carp or tench can be put in keep nets; you're expected to lay out an unhooking mat; and nuts are banned as baits – all good signs that the fishery is carefully watched over.

Season – open all year.

Tickets – these are available on site at £6 with some concessions for Senior Citizens and juniors. Phone 01487 740701 for further details. Tickets need to be pre-booked.

Directions – from St. Ives, take the A1123 eastwards. You will shortly come to Earith village. Take the B1050 on the left. Take the second left and then the first left down the Earith Fen Drove. Car parking is on the left.

Accommodation – contact the Tourist Information Centre in Huntingdon on 01480 388588 for details of accommodation in the area.

Northey Park – Peterborough

Those that live around Peterborough sometimes lament about the quality of fishing, but with the opening of Northey Park – a three-lake complex – they've got something special now. These were originally gravel pits, but they've been left untouched for nearly thirty years and have matured magnificently. Today, they are reed-fringed and look as mature as any estate lake.

Rudd are the main species – a very overlooked fish in this day and age. The heavy stocking with carp in so many waters has tended to push rudd to the very fringes of existence in many areas. A tragedy, especially when you fish a place like Northey and see just what beautiful fish they are.

The rudd here, unfished for so long, are not particularly canny – yet! You can take them on a waggler outfit with corn, flake or maggots. There are some good fish and, although keep nets are allowed, do remember that rudd are fragile. My own advice is always to return them immediately after an admiring look. Feeder tactics will also work and why not drift out some floating bread and watch the shoals hammer into that. If you've got some casters that have gone off, let them float down with the breeze as well, and chances are that you'll see some cracking rudd come to the surface. In short, this is just the place to make you realise that the present day fixation with carp, barbel and pike is a blinkered one.

SEASON – open all year round.
TICKETS – day tickets cost £5 on the bank. Contact 01733 558329 for further details.
DIRECTIONS – Northey Park is situated on the Northey Road, Fengate, Peterborough off the A1139, but it is advisable to contact the fishery for detailed directions.
ACCOMMODATION – try the Peterborough Tourist Information Centre on 01733 452336 for details of suitable accommodation.

THE FENS

To be quite honest, I've never personally really come to grips with the Fens, so I suppose I'm dubious about recommending them as a day-ticket venue to the more casual visitor. The endless drains and canals demand a specialist approach and are difficult to read. Location is always the problem, and in the deeper, more turgid waters there's rarely much visual sign to give you a clue. However, the rewards can be great. The bream and roach fishing can be sensational at times and, of course, predator action can shake the record books.

The Twenty Foot Drain, in Cambridgeshire, however, does buck the trend to some degree. Fish stocks are prolific and it does have some character, so if you do find yourself in this part of the country, it's well worth a look. As ever, location is something of a problem, but the Twenty Foot does have pointers. There is, for example, marginal weed growth, and you'll often find tench and bream very close in to the bank. Pole fishing is a favourite here. Look also for the bridges: historically hot spots and magnets to all fish species. Matches are frequently held along the length, so it pays to take a walk, talk to the competitors and see how they're fairing. And those that are doing well with silver fish could well give you a clue to the whereabouts of the zander and pike.

Feeder fishing is also a favourite: try casters, redworms or pink maggots on the hook. Don't expect bites to be tear-aways – look for slight nudges and concentrate like a hawk. And if you're new to the Fens, don't be alarmed if the flow suddenly speeds up – it simply means the pumps are in operation. Remember that you can be fishing something like a pond one moment and a roaring river the next. If it's any consolation, a change in flow can often mean a change in luck.

There are many who find Fenland fascinating. Perhaps to some eyes its unbounded flat acres appear bleak and uninviting, but you'll never see sunrises or sunsets anywhere else to compete. In fact, the skyscape is endless, only broken by occasional troops of poplars. It's an experience no angler should really miss.

Season – closed season March 14th to June 16th.
Tickets – day tickets cost £3 on the bank. The fishing is controlled by Whittlesey AA, which can be contacted on 01733 203800. Please note that bloodworm is banned.
Directions – from Whittlesey, take the A605 eastwards towards Wisbech. There are several roads leading off to the right that take you down to the water. Park close to the bridges or cross the drain and park even closer to your swim.
Accommodation – the Tourist Information Centre in Cambridge, on 01223 322640, will give advice on suitable accommodation in the area.

Glen Mere Lakes – Norfolk

I'm including this serene water simply because it's so very pleasant to visit and also because it's near to the north Norfolk coast, Cromer in particular, which is such an important holiday area. Glen Mere is a jewel. There are two lakes – one a syndicate water . They are both small, but with extraordinary stocks of fish.

Glen Mere is all about crucians – one of our most attractive, yet unsung, heroes. Here, they grow to about two pounds, but you will catch lots of fish beneath that weight. The fish fight well and also look stunning. All the more so when set against such a beautiful background.

There are carp – not particularly big ones – bream, roach and rudd, but none of them will make it into the record books. But does that matter? Fishing doesn't always have to be about earth-shattering experiences, especially if you can find a gorgeous little hideaway like Glen Mere.

Season – open all year round.
Tickets – these cost £3.50 for adults and £2.50 for juniors. You pay on the bank. It's sometimes wise to contact the owner on 01263 761303 to check on availability.
Directions – from Norwich, take the A140 north towards Cromer. At the roundabout before Aylsham, turn right and continue until you see the sign to Hanworth by the old stone cross. Turn left, cross one cattle grid and at the crossroads follow the sign to Sustead. Pass over the second cattle grid and after two hundred yards turn right into the fishery. You will see it signposted.
Accommodation – Cromer offers a wealth of bed and breakfast, guesthouse and hotel accommodation. Close by is the delightful country inn – the Saracens Head. Phone 01263 768909. The Tourist Information Centre in Cromer, on 01263 512497, can supply details of other accommodation in the area.

Bure Valley Lakes – North Norfolk

Bure Valley, situated in a wonderfully quiet, green part of North Norfolk, has splendid fishing. It consists of two lakes – one at a couple of acres and the larger one some four or five acres. The roach fishing in the smaller lake is superb and has been described as the best available on a day ticket anywhere in England. This small lake also holds good tench and plenty of carp.

The larger lake is a carp fisherman's paradise. The lake record is thirty-two pounds, but there are many fish over twenty pounds in weight, most of which can be seen cruising in the surface layers on warm days. As a bonus, pike fishing is soon to be allowed on a limited basis on the trout lake that is also situated within the fishery. It's confidently expected that twenty-, and even thirty-, pound pike will be caught there.

The big roach are generally caught on maggots or casters, float fished over a bed of ground bait or hemp. This doesn't mean to say that a lump of flake ledgered out in the middle might not pick up some fish. However, the water is usually clear, so a softly-softly approach generally works best.

Most carp fishermen approach the bigger lake using fairly standard tactics and bait, but success is to be had off the top with floating baits and fishing very close in around the margins, where there is a pronounced shelf. Particle baiting in these areas pays dividends for the careful angler. Above all, however, Bure Valley is an idyllic place to escape the pressures of the world and enjoy an entertaining conversation with fishery owner Mike Smith.

Season – open every day throughout the year.

Tickets – carp lake £7.50 for twelve hours and two rods and £12.50 for twenty-four hours. The roach lake costs £5 for the day for two rods. There is no night fishing on it.

Records – pike thirty-four pounds, roach two pounds twelve ounces, tench five pounds twelve ounces, carp thirty-two pounds eight ounces.

Directions – Take the A140 from Norwich to Aylsham, then the B1354 to Saxthorpe. The fishery is on the right-hand side four miles out of Aylsham. You will find it down a mile long cart track.

Accommodation – The Buckinghamshire Arms on 01263 732133, The Saracen's Head on 01263 768909, or contact the Tourist Information Board on 01263 733903.

Blickling Lake – Norfolk

This great, crescent-shaped lake is the essence of an estate water. To the south lies Blickling Hall, one of the National Trust's prize mansions. The banks are heavily wooded. There are fields where sheep graze. To the north, beyond the dam, rolling countryside stretches to the coast. Blickling Lake, built over a chalky bottom, is fabulously rich and generally crystal clear unless clouded by swarms of daphnia.

This fertility is reflected in the fish stocks. Tench and bream are both numerous and very large. Double-figure bream and tench to eight pounds are always possible, along with excellent roach, big perch, massive pike and extraordinary eels. Carp, just a few ounces in weight, were stocked back in the mid 80s, and these have now grown into twenty- and thirty-pounders. Mind you, just because there are a lot of fish doesn't mean to say that Blickling is always easy. Far from it: the clear water and rich natural food stocks both make for fish that can be very picky. Yet, at the same time, to go too light is absolutely asking for trouble, especially from mid-summer onwards, when weed growth can be heavy.

So what do you do? Well, you can consider fishing at range from the dam, where the water is deep. A swim feeder with maggots or a small redworm on the hook often work well. Alternatively, patrol the margins with Polaroid glasses and actually look for feeding fish. You'll often find groups of tench browsing on the bottom, sending

Estate Lake Tench

Estate lake tench might not grow quite as big as some of their gravel pit brethren but, believe me, they are in marvellous condition, fight well and can be very difficult to outwit, especially in clear water.

The best times on most estate lakes are from dawn to about eleven in the morning.

- *Try to visit the water before you are going to fish, to reconnoitre swims. If you can put some bait in beforehand, so much the better.*
- *Estate lake tench tend to be fairly territorial. You will find the same group of fish patrolling the same length of bank most days. If the water is clear enough, you can target groups of fish.*
- *If you're not getting bites, it's tempting to go light but remember these tench fight very hard and if there's weed about you will lose them.*
- *The top baits here tend to be maggots, casters, sweetcorn, lobworm, redworm and mini boilies.*
- *Float fishing is the traditional way to catch these fish but in very clear water they can be wary of both the float and the line in mid water.*
- *If you suspect that this is the case, it makes sense to ledger. Bolt-rigged tench baits are now very popular and bites do tend to be unmissable.*
- *Look for tench close to reed beds, especially bulrushes. Tench like to feed over relatively hard bottoms – sand, gravel and the like.*
- *To rake or not to rake! The traditional practice of raking a tench swim to stir up the bottom and excite their inquisitiveness has long been out of fashion, but my diving experiences suggest that a big cloud in the water does attract tench in.*

up bubbles. Bait sparingly with casters, mini boilies or anything that doesn't cause too much commotion on entering the water. Bream seem to hang halfway up the lake, often rolling on the surface. Steady baiting up with a swim feeder can often get them down onto the bottom where they'll feed hard. This is how the big bags are amassed.

Top tench feeding times are from dawn till around ten or eleven o'clock in the morning. On a dull, windy day, you'll find the bream feeding well on into the early afternoon. Dusks can be productive but probably not quite as dynamic as the early morning period. The one problem can be a cold northerly that often blows in from the sea through the summer months, bringing with it a chilling mist. The whole lake can go quiet during these periods but once the winds swing round and the temperatures rise, look out for frantic feeding periods.

If you need any incentive to fish one of England's most beautiful lakes, be warned that the tench here fight probably better than anywhere else I know. Perhaps it's their general fitness or the clear water, but hooking one is like catching a tiger by the tail.

Season – open 16th June until March 14th, though for past few years has not closed until 31st March.

Tickets – contact David Cooper, the park warden on 01263 734181 for details. £4 a day, £2 concessions. Tickets can be purchased on the bank.

Directions – take the B1354 off the A140 from Norwich/Cromer road, which leads you through the town of Aylsham. Continue for approximately 1¼ miles to the north-west of Aylsham. Blickling Hall and lake is clearly signposted.

Accommodation – the Tourist Information Centres in Aylsham, on 01263 733903, or Cromer, on 01263 512497, can advise on suitable accommodation available in the area.

Gunton Park Lake – North Norfolk

Gunton is a treasure of a water, some fifteen acres in extent, with depths varying between two and five feet. Created back in the 1700s as a feature for the grand house still standing today in the background, it is typical of the string of estate lakes to be found in this part of Norfolk. The lake and its surroundings are steeped in history: the car park is close to the ancient and unique water-driven sawmill, and you will almost certainly be fishing in view of the delightful two-century-old bridge that leads from the water up to the big house itself. In the north-east corner of the lake is an ancient, submerged boathouse.

Even the fish stocks are relatively ancient: the bream shoals, for which the water is justifiably famous, have been fished for decades. And there are scores of wild carp that escaped from a private lake deep in the estate and have flourished in the larger water. These wildies now often approach double figures, and you might even pick up the odd one going to twelve pounds or more. Thrilling stuff, especially if hooked on lighter bream gear. There are also roach, perch, pike, tench and a few crucian carp present.

Gunton Lake is fairly heavily fished, and most anglers use quiver tips, feeders and light hooks with maggots or caster as bait. This system works well, especially for the bream shoals that generally hang further out from the bank than the roach, carp or tench. However, it can pay to have a change: why not straight lead with a big lump of flake, for example? Or try a big worm over a bed of hemp and maggots. Hot areas include the eastern bank, the reed-bed bank and the north bank, but fish are also to be caught by the sawmill itself. My advice is not to put your basket down at the first free peg but have a good walk, watch the water closely, and you might see signs of feeding fish. This is where binoculars come in.

For the carp, try fishing close in amongst those reed beds. Particle baits of all sorts work well. But be warned – these fish aren't fools and you're going to have to present bait very tightly and delicately to trick them. My favourite would probably be a float-fished redworm over a carpet of hemp and casters.

Season – the old close season of March 14th to June 16th is roughly adhered to.
Tickets – these are available on the bank and at present cost £3.50 per day for adults and £2 for children. The bailiff, the excellent Mr John Waite, will come round for the money.
Rules – please note that there is no night fishing and that boilies, keep nets and barbed hooks are also frowned upon!
Records – bream run to eight or nine pounds, with rumours of ten-pounders. The wild carp generally plateau out at around eight to ten pounds but there is the odd mirror carp exceeding twenty pounds. Pike are rarely caught above twenty-two or twenty-three pounds. Roach average small but pounders are taken. The perch fishing is something of an unknown quantity, but big ones are present.
Directions – turn right off the A140 from Norwich to Cromer about five miles north of Aylsham. The road to Gunton is called White Post Lane and is signposted Suffield. After a mile, you will see the gates of Gunton on a sharp right hand corner. Turn this corner and the fisherman's entrance is a hundred and fifty yards or so on the left. The lake is in front of you.
Accommodation – the Elderton Lodge, on 01263 833547, is situated on the estate itself and is personally highly recommended. The nearby Saracen's Head, on 01263 768909, offers excellent pub food and comfortable accommodation.

Great Witchingham Lakes and River Wensum – Norfolk

So much to say here I hardly know where to begin! Let's start with the Wensum, the scene of some of my own personal happiest fishing memories. But I'm going back a fair bit – to the 1970s to be exact. It was during that decade that I took hundreds – yes hundreds – of Wensum two-pound roach. There were also some threes thrown in and in fact I guess the Wensum was at that time probably one of the best roach rivers in history. Then came the bad times for all

manner of reasons – mainly, I guess, because of ill-advised river management – and the roach stocks declined almost to the point of extinction in many places. The good news? Well, little by little, it seems that pockets of roach are spreading and there are now fish to be caught.

In large part, this is due to changing attitudes. The Norfolk Anglers' Conservation Association has been at the forefront of this, and the Environment Agency also takes river management much more seriously and sensitively than it did before. So, there is hope for the future. A problem for the visiting angler is that most of the best stretches are not day ticket. However, there are still some opportunities. In Great Witchingham, about eight miles north of Norwich, there is a good stretch of water that holds a good head of chub and roach. It's controlled by the Great Witchingham Fuel Allotment Charity, who run both the river and the three lakes under their supervision with care.

How do you go about catching those fish? The chub are comparatively easy. I'd recommend roaming with a sensitive quiver tip, four-pound line and a loaf of bread. One or two swan shot, six inches from a size six hook should do the trick. Simply squeeze on some flake, cast it in all the likely spots – and there are many here – and if you don't get a response, move on. You could bait up a patch to come back to at dusk.

The roach can be more difficult. You will probably catch many chub to every single roach but, it could be that you might hit the jackpot. In fact, if you scale down the tactics I've mentioned above so you were using a size ten hook and a smaller piece of flake, you'll stand a chance of picking up both chub and roach. It's worth a try.

The lakes at Lenwade have been famous for at least forty years as this was a centre of extensive gravel workings just after the Second World War. Most are now, sadly, private but these three at Great Witchingham remain open to the public. They are beautiful lakes, and each offer something special. The lake on the right is primarily designed for carp and tench fishermen. It can get clear in the summer and is sometimes weedy, but you'll see fish gliding around. There are also a few, elusive very big crucians. The large lake to the left is an excellent bream water and the far lake – the long thin one – has good pike and some tench.

If you're really going to get after the bream, it's probable that you'll have to night fish. Put in a decent amount of bait – I don't recommend cereal – preferably on one of the bars. It pays, therefore, to get to the water early and do a fair bit of plumbing. Best baits include maggots, redworms and casters. If all else fails, try a good dollop of flake on a size eight. When a bream picks up your bait and runs, my advice is to have the reel on backwind and let the handle turn a few times before striking. It takes nerve to let a bite go on so far but you'll hit it in the end.

SEASON – Open all year round.

TICKETS – these are available on the bankside. They cost £5 per day for adults and £1 for Senior Citizens and juniors. Night tickets cost £10 and £3 respectively. Please note that no carp are to be held in keep nets. Also obey the rule that says you must not drive up and down the very bumpy track between dusk and 6.30am, for the sake of the nearby residents.

→ **Directions** – from Norwich, take the A1067 northwards towards Fakenham. You will come into Lenwade (often called Great Witchingham) and cross the river bridge. Go past the garage on your left and in quarter of a mile or so you will come to a butcher and a bakery. Take the first left immediately after these shops and follow the bumpy track down to the waters.

Accommodation – the nearby Wensum Country Hotel (01603 872288) offers super accommodation with its own fishing – both river and lake. Also apply to the Tourist Information Centre in Norwich (01603 666071) for details of accommodation in the area.

Woodrising Water Meadows – Norfolk

If you're holidaying in Norwich and fancy a quick spin out, you can't do better than visit this very attractive two-acre fishery. It's set well out in countryside and surrounded by woods and meadows. It is man-made but you wouldn't really know it: there are lots of features and nice depth changes. The fish stocks are also excellent – good sized and very well-conditioned carp, tench and roach. Pole fishing is a favourite here, but waggler and swim feeder also work well. On a small water like this look for features – remember that tench hug the margins of both the bankside proper and the islands. There's deeper water away from the car park and fish tend to migrate down there as autumn turns into winter. Get to the water early, however, and you can see a lot of action up in the shallows near the car park.

There are times when small waters can prove surprisingly difficult. You know the fish are there and you can often see activity, but you cannot buy a bite. What do you do? It's not always a case of going finer – what's the point if you're just going to lose a good fish? Try different baits, obviously. Perhaps a cocktail, perhaps the tip of a worm. Change your depth – come off the bottom, or even fish in mid-water. Put a couple of handfuls of bait close in just a couple of yards or so up the bank from where you are fishing and watch out for clouding or bubbles. Take a careful walk round the fishery and see if there's any surface activity whatsoever. Talk to other anglers, especially locals who know the place. Try to seek out the owner: every fishery boss wants to see satisfied customers. Above all, don't panic – fishing is a learning experience and a blank day can be as important as a successful one.

Season – open all year round.

Tickets – these cost £3.50 and are available at the water. Contact David Bunning on 01362 820702 for further information.

→ **Directions** – from Norwich, take the B1108 to Hingham. You will soon see Cranworth signposted on the right. Just before the village you will see a sign indicating the fishery.

Accommodation – details of accommodation can be obtained from the Norwich Tourist Information Centre on 01603 666071.

Hickling Broad – Norfolk

Every coarse fisherman had heard of the Broads, these large stillwaters dug centuries ago for supplies of peat, then filled by rain and spring water. The Broads are a shifting, fragile environment, largely because they are so close to the North Sea and subject to periodic flooding. This can lead to a boom and bust sort of situation but when the fishing is good, it can be tremendous. Perhaps the most accessible and most charming of all the Broads for the visitor is Hickling. This is a vast body of water connected with Heigham Sound – another large broad – by a deep dyke. Horsey Mere is also part of the same water complex.

Hickling is riding high at the moment, and any anglers going there can, very frequently, reap bonanza catches. There are, however, certain gold rules. For example, try to fish early and late and always make sure that you moor up – because nearly all fishing is done by boat – well away from the main cruiser channels. Ground bait thoughtfully. Fish as light as you can get away with – especially when the broad goes gin clear. Above all, manoeuvre your boat quietly and gently, and try to keep it from rocking and sending out telltale vibrations throughout the day. Use binoculars to scan the water from time to time for any signs of topping fish. This is a big water and the shoals are nomadic. If you're not catching, it could well pay to explore new areas.

I don't think we need look at any particular, special baits or methods. The bream, roach and rudd all fall to traditional baits though float fishing is probably easier than ledgering when afloat. Go for a comparatively heavy waggler that allows you to cast a good distance and still maintain control. Perch are making something of a comeback, so it pays to have a supply of lobworms with you and use one especially if you see small fish scattering before a cruising predator. There are some very, large pike and even if you are fishing for the roach and rudd, it pays to have pike gear set up with dead bait perhaps, in case there's esox activity!

The North Sea coast is close by, so the weather can be variable. North-easterly winds in the summer can bring severe chill and in the winter, watch out for northerly and easterly winds. If it's the traditional Broadland experience that you are looking for, there is no better place left to enjoy it than on the wild expanses of Hickling Broad.

Season – June 16th to March 14th

Boat Hire – Whispering Reeds Boats Ltd., Hickling, Norfolk, NR12 0YW. Phone/Fax 01692 598314.

Tickets – these are £1 per boat and are bought from a bailiff who motors round to collect the fees. Two rods per boat are allowed.

Records – there are few precise records but it is safe to assume that roach top one pound, rudd grow to two pounds and over and perch reach three pounds. Bream seem to level out around eight pounds and thirty plus pike are always on the cards. A wonderful mixed fishery. Tench can also grow large.

→ **Directions** – follow the Hickling Broad sign off the A149 between Potter Heigham and Stalham just to the northwest of Great Yarmouth.

Accommodation – Whispering Reeds offer a wide range of houseboats and cruisers. You can't beat living afloat for getting the very best out of the weather.

Fritton Lake – Suffolk

This is a beautiful and largely undiscovered water around about two and a half miles long and approaching two hundred acres in extent. It's likely Fritton was dug for its peat reserves and is, therefore, in reality a Broad rather than a lake. It averages eight to twelve feet deep – much like some of the Broads themselves – and the water too is usually well-coloured.

There are huge shoals of bream in Fritton and these are the major target for most visiting anglers. However, the roach are also widespread and run to well over the pound. There is some excellent perch fishing, a few carp and some tremendous sport is to be had with pike.

Dawn and dusk are almost certainly the best times to get down to fishing on Fritton. This is when you'll find the bream most active and really feeding hard. It pays to scan the water – preferably with binoculars – to look for any sign of rolling or priming fish. Then get to them as quickly as you can, bait up close by and wait for the fish to move over the feed. Alternatively, bait a well-known area for a day or two and then move in at first light to await your reward.

For the bream swim feeder and quiver tip is the usual approach but the roach respond well to float fished maggot or caster a couple of rod lengths out. If it's bream you're after, don't go too light because some of the fish run to a very good size indeed.

Season – Fritton is now open all year with no closed season. No keep nets are allowed and no live baiting for pike.

Tickets – the bailiff, Edward Knowles, can be contacted at Fritton Lake Country World, Church Lane, Fritton, Great Yarmouth NR31 9HA or phone 01493 488288. It's best to telephone beforehand to make arrangements. Tickets cost £5.20 per day for adults and £3.80 for children. You are strongly advised to book a boat for that extra mobility at £5 per day.

Records – pike are common between twenty and thirty pounds. The bream run to twelve pounds, the roach to one pound and perch of four pounds are present. Occasional carp to the mid twenties are also landed. Eel fishing is little practised but there are certainly some big specimens here.

→ **Directions** – Fritton is signposted off the A143 between Beccles and Great Yarmouth.

Accommodation – you really can't do better than stay in the holiday cottages which are available close to the lake itself. Once again, phone Mr. Knowles on 01493 488288 for details. Living on site, as it were, gives you the flexibility to really bait up for the bream shoals and make proper headway with them.

Yew Tree Lakes – Norfolk

Yew Tree rubs shoulders with some very famous waters. The two lakes here are situated in this extraordinary length of the Waveney valley between Harleston and Bungay. There's good river fishing still available if you're prepared to hunt it out but it's the pits and lakes in this area that have made angling history in the past. Waveney Valley Lakes (01986 788676) have produced big carp now for generations. The Highfield Fishery (01986 874869) holds real specimen fish. Weybread Pits have traditionally produced monsters. Homersfield Lake is another name instantly recognizable amongst specimen hunters. However, Yew Tree offers a really accessible way into this hallowed area. Many of the other waters can be difficult. I'm not saying Yew Tree doesn't offer a challenge, but it's comparatively small, feels intimate with all its features and has good fish stocks. It's a two lake complex – Yew Tree Lake is four acres and the Marsh Pool is an acre and a half. There are islands, overhanging trees and there's an undeniably fishy feel about the whole place.

I suppose what makes Yew Tree particularly exciting is the stock of catfish. Both lakes hold them, and they go to over twenty pounds. Twenty pounds might not sound a huge weight to anybody who hasn't played a catfish but, believe me, get one on the end and you'll know all about it – for the next forty minutes! There are also good carp, and both waters hold fish to around thirty pounds. Yew Tree might not quite be up to the big boys around it in terms of big fish reputation but it's getting there and it does offer a realistic chance of action.

You'll find that the catfish fight hard and doggedly. You'll need the very heaviest carp gear you've got. Remember also that they are afraid of any resistance and will drop a bait instantly if at all suspicious. They'll sometimes pick up boilies – especially fish-based ones. Try a bit of squid, a roll of anchovy or perhaps a couple of meatballs. Pepperami can work, and one of my favourites for cats is garlic sausage. Do remember that a nylon hook length isn't enough for catfish: their small rasping teeth will fray it quickly. Instead, use something abrasion-resistant such as Kryston Quick Silver.

Location is also important for catfish – even on small waters where they are plentiful. You'll often find them very close in to the bank or near to islands or lying in deeper channels. For this reason, it often pays to plumb a water before fishing, especially if you've got the time to put in a few days. Look very hard for surface activity. You'll often see the water colour as catfish begin to feed and sometimes even the tip of a tail will break surface momentarily. If you're very lucky, you will see a fish roll or even chase fry. Catfish are frequently considered nocturnal feeders but don't be put off fishing in the daytime. It's surprising how many blindingly hot afternoons will see a run develop.

One word of caution – Yew Tree is commendably harsh on litter depositors. Long-stay anglers do sometimes have something of a dubious reputation and rubbish won't be tolerated here.

Season – the fishery closes between November and March.

Tickets – these are £10 for four hours and can be obtained on the bank. Phone 01986 788570 for further details.

Directions – take the A140 from Norwich to Scole and turn onto the A143 towards Lowestoft and Bungay. At the second roundabout, turn into Wortwell Village and the lakes are well signposted on your right hand side.

Accommodation – the Tourist Information Centre in Lowestoft, on 01502 533600, will be able to supply details of suitable accommodation in the area.

Alton Water and Ardleigh Reservoir

I'm treating these two superb waters as one entity because they are both controlled by Anglian Water and they are both prime examples of how wildlife, sailing, birdwatching and fishing can all be accommodated together in glorious surroundings. Alton is slightly to the north of Ardleigh – the first being in Suffolk and the latter in Essex – but they are very similar in feel. Both are set in green, rolling countryside and they're both approximately the same sort of size – both over a hundred acres but not so large as to intimidate an angler.

Alton was always designed as a coarse fishing water and now boasts large stocks of bream, roach, rudd and pike. It's a perfect match venue but also excellent for the visitor. The quality of fish is fantastic. The pike at Alton are getting steadily bigger: every year sees twenty pound fish as the norm and much, much bigger specimens lurk.

The same applies to Ardleigh. In fact, Ardleigh once held the British pike record with a monster of forty-four pounds. It is Ardleigh that has always attracted my own eye, possibly because it has doubled as a trout and a coarse fishery for most of its life. And we all know how pike thrive on stocked rainbows. Now, sadly, the trout fishing is being phased out, but that doesn't necessarily mean that the pike fishing will suffer as a result. The big fish still have plenty of roach and bream to sustain them. In short, I expect Ardleigh to carry on being a premier pike fishery for years to come.

But it's not just pike that make Ardleigh so special. A two pound roach is nothing in this sensational water. Bream and tench grow big, and carp are on the increase. A few years ago Ardleigh was also nationally famous for its extraordinary perch fishing and, who knows, these may well return in the same strength one day.

There's something rather liberating about fishing these waters – you know that you're in for a rewarding day. The calibre of the fish is always excellent. The birdlife is extensive. There's a feeling of openness, of freedom and you never quite know what's going to take your bait next. Believe me, the chances are there that it could be a fish to make the national headlines.

Season – Ardleigh is open all year round. At Alton, the fishing season runs from Spring Bank Holiday Saturday until 14th March the following year.

Tickets – for Alton ring the warden at Alton Water Treatment Works on 01473 589105. For Ardleigh, contact Barry Bartholomew, the bailiff. You can buy tickets from the fishing lodge at Ardleigh or the self-service kiosk outside the lodge. Tickets are £6 per day for an adult and £3 for juniors under sixteen years of age. Half-day tickets are also available.

Rules – these are showcase waters where fishermen should remember to be on their best behaviour. Co-operation with sailors and birdwatchers is most important and do not fish in areas that are restricted for wildlife.

Directions – Alton is found just off the A137 south of Ipswich. Ardleigh is three miles outside Colchester on the A137 to Manningtree. They are so close together it is possible to take both in in a single day or certainly over a weekend.

Accommodation – the Tourist Information Centres in Ipswich (01473 258070) and Colchester (01206 282920) can supply details of accommodation in their area.

Highly Recommended Fisheries

- *Decoy Lakes, Whittlesey, Cambridgeshire. Six waters here with huge heads of carp from small to around the twenty pound mark. Some roach and tench but carp are the main attraction. Tickets cost £5, contact Diane Band on 01733 202230.*
- *Middle Level Main drain, Three Holes, Upwell, Norfolk. A long straight drain controlled by King's Lynn Angling Association which holds some great pike and zander. Also good shoals of roach and bream. Good perch and also some tench. Contact Mike Grief, King's Lynn Angling Association Secretary on 01553 671545. Tickets £3.50 on the bank.*
- *Old River Nene, March, Cambridgeshire. Some great roach fishing to around about a pound with very good perch as well. Free fishing but enquire about parking and matches on 01354 658747.*
- *Gimmingham Lakes, Nr. North Walsham. Contact 01263 720432. Small lakes but very intimate with some cracking fish available – especially carp and tench.*
- *Revesby Reservoir, Lincolnshire. A thirty plus acre reservoir. Good pike, bream and tench. Plentiful small roach and perch. Red maggot and worm score well. Tickets £3 a day on the bank. At present closed season March 14th–June 16th is maintained and no fishing on Sundays. Contact 01507 568395.*

Coarse-Fishing Sites in The Midlands

1. *Moccas Fishery*
2. *Docklow Pools*
3. *Baden Hall Fishery*
4. *Fisherwick Lakes*
5. *Packington Somers*
6. *Alvechurch Fisheries*
7. *Bishops Bowl Lakes*
8. *Clattercote Reservoir*
9. *Butlers Hill Farm*
10. *Blenheim Palace Lake*
11. *Hollowell Reservoir*
12. *Bluebell Fishery*
13. *The River Trent*

Just because I caught my record carp over on the Welsh borders and I've done a bit of pike fishing up on Loch Lomond, people tend to think of me as a great traveller, but this isn't really the case. In fact, John, I'll let you into a secret. That is, I don't really like travelling a great deal. I see this as a major bonus, living as I do in Hertfordshire. I've got all manner of waters pretty much on my doorstep and if you read my articles you'll realise that ninety-five percent of the time I'm fishing almost within casting distance of my own sitting room. I'm not saying the fishing is necessarily as good as it was when I was a lad, but there's still some really interesting sport to be found, especially if you keep your ear to the ground and you've got a network of good friends. My sneaking suspicion is that the fish themselves are probably getting bigger as the years go by. I'm not sure why this is – it could be something to do with nitrates enriching the water or perhaps increased food supplies, possibly from anglers' baits. I know you've got some great fishing close to you up in Norfolk but, I guess, on balance I'm just about as fortunate.

LETTER FROM THE LATE RICHARD WALKER TO THE AUTHOR

Richard Walker was the greatest angler – either coarse or game – of the 20th century, and his list of big fish will probably never be equalled. There was hardly a species that he hadn't caught really breathtaking specimens of in the 1980s. And yet, Richard rarely travelled more than an hour or two from his home in Hitchin. The simple reason was, as he said, there was so much good fishing on his doorstep, so why on earth would he want to travel long distances? And he was right then, just as he would be correct now. Just think: the Ouse in Bedfordshire – home of record barbel; the Derbyshire rivers just brimming with dace; the Wye and the Severn over to the west; the reservoirs of Leicestershire; the Trent; the Meres of Shropshire; the Warwickshire Avon; the gravel pits of Oxfordshire; and, of course, the Thames.

Moccas Fishery – Bredwardine, The River Wye

Beat six of the famous Moccas Fishery is well known among barbel anglers throughout the country. I ought to explain that the fishery is actually made up of ten beats in all, but the public are only allowed onto this one day-ticket water. Never mind – at more than a mile in extent, it offers some excellent opportunities for the specialist angler or a small club match.

The barbel are large; school fish are between six and eight pounds and there are plenty bigger than that. Above all, the fishery is widely varied, offering scope for all manner of methods. Try the deeper, slower water at the head of the beat if you want to fish static baits. From the bridge upwards, however, the quick, dancing shallows allow you to float fish or even free-line a bunch of lobs, or a dead minnow perhaps.

The pike fishing is also interesting and the chub are numerous and large. There's also the chance of a perch or two, and dace are on the comeback trail. But above all, beat six is just a beautiful place to fish, surrounded as it is by lush, rolling farmland and towering, amphitheatre-like hills.

Best times tend to be early and late (remember there is no night fishing) but barbel can be caught here throughout the day, especially if there's a bit of a tinge on the river. A careful approach makes a world of difference. Too many anglers clump to their swims, swing down heavy baskets and cast in football-size feeders. To get the best out of this water, approach with care, fish as light as you can get away with and try to do something different. That's why I mentioned worms – the natural bait approach can often work wonders here. As a final thought, don't ever fish a main line under six pounds breaking strain, as barbel fight like tigers and the winter floods bring down all manner of material to create large snags.

Season – fishing season for barbel runs from June 16th to March 14th. Keep nets are strictly banned. Also, take great care with gates and litter here. The beat runs through pastureland and the cattle and sheep must be protected. No night fishing.

Tickets – day tickets cost £6 and are available from Mike Taylor at the Red Lion Hotel, Bredwardine, on 01981 500303. Prior booking, though not essential, is certainly advisable, especially during busy periods.

Directions – from Hereford, take the A438 Brecon road. Around ten miles from Hereford, you will see a signpost indicating Bredwardine to the left. Follow this road for a mile and a half until you reach the river bridge. The Red Lion stands another four hundred yards further on at the T-junction.

Accommodation – good accommodation can be found at the Red Lion Hotel itself – see above for details. Residents to the hotel are also allowed to fish beats one to five, an area of water excluded to day ticket purchasers. I also run barbel-fishing courses along the whole length of the Moccas Fishery. Mike Taylor will furnish dates and prices.

Docklow Pools – Herefordshire

Docklow Pools really do represent a true labour of love: the complex is made up of an assortment of different waters, each offering a different level of challenge. Add to that some excellent accommodation and catering services on site and you really do have something a little bit special. In fact, Docklow Pools offer tremendous value for money to the holidaying angler. You've even got a well-stocked tackle shop and pub! And it's all set in beautiful countryside.

The Old Pool is ideal for children. It's attractive, safe and simply crammed with fish. Moby Dick is somewhat bigger and has a larger stamp of fish – carp, for example, go to twenty pounds plus. It's also a very appealing venue to fish, totally surrounded as it is by trees and reeds, and a place that definitely responds to the stalking, easy-does-it approach. Try fishing on the surface for the carp or close in to the margins.

Stalking for Carp

Most carp fishing is done in a relatively static fashion sitting behind fixed rods and baits. However, stalking can be efficient and is great fun. All you need is a rod, reel, float, hooks and bait, and off you go.

- *Always wear Polaroids – you just can't see anything without them.*
- *Only go stalking in quiet areas of the lake where you are not going to interfere with any other anglers.*
- *Look for browsing carp well away from all human activity. Remember even big fish will come into just a few inches of water. Look for them around fallen trees, weed beds and anywhere else they might feel secure.*
- *Sometimes you see the fish or its fins. At other times you'll see clouds of silt disturbed by feeding fish. Skilled stalkers can often tell the presence of carp just by the way the water stirs and rocks gently, indicating a big fish just subsurface.*
- *Stalking calls for an instant bait – try a couple of lob worms on a size 4 hook.*
- *Don't attempt to catch a carp from a swim where you know there is hardly any chance of landing it.*
- *If a fish becomes weeded, try hand lining. Point the rod straight at the problem area, hold the line tightly between the fingers and pull in a sawing motion. This will exert far more pressure than the rod can put on itself and could get the fish moving.*
- *If this does not work, let the line go slack for up to five minutes and you might find that the carp swims out of the weed or the tree root on its own accord.*
- *The best time for stalking is at dawn, when the fish are still actively roaming and feeding.*

Snake Lake is ideal for pole fishing, whereas the Figure of Eight Pool is another cracking venue for children or novices. There are also other pools at Docklow that are only open to membership tickets, and these even hold the exotic catfish. In short, membership is well worth thinking of taking out if you live locally or you think you're going to holiday in the area on a frequent basis. The countryside hereabouts is a birdwatcher's dream, the fishing is absolutely top rate and the accommodation is hard to beat.

SEASON – open all year round.
TICKETS – apply to Docklow Pools, Docklow, Nr. Leominster, Herefordshire HR6 0RU, or phone 01568 760256. Or phone the tackle shop (open in the summer) on 01568 760544. Day tickets cost £5 for adults.
DIRECTIONS – Docklow Pools is situated on the main A44 between Leominster and Bromyard. If you are travelling from Leominster, the clearly signed entrance is on the left-hand side, about four miles before reaching Bromyard.
ACCOMMODATION – there is excellent accommodation on site in either static or touring caravans, or lodges that all retain beams, sloping walls and old world charm. Alternatively, apply to the Tourist Information Centre in Leominster, on 01568 616460, for details of other accommodation in the area.

BADEN HALL FISHERY – STAFFORD

There's a really go-ahead management here at Baden Hall that has turned a promising fishery into a really exciting one. There are comprehensive club facilities and you certainly won't go short of food and drink when you're on the complex. You won't go short of fish either. Middle Pool is as nice as they come – very natural looking, and at around ten acres it holds some great fish, including double-figure bream. But there are also good carp (along with original wildies), tench to eight pounds and quality roach to over two pounds. Try maggots, worms, luncheon meat and bread. Floating bread is also a deadly method – would you believe it for the bream, I'm told! Keep nets, happily, aren't allowed on the water, so the fish are always in cracking conditions.

The Wetlands, the Match Pool and Duck Pond all provide equally satisfying fishing – each with their own particular slant and challenge. In short, there's something here for everyone. Do, however, check out the fishery rules before beginning. Keep nets, basically, are reserved for matches only, and there are restrictions on several baits. Anglers are also requested to take unhooking mats with them, especially if they are after the carp. But don't be put off. Baden really is a welcoming place and all these rules are simply designed for the good of the fish themselves, and the management should be applauded for that.

SEASON – open all year round from 7.00am until 9.00 in the evening and later by arrangement.

TICKETS – contact Baden Hall Fishery, Eccleshall, Stafford ST21 6LG, or phone 01785 850313. Coarse tickets range from about £6 for adults to £3.50 for juniors.

DIRECTIONS – from the M6, take junction 15, which is the A519, towards Eccleshall. Follow the signs to Swynnerton. Drive through Swynnerton itself, through Cold Meece and across the railway line. Go up a hill and Baden Hall is on the left, but please note that you should enter through the fishery entrance and not down the private drive.

ACCOMMODATION – details of accommodation available in the area can be obtained from the Tourist Information Centre in Stafford, on 01785 619619.

FISHERWICK LAKES – STAFFORDSHIRE

Fisherwick Lakes are situated in the grounds of what used to be Fisherwick Hall, though the original building has now been pulled down and all that remains is the former coach house. There are still thirty-two acres of land, in which nestle seven lakes and pools – most of them designated for coarse fishing. And there's something here for everybody. There are deep pools, shallow pools, long pools and round pools. There are pools overhung with trees and lined with thick marginal reeds. And there are the fish species – mirror carp, common carp, ghost carp, crucians, tench, bream, perch, roach, rudd, chub, golden orfe, dace and even the odd barbel – that make for a fishery where you really don't know what you're going to catch next.

At one end of the spectrum you've got waters like the Deep Hole Specimen Lake, which offers challenging fishing for carp well into the high twenties and tench to seven pounds or so in weight. Note that unhooking mats are obligatory here – excellent for the care of these very special fish. Most of the big carp are caught with mainstream methods, but there's still a real opportunity here for stalking amongst the extensive reed-beds. Also, look out for fish near the surface, especially in secluded bays.

Then you've got the Short Stream – more like a lake really, and full of fish. The water is comparatively shallow and absolutely teeming with small perch and tench, which makes it a real favourite with kids. Mind you, they could easily land a decent crucian carp, a good tench, a good mirror or even a passing chub or two.

With waters like Fisherwick it's a good idea to take your time before selecting a swim. Too many anglers are just in too great a hurry to get started, and half an hour or so spent walking the banks, looking for fish activity and deciding on a sensible approach for the day, really does pay dividends. Don't always be too keen to fish as close to your car as possible: the chances are that the more remote, peaceful areas of a fishery like this will hold the better specimens. Polaroid glasses are an excellent aid: often they'll help you actually see the fish you're hoping to catch. Also, look out for clouds of disturbed silt, twitching reeds or moving lily pads. If you are

even a few barbel, so I'm told, though I remain to be convinced. My own plea is this: if you were to latch into a barbel, please, please do not consign it to the keep net! And that goes for rivers everywhere,too.

Season – open all year round.
Tickets – apply to Alvechurch Fisheries, Bittell Road, Barntgreen, Birmingham B45 8LT, or phone 0121 4454274. Day tickets run from £5 for seniors to £2.50 for juniors.
Directions – from junction 2 of the M42 motorway, head towards Birmingham and Cadbury's World. At the first island, turn left towards Alvechurch. At the second island, turn right. The entrance to Alvechurch Fishery is about two hundred yards on the right.
Accommodation – the Tourist Information Centre in Birmingham, on 0870 599 2244, will be able to supply details of accommodation available in the area.

Bishops Bowl Lakes – Warwickshire

There's a real buzz about Bishops Bowl now it's under new management and making great strides forward again. The complex is just outside Leamington Spa, situated in a hundred acres of verdant countryside. There are five lakes, and their diversity means there's something for everyone. It's especially a great place in winter – there's a super café and a coffee shop available that offer a great range of hot breakfasts and even bowls of chilli-con-carné for those winter afternoons when you're both freezing and famished!

Back to the fishing! Blue Pool is a flooded quarry going down to over twenty feet and holding thirty-pound-plus mirror and common carp. The depths make floater fishing a popular line of attack, but if you are fishing on the bottom, it pays to long cast against the far wall of this former quarry where the bank is inaccessible and many of the bigger fish congregate. Blue Pool has got more to offer than carp, and you'll find tench to six pounds and perch – cracking, bristling creatures – to three pounds plus.

At around three acres in size, White Bishop Lake is probably the most popular match fishery, and it holds plenty of double-figure carp, good-sized tench and quality roach. Pole fishing is a favourite method on the lake, but be careful you aren't taken by surprise by one of those good carp that wander along very frequently. Tench go well on trout pellet paste and corn. Try laying on a couple of rod lengths out and you can build up a really good day's sport.

It can pay you to look very carefully at any bubbles that break on the surface. Reading bubbles is quite an art form and will tell you the fish species that are feeding over your bait. If, for example, the bubbles are tiny and fizz on the surface, then you can be fairly sure that there are tench about. They also come up in small clusters.

If the bubbles are larger, however, and follow a mazy trail, then you've probably got a carp or two grubbing about. If you see a big cloud of silt ballooning up, and one or two very large bubbles, it could be that a group of bream have moved in. These are generalisations and there are always exceptions to the rule, but remember that pointers like this can help improve your sport.

We should mention Lodge Pool and Dinosaur Dip – two small, comparatively shallow waters situated close to the car park and ideal for disabled anglers, senior anglers and especially children. The waters are full of fish. Ideal venues for the young where you know they can fish with confidence and in safety. Children are the future of the sport and this is realised at Bishops Bowl, where they are very well looked after.

SEASON – the lakes are open year round but do note that night fishing is by prior arrangement with the fishery manager on the number below.
TICKETS – contact Bishops Bowl Lakes, Station Road, Bishops Itchington, Leamington Spa, Warwickshire CV33 0SR, or phone 01926 613344. Summer tickets cost £5 and winter tickets £4, with concessions for senior citizens, juniors and disabled anglers.
DIRECTIONS – from junction 12 of the M40, turn right onto the B4451 to Southam. Bishops Bowl Lakes is about three miles along the road on the left. It is well signposted.
ACCOMMODATION – the Tourist Information Centre in Leamington Spa, on 01926 742762, will give advice on accommodation available in the area.

Clattercote Reservoir – Oxfordshire

Clattercote is a feeder reservoir for the Oxford canal, with depths down to about twenty feet at the dam end and less than five feet up in the weed-strewn shallows. What makes Clattercote instantly recognizable is the wooden walkway that rings virtually the entire water, so that anglers actually sit over the water rather than on the bank. Okay, in theory this sounds artificial to the point of the ridiculous, but in practice it creates a pleasing effect and, being totally surrounded by water, you do feel that you're very much a part of the lake.

Stocking has been prolific in the reservoir. The carp go into double figures, and there are plenty of them. Tench reach about six pounds, the crucian carp are beginning to head towards two, and there is a large head of perch, roach and bream of decent sizes. In fact, this makes the ideal match water, and bags of a hundred pounds plus have so far been recorded.

Clattercote is much more than a match fisherman's water. The roach fishing goes on well throughout the winter, and in summer it's quite possible to stalk both carp and tench in the weedy shallows. The water up there is only around four or five feet deep, and you can single out individual fish if you take your time and approach carefully.

All the usual techniques work well at Clattercote, but do make sure that you don't use cereal type ground bait. Loose feeding, anyway, is all that most anglers need on the vast majority of stillwaters. Also, and I'm well behind this, keep nets are only allowed at Clattercote during matches and then two have to be provided. This is very necessary, especially if the bream are on the feed.

Clattercote is a pleasant, interesting and rapidly-improving fishery. Specimens are already appearing, and it's only going to get better, especially given the enlightened management of the place. You don't feel crowded and the walkways do give a very interesting perspective of the entire water. In short, it's a fine example of what can be done with a little imagination and a great deal of commitment.

SEASON – open all year round.
TICKETS – contact Clattercote Reservoir, Clattercote, Nr. Claydon, Banbury, Oxfordshire, or phone 01442 278717. Permits are available on the bank from the patrolling bailiff and cost £5 for an adult and £3 for senior citizens, disabled and junior anglers. Night fishing is also available, again at a cost of £5.
DIRECTIONS – leave junction 11 of the M40 motorway. Take the road for Banbury but well before the town, take the A423 signposted to Southam, which you will find on the right-hand side. About five miles down this road you will find a turning on the right signed for the Bygones Museum and Claydon. Take this, and the entrance to Clattercote is on the right about a mile down this road.
ACCOMMODATION – the closest Tourist Information Centre is in Banbury, on 01295 25999855, but the Oxford Information Centre, on 01865 726871, will also be able to give details of various kinds of accommodation available.

BUTLERS HILL FARM – OXFORDSHIRE

Situated deep down in the beautiful Cotswolds, Butlers Hill is a tremendous holiday venue for the whole family. The lovely towns nearby are excellent for shopping and browsing, whilst the pools at Butlers Hill provide entertainment for the budding angler.

Number 1 pool, once an irrigation pond for the fruit farm, holds some tremendous fish. It's only an acre but it goes down to twelve feet deep and has carp to just under thirty pounds. There are also nice surprises – grass carp, for example, and chub that go over the four-pound mark. It's a pretty lake and is well established. Fish it either on the pole or for carp with trout pellets, boilies or floaters.

Number 2 pool is shallower than number 1 but has some tremendous attractions. Roach go close to two pounds and there are also grass and ghost carp. Number 2 pool has a predominantly muddy bottom and this colours up ferociously when fish are on the feed. It's not a bad idea, therefore, to walk the circumference of the pool looking for signs before settling down to fish.

Number 3 pool is only a quarter of an acre in size and, being so intimate, is ideal for kids. It's stocked with a host of carp, roach, rudd, chub, tench and bream, and as there are very few snags, it makes for ideal fishing conditions for the inexperienced. Moreover, the pool is close to the other two, and it's shallow and secluded so children can fish on their own with a great degree of safety.

Don't expect world-shattering fishing at Butlers Hill: it's rather a gentle, interesting place to fish, full of quality specimens in lovely countryside. And you can't get much better than that, especially on a family holiday.

SEASON – open all year round.
TICKETS – apply to Butlers Hill Farm, Great Roll Right, Chipping Norton, Oxfordshire OX7 5SJ, or phone 01608 684430. Day tickets are £3.50 and juniors £2.50. Night fishing is available at £5 per night but only by prior arrangement with the fishery manager. Ticket money is collected on the bank.
DIRECTIONS – Butlers Hill Farm is three-quarters of the way along the A34 between Shipston on Stour and the road to Chipping Norton. Travelling south, continue through Long Compton and start up the hill as soon as you pass the village. Halfway up is a road, to the left, signed Great Roll Right. Take this and then the first left turning will have Butlers Hill Farm on the corner. Continue down the lane for two hundred yards and the entrance to the fishery car park is on the right.
ACCOMMODATION – advice on various kinds of accommodation in the area can be obtained from the Chipping Norton Tourist Information Centre on 01608 644379.

BLENHEIM PALACE LAKE – OXFORDSHIRE

Blenheim Palace Lake is stunning. It's set triumphantly in the grounds of the main house and twists and turns its way through some of the most wonderful landscaped parkland. Just to look at it, spanned by noble bridges and dotted with exquisite islands, takes the breath away. The problem with fishing Blenheim is that you can't just turn up and buy a ticket on the bank – tickets have to be booked in advance and this does need a little prior planning. But believe me, it's well worth the effort.

Fishing is by boat, and this way you can get to the most hidden little bays and mouth-watering areas. There are favourite swims, of course, but there are so many fish that it really does pay to explore and it's no real handicap being a newcomer on the water. Get there as early as you can. If you can get out before the sun is up, you will see fish on the move. The bream and tench, especially, love to give themselves away around the shallower margins. You'll spot their fins and clouds of eddying silt as they feed.

Don't get your boat too close to feeding fish or they will spook – you probably won't see them arrow off, but there will be a general decline in activity. Feed sparingly. Remember, anyway, that ground bait is banned. Simply scatter in loose feed a few yards away from the bulk of feeding fish and let them come onto it. You're always up against it if you want to ledger from a boat, although quiver-tipping is possible. Much better, and much more fitting at such a lovely water, is float fishing. Set your waggler a few inches over depth and you'll pick up both bream and tench. And who knows what else might wander along during the course of the day?

All the usual baits work very well, but try a cocktail occasionally – say sweetcorn and redworm on a size twelve, or two casters with a tiny shard of luncheon meat. Don't be afraid to experiment.

Pike fishing comes into its own from October onwards, and there really are some magnificent fish to be caught. Don't be afraid to try lures out on Blenheim, because they really do work – especially on calm, still days when you can work something close to the surface. Alternatively, try a dead bait trolled very, very slowly behind you under a float. Set the fish so it doesn't quite touch bottom and snag up all the time, and work the boat at no more than wind speed under your oars.

I fished Blenheim in July 2000 and a perfect day made me realise how privileged we anglers are to fish such a place. During the course of the day – particularly before eleven o'clock in the morning – I picked up some half a dozen tench to over five pounds and three beautiful bream. The odd roach and perch also came along. The fish fought magnificently – even the bream – and all the time there was a stunning backdrop. Blenheim is one of the places where anglers are very much on show, so do constantly be aware of that. Remember that loud voices and bad language travel particularly well across the water.

SEASON – Blenheim is closed from March 14th to June 16th.

TICKETS – these must be booked in advance from the Blenheim Estate Office. Phone 01993 811432. You will be sent a provisional booking letter and form. You will need to fill this in, make out your cheque, and return it. Your permits and instructions will be sent on to you. One angler and boat costs £25 for the day and two anglers and a boat cost £30 for the day. You can book three anglers into a boat but this does tend to get uncomfortable.

DIRECTIONS – take the A44 north out of Oxford. This passes through the village of Woodstock, and Blenheim Palace is impossible to ignore on your left hand side. The actual instructions to the anglers car park will be given on your permit.

ACCOMMODATION – there is a great deal of hotel, guesthouse, and bed and breakfast accommodation in the area, including Woodstock itself. Contact the Tourist Information Centres in Woodstock on 01993 813276 or Oxford on 01865 726871 for details.

HOLLOWELL RESERVOIR – NORTHAMPTONSHIRE

Hollowell is one of those rare finds – a really prolific reservoir fishery where big fish can be taken in enough numbers to make it not too much of a specialist game. Hollowell is attractive too. Set in rolling countryside, it's a good-sized water at a hundred and forty acres, rarely gets crowded and always offers a feeling of peace and space.

Hollowell has been making the news for many years now, ever since its extraordinary roach-rudd hybrids appeared. These fabulous creations, often weighing over three pounds in weight, look sensational and fight like fiends. But that's not all

Hollowell has to offer. There are tench up to eight pounds, and huge shoals of bream between five and twelve pounds in weight. The carp also do well. The record common is a monster of nearly thirty-five pounds and the mirrors go well over twenty. Feeder fishing with maggot, caster, corn and boilies is the traditional way of fishing at Hollowell but it is possible to float fish, especially where there is deeper water close in.

Part of the reason for these stunning big fish weights is the fact that Hollowell is a very fertile environment. The silty bed of the water is heavily colonised with bloodworm, shrimp, beetle and corixa, and so the natural larder is a full one. Considering this fertility, it is not surprising that weed growth can be heavy, and it sometimes pays to fish early or late in the year, especially if you're using swim feeder tactics at long range.

It wouldn't be fair to leave Hollowell without a mention of the pike fishing. The pike are prolific, feasting on a diet of smaller fish. They are also large, and twenty-five-pound-plus specimens are caught frequently. The fishing really takes off in the late autumn when the weed growth dies back to allow you to drift float a dead bait away from the bank and explore distant features. Always remember when dead baiting, though, to take a pair of binoculars with you so that you can see a take very early on. Strike at once, or you risk deep hooking when the range is eighty yards or more.

SEASON – the fishery opens on 1st April and closes on 28th February. Note that night fishing is not available on a day ticket but is restricted to season permit holders.

TICKETS – for all bookings and advise on ticket prices, contact the Fishery Warden on 01604 781350, or c/o Pitsford Water, Holcot NN6 9SJ.

DIRECTIONS – Hollowell Reservoir is on Guilsborough Road, Hollowell, Northants. Hollowell itself is easy to find. It is seven miles north of Northampton, just off the A5199 and A14 motorway link.

ACCOMMODATION – the Tourist Information Centre in Northampton, on 01604 622677, will be able to supply details of suitable accommodation in the area.

Bluebell Fishery – Northamptonshire

Bluebell Fishery is nationally famous for its Kingfisher Lake, which has produced a whole array of very serious carp, including fish of over forty pounds. There are also very big catfish, huge grass carp, and bream and tench both well into double figures. Bluebell Lake, supposedly easier than Kingfisher, is also a prime big-fish venue that also holds big mirrors and large bream, along with tench, golden orfe to four pounds, and perch and crucian carp, both of which top three pounds, as well. With roach to two pounds plus and eels to seven and a half pounds, you can see that this is a very serious fishery indeed. There's also Wood Pool, which is a more run-of-the-mill match water. There are also a couple of miles of the River Nene, a stretch that can produce carp to thirty pounds, big bream and very good chub, along with tench, perch and

roach. So, as you can see, there's something for everyone at Bluebell. And I haven't even mentioned the pike! Sand Marten and Swan Lakes hold specimens to over thirty pounds, and are regular venues for Pike Anglers' Club events.

Of course, waters as successful as this do not yield up their prizes easily, and it pays to take time out to plan a successful approach. Don't rush to the first available swims. Think carefully about bait, rig and loose feed. Go the boily route by all means, but don't neglect float fishing in the margins or floater fishing in calm bays. Kingfisher Lake is very weedy in the summer and so you have to take this into account. It's no good casting a heavy lead into thick weed, because your bait will simply be hidden. Look for those areas where weed is at its thinnest, perhaps on the top of bars for example, where water fowl can keep patches clear. Or fish with suspended baits – pop-up boilies or maggots glued to a cork ball. Don't neglect natural baits: worms, especially lobs and brandlings, work very well at the complex for all species of fish. It's sad that lobworms have disappeared from the carp angler's list of bait these days, because for many years they were hugely successful and would be again, given a decent run. Take note of the wind – if at all possible, fish with it in your face. Don't neglect the margins – the fish here are great patrollers and are looking for food close in. In short, fish with as open a mind as possible and don't be afraid to experiment if you want to get the very best out of this fascinating complex of waters.

SEASON – open all year round, twenty-four hours a day.
TICKETS – apply to Bluebell Fishery, Tansor, Nr. Oundle, Northamptonshire PE8 5HN, or phone 01832 226042. There is a whole scale of charges depending on the water in question and whether night fishing is included. Prices start at about £15 for an all-night ticket and go down to less than £3 for a river half-day ticket.
DIRECTIONS – on the main A14 take the A45/A605 junction at Thrapston. Follow the A605 north towards Titchmarsh, Oundle and Peterborough. Continue along this road for several miles until you pass a turning to Oundle on the left. A little further on, again on the left, is a turning for Tansor. Drive through the village and, as you leave it and head into the countryside, the white railings marking the entrance to Bluebell Lakes can be seen on the left. The drive to the fishery is a mile through the fields.
ACCOMMODATION – the Tourist Information Centres in Oundle, on 0870 1515500, and Peterborough, on 01733 452336, will be able to supply details of various kinds of accommodation in the area. Caravans and tents are catered for on the fishery site.

THE RIVER TRENT – MIDLANDS

The Trent is the largest river system in England, rising in Staffordshire, crossing the country west to east, and emptying into the Humber. Years ago, fishing in the Trent was severely hit by pollution, but it recovered and, during the 1970s and 1980s, hit unprecedented successes. At the start of the 21st century, fishing

has become difficult and some doubts have been voiced as to whether the fish are simply hard to catch or are no longer there.

However, the Trent remains a cracking river and it's simply the case that certain matches are fished in the wrong conditions at the wrong time of the day and therefore the wrong impression has been given. In fact, there are huge barbel and chub still to be caught throughout the Trent. Double-figure barbel are not unknown, and chub to well over six pounds exist.

It's probably true to say that there are two main attacks on the Trent. Firstly, you can use a stick float close in with single or double caster or bronze maggot on light tackle. Don't be afraid to change baits when bites begin to slow down. Bread, a redworm, the tip of a lobworm or even stewed wheat can work well. They can easily produce an unexpected large barbel as well. You're more likely, however, to catch roach and the smaller chub and bream for most of the day. Nonetheless, if you've built up some feed, expect the barbel and bigger chub to move in as the light fails.

It's fair to say that most big fish still come to quiver-tip and feeder techniques. For big fish, don't be afraid to experiment. Spice up your feed – the commercially bought ground baits all work well, but try introducing chopped worms, crushed trout pellets, crushed hemp, minced meat or pulped meatballs. In winter especially, when there's a tinge to the river, a good smell is vital.

Similarly, experiment with your hook baits. Double lobworm, a huge knob of cheese paste, two or even three meat balls on a hook length, a strip of bacon, half a sprat – anything that makes a big barbel or chub sit up and take notice. Of course, most fish will continue to come on triple bronze maggot, perhaps, on a size fourteen hook, but that doesn't mean to say that you can't play different options.

Think about your tackle, too. A swim feeder, either open or block-end, is the most common form of attack, but there are times when a straight lead will be an advantage. Fish do wise up to the feeder, and a lead can help allay suspicions. Also, if you're going for a big, bold bait, you don't need quite as much loose feed around.

Think carefully about where you're going to fish the feeder. Sometimes the deeps of mid river are where you'll want to fish, but there are other occasions when trees on the far banks, for example, should hold your attention. Remember that if you're fishing at range, a flat lead is going to hold bottom much better than anything else.

Think hard about the conditions. In summer, if the water is clear, there's not a great deal of point fishing during the heat of the day. Try and get out very early, around dawn, and stay till breakfast time. Alternatively, arrive at teatime and fish till the last knockings.

The same applies in winter if water conditions are clear, but if they're murky and there's a good flood on, fish can be caught throughout the day. It's probably better to arrive about noon when the water temperature is at its highest and then have a concentrated attack for the last four or five hours or so. That way you don't get too cold and your concentration doesn't disappear.

There are times in the winter when you just have to be out on the river. If there's been a period of warm, damp weather with air temperatures consistently between eight and eleven degrees it's criminal not to be on the riverbank. You'll find that all fish species fish well during this period and you can even pick up a bonus big barbel or two. A winter carp is also very much on the cards.

SEASON – open June 16th to March 14th.

TICKETS – there is a huge amount of access open to the visiting angler along the Trent. In fact, the vast majority of this huge river is available on day ticket and a good amount of this is simply payable on the banks. Expect to pay between £3 and £5 for a cracking day's sport. Robert Hardy, on 01636 525265, is a good contact. Robert controls a great stretch of the Trent at East Stoke in Nottinghamshire, not far from Newark. The Nottingham and District Federation of Angling Societies also controls huge amounts of river. Write to W. Belshaw, 17 Spring Green, Clifton Estate, Nottingham. Also contact the Nottingham Anglers' Association via I. Foulds, 95 Ilkeston Road, Nottingham. Scunthorpe and District Angling Club, on 01652 655849, also controls good water in the tidal stretches. Newark is also a great centre. Contact the Newark and District Piscatorial Federation on 01636 702962. The Worksop and District Anglers' Association, on 01909 485176, also has good water in the area. The Nottingham Piscatorial Society has good water around Rolleston in Nottinghamshire. Contact them on 01623 759589. In Nottingham itself there is good mixed fishing, and several miles of the river is free within the city. The Midland Angling Society, on 0115 9634487, has good water at Thrumpton. In Staffordshire, contact the Stone and District Angling Society on 01785 819035. In Stoke, the Stoke City and District Angling Association, on 01782 267081, has a whole list of fishing in the area.

ACCOMMODATION – the Tourist Information Centres in Stafford, on 01785 619619, Nottingham, on 0115 9155330, and Lincoln, on 01522 579056, can all supply details of suitable accommodation in your chosen area.

HIGHLY RECOMMENDED FISHERIES

- *Himley Park, Dudley, West Midlands. Good tench, excellent crucians, carp and, notably, grass carp. A really great setting. Tickets £4 on the bank. Phone 01902 324093.*
- *Larford Lake, Stourport, Worcestershire. Nearly thirty acres. Big bream, roach and tench. Good perch fishing with crucians and some good carp. Also included is two miles of the River Severn with barbel, chub, dace and roach. Day tickets cost £5. Contact Arthur Field on 0374 703067.*

- *Chasewater, Brownhills, Staffordshire. This is set in Chasewater Country Park, a very pleasant setting. It is a large water with great roach fishing and some very good perch. Also some good pike. Tickets at £2.20 are available on the bank. Contact the Ranger on 01543 542302.*
- *The River Avon, The Lido, Stratford, Warwickshire. A good stretch of the Avon just outside Stratford offering excellent chub, plentiful roach and dace. There are also some decent bream and a few barbel. A good winter fishery after heavy rain. Waggler, stick float and swim feeder all work well. Day tickets £1.80 on the bank. Contact Dave Jones' Angling Centre, Stratford, on 01789 293950, for bait and up to the minute advice on conditions.*
- *The Erewash Canal, Dockholme, Nottinghamshire. A really steady venue with plenty of fish including chub to around three pounds, roach, skimmers, perch and some big carp. Try caster and worms for the larger fish, with meat for the carp. A good winter fishery but fishes well all year. Tickets cost £2. Contact Eric Aynsworth of Long Eaton Federation on 01159 256270 for further details.*
- *Earlswood Lakes, Earlswood, Warwickshire. This is worth mentioning as it is just south of Birmingham and the complex offers some great fishing. Plenty of fish and some really good specimens. Good pike, for example, to around the twenty-pound mark. Note there is no live baiting. Also famous for eels. Tickets cost £5. Contact John Howse on 01217 834233.*
- *Hooly Farm Fishery, Ashby Magna, Leicestershire. Three characterful lakes here. Tremendous match waters with plenty of fish for everybody. Also included are some splendid exotics such as golden tench. Tickets cost £4. Phone 01455 202391 for further details.*
- *Rolf's Lake, Holton, Oxfordshire. A really attractive, matured venue. Carp, tench, bream, roach, big chub and occasional golden orfe. Note that fishing is only available by prior arrangement. Contact Rolf Wobbeking on 0802 708937.*
- *Rudyard Lake, Staffordshire. A lovely lake – I caught my first bream here. Very good pike fishing, plenty of roach and bream, and reputedly some very big perch. Phone 01538 306 280.*
- *Milestone Fisheries, Gloucestershire. A big pike water – live baits available on site. A small coarse lake with big bream and very decent carp. Phone 01285 713908 for further details.*
- *Chad Lakes, Bleddington, Gloucestershire. This is an excellent commercial fishery opened back in the mid 1990s, holding good carp, tench, bream and roach. All usual methods and baits – try floating baits for carp in the summer. Bream, apparently, to seven pounds and roach to over a pound and a half. Close to Stow on the Wold – an excellent shopping centre. Tickets available on the bank, or contact Dave Wren on 01451 831470. No keep nets.*

Coarse-Fishing Sites in Wales

1. *Anglesey Lakes*
2. *The River Dee*
3. *Llangollen Canal*
4. *The River Teme*
5. *The River Irfon*
6. *The River Wye*
7. *Llangorse Lake*
8. *Pembrokeshire Fishing*
9. *Half Round Pond*
10. *Darren Lake*

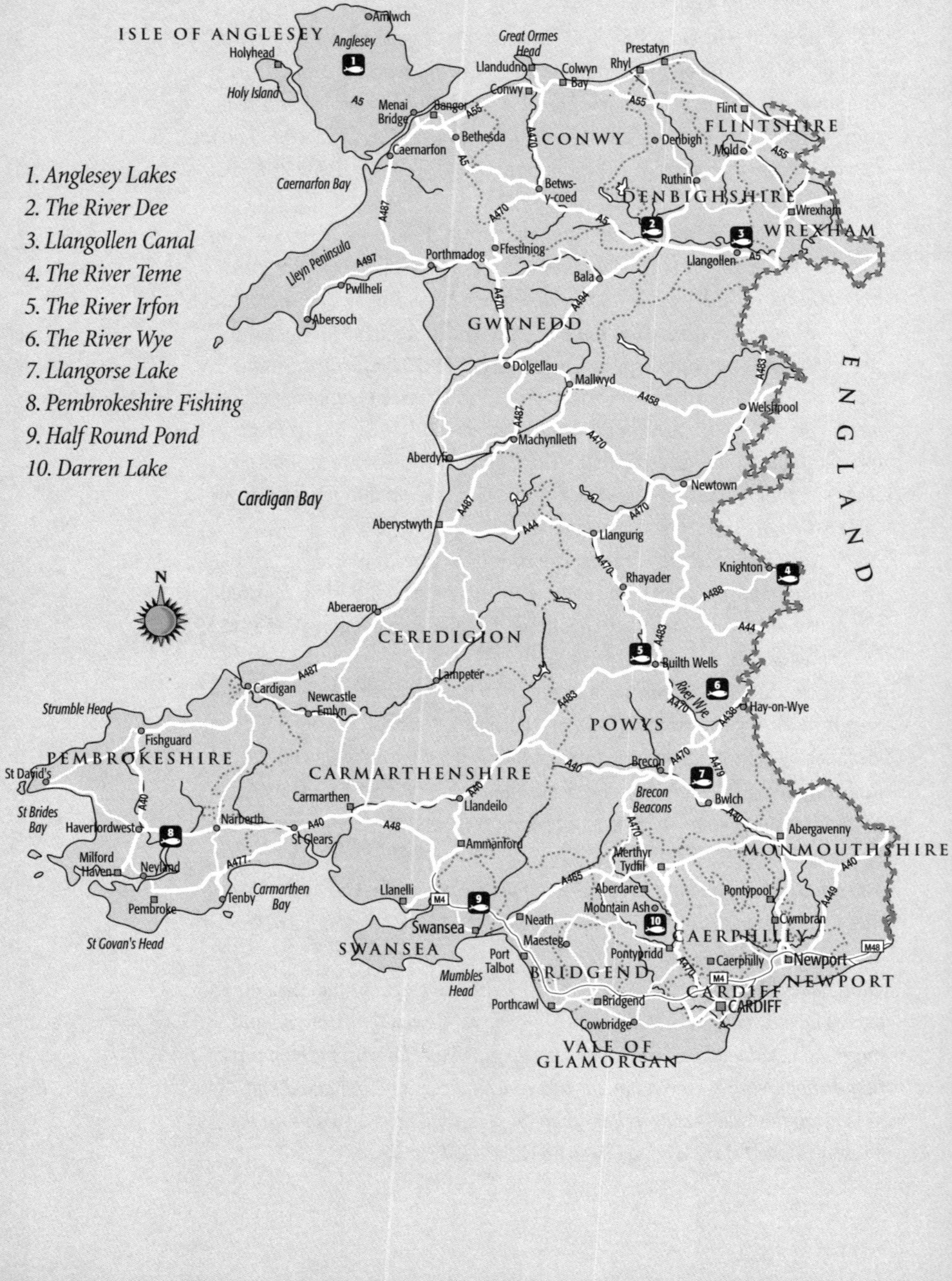

"I just love being down here in Wales even though I was lucky enough to live for many years right by the Avon. Even that doesn't compare with the fishing I've got hereabouts. Of course, the Wye is special, you know that, but there are all manner of little places tucked here and there around this fabulous country. And what countryside it is. It never ceases to amaze me just how secretive some of the valleys are. And you never quite know what's going to happen. For example, this morning I woke up and there was snow on the ground. I walked outside and found that the Wye was still running low and clear. Or at least I think it was. Believe it or not, it was frozen for at least seven-eighths of the way across. Needless to say there wasn't much to be caught, although I did pick up a few grayling. Wales is a wild, wonderful place. If you can't live here, then at least try it for a holiday."

BOB JAMES, AUTHOR, TV STAR AND BEDROCK OF THE ACA, ON THE PHONE TO THE AUTHOR

I lost my own heart to Wales many years ago when my fishing club up in Lancashire used to make its annual journeys to the River Dee. I'd never fished a river that was so clear and so quick-flowing. And, until those days on the Dee, I'd never come across dace. What beautiful, silver, dart-like fish they are.

Other favourite fish here? The grayling are crackers and again tend to be overlooked. Most of the game fishermen spend their life after trout, salmon or, especially, sea trout. The coarse fishers tend to concentrate on carp, pike, tench and barbel. That leaves grayling in a vacuum, ignored by both camps. What a mistake!

There's also brilliant chub fishing, often in rivers that have hardly ever been fished. This is marvellous, creepy-crawly sort of stuff that takes you back to the days of childhood. Yes, Wales is very much a land for the explorer: you'll find secretive pools and small streams if you look hard enough. Okay, some are private but with a bit of investigation and politeness you never know what doors might open to you.

ANGLESEY LAKES

Anglesey is one of the country's major tourist attractions, but those holiday-makers flooding along the A5 needn't only think about buckets and spades! There is now some very appealing coarse fishing available on Anglesey. It's not on the grand scale, and don't expect to see yourself featuring on the front page of the angling press. That's not what Anglesey is about. Rather it offers some very appealing small stillwaters, generally set in super locations. And, most importantly, there's frequently a great deal for the family to do in the area. Anglesey has plenty of hotels, bed and breakfast, and guest houses. For general information about accommodation on the island, contact the Tourist Information Centre in Holyhead on 01407 762622.

CWM RESERVOIR

This is a two-acre reservoir only a short way outside the town of Holyhead. It's picturesque and is close the South Stack landmark – well worth visiting in its own right. Stocks are dense: you can hope to catch carp, rudd, bream, perch, roach and tench. Individual sizes aren't great but you can expect bites throughout the day, which makes it a great water for the family. Please not that, in common with most of the waters on Anglesey, barbless hooks are obligatory, and don't use a keep net unless you are fishing in a match. The glorious Anglesey rudd is particularly susceptible to the chafing of net mesh.

SEASON – the lake is open all the year round, dawn till dusk.
TICKETS – these cost £3 per day and are available from the Tackle Bar Shop, William Street, Holyhead. Further information can be obtained on 01407 765479 or 01407 860239.
DIRECTIONS – in Holyhead, take the minor road west toward South Stack Cliffs. You need the signposts for Llaingoch and South Stack opposite the Cambria pub. After a quarter of a mile or so, you will see the turning to the reservoir on the right.

LLYN BRYNTIRION

Bryntirion is a working farm situated down in southwest Anglesey, so it's perfect for the whole family. There is always something going on and always animals to feed. The fishing isn't bad, either! There are three ponds offering prolific carp fishing and some splendid perch. The carp don't grow large but their numbers make it ideal for a family outing. Perch, though, are reputed to be serious. There are certainly two-pounders and the place calls for a bit of investigation. Fish a lobworm on a size four hook, and you stand a good chance of picking up either a good carp or a cracking stripy! A really good venue for all the family.

SEASON – the lake is open from March through to October. Note that fishing times run from 8.00am until dusk.

Tickets – these cost £3 a day and are available from Mr Naylor, Bryntirion Working Farm, Dwyran, Anglesey LL61 6BQ, or phone 01248 430232.
Directions – from Bangor, take the A5 across the Britannia Bridge and turn off on the A4080, following the signs to Brynsiencyn. In the village, follow the road to the right and the brown signs to the Working Farm.

Llyn Dewi

This is another small but very attractive water, absolutely packed with fish. You'll find carp into double figures and some superb rudd fishing. The rudd is, as it were, the national fish of Anglesey and you won't really find better specimens anywhere else in the country. It doesn't matter how big a rudd is – it's a beautiful fish! Try for them on the surface with tiny bits of floating bread. Or catapult maggots out letting them sink slowly and then fish a shotless float rig in the area. You'll find that rudd love to come up off the bottom to intercept baits in mid water and above.

Season – open all year round.
Tickets – these cost £4 and are available from Mr Hughes, Fferam Uchaf, Llanddeusant, Anglesey, or phone 01407 730425.
Directions – From the A5, turn right, signposted Bodedern. Go through the village and take the signs for Valley. After the 30mph-limit sign, take the first turning right and follow the road down to Llanddeusant. Follow the Llanbabo road and Llyn Dewi is between one and two miles along the road. It is signposted.

Llyn Y Gors

This really is one of the star lakes of Anglesey, situated just outside Beaumaris. There is some wonderful water here with excellent fish stocks – carp, catfish, rudd, tench, roach, perch, golden orfe and bream – and that's not mentioning the tremendous stock of ghost carp, another favourite on Anglesey. The carp certainly exceed twenty pounds and the catfish are rumoured to be doing well. But it's a big bag venue in essence. There's a match lake, recently opened, and stocked to the hilt. This is definitely a place for the holidaying angler, probably with a couple of mad-keen youngsters at his or her side. Action is guaranteed.

Season – the fishery is open all year round, 7.30am to dusk. There is a shop on site.
Tickets – these cost £8 a day and are available from Roger Thompson, Llyn Y Gors, Llandegfan, Menai Bridge, Anglesey LL59 5PN, or phone 01248 713410.
Directions – take the A5 over the Britannia Bridge and follow the flyover towards Benllech. Go straight ahead at the Four Crosses public house roundabout and follow the road towards Beaumaris. Turn right before Pentraeth garage. Keep left towards Beaumaris through Hen Llandegfan. You will see the sign to the fishery on the right after the village.
Accommodation – contact the Tourist Information Centre in Holyhead on 01407 762622.

Ty Hen

This is a brilliant water – quite small at one and a half acres, but fed with natural spring water, which gives the place its own life and lustre. The place is very well stocked with common, mirror and ghost carp. Twenty-pounders have reputedly been caught. There are also some cracking tench going well above six pounds. It's a comparatively new lake – about twenty years or so – but is well matured. There's an island that attracts many of the carp, especially during hot, still, summer days. Please note that barbless hooks are the rule here and no keep nets are allowed.

Season – fishing begins on 21st March and runs through to the 30th October. Dawn till dusk.
Tickets – these costs £5 a day with an evening ticket of £3. Apply to B. J. Summerfield, Ty Hen, Rhosneigr, Anglesey LL64 5QZ, or phone 01407 810331.
Directions – driving along the A5, turn left after Gwalchmai onto the A4080 to Rhosneigr. Turn sharp right before Llanfaelog Post Office. Drive a mile along this road and you will find the entrance to the fishery a hundred yards on the left after the railway station.
Accommodation – there is accommodation on site.

Tyddyn Sargent

This is only a one-and-a-half-acre lake but it's attractive and well stocked. There's a good head of carp, generally quite small but easy to catch, along with roach, rudd, tench and bream. There are crucian carp and some very attractive ghost carp that give the fishery a real feeling of the exotic.

Season – all the year round. Note barbless hooks only. No keep nets.
Tickets – these cost £5 a day. Contact K. Twist, Tyddyn Sargent, Tynygongl, Nr. Benllech, Anglesey, or phone 01248 853024.
Directions – from Bangor, take the A5 express way into Anglesey. Turn up the slip road signposted Benllech and turn right at the roundabout. Go straight ahead to the village, where you will come to a crossroads. Turn left, signposted Llangefni. Continue for a mile and then turn right, signposted Llanfair ME. Turn right after the telephone box and Tyddyn Sargent is the second house on the left. Drive through the gates to the parking area.

Grayling Fishing in Wales

If you want to sample some real wild Welsh fishing, how about pursuing grayling, especially in the autumn when the brown trout fishing has finished? Some of my best days have been spent searching for these delightful fish on both fly and bait. Welsh grayling really are the world's best-kept secret: there are big grayling available in Wales, at least as large as those from the Wessex chalk streams. The only reason that the angling fraternity doesn't really know about these fish is that they haven't been extensively investigated.

Whether you're fishing for the grayling with fly or bait, my advice is to be mobile. Okay, you'll sometimes settle on a deep pool that proves to be full of fish, and you'll catch one after another, all day long. But this is rare. Mostly, you'll find grayling scattered along a length of river in small groups of perhaps ten or fifteen fish. Catch a couple and you'll scare the rest – you've just got to move on.

Long-trotting techniques are as good as any when it comes to locating fish on stretches of river that you're not sure about. Perhaps a couple of brandlings on a size fourteen under a buoyant, highly visible float add up to the best approach. A twelve- or thirteen-foot rod, three-pound line straight through to the hook, and you're in business. Simply long-trot every glide you come across and look for that float shooting away. If you do hook a fish, keep your rod low to avoid the grayling splashing, and try to hustle it out of the area before it disturbs its shoal members. You'll find that a one-and-a-half-pound grayling puts up a real struggle in a quick river – in fact you could well think you've got a four-pound chub on the end, which isn't an impossibility!

If you're fishing worm, you probably won't be able to get away with a barbless hook, but just dampen the barb down a little bit and try to unhook all grayling in the water. If you think grayling fight hard in the water, wait till you try and touch them! They squirm like an eel and do themselves no good at all.

The only time you're likely to come across real concentrations of grayling is towards the end of their season in March, when they are grouping ready for spawning. If you do hit into these huge shoals, take a few fish and then move on. It's not fair to hammer fish near their spawning beds.

Bait fishing for grayling is not universally allowed, so do check very carefully when you buy your permit. Ensure also what bait restrictions are in place. For example, the most commonly-banned bait is the maggot. This isn't an attempt to be difficult – it's simply trying to protect the stocks of salmon parr in any water. If there is a problem, don't neglect a piece of sweetcorn. Grayling love the yellow grains and they are pretty well parr-proof. Also, make sure that you are fishing within the prescribed limits. On some of the wilder rivers, it's all too easy to wander into a restricted beat. This is some of the most glorious fishing that Wales has to offer, but remember that you can get coarse fishermen a bad name unless you stick to the rules.

Before moving on to the logistics, let me just put in a little plea here for fly fishing. It could well be that you've been a bait fisherman all your life and have disregarded fly fishing altogether. I honestly believe that you are making a mistake here. Fly fishing is not difficult – fly casting can certainly be learnt in half a day – nor does it need to be expensive. You can kit yourself out for well under a hundred pounds, and day tickets for autumn and winter grayling in Wales, as in many parts of the country, are very cheap indeed. So, if you are a keen freshwater fisherman, do think about taking up the fly rod. It will give you immense pleasure and open all manner of doors. Remember, too, that all sorts of coarse fish can be taken on the fly – perch especially are suckers for a big, flashy lure. Fly fishing for pike is becoming more and more popular and I personally am beginning to master the techniques of catching barbel on a nymph. Believe me, there's no more exciting way of catching these sporting fish.

SEASON – note that the grayling is out of season between March 14th and June 16th. It is often difficult to secure grayling tickets, however, before the end of the trout season in October. Fortunately the grayling bites well in the coldest of weather.

TICKETS – many of the best grayling stretches are on protected waters, but day ticket possibilities do exist. One of the most exciting is in Llangollen, where the Llangollen Angling Association has fourteen miles of water, much of which can be bait fished. Tickets are available from S. Hughes, Newsagents, 12 Chapel Street, Llangollen, or phone 01978 860155. Also on the Dee, contact Derek Cycles on 01978 821841. You could also try the Tytandderwen Farm stretch near Bala – contact Mr Davis on 01678 520273.

For the River Wye, contact Mike Morgan of the Groe Park and Irfon Angling Club in Builth Wells, on 01982 552759. The club offers water upstream of the bridge in the town. There is some good grayling fishing along several hundred yards of streamy water. Some of the fish can grow big.

You could also contact Peter Smith at the Caer Beris Manor Hotel on 01982 552601. There is a mile or more of private water, the River Irfon, running through the grounds of the hotel, and there is some excellent grayling fishing in the pools. Fishing is primarily for hotel guests, and the accommodation is superb.

Just outside Wales, at Ludlow, flows the River Teme with some good grayling trotting water. Phone Ludlow Tackle on 01584 875886. There is also free fishing on the town water in Ludlow downstream of Dinham Bridge. This beat extends for approximately one and a half miles, and is good trotting water.

LLANGOLLEN CANAL

This canal is an absolute delight, almost unique in my experience. Your access is likely to be in the busy town of Llangollen itself, which is all of a bustle from spring through to autumn, but once you've walked away out into the countryside, the whole scene changes dramatically. In fact, this can be like coarse fishing on a southern chalk stream, so clear runs the water. Yes, runs. Through the canal there's a constant flow of water seeping in from the Dee itself, the river that marks the beginning of the canal.

Roach and bream are the prime targets, and what fish they are – especially the roach. Groups of fish of way over a pound and nudging the two-pound mark are quite visible to the angler who stalks them carefully in good light conditions with Polaroid glasses. The bream, too, respond to this approach, and you'll often see patches of water muddied by their feeding.

But how to approach these really super canal species? My advice is to fish as light as possible with tiny baits and just a scattering of loose feed. I remember one morning around about a mile from the town where I took four bream to five pounds on just a tiny pinch of breadflake with an anchoring SSG shot eight or nine inches up the line. Bites were infinitesimal. The line would simply tighten minutely or shake as though a breeze had caught it. Each time I struck, a big bream was wallowing in water just a couple of feet deep.

The same sort of technique works for roach – a caster or a couple of maggots, on a size eighteen perhaps, flicked under a far bank bush or into the deeper water where the canal occasionally narrows.

The angler who stays put isn't likely to catch a great deal, because the shoals of fish can be very nomadic, especially during the day when the passenger barges are being pulled up and down the canal with sickening (for the angler) regularity. Fish aren't stupid, though, and they soon get used to the disturbance. In short, I find there is something totally magical about this canal and, with its challenging fishing and superb roach and bream, it's a treasure of a venue.

SEASON – this is now a year-round fishery.
TICKETS – the Northwest Region of British Waterways has introduced the Waterway Wanderers Permit to cover most of the canals in their region. Tickets are obtainable at £10 a season or £1.50 a day. Contact Northwest Region, Navigation Road, Northwich, Cheshire CW8 1BH or phone 01606 723800.
DIRECTIONS – you'll find the canal in the centre of Llangollen, close to the station. It then winds its way through the town into the countryside towards the Dee itself. You can't miss it.
ACCOMMODATION – Llangollen is very much a holiday town with, many bed and breakfasts, guesthouses and hotels. The Royal Hotel, on 01978 860202, by the river bridge is personally recommended. Alternatively, contact the Tourist Information Centre in Llangollen on 01978 860828.

THE RIVER WYE

Now I know that the River Wye is traditionally regarded as an English river, but in my heart I feel it's Welsh, and in the general layout of this book I feel it is perfectly logical to include it here in the Welsh section as well as in the Midlands section (see page 66).

A little history might not go amiss here. For most of the 20th century, the Wye was one of the country's leading salmon rivers. If we look back to the 1920s, catches were legendary. Salmon were not only prolific – they were huge. Thirty-pounders were commonplace, and forties were caught each and every year. This meant that for whole decades, coarse fishing on the Wye was rendered next to impossible as nearly all the beats were private and fished for salmon. Okay, here and there, in the town centres especially, coarse fishermen could be accommodated and there have always been big catches of chub, perch and pike with roach further down river.

However, it was only from the 1990s and with the tragic decline of the salmon stocks that a little water began to trickle onto the coarse market. It would still be a mistake to think that there is a lot of coarse fishing available on the Wye but the amount is increasing annually. And what fishing it is.

We are primarily talking about chub fishing, which can be splendid. All the usual methods work and you will find huge numbers of fish between three and five pounds in weight. I've often been sceptical about the legendary monsters of the Wye, but in recent years there have been more fish of six pounds turning up, with at least one genuine seven-pounder recorded. Why not try floating crust in the summer? Throw twenty or thirty pieces in and simply follow them downriver until they're attacked. You can be quite sure they will be attacked before long!

Pike fishing is also excellent in the Wye and is frequently ignored. Of course, one of the great benefits of the Wye is that there are so many sanctuary areas for the fish. If the pike feel pressurised in one area, they can simply move up- or downriver until they slip away into the unknown – very easy, as so much of the Wye bankside is heavily wooded and impenetrable.

Barbel On A Float

Most barbel are caught on swim feeders or leads, but float fishing can be great fun. Choose a meaty rod, a minimum of 12 feet in length.

- *Centre pins are ideal for the job.*
- *Main line ought to be around about 6 pounds breaking strain.*
- *Choose a float that is well up to job. There is no point in going too light or you will struggle with control.*
- *An Avon-type float is ideal for streamy water. A big stick float will suffice if the flow is more placid.*
- *It generally pays to fish quite a way over depth so that the bait is dragging bottom – exactly how the barbel expect to find it.*
- *If you are fishing over depth, then a long trot is not possible. Instead, try to work up the five or so yards of water in front of you. Fish this neatly, tightly and the barbel should come.*
- *Don't worry too much about differentiating between a bite and the shot catching on the bottom – a bite will generally pull the rod out of your hands! At the least, you will certainly know about it.*
- *Loose feed tightly and consistently – for example, ten or so grains of sweetcorn each cast, or a small handful of maggots. Make sure that the bait is getting down to the riverbed in the right place. It is no good baiting the next swim downriver.*

Lure fishing works very well when the water is clear, and in flood time, search out the bays with dead bait. Don't expect twenty-pounders each and every visit, but they're there in good numbers and a thirty-pounder is always on the cards, especially at the back end. As ever, treat your pike with the greatest respect and care, and don't let a big fish flop around on a hard bank and injure itself. Flatten down the barbs on those lure trebles. If you're dead baiting, strike quickly once a bite develops. Don't delay the strike: if you miss a take, then in all probability it's a jack pike and of no interest. A big fish will almost certainly be hooked.

There are other treats, too. Perch seem to be coming back – at least in the middle Wye, which I personally know best. Dace stocks are also recovering, and trotting with maggot can give you a tremendous autumn day's sport – in the summer the minnows probably tend to be too prolific to even think of using maggot as bait! You'll find bream here and there, and even the odd wandering carp. But, above all, the Wye is now gaining a huge reputation for its barbel stocks.

Barbel haven't been in the river very long – perhaps twenty years or so – and they're not well established throughout the river but are still found in pockets. Mind you, those pockets are now extending rapidly, and much of the middle Wye is now a barbel fisher's paradise – providing, of course, that access can be gained.

The Wye is generally low and clear in the summer and this allows for stalking techniques. Walk your stretch of river very carefully with Polaroids, looking for any of the giveaway signs. Flashing fish, rolling fish and even jumping fish are quite common. Try and get out at dawn and perhaps you will see barbel working on the shallows. Don't rush this side of the business: barbel aren't spread randomly like currants through a cake on the river Wye and you need to locate their swims.

Once located, the barbel tend to be somewhat less pressured than on many typical English rivers. This means that you can often get away with more clumsy tactics than you would want to employ on, say, the River Kennett. This does not mean they are stupid and that they don't learn quickly, because they do. Still, the fact remains that in many areas you can still catch barbel on sweetcorn and feeders. And let me make a plea here. The barbel of the Wye, in places, are naive and can be caught comparatively easily. If you do happen on a near-virgin shoal of barbel, please don't hammer them. Take two or three fish and then leave them alone. That way you can come back to them over and over again over many seasons without disturbing them too greatly and pushing them up the ladder of knowledge.

If you've been used to the river in low summer conditions, don't be too frightened when autumn comes and the river rises dramatically. It might look very scary, but you can still catch barbel. They do tend to push out of the main flows to some degree, but don't just look for slack water. The barbel is shaped to hug bottom in pretty quick currents, and if you can hang a bait out a few yards from the bank then you could well catch fish. In the winter, or when the water is coloured, go for the smellier baits, such as meatballs or big hunks of luncheon meat.

SEASON – June 16th to March 14th.

TICKETS – you have to search along the Wye to find areas where you can barbel fish throughout the season between June 16th and March 14th. Some areas do allow you on when salmon fishing ends in October. There is excellent fishing in Hereford itself and double figure barbel are caught there most weeks. The fishing is controlled by the Hereford and District Angling Club and day tickets are priced at £3.50. Obtain these tickets at Woody's Tackle Shop in the town of Hereford, or phone 01432 344644. Woody is an expert on this stretch of the river and he will advise on other day ticket areas in and around the town. He also sells top quality maggots, so no need to bring your own. Moving upstream, you can also contact Richard Pennington on 01544 327294 at the famous Letton Court stretch. There are about one and a half miles of water here with some good pegs. The opposite bank is controlled by the Red Lion Hotel, where I have been giving barbel fishing courses now for

STALKING CHUB

The small, clear, overgrown rivers of central Wales in particular are often undiscovered havens for big chub. And I mean big! Catching them, though, can be another business and stalking individuals can often prove highly effective and thrilling.

- *Travel as light as possible. You don't want to tote unnecessary gear long distances along pretty well untended bankside.*
- *Rod, reel, bait and bag of assorted items are all you're likely to need. Carry a trout-type landing net that you can hang from your waist.*
- *Polaroid glasses are essential for spotting individual fish.*
- *Look for chub anywhere there's cover – deeper water, overhanging branches, fallen tree trunks, heavy weed – the sort of places chub can hide and mount an ambush. Make sure your gear is reasonably heavy – bullying a big chub from its tree-root sanctuary can be a difficult job.*
- *Best baits are slugs, lobworms, breadflake and even small, dead fish like minnows. Big, bold baits attract a chub's attention.*
- *Try the floating crust technique for flushing chub out of hiding. Break up twenty or so pieces of floating crust and throw them into the flow, watching them carefully as they go downstream. Frequently you'll find that they are taken at a point fifty, a hundred or even two hundred yards from you. Move down carefully and you know where the fish will be.*
- *If you try for a chub and scare it, you can always go back later. Richard Walker used to say chub become secure again at about ten minutes to the pound! Double it, I guess, for these pressurised days!*

ten years. Most of the water is reserved for hotel residents or course members, but there is about a mile of day-ticket river available. Contact Mike Taylor on 01981 500303.

Most of the river upstream is protected but there is some fishing available in Hay town centre with a few barbel showing there. There are also reports of barbel way into Wales at Builth Wells. Contact Pete Smith at the Caer Beris Manor Hotel, on 01982 552601, for details of fish appearing on the Irfon, a major tributary, and for accommodation.

ACCOMMODATION – both the Caer Beris Manor Hotel, on 01982 552601, and the Red Lion Hotel in Bredwardine, on 01981 500303, are highly recommended.

Llangorse Lake

I have no hesitation in including Llangorse in this guide because it's a water that has given me some fabulous days. I just love it. Primarily, this is because you just won't find a more beautiful water anywhere, situated in its own little valley just to the west of the Black Mountains. It is a large water and, as fishing is by boat, you do feel as though you can get away from the rest of the world. When the day is fine and the sun is out, you just look around and realise coarse fishing doesn't come any better.

There's a good head of coarse fish in Llangorse, bream, perch and roach particularly. I've never targeted the bream but I've frequently seen them, especially in the shallow water where they've been muddying the water up as they feed. My plan for them, if I were ever to attempt them, would be to moor up at around twenty yards range and fish a moderate to heavy waggler on the fringe of their activity. By catapulting very small balls of ground bait laced heavily with maggots and casters I'd expect to pick up fish.

But it's the pike that have always attracted me to Llangorse. If we go back to Fred Buller's classic book, Domesday Pike, we'll find that is Llangorse mentioned there. Once upon a time, there was a run of salmon through the lake and, undoubtedly, pike did grow more massive in those days on the runs of classic silver tourists! Today, presumably, roach, bream and perch are there main fodder and their sizes have scaled down accordingly. There are still big pike to be had, though. As for methods, well all methods work at Llangorse, but my own preference is to drift slowly, working the water with a lure until I make contact. I might then anchor up and put a dead bait out while I search the area a bit more thoroughly.

Major words of caution here. Llangorse is beloved by the Welsh pike angler. It's the jewel in the crown. Please remember this and make sure that every single pike you hook in Llangorse is returned in the pristine condition you caught it in. You must take an unhooking mat along with you in your boat. Make sure that you have strong enough forceps or long-nosed pliers. Don't tackle Llangorse unless you know that you're a confident and competent pike angler. It's simply not fair to raid a water as fragile as Llangorse and harm the fish stocks.

Preaching over! A lovely water, whatever you are fishing for, and even on wild weather days the atmosphere remains. Just half close your eyes, take yourself back a hundred years or so and think of the monsters that once swam beneath your boat.

SEASON – the closed season is from 14th March for six weeks.
TICKETS – tickets and boats can be obtained from Ray Davies, Lakeside Caravan and Camping Park, Llangorse Lake, Brecon, Powys LD3 7TR, on 01874 658226. It is heartily advised that you plan a trip to Llangorse well in advance and make sure that everything is in order.
DIRECTIONS – Llangorse can be found off the A40 from Brecon to Abergavenny, to the northeast. From Abergavenny, turn right at Bwlch onto the B4560 and you will see Llangorse signposted on the left.
ACCOMMODATION – there is caravanning and camping on site. Alternatively, contact the Tourist Information Centre at Hay-on-Wye on 01497 820144 or at Brecon on 01874 622485.

COARSE FISHING IN PEMBROKESHIRE

Pembrokeshire is primarily a game-fishing area, but that doesn't mean to say that the coarse angler on holiday or visiting the area doesn't have some possibilities. There's some lovely fishing available. It's generally stillwater stuff but nicely controlled and, in places, with a pleasant, wild feel. Pembrokeshire itself is a stunning holiday area, and it's nice to know that sport and relaxation can be combined.

Breaking the mould, I'm simply going to give a list of the waters available along with contact phone numbers. Enquire for more specific details, such as directions and accommodation, when booking tickets.

BOSHERSTON LILY PONDS

Situated near Stackpole in the south of Pembroke, this is a flooded limestone valley managed by the National Trust. There's some interesting wildlife, with the rumour of otters. The ponds here have good stocks of coarse fish and the tench fishing is considered excellent. There are also roach, perch and good pike. You've got to get your permit first and this is available from Ye Olde Worlde Café, Bosherston (01646 661216) or the National Trust Office in Stackpole (01646 661359). Also contact the Pembroke and District Angling Club (01646 622712) as this excellent club also has the lease on nearby Decoy Pond, a thirteen-acre water with some permits available.

PENHOYLE FISHING PARK, PENALLY, TENBY, SA70 7RG (01824 8422550

There is some good coarse fishing here in a carefully planned lake landscape. The scenery around is beautiful and the parkland that has been planted is maturing into a wilderness.

Premier Coarse Fisheries, Holgen Farm, Llawhaden, Narberth SA67 8DJ (01437 541285)

This is a fishery managed by Ian Heaps himself. I've met Ian at many of the game shows and he speaks very highly of the water, as well he might. As a former world-champion match angler, he certainly has the experience. There are three lakes here and they're all well stocked with good carp and especially tench. Strongly recommended.

Roadside Farm, Templeton, Narberth, Dyfed SA67 8DA (01834 891283)

This is another appealing water that holds common carp, mirror carp, bream, roach and crucians. It is well stocked and set in serene surroundings. Contact Mr D. Crowley at Roadside Farm.

West Atheston Coarse Fishery, Valley Farm, Narberth, SA67 8BT (01834 860387)

This is only a one-and-a-half-acre lake, but it is very well stocked indeed with carp, tench, perch, bream and roach. There are also rumours of grass carp, which are a personal favourite of mine. Try hooking one on a thistlehead and you'll know what I mean! I may not have caught many grass carp, but I really did catch one on a thistlehead, and I also caught one on a four-inch piece of reed. You'd hardly believe it was possible until it happens to you!

Half Round Pond – South Wales

If you find yourself down in the Swansea area and you are looking for a spot of very pleasant fishing indeed, you can't do better than Half Round. This is a really good fishery, roughly in the shape of a horseshoe but divided by a narrow promontory to create two adjacent waters. The fishery extends to nearly three acres and is set in a valley bordered by trees. In fact, you would never guess that you were slap in the middle of a modern trading estate! It's a perfect venue for children, especially with a bailiff to keep a watchful eye and good, sound banks.

The fishing can also be well worthwhile. We're not talking huge fish here – the carp go to double figures, though, and the tench reach nearly five pounds. There are decent perch and, in common with most Welsh waters, some big eels. Even better for children, there are masses of tiny roach, always very willing biters on simple maggot. In fact, simple baits are the order of the day. Bread, worm, maggot and sweetcorn are pretty much all that you'll need. Floating baits are not allowed – sensible when you consider the amount of waterfowl on the ponds – and nor are barbed hooks.

Half Round isn't going to provide you with the most earth-shattering fishing in the world and you're not going to rewrite the record books but, considering its setting and how close to urbanization it lies, it really does offer a breath of the countryside. And above all, it's a tremendous stamping ground for children. Highly recommended.

SEASON – open March 1st to February 12th.

TICKETS – these cost £2.60 and the money is collected on the bank.

DIRECTIONS – from junction 45 on the M4, follow the A4067 to Swansea. Turn left at the second exit. Turn right at the first roundabout and cross the second roundabout past Fendrod Lake. The ponds are behind the Wyevale garden centre at the next roundabout.

ACCOMMODATION – contact the Swansea Tourist Information Centre on 01792 468321 for details of various types of accommodation in this area.

DARREN LAKE – SOUTH WALES

An interesting lake, set close to the industrial areas of South Wales. In fact, the lake itself is on the site of a disused coal mine. There were two very deep lift shafts and these were left to overflow. As a result there now exist around four acres of very cold spring water, some four feet deep around the margins and plunging rapidly to a zone that is twenty to thirty feet deep – an interesting area of water to investigate when it is bakingly hot or achingly cold!

The stocks in the lake are good. There are big bream and tench nudging at least six pounds. The perch are reputed to be sensational. Locals say five pounds, but even if this is wishful thinking, you can still stake your hat on some big ones being present. There are also decent roach and rudd, some big eels and a few small pike that don't seem to attract much attention at all.

The carp fishing has potential. There are, almost certainly, fish to thirty pounds plus present. It's not an easy lake though, if only because it is situated in a park and there is a good deal of bankside disturbance. Also, you've got that extraordinary depth range to take into account. You've got other problems to contend with, too. For example, the fishing is only available during park opening times, so it's difficult to get away from the madding crowd at times.

Nevertheless, this is a fascinating lake and it serves the area very well. It's run by the Glyncornel Angling Association and they keep a very careful eye on the water. Note that barbless hooks are mandatory.

SEASON – open March 1st to February 12th. It's only closed for a short time between February 13th and 28th/29th.

TICKETS – day tickets cost £5, season tickets £20 for adults and £15 for children/concessions. Contact Paul's Army and Navy Stores, Tonypandy, on 01443 432856, or David Piction-Davies on 01443 432289..

DIRECTIONS – from the A465 at Hirwaun, take the A4059 to Aberdare. Follow the A4233 through Maerdy to Ferndale and turn right by the Rhondda Hotel. Darren Park is just past the school on the right.

ACCOMMODATION – the Tourist Information Centre in Pontypridd, on 01443 490748, will give advice on suitable accommodation.

Highly Recommended Fisheries

- *Nine Oaks, Oakford, Aberaeron, Cardiganshire. Plenty of good carp, roach, tench and bream in an area of Wales not overly blessed with good coarse waters. Phone 01545 580482 for details.*
- *Gowerton Carp Lake, Swansea. A good carp water close to the city situated on the Gowerton golf course. Plenty of carp including some good fish, averaging double figures. Fishes well in winter. Phone 01792 875188.*
- *Fendrod Lake, Swansea. This is situated in Swansea's Enterprise Park and is occasionally flooded by the adjacent River Tawe. This means that there are plenty of dace to be caught, along with the usual species. The contact number here is 01792 202245.*
- *Hazel Court, Cowbridge, South Glamorgan. Plenty of carp and some good rudd fishing. Also exotics like koi. Phone 01443 229601 for details.*
- *Riverside Maesycwmmer, Mid Glamorgan. A tremendous coarse lake with plenty of fish. Carp a target species but also roach and, notably, ide. Contact 02920 867513 for further details.*
- *Warren Mill, Nr. Cardiff. Excellent carp fishing and good roach in the winter. Also tench, bream and some big perch. Search out the deeper water along the dam. Phone 01446 781274.*

Coarse-Fishing Sites in The North

1. *Longtown West Pond*
2. *The Lake District*
3. *Wyreside Lakes*
4. *Woodland Pool*
5. *Winsford Flash*
6. *Wall Pool Lodge*
7. *The River Swale*
8. *The River Ure*
9. *The River Ouse*
10. *Harthill Reservoirs*

'You know, for my job I travel all around the country, but I can never really wait to come back up north here, to my home. It's the wild waters, you see. All right, there is fishing pressure everywhere these days, but up here you can find stretches of river that you just know haven't been fished, at least not heavily, recently, if ever. And that reflects on the specimens themselves. Where else do you find chub so beautifully marked, in such cracking condition? There's plenty of variety too – enough to keep me going for a good few more years I'll tell you.'

MARTIN JAMES

Martin James, the radio presenter, once explained to me why he left his native Kent and put down roots in the north. How right Martin is. Just look at the dazzling array of waters available. The Lake District is full of mystery. Windermere is beginning to open up as a really extraordinary pike water, and there are big, big perch in many of the other deep, clear lakes. My own best fish came from Bassenthwaite back in the 80s and what a beautiful fish it was. I was brought up on the lakes, canals, meres and rivers of Cheshire. In fact, I saw my first two-pound roach from the Peak Forest canal, a rural stretch just outside Macclesfield. I also saw my first big bream from Tatton Park, weighing in at six pounds and two ounces. Martin James himself is a dab hand on the River Ribble and has made real inroads into the chub, roach and barbel populations there.

Yorkshire, too, has a whole lot to offer. Rivers like the Swale, Ure and Nidd are spate waters, up and down like a fiddler's elbow and constantly asking questions of the angler. The barbel aren't colossal there, but they're fighting fit and live in large shoals, and there are great chub, super grayling and dace – in fact pretty well everything a river angler could want. And with the onset of commercial fisheries, there's now much more in the way of really big carp than there was just twenty or so years ago. In those days, you really had to sweat for a big fish, perhaps sitting for a season or more on a water like Redesmere .

Longtown West Pond – Cumbria

I'm including this water because it's perched right in the north of the county, virtually on the borders with Scotland, and offers some excellent coarse fishing in an area that generally has little coarse fishing. West Pond is around twenty acres in extent, an old gravel pit going down to fifteen or sixteen feet in places. However, it's well matured and tree-lined, with a profusion of bars, plateaux and drop-offs. Also, most of the water isn't particularly deep and so is easily fished with a float. Partly because it is so shallow, it does get weedy in summer, and it might be an idea to take a drag, especially if you're fishing close in for the tench. There are good fish in the water. Carp reach twenty pounds, and bream have been recorded to double figures. The tench aren't very prolific but they are quite big, and the same goes for the perch. I'm also told there are some good stillwater chub in the water, genuinely reaching six pounds or so in weight.

All the usual pit techniques work here, and if you can find clear areas, especially at range, feed them up carefully with maggot, caster and corn. Swim feeder tactics also work well. Most carp, as expected, fall to boilies or, occasionally, luncheon meat.

Pike come to lures and dead baits – sardines are a favourite. (Please note that no live baiting is allowed on the water.) The chub are a different matter altogether. Stillwater chub virtually everywhere are very difficult beasts, and they're no different here. However, considering the sizes they run to, they are worth a bash. Try for them very early, at dawn, perhaps with a floater. Alternatively, go for dusk with perhaps a portion of dead fish. Do be careful of pike, though. Feed heavily with maggots in the hope of drawing chub into the area and getting them to intercept bait on the drop.

Season – open all year.
Tickets – these are £4.50 a day and it is best to phone in advance, on 01228 674519.
Directions – from Carlisle, take the A7 north to Longtown. Look for the A6071 signposted to Gretna. West Pond is at the bottom of the first turning on the left. The track leads to a car park.
Accommodation – for advice on suitable accommodation contact the Tourist Information Centre in Carlisle on 01228 625600.

The Lake District – Cumbria

Anyone holidaying in the Windermere area with coarse fishing tackle in their car is in for a real treat. There is some really excellent coarse fishing within just a few miles of the town, invariably set in the most wonderful surroundings. You probably won't break national records, but that doesn't matter: the fish are fighting fit, in beautiful condition and there are backdrops to take your breath away. In large part, this access to such good fishing is a result of the splendid clubs in the area – most notably the Windermere, Ambleside and District

Angling Association. This worthy organization has several very good waters and offers day tickets to the visitor. You should try Ratherheath Tarn – a beautiful, tree-lined lake of about five acres in extent. Ratherheath offers tremendous tench fishing with individuals to about three or four pounds in weight. There are good bream, too, running well over five pounds and the carp are nudging their way into the upper doubles. There are also crucians, roach, rudd, chub and perch.

You don't have to fish too far out, and most people simply fish a waggler three to four lengths from the bank. Also, it pays to investigate marginal, snaggy areas. Try to get out to deeper water if you can – some of the longer platforms will take you to convenient drop-offs.

Ratherheath does attract the wind and this can make waggler fishing difficult. If it is windy, try either a straight lead or a small feeder, a method particularly favoured for the bream. All traditional baits work well, but maggots – especially red ones – and casters seem to pick up the bream. Small worms are also attractive to the bream, crucians and tench, and will occasionally attract a passing carp. All the traditional carp baits work well. In the very early morning, during warm weather, look for the carp in the shallows. They'll often come into water less than a foot deep and you'll see them feeding, throwing up mud clouds. Exciting stuff. A lobworm fished on a size six can often do the trick.

Holehird Tarn is another cracking WADAA water. It's an estate lake, dating back to the late 19th century. You have to buy tickets for Holehird before fishing. Only four day tickets are allowed, and this means that a serene day is pretty well guaranteed.

It's around three acres in extent and beautifully landscaped. It was made by damming a small stream, and this means that depths are about six feet at the dam to a mere foot or so near the inflow. There is plenty of bankside cover – lots of overhanging trees, along with lilies, weed beds and reeds.

There are some very good carp in Holehird, certainly reaching well into double figures. The crucian carp get to a pound or so and the tench are knocking five pounds. There are good roach, rudd and some pleasing bream.

Once again, look for the carp up in the shallows, especially early and late. You can get them on surface baits, but I'm told they are 'wising up'. Perhaps a bed of maggots will get them down or, once again, don't overlook that trusty lobworm.

Do make sure, however, that your tackle is up to the job. The carp fight very well indeed and they're rarely far away from snags. The association takes pride in the water and its fish stocks and it's only fair that you leave the place in as pristine a state as you find it.

The same goes for Grasmere. You just won't find a more beautiful water for pike anywhere in the British Isles. I promise you that. Weed can be something of a problem, especially in the summer. Grasmere is a prime tourist attraction so it often pays to get out early on the water, especially if you're fishing from the very accessible east bank.

Grasmere holds great stocks of perch and roach – both of which can reach a couple of pounds or so – but it's the pike that really make the fishery. Genuine thirty-pound fish have been caught and there are plenty of twenties every year. Smaller fish, just into doubles, are also prolific.

The fish come well to lures – try a surface lure, perhaps at dawn during settled weather conditions. Dead baits also do very well. (Please note that live baits are not allowed.) Try to vary your dead baits – eel sections are good, or even a lamprey or a small rainbow trout. Think carefully how you're going to present your dead bait. Make sure, for example, that you're not simply heaving it out into an extensive weed bed. Perhaps you can try one popped up with some polystyrene inserted in its throat?

Grasmere is the jewel in the crown of the WADAA so do take care of the pike stocks here. They are quite heavily fished and, although they may look ferocious with all those teeth, they are highly susceptible to bad handling. Always lay pike out on an unhooking mat – especially important if you're out in one of the rowing boats. Make sure that you have strong forceps or long-nosed pliers with you to get any deep hooks out. Ensure that you've flattened all the barbs on your trebles. If you are wary of going too near a pike's mouth, don't be afraid of wearing a good, stout, leather glove. When unhooking a pike, you've got to be confident. Don't dither. Lay the fish down, and if necessary, straggle it with your legs. If you've struck quickly and cleanly when dead baiting you should have the hooks close to the lips and they're much easier to remove here. Get that pike back into the water as quickly as possible. If you need a photograph, let it rest in the margins, in a net perhaps, while you set up the camera. Don't bother weighing every fish that comes along unless you think it's a personal best. Remember that every second out of the water causes these precious pike that extra bit of stress.

There's far more to the area than I've mentioned – Clea Barrow Tarn, Rydal Water, Blelham Tarn, Bassenthwaite, Coniston, Bigland Hall, the Ulverston Canal and so on. In fact, you can hardly do better than join the WADAA itself – you'll find this brings many benefits and the annual membership is very reasonable indeed.

SEASON – in general, often all year but check with the WADAA.

TICKETS – for Holehird, permits must be bought in advance. You can get them from Go Fishing, Robinson Place, Bowness on Windermere, Cumbria LA23 3DQ. Enclose a cheque and stamped addressed envelope. Day tickets cost £4 for adults and £2 for juniors. Phone 01539 447086 with enquiries. For Ratherheath, you can buy your permit at the Plantation Bridge Filling Station, which is just south of the fishery. For Grasmere – where day tickets are £3.50 – you can buy permits from the local Tourist Information Centres (of which there are many) or contact the WADAA direct. Contact Chris Sodo, Ecclerigg Court, Ecclerigg, Windermere, Cumbria LA23 1LQ on 01539 442708.

DIRECTIONS – from the mini roundabout on the A591 outside Windermere, take the A592 Ullswater road. Holehird Estate is on the right just after St. Anne's School for Girls, about half a mile from the roundabout. The fishery car park is clearly signed just inside the entrance to the estate. The Tarn is a short walk through the trees. To reach Ratherheath, go north on the A591 from the main Kendal roundabout. After half a mile the road becomes dual carriageway. A hundred and fifty yards into this section, turn left onto Ratherheath Lane. The fishery is on the right. Grasmere is found on the A591 north of Ambleside. You will come to it on the left, shortly after passing Rydal Water.

Accommodation – all of the following can supply details of accommodation in their areas: Windermere Tourist Information Centre, Victoria Street, Windermere, on 01539 446499; Kendal Tourist Information Centre, Town Hall, Kendal, on 01539 725758; Ambleside Tourist Information Centre, Central Buildings, Market Cross, Ambleside, on 01539 432582.

Lake Perch

The Lake District in particular has had an outstanding reputation for large perch over the course of many years. These are fine, bristling fish, but how do you go about catching them?

- *Location is vitally important. You won't catch perch on large, deep waters unless you know where they are.*
- *Ask around and get as much local knowledge as you can. Trout fishermen are often particularly approachable. Perch don't mean too much to them!*
- *If you can, get afloat and take a fish finder with you. Remember that perch are shoal fish and they will frequently show up on the screen. Failing that, be as mobile as possible until you find fish. Explore by both bank and boat fishing as much acreage as you can. A good way to do this is to use lures. Perch like small spinners – especially with red wool around the tail. Try bright silvery plugs as well. Use Polaroid glasses and watch your lure as it comes into the bank. Perch will often follow without actually taking.*
- *Try trolling for perch – that is pulling small lures behind a moving boat. This way you're covering a lot of water rapidly and if you do contact perch, anchor up and fish the area carefully.*
- *Remember that top perch baits are small dead baits – minnows, gudgeon and the like, and also lobworms. One or two lobworms on a size four hook are difficult to beat.*
- *Try and get out a t dawn if you possibly can. This is a prime perch feeding time and you might well see perch on the prowl, chasing small fry around the margins or even bow waving after their own baby brethren. Remember that perch are very cannibalistic and a four inch dead perch is hard to beat for a grandmother.*
- *Perch are particularly susceptible to stress. Don't keep them in a net but photograph them and, if necessary, weigh them and return them as quickly as possible.*

WYRESIDE LAKES – LANCASHIRE

Sometimes commercial fisheries really do hit the jackpot and offer fishing that is way beyond anything that so-called natural waters can produce. This is certainly the case at Wyreside. The Wyreside complex, just off the River Wyre, holds seven waters, each offering vastly different challenges. The predominant theme, however, is carp fishing. There is a staggering number of big fish in the lakes – carp reaching almost forty pounds, very large indeed for the north.

However, you don't have to leap in big-time. This is what makes it such a perfect place for a holidaying angler, perhaps with children who want to know the ropes. Tuition, by the way, is also available. It's generally considered by the regulars that Foxes Lake is the best place for the general angler. There are carp there in numbers and size, but they're not too desperately difficult to catch. Moreover, there are big tench, lots of bream, huge stocks of roach and rudd along with perch, crucians and chub in this very prolific four-acre water.

There are well-known hotspots – the outflow pipes especially – but fishing a feeder at range is generally considered one of the surest ways of building up a bag. Hemp is considered an important base to fishing at Foxes and is available on site if you can't bring yourself to cook your own! Maggots, sweetcorn and worms all work well also.

Foxes is a favourite venue so, as on all comparatively pressurised waters, it doesn't pay to be stereotypical. Try something just a little bit unconventional and you could get a surprise. Why not, for example, mix casters in with your feed and then try ten or eleven of them squeezed onto a size six or eight hook.

There are other lakes all the way up the ladder of difficulty. Sunnyside One holds plenty of better-sized carp and is considered the next step to take. At the top of the pyramid is Wyre Lake, a real big-fish water, holding several carp over thirty pounds.

A really great complex, attractive to look at, very welcoming, with great fish stocks, and altogether highly recommended.

SEASON – open all year.

TICKETS – there is a whole scale of charges depending on which lake you are fishing and how long you are at the waterside. For Foxes – the most popular family choice – a full day costs from as little as £4.50. There's also a children's lake where under-twelves fish free if they have a parent on the fishery. Phone Wyreside Lakes on 01524 792093 for full details.

DIRECTIONS – take the M6 northwards from Preston. At Junction 33, just after the Lancaster Service Station, turn left at the first roundabout, and then immediately left onto Hampson Lane. At the end of the lane turn right (you will see the signs to the fishery). Go past the Fleeced Inn pub and then right and left and you will come to the waters.

ACCOMMODATION – there is camping on site. Details of other accommodation can be obtained from the Tourist Information Centre in Lancaster on 01524 32878. The fishery is also reasonably close to Morecambe, where there is a host of various kinds of accommodation. Phone the Tourist Information Centre there on 01524 582808.

WOODLAND POOL – SOUTH WIRRAL

There are four lakes at this day ticket venue but this is probably the most beautiful. All the lakes are mature and they have become hugely popular in the area. There are islands, weed beds, reed margins and lots of overhanging trees – a real gem of a pool.

Fish stocks are generous. The crucian fishing is excellent and you tend to find these in the margins, especially under the weeds and in the tree roots. The tench – some of them very good fish indeed – tend to hang around the islands, and the carp are absolutely suckers for floating baits when the temperatures are reasonably stable. Mind you, they can be infuriatingly fussy. Make sure that your line immediately preceding the hook bait is under the surface, because if they see it in the surface film you are unlikely to get a bite. There are even a few catfish in the lake and chub have recently been introduced. Please note that keep nets are not allowed – another sign of pride in a fishery.

SEASON – open all year.
TICKETS – day tickets cost £6 for one rod. Night fishing costs £10. Phone 0151 353 0115 for further details.
DIRECTIONS – from Chester, take the A540 northwest toward Hoylake. After the junction with the A550, take the third turning on the left signposted Burton. The fishery is well signposted in the village.
ACCOMMODATION – contact the Tourist Information Centres in Birkenhead, on 0151 647 6780, and/or Chester, on 01244 402111, for details of accommodation in the area.

WINSFORD FLASH – CHESHIRE

This is a spacious, seventy-acre flash that is fed by the River Weaver. Forty-five acres of the water are available on day permit. Depths average around about six feet but there are deeper pockets, especially out in the middle, which reach twelve and thirteen feet. The fish stocks, though, are excellent. Carp are a big draw with lots of doubles and big fish approaching thirty. The water is full of bream, which are not generally large, but there are rumours of double-figure fish here. There are many pike and numerous doubles, along with tench, big perch and two pound roach.

Both pole and waggler approaches work well, but if you really want to get into the bream, the ground bait feeder attack is probably the best. Remember that the bream stocks really are prolific and this isn't the sort of water where you build up a big bag with just half a pint of maggots or so. Keep the feed going in but, as always with bream fishing, beware of putting big balls directly above a feeding shoal's head. Bites can get a bit twitchy as water temperatures drop later in the year and this is where sensitive indication and the very best quality bait begins to pay off. A single caster on a size sixteen hook, along with a small redworm, has long been one of my own personal favourites for temperamental bream. Waters like this are a lot of fun: when your float goes down you simply don't have a clue what species could be next to come to your waiting net.

SEASON – open all year.
TICKETS – these cost £3 per day and are available down on the bankside. Junior tickets are £1.50. Night tickets are £5 and £2.50. Phone 01606 558475.
DIRECTIONS – on the A54 from Middlewich to Winsford, you will come to the central Winsford roundabout. This crosses the River Weaver. Continue up the hill and at the second set of traffic lights turn left along Dene Drive. Turn left at the first roundabout into Queensway and on into Ways Green. You will see signs now for Winsford Flash. You come to the dirt road and turn right before the caravan park. The Flash is on your left and parking is ample. Do note, however, that certain areas of the Flash are out of bounds.
ACCOMMODATION – there is bed and breakfast accommodation very close to the site. Phone 01606 592186, or contact the Tourist Information Centre in Nantwich, on 01270 610983, who can supply details of further accommodation in the area.

CHOOSING SWIMS ON BIG WATERS

Huge reservoirs and gravel pits can be intimidating places to fish simply because the location is so daunting.

- *Fish of most species tend to follow the wind. Most winds in this country blow from the south and west so banks to the north and east are generally favourite.*
- *Look for any possible features, islands, bays, shallow bars, water towers, inflowing streams. Fish might not necessarily be around these features but they do give you a starting point.*
- *Look intently for signs of surface activity. You might see a crashing carp, or the backs of rolling bream.*
- *Binoculars are a great help when looking for fish.*
- *On a windy day you will sometimes see a large flat area of water appear. This is a sign of a big fish turning underneath.*
- *Remember that even on the largest of waters fish aren't necessarily always out on the horizon but can be close in to the margins.*
- *If you are pike fishing, a drift float rig can get your dead baits one hundred and fifty yards or more out from the bank. A great method.*
- *Don't be afraid to ask bailiffs for any information they might be able to give. It is their job to make sure you're a happy fisherman!*

WALL POOL LODGE – CHESHIRE

Gawsworth is the most gorgeous of rural villages, set deep in the Cheshire countryside, and the lakes there, when I was a child, were always something of a dream for me. This is real, sleepy, rural fishing. Wall Pool Lodge offers three well-stocked and very beautiful woodland pools. They're exactly as I remember from childhood, girt by rushes and ornamented by lily pads.

Wood Pool is probably the largest of the waters, followed by Park Pool and Wall Pool, and they are all well stocked. Wall Pool, however, has a real reputation for ghost carp. These beautiful and shy fish average about five pounds. There are also good tench, roach and rudd. All the lakes hold big crucians and interesting perch. There are carp to approaching twenty pounds and good bream.

Despite the number of fish, they're not always that easily caught – it pays to fish close to features and to get to the water early.

SEASON – open all year.
TICKETS – these cost £5. They are best pre-booked, on 01260 223442.
DIRECTIONS – Gawsworth is just outside Macclesfield on the A536 Congleton Road. In the village, follow the signs to Gawsworth Hall. Go through the gate and the fishery is well signposted.
ACCOMMODATION – advice on various types of accommodation in the area can be obtained from the Tourist Information Centres in Macclesfield, on 01625 504114, and Buxton, on 01298 25106.

THE RIVER SWALE – YORKSHIRE

Go back thirty years or so and the River Swale was the barbel Mecca of the north. In fact, my first trips after the species were spent at the then very famous Topcliffe stretch. I was never successful myself, though nearly... One glorious morning I actually hooked what was obviously a barbel. It tore off against a clutch that couldn't have been screwed down more tightly with a pair of pliers. There wasn't much stretch in the nylon lines of old and the result was simply inevitable. I received a justified ticking off from the adult club members that I've never forgotten.

It is a fact that too many barbel are lost, especially by those that haven't had a great deal of experience fishing for them. Always make sure YOUR CLUTCH is set properly and can give line if it has to, your knots are secure, your hook point is sharp and that you're not going too light on the breaking strain.

Also, watch out for that famed last rush, because it is a fact. Well over ninety percent of barbel will make another strong, spirited run when they see the landing net. Be ready, and have your rod up and your clutch set lightly so that you're not going to leave a hook in a tired fish.

The Swale has always responded well to maggots and casters – and you'll pick chub, grayling and roach on these. In some stretches, bream have also been stocked, and these are beginning to grow and to spread. Don't neglect the usual baits: meatballs work well, and if the water is high and coloured, try two or even three on a big hook.

SEASON – phone 01609 776850 to check on the current situation.
TICKETS – an excellent stretch can be found at Morton-on-Swale. Day tickets cost £5 and must be obtained from Morton Service Station before fishing. You'll find this at the river end of this small village. In case of problems, phone 01609 776850. Obviously, if you are contemplating an early start, get your ticket the day before.
DIRECTIONS – turn off the A1, south of Scotch Corner onto the A684. You'll be heading eastwards towards Northallerton. In about three or four miles, you will come to Morton Bridge where there is good parking in the lay-by adjacent. The river can be reached along the paths at the bridge, at Swalefields Farm or Fairholme Farm. These are all situated down the lane on the right after passing over the bridge. Morton village will be just in front of you.
ACCOMMODATION – advice on various kinds of accommodation can be obtained from the Tourist Information Centre in Northallerton, on 01609 776864.

THE RIVER URE – YORKSHIRE

I have the happiest memories of the Ure, this sparkling Yorkshire river. Find the right stretches and you'll be in a wonderland. Nice, eddying deeps, glistening shallows and enticing, steady glides. And, generally, flowing through stunning countryside. What can you expect on the Ure? Well, barbel certainly. These might not run as large as in some of the southern rivers, but they're cracking fish nonetheless and fight spectacularly. You can catch them in all sorts of ways but, if you can, try and get out early in the morning and stalk them in the shallows. They come from the deeps during the night to feed on caddis, loach, leeches, anything they can find in and around those gravely margins. Approach them really cautiously – you'll often see their fins on bow waves – and free-line a single lobworm just upstream of them. Watch that line streak tight!

You'll find grayling, too, and what's better than float fishing for them on a crisp, autumn morning? And, of course, like all the Yorkshire rivers, the Ure is famous for its chub. These can grow large, but be satisfied with any fish over a couple of pounds or so. Of course, chub will come on maggots and casters, but never neglect a really big lump of flake. And I mean big. A piece the size of an orange will often overcome the suspicions of chub that are used to light gear and small baits. In short, summer or winter, a brilliant river.

SEASON – at present, rivers still have a closed season but a change is threatened. Check on your ticket for the latest details.

Tickets – there are several places where day ticket access is available. Ripon is a good place to start and Ripon Piscatorial Association sells day tickets for £4. A useful contact here is Bernard Thain at the Ripon Angling Centre, on 01765 604666. There are also day tickets available on the Newby Hall Estate at Boroughbridge. Phone the tackle shop Fish-n-Things on 01423 324776. Day tickets cost £4.50.

Directions – for the Ripon stretch, take the A61 or B6265 east to access points. You will see the parking areas shown on your ticket. Fish-n-Things (see above) will give detailed instructions on purchase of ticket.

Accommodation – the Tourist Information Centre in Ripon, on 01765 604625, can give advice on suitable accommodation.

The River Ouse – Yorkshire

I've never done nearly as well on the Ouse as I feel I should have done and in part this is because it is bigger, deeper and less easy to read, I guess. Still, it does have very good fish in it. You'll find roach, bream, perch, chub, barbel and good pike in most stretches of the river. Perch can grow large and the barbel, though not that easy to contact, can be huge.

There's some excellent free fishing just northwest of York itself. So, if you are visiting this wonderful, ancient town it is worth putting a selection of gear into the car. The pole works very well here, as do both waggler and stick floats. Probably favourite, however, is feeder with maggot. Good bags are possible, especially if you get out of the city early in the morning and catch that early feeding spell.

Season – phone 01904 654484 to check on current situation

Tickets – these are free, but the nearest tackle shop, Mitre Pets, Shipton Road, York, will give further details. You can contact them on 01904 654484.

Directions – from York, take the A19 road to Thirsk. In a very short while you will come to a road on the left called Waterend. Park in the lay-by on the left, just before the bridge.

Accommodation – contact the Tourist Information Centre in York on 01904 621756. They can give details of various kinds of accommodation in the area.

Harthill Reservoirs – South Yorkshire

I've never actually fished Harthill, but a couple of visits there without tackle have impressed me immensely. There's something noble about these reservoirs so close to the city of Sheffield. Number One reservoir is large and deep, especially by the main dam where, with depths approaching thirty feet, you can catch roach in the coldest of winter weather. The opposite end of the reservoir is shallower with a deep channel running through it. There are all sorts of fish here to be caught, often good-sized ones. The carp and pike both pass twenty pounds and

there are reputedly double figure bream and tench approaching that mark. There are good roach, as well, in the reservoirs – some say two-pound fish.

Number Two reservoir is both smaller and shallower than Number One, but it nonetheless offers some good sport, especially with carp. Reservoir Number Three is the shallowest of them all.

The local anglers fish the water intently. Hemp, ground bait with casters and redworms seem favourite for roach and bream. Occasionally, try just turning the reel handle a couple of times so that the hook bait inches back along the reservoir bed. All manner of carp baits seem to do the trick, but for pike you've got to think of presenting a dead bait in an untypical fashion if you're going to get the best out of the water. They've simply seen too many dead herrings presented hard on the bottom. Perhaps you could use a drifter float, moving a sardine slowly through the mid-water regions. Or go for a more exotic dead bait – really search your tackle dealer's freezer or the local fishmonger. And don't forget eel sections – tremendously effective. I've also got a feeling that very small flat fish could prove interesting!

Season – open all year.

Tickets – these are available on the water. They cost £3 for a day and £6 for a night. Phone 01142 207352 for details. There are many concessions.

Directions – take the A618 south from Rotherham. Just before you reach the M1, turn off left towards Woodall and Harthill. Turn onto Carver Close and you will find parking by the first reservoir.

Accommodation – the Tourist Information Centre in Sheffield, on 01142 211900, can advise on suitable accommodation.

Highly Recommended Fisheries

- *Pebley Reservoir, Harthill, South Yorkshire. At around twenty-five acres, Pebley is a large water and very picturesque, nestling in its wooded valley. Big tench and bream, including roach around the two-pound mark. There are some big pike and good perch. The carp now are plentiful. Contact Dave Downes on 0966 361005.*
- *The River Swale at Cundall Lodge Farm, Boroughbridge, Yorkshire. A tremendous piece of the river, offering very good chub fishing. There are also good numbers of barbel, roach and perch. Worm is seen as a good bait, along with the usual luncheon meat. Day tickets cost £3 and you pay in the farmyard. Contact Fish 'n' Things, Boroughbridge. Phone them on 01423 324776 for bait and up to the minute advice on conditions.*
- *Tyram Hall Fishery, Hatfield, South Yorkshire. Four pools available. Some big carp, plenty of doubles, and the main lake holds good numbers of roach, bream and tench. Also some good pike and fish approaching twenty-five pounds have been landed. A good all-round fishery. Tickets cost between £3 and £6. Phone Phil Johnson on 01302 840886.*
- *The River Don, Doncaster, South Yorkshire. Not the most elegant of fisheries, but worth trying as it's pretty well come back from the dead. Today there are good roach, perch, chub and even the occasional barbel. Day tickets cost £2.50. Contact Doncaster Match Secretary, Lee Granta, on 01302 781016 for further details and directions.*
- *Flylands Pond, Bishop Auckland, County Durham. A small two-acre pond with a central island and depths to around four or five feet. Small carp, tench and skimmers but some good roach. Plenty of fish. Good for beginners. Tickets are £5 a day on the bank. Contact 01388 832362.*
- *Fir Tree Lodges, Appley Bridge, Wigan, Lancashire. Two lakes here. Nicely matured. Carp to mid twenties, big tench and chub. Reputed three-pound roach and perch and some good crucians. Also some golden and blue orfe. Lots of fish, lots of potential surprises. Tickets £5 a day on the bank. Phone 01257 252607 for further details.*
- *Borwick Fishery, Carnforth, Lancashire. A ten-acre gravel pit holding big carp and bream plus good tench, roach and perch. Not a particularly easy water but the rewards are impressive for the specialist angler. This is a popular fishery, so check on availability and ticket prices by phoning 01254 720844.*

Coarse-Fishing Sites in Scotland

1. *River Tweed*
2. *Barend Loch*
3. *Oauchenreoch Loch*
4. *Duddingston Loch*
5. *Clatto Country Park*
6. *Glasgow Fishing*
7. *Loch Lomond*
8. *Loch Awe*
9. *Loch Garry*
10. *Loch Ness*
11. *River Tummel*

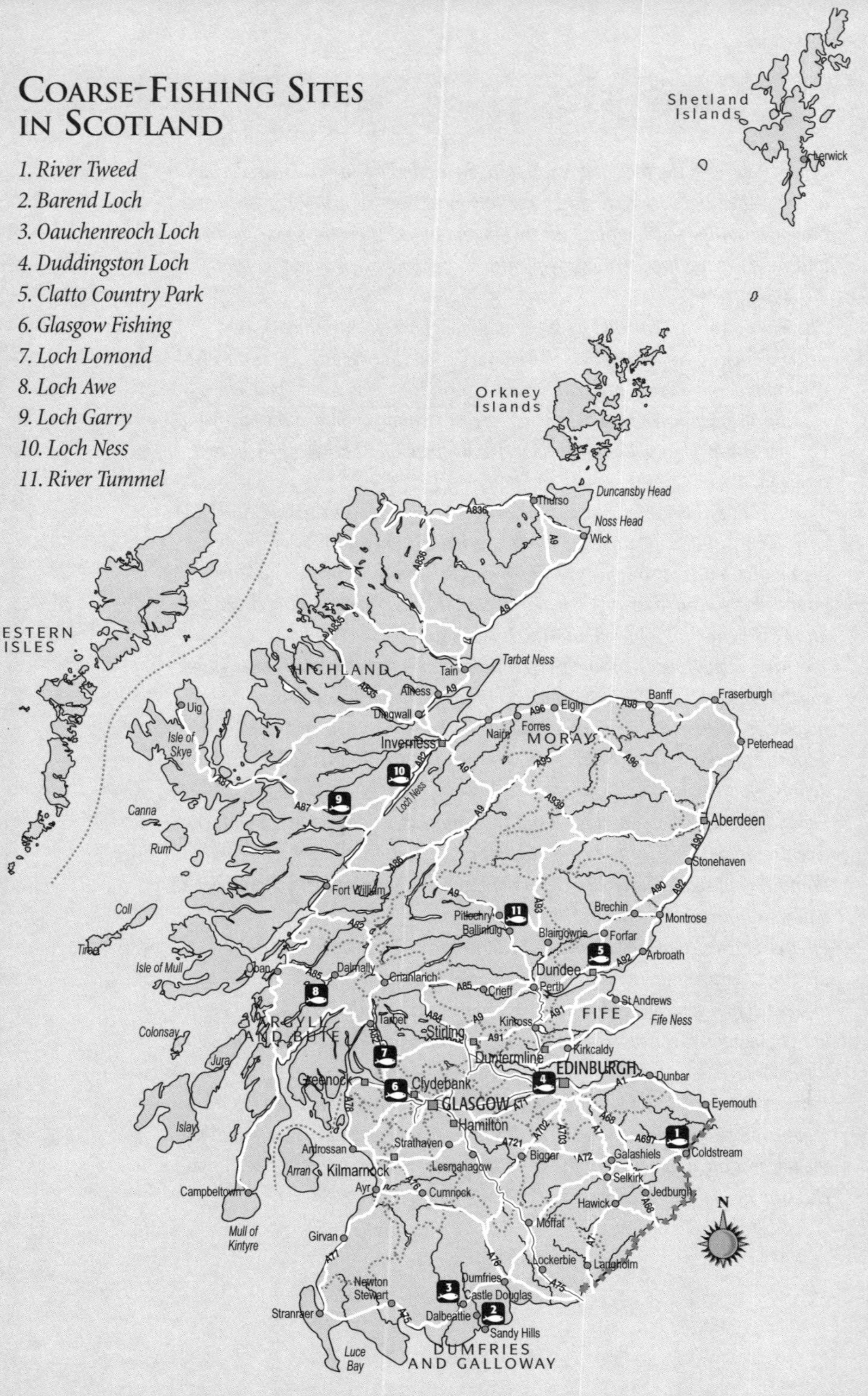

For the man who really wants a bit of adventure, my guess is you can't do better than coarse fishing in Scotland. The point is there are just no signposts up here. Everything is fresh and new, and most things you've got to find out for yourself. I've been coming up to Scotland for around fifteen years – mostly with pike gear – and there's still hardly anything I do know, never mind things I don't. Mind you, you will catch fish, Probably! What is definite is that you will never catch pike that look better and fight more magnificently. They really are tigers. Unbelievable. There's more, obviously. The perch can grow big here, and in the lowland belt you've got some very interesting roach and dace fishing for instance. But, for me, it's the Highlands every time.

ROGER MILLER – ANGLING AUTHOR

Roger is absolutely spot on with this assessment of Scottish fishing. The lowland belt does offer more conventional delights. Here you can catch bream, roach, dace, tench and carp, but it is as you climb north that the real lure of Scotland begins to grab you.

The lochs are vast, largely uncharted, bodies of water and it's only really Loch Lomond that anybody knows a great deal about. Trek further than that and you are beginning to break some new territory. But don't be too worried – you're not totally on your own. There have been enlightened fishermen for many years who have understood what piking in the north of Scotland is all about and have appreciated its possible, awe-inspiring boundaries.

Who can actually tell how big Scottish pike can actually grow? We know, of course, that twenties and thirties are to be caught. Nor do I have any doubt that there are forty-pounders in some lakes. And fifties? Well, rumours abound that pike of that sort of size were taken back in the last century, either on rod and line or in nets laid out to rid trout waters of them.

RIVER TWEED – SCOTTISH BORDERS

Naturally enough, whenever an angler thinks of the Tweed it's salmon that pulls his imagination. However, for the touring coarse fisherman, a lot more is on offer. It was back in the 1960s that the huge roach of the River Tweed really began to make ripples in the angling world. Roach of two pounds were common. Three-pounders were anything but rare. Dace of a pound littered the river. More and more anglers, especially from northern England, began to make their way to the Tweed, and huge catches were taken.

And so it was through the 70s, before catches began to decline somewhat in the early 80s. Now, there is a rumour that roach and dace are on their way back in both numbers and size. I'm not necessarily saying that the fishing you'll find on the Tweed is going to be easy. It certainly will be, though, if you search enough water and find the fish. Believe me, the roach shoals can be large and obliging. The key is to keep on the move, watch for any surface activity and, above all, take local advice.

If you can keep them fresh, swim feeder maggots can work very well where allowed, although bread and worms also take their fair share of fish. My own best bag was built up in Coldstream, just by the bridge on the crease of a huge slack a third of the way across the river. If I remember correctly, in a four-hour session I took some thirty roach over a pound, with two of them going over two pounds to just on two pounds and four ounces. Intermingled were some twenty or thirty fine dace.

I've included this entry because the rewards can be great for the angler willing to risk a slow day or two. But, of course, a day on the Tweed is never wasted. This majestic river in such wondrous countryside is a water to be loved no matter what the day's results might bring.

SEASON – there is no close season for coarse fish in Scotland, although it pays to check on local rules that may protect areas of water when migratory fish are spawning. Ring the secretary of Coldstream and District Angling Association, M. Young Esq., on 01573 226411 for up-to-the-minute information. He can also advise on day tickets for brown trout and grayling.

TICKETS – tickets can be bought for £2 a day from the Crown Hotel in Market Square, on 01890 882558, and from the Coldstream Guardian, on 01890 883164. The Norhambridge area is well worth a look for roach, perch and dace, and tickets can be bought for £4 a day from the Masons Arms, the Victoria Hotel, the Mace Shop and the Shepherd Shop all in Norham village itself. Kelso is also a centre for coarse fishing. Tickets for £4 a day can be bought from: Forest and Sons, 40 The Square; Intersport, 43 The Square; and Tweedside Tackle, 36–38 Bridge Street – all in Kelso.

ACCOMMODATION – a huge amount of bed and breakfast accommodation is available in the area along with some exceptional hotels. The Tillmouth Park Hotel, on 01890 882255, is quite spectacular and offers some excellent fishing of its own. In Kelso, try the Cross Keys Hotel on 01572 223303, or the Ednam House Hotel, which is right on the River Tweed itself, on 01573 223303.

BAREND LOCH – DUMFRIES AND GALLOWAY

Barend is one of those rare beasts up in Scotland – a carp-only fishery. It used to be trout but competition forced a change of use for the water, so the trout were taken out and the carp put in. Most of them are either ghost carp or commons, which makes for an interesting mix. The fish aren't yet of a huge size, but they're in good condition, there are plenty of them and they fight well in the clear water. Barend extends to around three acres. It's picturesque and surrounded by trees, and an island adds some focus. The lake is man-made but it is spring-fed and that accounts for its clarity. Most of the water is quite shallow, but there are areas that go down to nine or ten feet.

The pool can be approached in a variety of ways. For smaller carp, close-in float fishing with corn, scraps of meat and maggots, for example, works well. Try laying on or fishing just on the bottom under a waggler. For larger carp, look for the deeper water and try ledgering larger baits. Luncheon meat, again, works well as, obviously, do all manner of boilies.

Don't neglect floaters either. Dog biscuits and bread crust both work well, especially on warmer days when fishing on or near the bottom can be difficult. Ideal conditions, overall, are warm, wet, windy days when light values are low.

Barend is all part of a holiday village complex, so it's an ideal place to take the family, get away from everything, explore the lowlands and do a bit of carp fishing in the evening before or after supper.

SEASON – open all year.

TICKETS – day tickets cost £5 and are available from the holiday complex reception. Buy these before fishing. Contact Frank Gorley, Barend Loch, Sandy Hills, Dumfries and Galloway, Scotland, on 01387 780663.

DIRECTIONS – take the A710 from Dumfries towards Sandy Hills. Turn right onto the road signposted to Dalbeattie and you'll find the fishery shortly on the left. The holiday complex reception, which you must visit, is on the right.

ACCOMMODATION – either stay on site or contact the Dumfries and Galloway Tourist Board on 01387 245550.

OAUCHENREOCH LOCH – DUMFRIES AND GALLOWAY

This very picturesque loch, lying very close to the A75, offers some spectacular perch and pike fishing. It's a natural loch, long and narrow, averaging around fifteen feet. It does go deeper – reputedly to fifty feet – and the water is generally clear. It also gets weedy, which goes a long way to explaining why the perch stocks are so good. You can target them successfully when the weed dies off from October onwards.

There are several ways of approaching the water and for the small roach and small perch that proliferate, simply float fishing with maggots does well. For larger perch, try either lure fishing or drifting a dead bait. Should a small perch accidentally die through deep hooking, for example, you cannot find a better bait. If it is taken, don't delay too long in striking, as a two-pound perch can quickly gobble down one of its smaller brethren. I aim for about four or five seconds before striking with a slow deliberate sweep.

The pike average a good size and have been caught to mid twenties with plenty of rumours of the odd thirty-pounder being seen. Once again,perch is a good dead bait for them but in this clear water lure fishing always works well. One last tip: if you are fishing a dead bait for perch, always make sure that you use a wire trace in case a pike picks up the bait.

Boats are allowed on the loch, which gives you more scope to explore unfishable water. Bank fishing is only available on the road side of the water.

Season – all year round.
Tickets – these costs £3 and are obtained at the Loch View Motel before fishing. Phone 01556 690281
Directions – the loch lies between Dumfries and Castle Loch by the side of the main A75. Leave Dumfries heading towards Castle Douglas and you'll find the fishery on the right-hand side a little way through Crocketford.
Accommodation – the Loch View Motel is right on the water. Advice on other accommodation can be obtained from the Dumfries and Galloway Tourist Board, 64 Whitesands, Dumfries DG1 2RS, or phone 01387 245550.

Duddingston Loch – Edinburgh

How about this! Duddingston is a twenty-five acre loch set in the scenic grounds of Holyrood Park – owned by the Queen herself – and the fishing is free! It's basically a nature reserve and bird sanctuary, but you are still allowed free access to a hundred-yard stretch of the banks. You won't find much depth – in no place is the loch much deeper than six or seven feet – but you will find good fish. The primary species are roach, perch and carp that grow respectively to two, three and twenty-plus pounds. Ledgering further out is the best bet for the carp, but closer-in float-fishing tactics with maggots do well for the roach and perch. Alternatively, try a bunch of lobworms for a bigger perch or even a small dead sprat.

The rumours were that cormorant attacks had reduced the stocks somewhat, but fishing once again seems to be very well worthwhile and offers a real bonus so close to the centre of this great capital city.

Season – open all year round.

Tickets – the tickets are free but a permit to fish must be obtained from the park gates at Holyrood Park. Contact Mike Heath on 0131 657 3258. Under no circumstances leave litter, use keep nets or try to fish on after dark. And it is much appreciated if you do pick up any litter you should happen to chance upon. Remember that anglers are very much in the public eye in this sensitive area.

Directions – head south into Edinburgh on the A1 and turn off left to Duddingston village. Follow the road past the church, and park in the car park opposite the loch itself. It's easily found.

Accommodation – the Edinburgh and Lothian Tourist Board, Edinburgh and Scotland Information Centre, 3 Princes Street, Edinburgh EH2 2QP can supply information about accommodation in the area on 0131 473 3800.

Lure Fishing Tips

If you fish with multiplier reels, be very careful not to let them fall on sand or grit, as a single particle in the mechanism can destroy the smooth running of the reel and make casting very difficult. Remember when casting to use a progressive pendulum-type movement.

- *WD40 is perfect for getting a reel to run smoothly again. Spray the reel and allow half an hour or so for the oil to penetrate. Then wipe off the surplus.*
- *Look after your lures. Keep them neatly stocked away and use bonnets to mask the hook points, or you will get into terrible tangles.*
- *Keep big spoons and spinners well polished. A shiny lure reflects the light much more efficiently than a tarnished one.*
- *Try painting white blotches on a large plug with Tippex or a marker pen. A predator recognises white on a prey fish as fungus and a sick fish means an easy meal.*
- *Braid line is now an accepted part of the lure fisher's armoury – make sure, however, that you tie the right knots!*
- *Even if you are lure fishing for perch, always use a wire trace, as a pike can easily take a spinner not intended for it!*
- *Don't restrict yourself to plugs, spoons and spinners. Open your mind to jerk baits and especially jigs – rubber imitations of fish, frogs, lizards and so on. Jig fishing is great fun and highly effective.*
- *If you need lures, don't forget that the Harris Angling Company, on 01692 581208, are the country's leading lure experts and can mail anything to you within 24 hours wherever you are in the UK.*

CLATTO COUNTRY PARK – DUNDEE

Clatto is a former reservoir, around twenty-five acres in extent. It averages around ten feet and drops down to twenty feet plus. It is set now in a country park and so anglers are very much on view.

Only half the lake is actually open to anglers, so do make sure that you don't stray past the limits – the rangers office is close by, and you won't be fishing there for long!

The large amounts of smaller perch and roach are the main attraction of the water, but there are some real specimen perch lurking in the water – possibly topping the three-pound mark. There are also some very good tench and bream – reaching six or seven pounds – and carp are also occasionally taken. Do make sure that you obey the fishery rules here because they are strict – no live baiting and no spinning.

SEASON – open all year.
TICKETS – these cost £1.80. Phone 01382 435911 in advance.
DIRECTIONS – from the A90 Perth to Dundee, turn off onto the A923 on the outskirts of Dundee. This is signposted Angus Coupar. You will see signs for Clatto Country Park in approximately one mile.
ACCOMMODATION – information about various kinds of accommodation available in the area can be obtained from the Angus and Dundee Tourist Board, 21 Castle Street, Dundee DD1 3AA, on 01382 527527.

COARSE FISHING IN THE GLASGOW AREA

Glasgow is, today, a vibrant bustling city unmissable if you're into the arts, culture or simply shopping! It's a perfect holiday destination for a few days, and it's well worthwhile putting some coarse-fishing tackle into the back of the car. Of course, when you think of Scotland you tend to think of salmon and trout, but the Glasgow area has a lot more to offer. The Clyde itself has some cracking grayling fishing available, and in some parts offers free fishing. You also have the Forth and Clyde canal with good pike, perch, roach, tench, rudd and bream. There is no close season on the canal, and day tickets are just £1. For further details apply to British Waterways, 1 Applecross Street, Glasgow GP4 9SP, on 0141 3326936.

There's also plenty of free fishing in and around Glasgow city centre. You could try Uchenstarry Pond for tench, roach, perch and rudd. In the district of Milgavie, there's both the Mugdock Park Pond and the Tench Pool. At Seafar, there's a carp pond and in the middle of Glasgow itself, there's Hogganfield Loch. This is a big water at eighty acres. It's very busy indeed and although night fishing is allowed I personally wouldn't advise it, considering some of the characters I've seen wandering around after closing time! The choice is yours. Still, there are carp reputed to be over twenty pounds in the water, along with some big bream and eels.

Just a little east of Glasgow you can find Lochend Loch in Coatbridge. This offers good perch and pike fishing and you pick up permits from the waterside. The Monklands District Coarse Angling Club now manages Monklands Canal just west of the town. This holds good bream up to six and even seven pounds, perch, carp, dace, rudd and tench. Day tickets only cost £1 and are available on the bank.

SEASON – coarse fishing is open all the year round in Scotland.
TICKETS – most of the waters are free or tickets can be bought on the bank. The best ports of call are the excellent Glasgow tackle shops. Try Tackle and Guns, 920 Pollokshaws Road, on 0141 632 2005; The Anglers Rendezvous, 74–78 Salt Market; or William Robertson and Co. Ltd., 61 Miller Street.
ACCOMMODATION – the Greater Glasgow and Clyde Valley Tourist Board, 11 George Square, Glasgow G2 IDY, on 0141 204 4400, can advise on accommodation.

LOCH LOMOND

Where do you start discussing a water that has threatened to make so much history over so many years? Of course, Lomond is considered by the Scots themselves as primarily a salmon and trout water, but the pike fishing, especially, is dramatic. There are perch and roach as well, so let's start by discussing those briefly.

Perch are widespread and roach seem to be more closely packed – you'll often find them in bays where rivers or streams enter. I'm not sure about the roach personally. Way back in the 70s I was tempted up on several trips by stories of three- and four-pounders that proved to be totally false. I, myself, have never contacted much over a pound and a half, although I can't say I've got to the bottom of Lomond roach stocks by any means. The perch certainly are larger. I believe they've been caught over four pounds in nets in the past, and further big ones are always on the cards. There are also powan – a freshwater herring – which are now under severe threat and fishing is closely controlled. Mind you, if you catch something strange on a single maggot and size eighteen when you're trying for a roach, at least now you'll know what it is!

So back to the pike. You've got to remember that Lomond is only just north of Glasgow and therefore, at the weekends and bank holidays especially, it is a real city playground. You'll find that most of the shoreline villages and marinas are a hive of activity at these times. But don't worry: at nearly twenty-three miles long and up to five miles wide, Lomond is a big enough water to get away from the crowds and do a great deal of exploration in near solitude.

Of course, you'll need a boat. It is possible to fish for pike from the bank, but it's an uphill task and you really can't cover even a fraction of a water of this magnitude unless you can get afloat.

In the bad old days, going back twenty years or so, Lomond was a Mecca for English anglers and they used to bring up huge numbers of their local live baits – ruffe, crucian carp, dace and so on. Not only was that inhumane, but it also caused great problems to the ecology of the loch itself. No more importing of live baits please! In fact, you'll find really that dead baits and lures do the business.

It's not a bad idea to troll with lures until you find you hit on the centre of activity. Just a pull or two should be enough to make you want to anchor up and explore the area more thoroughly. Of course, you can put a dead bait out and still work a lure in order to cover all options. The great key to success on Lomond really is location, so it does pay to cover water and, especially, to ask for local advice, which is generally freely given. An echo sounder is also a good idea to pinpoint drop-offs, underwater reefs and anything that could give a key to pike location. Also watch for fish striking. A pair of binoculars is a good idea. The important thing is not to be scared of the water, and approach it confidently, with as much advice as you can glean before setting out. Try to put aside a week or so, so that you can really get to know at least some of the loch.

In the springtime, many anglers go up to fish the spawning bays, knowing that the jacks will come in first and the really big mommas will be lying outside in deeper water waiting for their time to come. Of course, this is when you can fish from the bank in relatively shallow water, but it's still a good idea to have a boat close by so that you can fish the drop-off where the big females are likely to be most of the time. If you do adopt this approach, remember that pike are particularly vulnerable at this time of the year. They have spawning on their mind and it's not fair to interrupt them too much.

How big do the pike on Lomond really grow? Well, we know there are twenty-pounders aplenty and thirty-pounders are caught occasionally. The question really is how much bigger than that can get? There are all sorts of rumours. Fish on graphs recorders have been seen at great depths that have looked huge, but are they in fact a single fish or two or three fish together giving out an enormous signal? How about the pike that Fred Buller lost back in the 1960s, which Richard Walker put at sixty or seventy pounds? Naturally, the realists would say that with so much fishing pressure over at least the last quarter of a century a big fish – I mean a truly colossal fish – would have necessarily succumbed. Perhaps. Probably. But you never know, especially as Lomond pike fight like terriers. You've got to remember that if you've been used to lowland English pike, you'll find a quite different animal in the Scottish beast. They really go like wildfire. You sometimes just can't believe that it's 'only' a twelve- or a fifteen-pounder on the end of your line. If you'd lost that fish, you would have sworn that it was Fred Buller's sixty, alive and well after all these years!

SEASON – you can pike fish year round.

TICKETS – the loch itself is under the control of the Loch Lomond Angling Improvement Association, c/o R A Clements and Co., 29 St. Vincent Place, Glasgow G1 2DT, on 0141 221 0068. It's a good idea to get in touch with them if you're planning a major campaign on the

Trolling for Pike

The pike fishing on the big Scottish lochs can be very rewarding and is one of the nation's best kept secrets. However, there are problems, not least of which is that of locating the fish, when you're talking about waters that can be miles long and hundreds of feet deep.

To get the best out of these lochs, you really have to go afloat and troll. Trolling is simply pulling lures or dead baits behind a moving boat.

These are potentially treacherous water, and safety is paramount, so that's where I'll start, with some simple do's and don'ts.

- *Always get an accurate weather forecast, and don't go out if heavy weather is expected during the day. It could come early and catch you out.*
- *Always wear a lifejacket.*
- *No matter how reliable your outboard motor is, always take oars and extra fuel*
- *Always start out against the wind in case your motor fails. It's easier to row home with the wind behind you.*
- *Always make sure that somebody knows where you will be fishing and your likely time of return.*
- *Don't try to fish more than two rods when you first start out trolling, or big tangles can occur.*
- *It is a good idea to have a depth recorder with you to help you avoid sudden shoals or submerged islands.*
- *Start by fishing big, flashy plugs and spoons that pike can see down deep. A good vibration is also recommended, so that they can pick up on a lure they can't initially see. Start off with one deep-working lure and another that fishes higher in the water.*
- *Don't travel too slowly. A slow walking speed is about right for a kick off.*
- *Vary your course a bit and look for obvious hot spots such as islands, the mouths of bays or inflowing streams.*
- *If you hit a fish, put the engine into neutral and try to get your other rod in quickly. This will help avoid tangles.*
- *Always have an unhooking mat in the bottom of the boat.*
- *If you hit one fish, patrol the area carefully, as there are likely to be more pike about.*
- *Gear for trolling has to be tough and reliable. Rods of about nine feet in length are perfect and don't go for anything too expensive and fancy – if you're going to break a rod, it will be when you're trolling.*
- *Multiplier reels are perfect. A sturdy fixed-spool reel is fine, but a bait-runner facility is an advantage.*

water. Day tickets are not difficult to come by and are available at all local tackle shops, boat hire yards and hotels. You'll definitely need a boat, and the traditional centre has always been the boatyard in Balmaha.

→ DIRECTIONS – Loch Lomond is northwest of Glasgow on the A82, which runs along the entire west bank.

ACCOMMODATION – there is a mass of accommodation ringing the banks of Lomond. There is everything from hotel accommodation to camping sites. Contact the Argyll, The Isles, Loch Lomond, Stirling and Trossachs Tourist Board, Dept. SUK, 7 Alexandra Parade, Dunoon, PA23 8AB, on 01369 701000.

LOCH AWE

Loch Awe, famous for its salmon and trout has also been a lure for serious predator men for at least a century! In Victorian times, it was the massive ferox trout – a huge cannibalistic brown trout – that drew the sportsmen so far north. In all probability, a monstrous fish of thirty-nine pounds was taken back in the 1880s, and since then there have been plenty of fish over twenty pounds recorded. These are magnificent creatures, and even though you're probably reading this for pike-fishing information, I'd urge you to take them on board and treat them very seriously. Of course, the bonus is that a massive predatorial brown trout is angled for in much the same way as a pike, so it's not exactly as though you've got to set your stall out for one or the other. No, you can fish Loch Awe pike-style in the secure knowledge that there's every chance one of these monsters could come along and make your angling life complete!

Awe is yet another huge Scottish loch and it is even more remote and, arguably, more inspiring than Lomond. There is no doubt that the ferox trout probably grow bigger in Awe than any other Scottish loch. So it occurs to me that the same could logically go for the pike. Pike fishing isn't over exploited, and that itself is a good sign: remember that pike thrive on neglect.

It doesn't matter which of these big Scottish lochs you are fishing, location is the key and, once again, you really will need a boat. These are easily obtainable from many centres, but do remember that when you're out on these very big waters you need to take every safety precaution. Mental attitude is almost as important as fishing ability. If you look at a water like Awe, Lomond or Ness and simply collapse within, then you're beaten already. You've got to tell yourself that there are plenty of pike, they are hungry fish, and that during the course of the day you're bound to cross the path of at least a few of them. Okay, these are big waters, but that just means that they have more fish in them. Keep your confidence high, keep working, and success beyond your wildest dreams could be the result.

I've fished Awe on dozens of occasions and, to tell the truth, have very frequently blanked. Mind you, there have been days when I haven't and they've been utterly splendid. My biggest ferox is a 'mere' ten pounds from Awe and I've only had pike nudging the twenty-pound mark, but I've seen much, much bigger. I was once up the northern arm where the River Awe itself runs into the loch. The water there is quite deep and crystal clear and I was fishing a dead brown trout, sink and draw. A pike – I thought it was a log at first – followed the bait in so close that I thought I'd be able to lift it out in a landing net. Of course, I couldn't: the pike was still deep down and it was vast. It would be unwise of me to put any weight on that fish because Scottish pike can be lean as well as mean. But, believe me, that was one big pike!

SEASON – pike fishing is open all year.
TICKETS – Loch Awe is protected and controlled by the Loch Awe Improvement Association and you have to have permits. These are available at most hotels and shops around the loch. Day ticket and weekly charges are modest. Contact D Wilson, Ardbrecknish House, Dalmally. Loch Awe Stores, Loch Awe, Dalmally BA33 1AQ, and any of the following hotels. You will need a boat, so contact the Taychreggan Hotel on 01866 833211. The owners have boats for the hotel's residents but also occasionally hire them out on a daily basis. The hotel, by the way, is absolutely excellent. Try also Cuil-na-sithe Hotel, on 01866 833234, or Portsonachan Hotel on 01866 833224. Contact also N. Clarke, 11 Dalavich, By Taynuilt, on 01866 844209.
DIRECTIONS – Loch Awe is situated on the A85 going west from Dalmally to Oban.
ACCOMMODATION – any of the hotels above offer splendid accommodation at differing rates. There is also a great deal of bed and breakfast and guesthouse accommodation around the loch. There are also some camp sites. The Argyll, the Isles, Loch Lomond, Stirling and Trossachs Tourist Board can give further advice and details on 01369 701000.

PIKE IN THE HIGHLAND LOCHS

This is a project for the fearless. Let's get it straight from the start, however, that I'm going to be talking about an area centred on Loch Ness that offers excellent holiday possibilities. This is the most wonderful countryside to explore with the whole family, and there is some charming accommodation available. Alternatively, for the single angler or party of piking pals, this area does offer a whole host of opportunities. And, you will be largely on your own. I've fished the area intensively for some fifteen years, but I don't pretend to know it well yet. In fact, when it comes to pike in general, I don't think there's anybody who truly does. Yes, I've had pike – good ones – and seen some monsters, but I'd never say it's easy fishing.

A real word of caution here. Remember that if you are going to take pike rods onto these waters you are stepping very much into the game fishing world. Do, therefore, behave with all consideration. If, for example, you are approached by a boat of salmon trollers then please do give way. If by chance you've strayed onto a bankside where you don't have permission to pike fish and you're challenged, please do explain the situation and be polite. Landowners will realise that mistakes are easily made providing you are not in anyway rude or aggressive. Don't leave any litter. Don't land a boat on bankside that is obviously anyone's private property. Always make every attempt to ensure that you have the correct permissions before setting out. Check also that Sunday fishing is permitted: in some areas it is still frowned upon. Don't just think that you can roll up to any water and launch your own boat. This is often not the case and it obviously raises local hackles. If you should hook a salmon on your pike spinners then return it. It's good to return them anyway, and if you don't have a ticket, it's a necessity.

Where do we begin? Loch Ness has some tremendous pike fishing on offer that is hardly ever tackled at all. Once again, this is best fished by boat, but I've always fancied Urquhart Bay near Drumnadrochit on the north bank. This is a shallow bay and it does attract numbers of prey fish. However, do check that you're not on prohibited territory. Ness looks forbidding, but isn't necessarily so. You can find quite fishable water not far from the margins and there are fish of thirty pounds plus in the water.

The whole Ness system is an exciting one. Moving south, you come to the much smaller Loch Oich. Now, a boat on Loch Oich really is an exciting prospect. This is predominantly a shallow loch and often quite weedy, and it has big pike stocks. Thirty-pounders are again present. Moving further south once more, we come to Loch Lochy, with some cracking fish available in the bays and on the extensive shallows. Neither should you ignore the stretches of Caledonian Canal that link the lochs together. The basins, in particular, can often provide dramatic sport.

There are rumours of big pike in some of the lochs to the south of the Ness system, for example Loch Duntelchaig, but I don't have personal experience of this water. I do know, however, the waters to the northwest. Loch Cluanie is a water with a big reputation and I know of at least one twenty-eight-pounder to come from it. Not bad when you consider how little piking pressure it receives. Some years there are pike matches on Loch Claunie and good fish are invariably taken – and this is from the bankside.

Moving further south, Loch Loyne is a mysterious, brooding sort of place. I have done well on Loyne, but to be honest it has been a struggle. I did see one enormous fish hooked, played to the surface and eventually lost down by the dam where it's possible to fish from the bank.

Loch Garry is a system that offers tremendous potential. Some four or five years ago, my fishing partner, Roger Miller, hooked a monstrous fish whilst spinning for char. He actually played it to the bank, but a group of Scottish fly fishermen appeared and began to start talking about killing the fish. Miller couldn't have that and pulled intentionally for a break, bless him. How big was that fish? Well, Roger has caught them to thirty–nine and a half pounds in England and guesses this fish was of the same ilk. I'm not surprised: a few years ago a couple of fish of forty pounds or more were taken by the nets of the local fishery management teams. And there is talk of a fifty-pounder that was caught some time back in the 1960s.

There are enormous fish certainly, and the potential in these farflung waters is colossal, but remember, you will be on your own. The chances of seeing other pike anglers are slim, so you've got to content yourself with what local advice you can glean and also explore off your own bat. No matter how 'piky' a place looks, if you don't get some action after a while, you've simply got to move on. Mobility is, as ever, the key.

SEASON – the pike season here is, I suppose, officially year round, but in practical terms fishing from the end of October to the beginning of April is rarely possible. It would take a hard man to fish the winter through.

TICKETS – the pike fishing is generally free around the area and, indeed, many fishery owners will be only too pleased to let you pike fish providing you agree to take the small fish out. I don't think this is too much of a problem providing that everybody agrees that fish of twelve pounds or more go back in for the good of the trout fishing itself. Contact, J. Graham and Co., 37-39 Castle Street, Inverness on 01463 233178 for information about boats and access. Try also Frasers, 15 Market Arcade, Inverness IV1 1PG, on 01463 710929. The Foyers Hotel, on 01456 486216, offers boats halfway down the south bank and there are boatyards in Drumnadrochit. On Loch Oich, the Glengarry Castle Hotel, on 01809 501254, at Invergarry occasionally has rowing boats for hire. Moving onto the Garry system, the Tomdoun Hotel, on 01809 511244, offers boats on Garry itself and the shallow Inchlaggan Loch that adjoins it.

DIRECTIONS – the Loch Ness system is situated on the A82 from Fort William to Inverness.

ACCOMMODATION – the Tourist Information Centre in Inverness, on 01463 234353, can supply details of accommodation available in the area. Alternatively, contact the Highlands of Scotland Tourist Board, Peffrey House, Strathpeffer, Ross-shire IV14 9HA, on 0870 5143070. All the hotels mentioned are highly recommended, especially the Tomdoun, which I've known personally for many years.

GRAYLING FISHING ON THE RIVER TUMMEL

From 30th June to 14th March you are allowed to fish for grayling on the beautiful River Tummel with bait or fly, of course . This is a tremendous privilege, because the Tummel is a top salmon and trout river. Always remember this, and please defer to anglers who are spending almost ten times more on a day ticket than you are yourself. That said, there are large stretches of the Tummel available and you will be able to hide yourself away and enjoy some pretty solitary sport.

Tummel grayling always excite me. I've caught grayling all round the British Isles – and in many countries abroad come to that – but I've never found bigger, more solid-shouldered, more deeply-coloured fish than in the Tummel. They fight savagely, too, in the quick currents, and take bait with true ferocity. Mind you, they're not everywhere and you've got to spend time locating them. Ask for local knowledge and it will be readily given if politely requested. Trout anglers, for example, often know where shoals of grayling are hanging up. But failing that, you've got to do it on your own and this means travelling light and fishing as you go. Don't, therefore, encumber yourself with a lot of tackle. Rod, reel, floats, hooks, shot, bait and a small landing net, and off you go. Thigh boots at the very least will probably be necessary, and chest waders will give you better access to some of the swims. Don't discount any stretch of water. Sometimes it's tempting to say that a piece of river is just too fast-moving, but don't dismiss it. Okay, concentrate on the slower, more seductive areas, but everywhere deserves fishing.

As for bait, my two favourites would have to be small redworm or, interestingly enough, sweetcorn! In fact, come to think of it, I'd be quite happy just fishing sweetcorn all the time on the Tummel. I would certainly say that the majority of my fish have fallen to this bait. It's also an easy bait to procure in Scotland, which is more than can be said for many other coarse-fishing baits.

SEASON – you can only fish for grayling with the fly before 30th June and from then on it's fly or bait right through to 14th March. There is no trout fishing between 7th October and 14th March, so apart from a few salmon fishermen, the grayling men will have the water to themselves.

TICKETS – these cost £4 a day and are available from that excellent tackle shop, Mitchells of Pitlochry, 23 Athol Road, Pitlochry, on 01796 472613. Other information is also given by Ross Gardiner on 01796 472157 in the evenings. Ross is a magnificent grayling fisherman and a marvellous man. Only phone him please with very serious inquiries. Do make sure that you study the map before setting off to fish. Your ticket will cover several miles of water but there are stretches here and there that are out of bounds. Do not poach.

DIRECTIONS – the River Tummel runs alongside a stretch of the A9 between Ballinluig and Pitlochry.

ACCOMMODATION – Pitlochry offers a whole array of accommodation from grand hotels down to homely bed and breakfasts. Contact the Perthshire Tourist Board, Lower City Mills, West Mill Street, Perth PH1 5QP, on 01738 627958.

Highly Recommended Fisheries

- *Castle Loch and Hightae Mill Loch, Loch Maben, Dumfries and Galloway. Contact the Warden, Loch Field, Loch Maben, Dumfries and Galloway. Both lochs offer excellent fishing for bream, carp, perch, tench and roach. Boat fishing only on Hightae Mill.*
- *Kelhead Quarry, Nr. Ecclefechan, Dumfries and Galloway. Good perch, roach, bream and pike. Some carp and tench. Phone 01461 700344.*
- *Strathclyde Country Park Loch. Close to the River Clyde. Carp, bream, roach, pike, perch and dace. Permits from the Booking Office, Strathclyde Country Park, Hamilton Road, Motherwell. Phone 01698 266155.*
- *Lochs Spectacle, Garwachie and Eldrig. All near Newton Stewart. Attractive lochs offering pike, perch, tench, roach and rudd in the main. Contact Newton Stewart Forest District Ranger on 01671 402420.*
- *Loch Ken, Dumfries and Galloway. Big pike, big roach and some good perch. Tickets available from local hotels and shops. A boat is advisable.*

Coarse-Fishing Sites in Ireland

1. *Lough Mark*
2. *Lough Comb*
3. *Lough Key*
4. *Corrick and Shannon*
5. *Lough Ree*
6. *Athlone*
7. *Lough Dog*
8. *River Bann*
9. *Lower Lough Erne*
10. *Grand Canal*
11. *Lough Muckno*
12. *Upper River Bann*
13. *The River Erne*
14. *The River Blackwater*
15. *Lough Allen*
16. *Royal Canal*
17. *Lough Muck*
18. *Clay Lake*

"The more I catch, the more I realise I know next to nothing about pike fishing in this country. Each season I learn more about old waters and find so many new ones that you hardly know where to cast next. Only the other day I heard about a lough – a small one, virtually unfished – and it produced a thirty-four-pounder to the first guys to go there. Just like that. I could tell you similar stories for a week on end."

DAVID OVERY, IRISH WRITER AND PIKE LEGEND

David Overy is one of Ireland's best known, and certainly most successful, pike anglers, and I well remember this conversation with him over breakfast in one of Dublin's finest hotels.

It is no wonder that Ireland has drawn pike fishermen to its waters for well over a hundred years now. The great trout-rich loughs and bream-infested rivers have produced some of the world's biggest pike – and if you only half believe the legends, there are pike to put shark to shame! Of course, Ireland is a bit like that: it's a land of mists and magic, and there are times when you are afloat on a water like Mask or Corrib when you can believe that just about anything is underneath you. Mind you, you would probably be right!

Even if pike are not your thing, Ireland is still bound to have a huge amount to offer. The bream fishing is probably the best in the world. There are rudd to die for. Where else can you catch endless amounts of five- and six-pound tench from scores of waters that are all but virgin?

Ask anybody who has been over to Ireland with a fishing rod, and they will tell you there is a lot more to the country than just the sport itself. The Irish are themselves a revelation and make any journey a pleasure. You won't find a more genuine people anywhere. And after the day on the water, go into any pub, order a Guinness, let the bar know that you are a fisherman, and you'll be inundated with information. You will be told about waters that aren't even on maps, and they are bound to be full of fish. Quiet roads, sumptuous farmhouse breakfasts, waters with not a footprint beside them. Get yourself over there!

THE SHANNON

The Shannon is a magnificent, extraordinary watercourse: a hundred and sixty miles long with a catchment area taking in the greater part of central Ireland. It's a limestone river, rich in weed and food, gently flowing for the most part, but with deep glides and, fascinatingly, an amazing number of loughs and lagoons off its spinal cord. There's just so much water to fish, so much of it hidden and secretive, only accessible by boat. The Irish adore the Shannon. It's a magnet to them; hardly surprising when you think of the huge number of specimen fish that it's produced: pike, bream, rudd and perch to name but four. In many ways, the Shannon is the core of coarse fishing in Ireland but, with my few attempts on the river, I couldn't begin to describe it. Enter my dear friend from Dublin, Charlie Stuart – who's lived his leisure life on the great river.

'Let's take the northern area first, from Lough Key down to Carrick-on-Shannon. You could spend the best part of a year exploring this area, if not your entire life. The list of species to be caught is quite breathtaking, from the humble roach to regular catches of big double-figure pike. Let's start at **Lough Key** where you can gain access to the water by driving from Carrick towards Boyle in County Roscommon. About four miles outside Carrick ,you will come across Lough Key Forest Park, which in itself is a most beautiful spot to visit. If you enter the park ,you will see a large tower, below which are jetties. It's from these that I've had some of my best bream and perch fishing ever. Lough Key produced an Irish record pike tipping the scales at thirty-nine pounds and three ounces, so it's well worth a visit for big predators. The lake is easily accessible for pleasure craft, so you won't have any shortage of company – what I'm trying to say is that even though I've had bags of bream well over a hundred pounds, being a night owl helps. You'll find they tend to feed after midnight until four or five o'clock in the morning later on a dull day.

'Moving downstream, we'll come to the smaller water of **Oakport Lough**. It's situated behind the village of Knockvicar. It's a lake that's an absolute must for any keen piker. You'll find boat hire available locally in the village and the northern shore of this reed-lined water seems to produce the best fishing. The best methods by far are trolled or wobbled dead baits. As the lake is virtually inaccessible overland, you've got to organise boat hire in the village. Just ask at the bar and you'll be sent in the right direction.

'A little further down the Shannon you will come across **Lough Drumharlow**. This is an ideal water for the general all rounder and the family on holiday. It produces bags of roach, tench and bream and, as you'd expect, significant numbers of good double-figure pike. The lake is accessible from the road but some anglers opt for the tranquillity of fishing from the island. Boat hire is essential to get you over and, once again, simply ask at that bar! I always say that the coarse fishing in Ireland is free but you've got to have a pound or two in your pocket for the odd Guinness!

'Having covered the local lakes of the northern section, I should add that there are sections of river here that are well worth a visit. Large areas of the banks are unfishable, but if you can get on the water, you will be surprised at the amazing clarity of the water, and you can actually see shoals of fish cruising along the riverbed. It's really brilliant to watch the bream and tench, moving slowly, tipping to feed, kicking up clouds of silt. It gets the heart beating, I can tell you. I should mention the area around Carrick-on-Shannon itself here. There are impressive bags of fish put together here, even in the harbour of the town centre, but the quality of the water does leave a lot to be desired and you won't get that clarity I was just talking about. Having said that, the town itself is well worth a visit after a session, because the hospitality and nightlife would rejuvenate the bones of the wettest fisherman!

'Moving down south from Carrick you enter a maze of waters that you could lose yourself in. The river splits in two directions, with the main section flowing through the settlement of Jamestown, while the other section is cut off through the Albert canal. The canal itself is not really worth a visit before reaching Albert Lough, due to the volume of boat traffic. Below Albert Lough, the canal rejoins the river to flow into **Lough Boderg**, which in turn flows into **Lough Bofinn**. It is at the meeting of these two waters that the river narrows. This is probably the best location on the two waters, as the shoreline is protected by a large forest, which gives you good shelter and comfortable fishing. The sport in this area is generally excellent, but be prepared to carry large amounts of ground bait – a good sharper would not go amiss! Bags include bream up to six pound plus and some pristine tench. Just north of Roosky is a beautiful village of **Dromod**. I've spent many a pleasant evening fishing in the harbour here, but again you have to be prepared to burn the midnight oil, as the place is very busy during the day. The fish move back at dusk and from about midnight onwards as things quieten down, large shoals of bream begin to reclaim the harbour as their own. Bags of over a hundred pounds are not uncommon and, with the added benefit of public lighting, you can fish and see what you're doing until the early hours.

'If we move on again south towards **Rooskey**, again we'll find a busy village for the boating fraternity. However, I would really recommend a visit to the lough here, as there is a lovely quiet backwater behind the lough keeper's cottage. I've caught some great perch here, many weighing over two pounds. If you prefer quantity, then the shoals of roach and perch will keep you occupied for hours – a great place for kids.

'Let's have a look at the middle Shannon now, the famous area around Athlone and Lough Ree. On the northern end of the lake sits the town of Lanesborough – which in recent years has become a honey pot for visiting anglers. The main attraction is the location of the local power station with its outflow of warm water. To say that you have to be up early to have access to a swim would be an understatement – this is a really serious hotspot! The fish are attracted to the warmer climate that the outflow brings and the anglers follow. Bags of even a hundred and fifty pounds plus are not unusual. You'll find roach, bream, roach/bream hybrids, tench, rudd and lots of perch. It's well worth a visit but, as I've said, you've got to arrive early or you'll be disappointed.

'Moving south on the lake down the eastern shoreline, you come across **Inny Bay**, where the River Inny itself enters the lake. This is a spot that has become renowned for massive shoals of bream. Indeed, one of my pals once said that he had to stop spinning for pike as he was foul-hooking so many bream. It's a must for the visiting angler if you have the nerve to put a really big bag together. On the opposite side of the lake you have **Hodson Bay**, another Mecca for big bream bags. There's a hotel just above the area and you can see people landing fish from the bar itself.

'Now, we're at **Shannonbridge**, about to move down to Lough Derg itself.

Night Fishing Basics

Night fishing can sometimes give you the edge, especially during hot weather. However, it is a specialised technique, and following a few basic guidelines can help to make your expedition successful and safe.

- *Don't go on your own for your first few sessions, but choose to go along with a friend. It is even better if he or she has night-fishing experience.*
- *Don't night fish in water that you don't have any experience of first. Always visit the swim that you intend to visit at night during the daytime, so you can get the feel of it and note down any over-hanging trees or other possible problems after dark.*
- *Lay everything around you that you might need during the darkness whilst it is still light. Make sure there is an order to all this so you know exactly where you can lay your hands on things in the blackness.*
- *Always have one big torch for emergencies.*
- *Always take a small torch for the little fiddly jobs such as rebaiting.*
- *A headlamp like miners used to use is a good idea, especially when you're playing fish and you need both hands free.*
- *Always take plenty of warm clothes ,even if the day has been hot. Temperatures can plummet after dark.*
- *Take plenty of food and warm drinks. No alcohol!*
- *If you do a lot of night fishing, it is a good idea to make sure your torch is mid red rather than white light. This can be done by using a red bulb or by colouring the torch face with a red marker pen. Red light is less likely to scare fish and is kinder on the eyes.*
- *Things that go bump in the night. Remember that the strange wheezing that is coming from that nearby bush is more likely to be a hedgehog than a werewolf! The world can seem weird after dark, but there is always a rational explanation for everything.*

Shannonbridge is a little village lying on the border of County Galway and even if it weren't for the brilliant fishing it would be worth a visit for its history. The main street crosses the river over an impressive nineteen-arch bridge – hence the name. Beside the bridge is a massive fortress built by the British during the Napoleonic Wars back in the early 19th century. From this building, you will be able to see most of the area that you'll want to fish. I have had many wonderful evenings fishing in Shannonbridge, but make a decision about what method you are going to use before you start.

'This is important, as different species abound in the area and the current tends to be a little faster on this stretch of the river. Trotting is a winner, but so is ledgering. I've had good bags of tench and bream, and endless amounts of roach and rudd. A little way downstream of the town you will come across a cutting that is used by boats navigating the river, and it's at the entrance of this cutting that I've had some of my best pike fishing in the area. Try a wobbled roach, drifting in and out of the current, and you can expect fish well into double figures.

'Now we're at Shannon harbour, which lies on the Grand Canal, just before its entrance to the river. Running alongside the canal is the **River Brosna**. I've had some really impressive fishing on this river just where it joins the main Shannon. In one session, for example, I caught nine pike to fourteen pounds, all falling to a float-fished dead rudd. I must hasten to remind you that live baiting on these waters is illegal. Moving downstream to the town of Banagher, you'll find a large harbour there and the river tends to pick up momentum. In fact, you've got really quite a strong current through the whole stretch. The banks around the town tend to be very difficult to fish because they're marshy, known locally as the Callows. However, below the town of Banagher you will come upon a large weir and lough known as **Meelick**. It's here that the fishing tends to become more comfortable and you'll find some well prepared swims on the western side of the river. If you read Fred Buller's Domesday Book of Pike you'll see that a fish of some sixty-nine inches in length was found dead here. The estimated weight was ninety pounds. I will leave that to your imagination and your scepticism, but remember that if you were to land a fish of half that weight you would hold the Irish record! It would beat the river record by over three pounds.

'The town of **Portumna** lies on the northern shores of Lough Derg; this stretch of water has produced some massive fish and excellent sport for visitors and locals alike. The river in the area of Portumna is very deep and in winter this acts as a magnet to the pike. Let's move now into **Lough Derg**, which is awe-inspiring! There's so much water that you could spend a lifetime exploring. The massive lough is riddled with bays and islands, and my advice is to search out secluded bays, bait up and wait for the bream to come in. Alternatively, pole quietly around in a small boat looking for the rudd shoals. I needn't say a word to you about the pike fishing. Just take one quick look at the Domesday Book: you'll see that there are thirteen entries for Lough Derg alone.

'Leaving Lough Derg – if that's at all possible – you'll come to the villages of **Killaloe** and **O'Brien's Bridge**. These are both popular venues for the coarse angler and you'll find many visitors there. Well worth a visit.

'In short, I've spent so many weeks holiday cruising the Shannon that you'd think I'd know most of the watercourse. I don't. Every time I visit, I discover a new venue and it's like starting over afresh. In fact, I don't think there's anybody that could know the whole Shannon system. You could spend a lifetime on it and still not scratch the surface. Mind you, that doesn't mean to say that you have to be an expert to catch fish. You don't. You won't find better coarse fishing anywhere in Europe.'

CONTACT – for angling information for the Shannon region contact Shannon Development, Shannon Town Centre, County Clare, on 00353 61361555. Garry Kenny, Palmerstown Stores, Portumna, on 00353 50941071, will advise on fishing in the northern Lough Derg area. At Shannonbridge, contact Dermot Killeen, Bar and Grocery, Main Street, on 00353 90574112. In Roosky, contact Key Enterprises and Lakeland Bait.
ACCOMMODATION – for information, contact Limerick Tourist Board on 00353 61317522, or Athlone Tourist Board on 00353 90294630.

BREAM FISHING – RIVER BANN AND LOUGH ERNE

The bream fishing in Ireland is arguably the best that you'll find anywhere in the world. There are huge shoals of fish in an endless number of areas. Moreover, these are fish that are rarely pursued – you'll generally find the Irish only interested in things with an adipose fin on them!

However, even though this is breaming paradise, the fish don't give themselves up easily and you've got to work quite hard if you want to reap the ultimate harvest.

There are several rules. In the summer, you've got to think about fishing early and late, if not through the night. If the water is clear and the sun is bright, don't expect to catch a good number of fish. Then you've go to ground bait heavily. These are very big shoals and they're hungry fish. If you just put out half a pint of maggots you'll hold a shoal of bream for half a minute. Work out an ambush area, feed heavily in the late afternoon and wait for the bream to move over it in the evening. Most bream in Ireland are uneducated when it comes to tackle but they do want a lot of food to go down over.

Bear in mind the weather conditions. Ireland can change dramatically from one moment to the next. If the winds are warm and wet from the southwest and the temperatures are mild, then you can expect to find bream in shallow water. If, however, there's a dip in water temperature, look for them in water of over ten feet deep.

Think carefully about what you give the bream. It's no good just ground baiting with a couple of pounds – you've got to pile it in and, above all, you've got to mix things into the ground bait to keep the fish interested. Casters are obviously good, but a gallon or so, which is what you'd need, does cost a fair amount. The same applies to a few pounds ofchopped worms. Instead, try a dozen cans of sweetcorn, stewed wheat, pellets and so on. What you've got to do is to keep a shoal of bream, anything up to five hundred fish strong, interested for hours on end.

Remember that the bream are not tackle shy and you'll find that they fight much harder in Ireland than they do in England. This means that you can go comparatively heavy – think about a size twelve hook and main line of four or five pounds straight through. There's also the point that a big tench could come along at any moment as well.

All the usual techniques do well but probably most big bags are built up with a swim feeder. It makes sense to cast your feeder to the perimeter of activity. If you put it right in the centre of the shoal, not only do you run the risk of disturbing the fish, especially in shallow water, but you've also got to get the hooked bream out. Fishing the edges, you might not get a bite instantly, but you won't break the shoal up.

If you don't fancy the idea of fishing through the night, try ground baiting at nine or ten o'clock in the evening. Put out a great number of small balls of bait and then return at first light – so not too much Guinness! With any luck, the bream will have moved in over the ground bait overnight and still be there – giving you three or four hours' hectic sport before packing up for breakfast. A nice compromise.

In Northern Ireland, **Portglenone** on the lower River Bann in Antrim has become a top venue. You'll find eighty purpose-made fishing stands there all with good access.

CONTACT – Smith's Tackle in Ballymoney, on 02827 664259.

Try also **Lower Lough Erne** at Trory, Fermanagh. Excellent in the springtime. There are several concrete fishing stands, and you can catch fish here nicely on the waggler.

CONTACT – Field and Stream in Enniskillen, on 02866 322114.

In the south, try **Ballycullian Lake**, Corrofin, Galway. A brilliant lake with big bays – a major venue for big bream. Fish to ten pounds. The Shannon Regional Fisheries Board has provided boat stands in several areas. Excellent.

CONTACT – Shannon Regional Fisheries Board on 00353 656837675.

The **Grand Canal**, Edenderry, Offaly. The Grand Canal flows close to this town situated thirty miles west of Dublin. It is a coloured water with masses of bream and some carp.

CONTACT – Padraic Kelly on 00353 40532071.

Lough Muckno, Castleblayney, Monaghan. This is a large lake with big bream stocks. Pre-baiting very important here.

CONTACT – Jim Mc Mahon on 00353 429661714.

Remember that bream are very well spread throughout the entire island, both north and south. There are huge numbers of rivers, loughs and pools with bream fishing freely available. Remember the old advice: go into the bar and order a Guinness!

Roach on the Blackwater, the Bann and the Erne

The roach fishing in Ireland has become a phenomenon. They've probably been present in the country for about a hundred and twenty years, and have spread rapidly – partly through natural causes and sometimes because of anglers transporting them for live baits (but not now that live baiting in the south is illegal). Roach have undoubtedly become an important part of the Irish angling touring scene, and some of my own first trips to Ireland were superb for the brilliant roach fishing down in the Munster Blackwater. What fishing it was back in the 1970s – the great roach explosion in the Blackwater around the Moy and Cappoquin. In fact, the renowned bacon factory at Cappoquin was the centre of it all. Dreadful times! By that I mean the river there fished best when the pigs were brought in to be slaughtered. A pipe ran into the river with gallons of congealed blood washing away in the stream. The roach, sea trout and seagulls went barmy! I confess, to my horror these days, I joined in the glut and had many a roach to just about two pounds and some big, big dace.

On the Blackwater, you didn't have to fish in such appalling surroundings to catch big roach. They were, and are still, freely available. In fact, today, the roach have spread so widely it's not difficult to find them anywhere. Only last year I enjoyed some fantastic roach fishing in Northern Ireland, around **Enniskillen** on Upper Lough Erne. The roach just seemed to come and to come. Fish all the way up to a pound on float-fished maggots just tripping bottom. Tremendous fishing.

Remember that, by and large, the roach in Ireland are less tackle shy than those in England. You can't always get away with heavier tackle and certainly not crude bait presentation, but you can afford to scale up a little bit. Feeding, too, must be done more heavily. In England we're used to scattering a pinch of maggots every now and again: over in Ireland you've got to be bolder if you're going to hold a shoal.

Try the **Upper River Bann**, Portadown, Armagh. Portadown used to be the hotspot for huge roach catches and is now recovering well after a bit of a slump. Big bags of roach are still possible, and you can catch fish nudging the two pound mark.

CONTACT – Premier Angling, Lurgan, on 02838 325204.

The **River Erne**, Enniskillen, Fermanagh, once rewrote the record books, and even today there is some magnificent fishing available in the area. It's a tremendous centre for all manner of species, but the roach fishing must be amongst the best in Europe. Plenty of fish, and some very big ones indeed. Local knowledge is important.

CONTACT – Field and Stream, Enniskillen, on 02866 322114.

Down in the south, the **River Blackwater** at **Fermoy** in County Cork is unbeatable. This is a big river running through the town, full of roach and dace. Look for swims around the main town bridge and the renowned hospital stretch. There's good trotting, providing you work at the swim with plenty of feed. Everybody is willing to give you advice here. It's a magnet for anglers, and championship matches are held. You might not catch the really big roach of yesteryear, but there'll be some cracking specimens.

CONTACT – Pat Barrie on 00353 2536187.

Don't be afraid to explore the entire Blackwater – Cappoquin still produces some brilliant roach. There are all sorts of access points along the river, a most attractive water and a roach fisherman's paradise.

Pike on the Loughs and the River Suck

Pike fishing in Ireland is still remarkable, though there have been problems in the recent past. At one stage, a great number of anglers from continental Europe were visiting Ireland, catching sizeable pike and killing them to take home the heads as trophies. Fortunately, this practice has just about ceased. Pike have also been remorselessly culled in some of the premier trout waters. This is still going on to some degree, but increasingly there is an acceptance that big pike actually do a water good and it's the jacks that have to be removed.

Having said all that, Ireland remains a pike angler's dream. Pike have been resident in Ireland for about four hundred years, and they immediately found Irish waters to their liking. Pike thrive on neglect, and for many decades they were certainly neglected! When the Victorians began to fish for them in the late 19th century they found pike fishing beyond their wildest dreams. The pike grow particularly quickly in the limestone loughs – rich feed for trout and coarse fish means good growing conditions for the pike. Not only is there plenty of day-to-day food for pike in most Irish waters, but there are also added bonuses such as salmon, sea trout, eels and even shad. In short, Ireland has everything that big pike need: large, rich, under-pressured waters, full of nutritious prey fish.

Catching very big pike from Ireland is not always an easy job. On some of the really large waters such as Mask, Corrib, Derg, Ree and Neagh, location is always a problem. You can either go on local knowledge – generally very freely given in Ireland – or take an echo sounder with you. You'll often be able to locate shoals of prey fish by bream and roach, and you'll certainly be able to discover drop-offs, plateaux and any other obvious fish holding areas. On watercourses such as Lough Erne, location is a little easier – the pike tend to follow the big shoals of bream and roach and so a good starting place is where you find general pleasure anglers doing very well.

To fish Ireland successfully for pike you have to have mobility, and that almost always means a boat. Fortunately, every single village in Ireland next to a waterway is well geared up for this. What I have found, however, is that it sometimes pays to take your own engine across. Irish engines are not always as reliable as they should be!

You've got to remember that live baiting is banned in the south but that doesn't mean that your chances are restricted at all. Dead baiting works very well and most of the waters are clear enough to provide excellent lure fishing.

I recently enjoyed wonderful pike fishing over a three-day period on **Upper Lough Erne**, just south of Enniskillen. My very first cast with a gold Super Shad resulted in a twenty-five pound pike! Things don't get better than that. For the rest of the stay I continued to do well with big, flashy plugs. It was largely a case of moving slowly around the waterways, exploring with a plug and, when fish were found, anchoring up and putting out a couple of dead baits. The fish averaged a very high size – around twelve to fourteen pounds – and another couple of twenties came to the net. All the fish were in superb condition, and even though it was at the peak of the fishing season, we only saw two other pike anglers out over the weekend. That is piking in Ireland for you: you can find yourself on a magnificent water and be virtually alone.

My other major experiences of pike in Ireland have been on **Loughs Corrib and Mask** and the potential here is awesome. Netting has reduced numbers to some degree, but my own belief is that this has only pushed up the possible potential size. I don't think anybody who fishes these waters is in any doubt that forties and even fifties possibly exist. Mind you, fishing can be heart-breaking. Because there aren't many pike in the waters, it's difficult to build up a picture of their movements. You're very much alone. The best bet, in my opinion, is to explore as much water as possible with big spinners and plugs. Once again, when you've found fish, it pays to anchor up and investigate more thoroughly with dead baits. In very heavy weather it's possible to moor up behind the islands on the big loughs, put out a couple of dead baits and wait. This can be slow fishing, but when the float cocks and the line begins to pull out, your heart really is in your mouth. This could certainly be the fish of your dreams.

It is very difficult to give precise locations for pike fishing. It is so widely available and people will help you in every way they can. For anybody taking their car over to Ireland, it could well be that you'll be landing in Dublin. If so, then Dave McBride is the perfect man to inspire you and set you on your way. He's a fund of information when it comes to all manner of pike fishing and general coarse fishing in Ireland.

CONTACT – Dave McBride, Clanbrassil Street, Dublin 2, on 00353 14530266.

One hot area is the River Suck around **Castlecoote** and **Athleague**, Roscommon. There are big bags of bream roach and hybrids, and these seem to attract large pike. In recent years there have been rumours of big thirties being caught – well worth checking out.

CONTACT – Mrs Holmes on 00353 4321491.

In the west, there is excellent fishing on **Loughs Corrib, Mask, Coolin and Nafooey**.

CONTACT – John O'Donnell on 00353 9246157 for information about boats in the area.

ACCOMMODATION – Fairhill Guesthouse, Clonbur, on 00353 9246176, accommodates anglers and arranges fishing trips with boatmen.

Cong is a fascinating area and offers excellent pike fishing.
CONTACT – Michael Ryan, River Lodge, Cong, on 00353 9246057, regarding boats. O'Connor's Tackle Shop in Cong also offers up-to-the-minute information.

Ballinrobe and **Tourmakready** are excellent centres on Lough Mask.
CONTACT – Dermot O'Connor's Tackle Shop on Main Street, Ballinrobe. There are centres for boat hire at Cushlough Pier, Rosshill Park and Cahir Pier.
Contact also Derry Park Lodge Angling Centre, on 00353 9244081, at Tourmakready.

The **Erne system** offers extremely good piking.
CONTACT – Field and Stream, Enniskillen, on 02866 322114, offers excellent advice.
ACCOMMODATION – Rossahilly House, on 02866 322352, is an excellent guesthouse right on the water, offering brilliant bream and pike fishing. There is also marvellous accommodation on Bell Isle, just south of Enniskillen on Upper Lough Erne, and boats are available. Phone Bell Isle Estate, Lisbellaw, Enniskillen, County Fermanagh, on 02866 387231.

In Ireland it is so easy to get off the beaten track and try a totally new water. How about **Lough Arrow** in County Sligo? This is revered first and foremost as a big trout water, there are also some excellent pike.
CONTACT – Stephanie and Robert Maloney at Arrow Lodge, Kilmactranny, Via Boyle, for details, on 00353 7966298.

TENCH, RUDD AND PERCH ON THE ROYAL CANAL AND THE RIVER INAGH

Most coarse fish species in Ireland were imported. Perch and pike probably arrived in the 16th and 17th centuries. Carp probably came across during the reign of James I, whereas roach were a fairly recent introduction – probably appearing in late Victorian times. It is likely that the tench came over with the carp, or possibly earlier when they were imported from monastic stew ponds. The belief is that rudd came over with bream, possibly around the time of the Norman Conquest. All species have certainly done very well, particularly tench and rudd. The clear, pure, rich waters produce great specimens, and the rudd do grow large. Two-pounders are common and the tench average a high weight, in most places between four and six pounds. The colossal tench of the English gravel pit scene have not appeared but Ken Whelan in his excellent Angler in Ireland records a fish between eleven and twelve pounds from the river Suck.

Both species are spread thickly throughout the north and the south of Ireland and you can find good sport in most localities. Once again we turn to Charlie Stuart:

'Tench fishing is probably the most exciting and frustrating of all the branches of angling that I know of. When things go well, however, you just do not ever pursue a more rewarding fish. I suppose some of my favourite venues are the canals of the Irish midlands, places where I've spent many an evening and early morning stalking the species. One of the great attractions of these canals is that there are so many stretches that have yet to be discovered. Truly there are places where no Irishman, let alone a visitor, has cast a bait. Let's look, though, at a few stretches along the **Royal Canal** that really are worth particular mention and have a good track record. The first one has to be the canal on the Dublin side of Mullingar. You'll find this stretch flowing along the side of the main road and the landmark to head for is Mary Lynch's pub and bed and breakfast – something of a draw for tench fishermen. Take a right turn at the pub and you travel alongside the canal for about half a mile. You'll find every yard is teaming with fish. There are huge shoals of roach and rudd that can prove difficult in clear water. But it's the tench that are really special. In the summer of 2000 I witnessed huge numbers of tench and their spawning ritual. I'll tell you this isn't a sight for the weak hearted. There were heaving masses of fish thrashing in the water, quite oblivious to my presence. It was pointless to take the rod out of the car but what a beautiful sight to behold.

'As any good tench fisherman knows, the best times for the canal are from dawn until about ten in the morning, and then late in the evening, from around eight o'clock until it is too dark to see a float. My tip is to use a common earthworm tipped with a single red or white maggot. Many is the time I've fished alongside other anglers who have been using different baits, and whereas they've blanked, I've almost invariably had a few good fish. Float fishing works very well indeed, and you won't be in any

Clearwater Rudd

Perhaps the most dramatic coarse fishing option in Ireland is rudd fishing on the limestone loughs. Fishing for rudd, however, can be frustrating.

- *Take your time on the water – you'll almost certainly need a boat.*
- *Drift more than you row.*
- *Scan the water with binoculars, looking for any surface activity.*
- *Choose warm, bright, comparatively still days.*
- *Look for reedy bays, water lilies – anything offering rudd some sense of security.*
- *Drift pieces of bread downstream and watch the rising fish through binoculars.*
- *If fish are located, use three or four pound line, a size eight hook and either a big piece of flake or a piece of floating crust about the size of a fifty pence piece.*
- *Dunk both the flake or the crust to give added weight for casting distance.*
- *Either attach a small float or watch the line for a take.*
- *When a rudd is hooked, hustle it away as quickly as possible. Release all fish caught immediately. Keep nets do nothing for the rudd's beautiful appearance.*

doubt when the tench are in your swim because they really bubble like crazy things here. Darkness and you pack up and make the short walk back to Mary's for a pint of the 'black stuff' and a wholesome supper. And then it's upstairs to bed, in all probability your room being one that overlooks the canal itself. A fisherman's paradise.

'Another extremely good spot for tench fishing is **Lough Patrick** outside Multifarnham. This village is between Mullingar and Edgeworthstown, and the lough is easy to find. Boat hire is available in Multifarnham itself and I'd really advise a visit if you're intending to travel to the area. My one word of advice is to bring along plenty of ground bait even though the lake itself is quite small. The fish need a little tempting to bring on the feed but, once you've cracked it, the rewards are endless.

'It is almost impossible knowing where to start giving advice on rudd venues. Rudd are almost everywhere. Perhaps they're at their best in the big, clear loughs, but you'll also find them in the Shannon, in the backwaters especially, and also in some of the rivers. The **River Inagh** in County Clare and the **Owenavorragh River** in County Wexford offer good sport. Once again, I'd advise going back to Mary Lynch's for some of the best rudd fishing sport that Ireland can offer. You'd be amazed at the number and size of the rudd that you can see there. Just to give you an example, I stopped over briefly one afternoon a couple of years back and caught four rudd, which weighed in jointly at over seven pounds! Not bad for about twenty minutes fishing.

'Before I go, John, I ought to say something about the perch in Ireland. Like rudd, tench and bream, they're pretty well everywhere and there really are some cracking specimens. But here's a last little tip. This little pond in the Forest Park at **Deonadea** in County Kildare was stocked by an enterprising individual some years ago and has become a place that turns up some amazing fish considering the water is so small. It teems with roach and that is obviously why the perch grow so big. I myself have had them up to three and three-quarter pounds, and one large perch that I caught coughed up a half-digested roach. So I don't have to say any more about the staple diet of the fish here. It's a tremendous place to visit if you're on holiday in Dublin. The park lies about four miles outside the town of Clane ,which is only about twenty minutes drive from the city centre itself. The water is shallow and how I fish it is to bait heavily with maggots and work the roach up into a feeding frenzy. The big perch then move in and you can pick them up on lobworm or, inevitably, a small roach dead bait.'

Highly Recommended Fisheries

- *Lough Muck. A thirty-five acre lake just outside Omagh with pike, roach and perch. Contact Kenny Alcorn for day permits on 0288 224 2618.*
- *Clay Lake, Nr. Keady, County Armagh. A hundred and twenty acres. Pike, rudd and perch. Controlled by the Department of Agriculture.*

Where to Sea Fish

Sea-fishing Sites from Lincolnshire to Essex

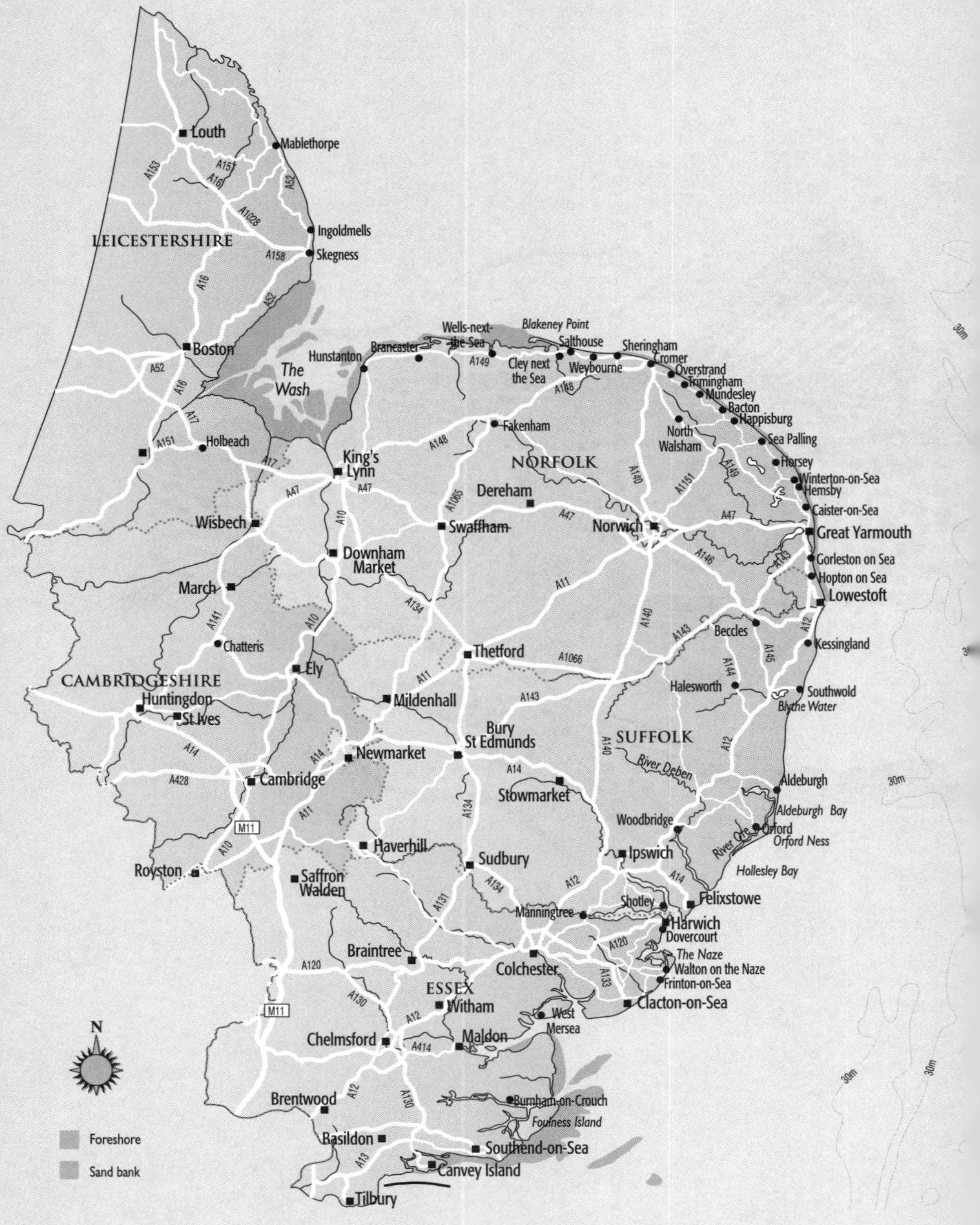

'I've known this coastline all my life. I was brought up here, and my whole life is concerned with conservation on the marshes at Cley. Okay, this east coast doesn't have the dramatic cliffs and huge surf of, say, Cornwall, but there's a quiet mystery and charm about it all. You should see it on a summer evening when the sea is molten and the marshes are on fire. Or during a winter storm when there's a gale blowing down from the north and nothing separating us from the Pole. It's a seashore of mists and seeping tides, and you've got to watch out for potential dangers. The fishing is thrilling. Obviously, there are those who say it's not as good as it once was, but it's still good enough for me and plenty of others. Perhaps the big cod aren't here in the numbers that they once were, but there are lots of other things to keep you occupied. Fishing for flatfish is as good as ever, and the bass fishing is certainly on the way up. Of course, we also have our secrets – it's not unusual to catch the odd sea trout, and we get great invasions of mullet during the summer.'

BERNARD BISHOP, NORFOLK WILDLIFE TRUST WARDEN FOR CLEY MARSHES

Bernard is quite correct. The east coast of England and dramatic sea fishing aren't always seen to go entirely hand-in-hand, but this is certainly a big mistake. The bass fishing in most areas can be absolutely superb – from spring right through to the early days of winter. Moreover, it seems that there are more and more bass appearing every summer, and the winter fishing for codling and whiting can, at times, be excellent. If you have access to a boat, then you can expect worthwhile skate fishing in places, and even the possibility of some good tope. There was a time when the Wash was considered one of the very best areas for these fabulous fish, and the rumour is that they're on their way back. Hopefully, conservation will ensure their long-term survival.

Mablethorpe

The area from Mablethorpe south to Skegness comprises miles of flat, sandy beaches. These beaches are very shallow and open to the winds, which doesn't make them particularly conducive to boat fishing. However, the beach fishing can be extraordinarily good. Mablethorpe is busy throughout the summer months when the tourists descend, but it dies a death during the winter, and the anglers come into their own.

Try the amusement park end of the beach and around the Trustville holiday camp. You will find that the beaches are clean and that they fish particularly well at low water. Worm is a favourite bait, but crab produces good catches of flounder.

Moving south, Chapel St Leonards, Chapel Point, Six Marshes, Nearby Creek, Mogs Eye and Huttoft are all popular fishing spots. The whole area can be very good for summer bass. Try lug – especially black lug – and don't make the mistake of trying to cast out too far.

You won't find any charter boats in this area, but the dinghy fishing can be very good for bass, eels and flatfish. There are thornbacks around, but you will have to go quite a few miles offshore to find these.

Accommodation – the Tourist Information Centre in Mablethorpe on 01507 472496 can advise on accommodation in the area.

Tackle shops – it's a good idea to have a word with the tackle shop in St Leonards, which is an absolute gold-mine of information; call Chapel Tackle on 01754 871657.

Skegness

Skegness isn't quite the magnet it used to be, since its famous long pier sank to a watery grave nearly quarter of a century ago, destroyed by gales and floods. There are still a few anglers that fish around this historic spot, but most of the locals move slightly further along the beach to Ingoldmells.

The Butlins holiday camp is a well-known mark, both winter and summer. The bass fishing can be very good, but also expect smooth-hounds and dogfish to feature. Crab is a winning bait. Come winter, there are plenty of codling and whiting about, with some big cod, well into double figures, occasionally showing up. Lugworm, fished on an incoming tide, is hard to beat. At high tide, cast shorter.

Accommodation – this is an area with plenty of hotels. For details, contact the Tourist Information Centre in Skegness on 01754 764821.

Tackle shops – contact Skegness Fishing Tackle on 01754 764404 for up-to-the-minute angling information.

THE WASH AND THE OUSE ESTUARY

The Wash can be featureless in places, but the Great Ouse River offers some tremendous possibilities. It flows northwards into the bottom right-hand side of the Wash at King's Lynn. You can find fishing within the town itself, as well as on the outskirts. What is also appealing about the place is that it's very much under-fished, and you're certainly unlikely to be struggling for bank space.

The Ouse Estuary was tremendously popular back in the 1950s and 1960s, when locals pioneered fly fishing for both bass and mullet. You'll be very unlikely to see anybody wielding a fly rod in the area these days, but the bass seem to exist in ever-increasing numbers. Basically, the bass move in from April, and you'll find mullet from May until September. You can also expect large catches of eels and flounder, and even the occasional sole. This is a perfect area for the exploring angler and one who is, perhaps, on holiday close by on the Norfolk coast – say at Hunstanton or Heacham.

Those that fish the area swear by peeler crabs, although bread can work for the mullet, and even maggots and garden worms do well at times. Obviously, standard beach gear will do the job, but you'll get far more out of your sport if you fish a little bit lighter. For example, try light spinning for the bass and coarse float tackle for the mullet. You'll even find that you catch far more eels on a five- or six-pound line, which is quite up to the job.

ACCOMMODATION – call Hunstanton Tourist Information Centre on 01485 532610.
TACKLE SHOPS – in King's Lynn, contact either the Tackle Box on 01553 761293 or Anglers' Corner on 01553 775852 for detailed information, bait or tackle.

CLEY TO CROMER

The long pebble beach between Cley next the Sea and Weybourne has long been a favourite area for local anglers pursuing bass and flatfish in the summer, and cod, codling and whiting throughout the winter.

There's easy access from the main A149 coast road down to these beaches, and there is convenient parking. However, it often pays to walk a little way from the main crowd – for example towards Weybourne cliffs, which have a great reputation for producing the bigger bass.

Sheringham is building up a good angling reputation, especially since the flood defences were erected at the centre of the town beach. You'll find abundant bass here, with a good number of spring cod. Flatfish are present all year, and there are plenty of mackerel between June and September.

Be careful at the main beaches, which are crowded throughout the holiday season. The same goes for Cromer. In the height of the summer, it's probably best to fish early or late and/or off the pier, which you can access for a small charge. You'll pick up occasional mackerel from the end of the pier and perhaps even the odd tope in the summer. There are also good skate and bass around.

Accommodation – for details of accommodation in the area, phone the Tourist Information Centres in Cromer on 01263 512497 or Sheringham on 01263 824329. Alternatively, try the George Hotel in Cley next the Sea on 01263 740652. Also highly recommended is the Dunn Cow – a small, family-run pub in Salthouse that offers excellent accommodation; phone them on 01263 740467.

Tackle shops – the Angling Direct shop in Cromer on 01263 513676 is the hub of sea fishing in this area and will offer you good advice.

Overstrand, Trimingham and Mundesley

Continuing south east, Overstrand and Trimingham offer good possibilities for codling, occasional bass and flounder. If you're fishing the promenade at Overstrand, long casting frequently pays dividends.

Mundesley is a charming little holiday town that offers some interesting fishing, too. The beaches are sandy, with odd patches of shingle and stone. There are gullies and sandbanks that dry out on large, low tides. You'll find the water shallow and very difficult to fish during rough seas.

The most productive time, locals agree, is three hours before high tide and two hours down. It's best to fish the gullies between the sandbanks and the shore – anywhere between fifty and 150 yards from the high-tide mark. You'll pick up good dabs and flounder, cod in winter and spring, and the odd bass and sole during the summer. Watch out for whiting once autumn comes. Mundesley is easily reached on the B1159 south of Cromer, and there are plenty of signs to the beach.

Accommodation – for various kinds of accommodation available in the area, contact the Tourist Information Centre in Mundesley on 01263 721070.

Tackle shops – the best is the Angling Direct shop in Cromer on 01263 513676.

Bacton, Happisburgh, Sea Palling and Winterton-on-Sea

All these locations further down the north-east coast of Norfolk offer good chances of some really good bass throughout the summer period

❧ Norfolk Bass ❧

The shingle bank from Blakeney Point down past the beaches at Cley next the Sea and Salthouse can, at times, provide some of the most stunning angling action imaginable. This is a very beautiful area, and a great favourite for holiday-makers drawn to the quaint Norfolk coastline, with its attractive little villages tucked away behind the marshes. The marshes themselves represent some of the most sought-after bird-watching territory in the United Kingdom.

The bass seem to come in quite early in the year, but the peak period is from June right through to October. One problem for anglers is the lack of real fish-holding features along this part of the shore. There are the occasional spots that are well known to the locals, but the casual visitor is advised to keep as mobile as possible. For this reason, it's a good idea to try spinning, especially when the sea is comparatively clear and weed isn't too much of a problem. You need something big and flashy – a big silver spoon isn't a bad option, providing you work it quickly so that it doesn't sink and foul the bottom. Above all, experiment. For example, on really calm days when you can see the bass splashing at the top, a 'popper' plug is worth trying; it's almost like American-style fishing for freshwater bass.

The bass do shoal quite tightly – I was talking to a local angler a few months ago who had managed to land eighty in one afternoon, admittedly from his small boat, but he was only some twenty yards out from the beach. I'm glad to say that he put back all but half a dozen. The fish were between two and seven pounds, about average for this area.

So, if you fancy some thrilling bass fishing in a wonderful, wild environment, then this could be just the place for you.

There's great accommodation around, too – Cley Mill Guesthouse is particularly in demand, with its wonderful views over the marsh. Phone 01263 740209 for details.

The angling shop in Cromer, Angling Direct (formerly known as Marine Sports), offers the most up-to-the-minute advice. Phone them on 01263 513676.

Lugworm can be bought locally from the many villages – simply look for the signs outside the houses. Lugworm can prove a very good alternative to the spinner. Simply use light gear, a weight just heavy enough to hold bottom, and feel for bites. You needn't cast far out – twenty yards is often far enough – and you can be in for a thrilling time if you locate the fish.

Lugworm Digging

Given the price of worms sold commercially, it makes good sense to get out there on the beaches and dig your own. The following tips may help:

- *Always check that digging on a particular beach is permitted as there are many restricted areas.*
- *Always ensure that you are down on the grounds at low water and leave well before the incoming tide.*
- *Never take any risks with the weather. If it looks as though it's going to be stormy, then don't go out.*
- *Never go far from the shore, especially in mist or foggy conditions as it's easy to become disoriented. If you're in any doubt, take a compass.*
- *As far as equipment is concerned, you'll need good thigh boots, a strong wide-pronged fork, and a net and a bucket to wash your worms. A good warm coat can be vital to keep out a piercing wind.*
- *Look for a dry area with many worm casts. Dig a trench some five yards long and then go back to the head and keep turning over in a rhythmical, methodical manner.*
- *Once your trench begins to flood seriously, turning the sand into liquid ooze, then it's time to pull out and look for another area to work.*
- *During cold weather, the worms will go deeper and you'll need to go down more than the normal eighteen inches or so.*
- *Don't rush your digging – you'll only tire yourself out and achieve lower numbers. Give yourself frequent rests to let your back have a breather.*
- *Watch your hands for emerging blisters. These can be very painful, especially if they crack and get sand and salt in them. It's a good idea to wear mitts with the fingers removed. (In my professional digging days, I once found myself putting thirty-two bits of plaster on my hands and fingers on a Saturday evening!)*
- *Ignore worms that you've broken. Leave them for the seabirds because they will only die and infect the rest in your bucket.*
- *Don't take immature worms and don't dig too high up on the marsh where the small worms create their nurseries. Move towards the sea where the worms are larger.*
- *Don't dig more worms than you need. You'll simply deplete stocks for yourself in the future.*
- *Treat your worms carefully. Keep them in cool, moist conditions in damp newspaper. Check regularly for any worms that have died or that you have nicked with the fork without realising.*

and well into the autumn. The area also fishes well for dab, flounder and codling. Try to fish this area after a good easterly blow, especially if you can fish into darkness on the flood. The Sea Palling and Waxham reefs offer really exciting new possibilities. They are part of a fifteen-mile scheme designed to protect those beaches of the Norfolk coast that are particularly susceptible to erosion. Something like 100,000 tonnes of sand and shingle are lost to the tides each year. Eight reefs have been constructed so far to steady this process. Four of the reefs are enormous – 250 yards in length and built on thick rock mattresses. These areas were always top bass marks, and the reefs have only added to the attraction.

The presence of the reefs has caused massive build-ups of sand, and this has created horseshoe-type bays of great width. Food tends to get deposited in these areas and this attracts great numbers of whiting, flatfish, dogfish, ray and, especially, bass. When the bass move in – as they do from May onwards – they are feeding hard and bites are frenzied. You can bait-fish on the lead or even use a float. Plugging has become increasingly popular amongst local anglers. All the reefs are producing fish, but the north reef to the left of Sea Palling is considered the top mark by many locals.

ACCOMMODATION – phone the Tourist Information Centre in Great Yarmouth on 01493 842195 for advice on accommodation in the area.

TACKLE SHOPS – see the entries for Great Yarmouth (below).

GREAT YARMOUTH

Great Yarmouth itself is a real hubbub of a place and not to everyone's taste. Nevertheless, however you view the bustling tourist trade in the town, you can't deny that Great Yarmouth has all styles of sea fishing on offer – two piers, miles of perfect shoreline and two mouths of well-wharved river from the harbour's mouth to the Haven bridge. You will also find plenty of boat angling.

There are lots of good marks around the Yarmouth area. The Pyramid, for example, gives up codling and bass. The Big Dipper and Green Shelter produce cod, with good numbers coming from the jetty. Altogether a pulsating area!

I've personally done well in the harbour at Gorleston on Sea for mullet during the summer. I haven't picked up any big fish, but the mullet swarm there in great numbers during the right conditions. And for a really special treat, you can't beat going out for a day afloat.

ACCOMMODATION – information about accommodation in the area can be obtained from the Tourist Information Centre in Great Yarmouth on 01493 842195.

TACKLE SHOPS – the tackle shops hereabouts offer really good advice – try Dave Docwra on 01493 843563. Gorleston Tackle Centre on 01493 662448 also gives up-to-the-minute advice. Tackle 'n' Tide on 01493 852221 has a good reputation.

BOAT HIRE – contact Bishop Boat Services on 01493 664739.

LOWESTOFT

Continuing south, Lowestoft is the next major centre, and it's noted for cod through the autumn, winter and spring, along with whiting and flatfish, and tope and ray from the charter boats.

Lowestoft harbour is a centre for really good flounder fishing, especially on crabs, with some codling and bass probable. There are good beaches to be found both north and south of the town, and the North Beach is a favourite mark.

ACCOMMODATION – the Tourist Information Centre in Lowestoft can advise on accommodation in the area; phone them on 01502 533600.

TACKLE SHOPS – Ted Bean Fishing Tackle on 01502 565832 and Sam Hook Sports on 01502 565821 are both excellent tackle shops offering good practical advice.

SOUTHWOLD

The Kessingland area has quite a bit to offer, but the fishing really comes alive again at Southwold. This is a lovely town, justifiably popular with anglers and tourists alike, so if you fancy a bit of a holiday with some excellent sea fishing thrown in, then you just can't beat heading down the A12 to Southwold.

Lying just twelve miles south of Lowestoft and forty-five miles north of Ipswich, Southwold is a delightful coastal town, small and quiet, but offering a great deal – good accommodation, great pubs, nice shopping and lovely scenery. The harbour to the south of the town is small, but bustling. You can fish along the harbour wall, and you will find some good flounders available in the spring and bass throughout the summer. Try spinning or float fishing, along with light legering. The pier was in a sorry state, but it's now being rebuilt, and this will add a lot to the shore potential of the town. Bass are almost certain to figure in captures.

There are beaches everywhere in Southwold and they produce a few sole in the summer. Bass, too, show up. In the winter, the favourites are cod and whiting. You'll find the sea wall as you head southwards, towards

Suffolk Bass

Go on, treat yourself. This really is one of the most highly recommended day's bass fishing you could possibly hope to have. Go out with Stewart Smalley, the Aldeburgh tackle dealer, who runs his twenty-foot boat out of Orford from May through to October.

This may seem a small boat, but it's supremely safe, very well skippered and highly manoeuvrable. Also, being a light craft, you do feel as though the fishing is very close and intimate. Stewart is extremely safety conscious and only takes very small groups, so don't worry. Enjoy!

This part of the Suffolk coastline is an absolute gem, and Orford itself is the prettiest village imaginable. Stewart generally, however, takes you from the quay, down the Ore estuary. You'll see birds and even the odd seal. He'll be heading for sandbanks about eighteen miles offshore where the bass really fight well on light gear. You'll be fishing on the drift, often with live sand eels. It's quick, lively, entertaining fishing, and if the bass are feeding you can expect quite a haul. Many of them aren't huge fish, but you can bank on five-pounders at the very least. And don't they scrap on light gear in that quick flowing water? It's a good idea, Stewart says, to use braid as main line. This keeps you in the closest of contact with what's going on and you will feel bites instantly. The thrill of the battle is also enhanced on non-stretch line.

During the day, there's also the chance to have a crack for the odd turbot or brill – in fact, Stewart says he's taking parties out now specifically for these. At around £200 to hire the boat, it's not the cheapest day out you'll ever have, but you won't regret a single penny of the cost. Stewart is a great character, with a huge knowledge of this part of the world and how the bass act in it. A day to remember. You can contact Stewart at Aldeburgh Tackle on 01728 454030.

To get the best out of your day with Stewart – or any day after bass, come to that – make sure you have the necessary gear. If you fancy lure fishing, which is truly sporting and great fun, you'll need a variety of spoons, spinners, plugs, pirks and jelly lures. Phone Cornish Lures on 01872 223346 and try their Scandinavian-type mini pirks. Eddystone (on 01752 696161) make the fabulous Eddyjelly sandeel lures that are almost better than the real thing. The Harris Angling Company (on 01692 581208) still offer the widest range of lures for the bass angler, and their brilliant catalogue is a must. Finally, if you want to go the full mile and try fly fishing for bass, contact Danny at Sportfish on 01544 327111.

PIER-FISHING TIPS

Preparation

• If the pier dries out at low water, it pays to walk around looking for fish-holding features. Check out gullies, rough ground and mussel beds.

• Familiarise yourself with pier rules and restrictions. Some only allow underarm casting or one rod per angler. Check closing times and charges.

• Ask a local tackle dealer to point you in the right direction as to the best parts of the pier and the best stages of the tide to fish them. Check out the weather – high waves can sometimes crash over exposed areas.

Equipment

• You'll always need a drop net because you just never know when that monster might come along.

• If you're after mullet or garfish, take ground bait and a suitable bag.

• A length of thin rope is always useful for lowering a bucket down to the water if you need to keep bait or fish fresh during the day.

• As you can't rely on seating, it's a good idea if your tackle box can double up as a chair.

Methods

• If you need to cast long, use a longer leader than you would consider for beach fishing. When you're swinging a decent fish up towards you, you want the security of knowing that the leader knot is on the reel and not halfway down the pier stanchions .

• Fish next to the girders for pollack, wrasse and pouting.

• During the summer, try float fishing on freshwater gear for pollack, mackerel, garfish and bass.

• Experiment with baits – a live prawn, for example, can work wonders. Also, twitch baits back and keep them on the move – guaranteed to attract the attention of a flatfish.

The Net Result

• If you've got a good fish on, try to get help from a nearby angler. He can lower the net down into the water, downtide of the fish, so that you can bring the fish to the net and not vice versa.

• If a big fish goes with the tide under the pier, try to get a fellow angler to net it as it comes out the other side. Don't drag it back against a heavy tide or you're almost bound to lose it.

the pier, and this fishes well throughout the year. Here you'll get bass, again, from May right through into the autumn, along with sole. If you want to go out, charter boats run from the town. You can expect some great sport from tope, pollack and cod. You'll also pick up some very nice bass indeed.

Just to the south of the town lies Blythe Water, an expanse of water that opens to the sea and forms a safe mooring area for commercial working boats. These are available to take you out over the numerous wrecks off the East Anglian coast. Many of the wrecks are old World War II hulks. Summer wrecking, in particular, can be excellent. Summer perking, therefore, is a real possibility – the local skippers have the latest gear and know exactly where to go. Cod to twenty pounds are more than possible.

It's also worth having a look at the mouth of the River Blythe itself if you fancy doing a little bit of exploring. Access isn't always easy and do take great care of the sometimes treacherous marshes hereabouts. Don't take any risks with the tide, as it can come in very quickly. You'll find eels and flatfish in the area and, from June onwards, increasing numbers of mullet.

The coastline all the way from Southwold down to Dunwich throws up some very good whiting during the winter months, albeit fish that move in small shoals. Dunwich is also a very popular flounder venue. Don't discount the Minsmere area, either, for the odd good cod and flounder once the colder weather moves in.

All in all, this is a very interesting piece of coastline with Southwold at its core. It is an area of outstanding natural beauty, and if you're one of those sea anglers who takes an interest in bird life, then you're in for a magnificent treat.

ACCOMMODATION – call the Lowestoft Tourist Information Centre on 01502 533600.

TACKLE SHOPS – the local tackle shop, Southwold Angling Centre, is a mine of information; phone them on 01502 722085.

BOAT HIRE – contact Nigel Hayter on 017885 316429 or Dave Wright on 01502 722411.

ALDEBURGH, FELIXSTOWE AND HARWICH

Travelling south, the town of Aldeburgh is well worth a look. This beautiful old town offers really consistent sport with codling and gives up some good bass. Also look for mullet in the summer months. You'll find these fascinating fish all the way down the coast past Orford and along the River Ore. The River Deben, too, is home to swarms of these fish during the summer months. They're not easy to catch, but the sport can be tremendous if you pick the right method at the right height of the water.

Felixstowe and Harwich both offer marvellous opportunities. Bass well into double figures have come from the sea front at Felixstowe and from marks close to Harwich harbour and Dovercourt. Codling tend to dominate Suffolk's beach catches here, but from the boats that can be chartered locally you'll pick up plenty of stingray and thornback.

A word here about the pier at Felixstowe, which has become a really popular sea-angling venue throughout the year. It's easy to fish and easy to find, just down the A14 from Ipswich. It doesn't matter what the conditions, you'll find the fish. It's a great place for garfish, and you'll pick up sole after dark during the summer months. There's always the chance of a specimen bass as well. After dark is the best time, once everything becomes a little bit quieter, but do check closing times so you're not locked on! Generally, it closes around 10:00pm. If you're fishing during the daylight, try to pick a day when there's a bit of a chop and not too much sunshine. The best baits are lugworm, squid and mackerel, although the soles go well on ragworm, and peeler crabs can't be beaten for big bass. The pier also allows for fishing during rough weather when you'd be forced off the beach.

This area is particularly renowned for boat fishing, especially in the winter, when the weather can be somewhat inclement. The rivers Orwell and Stour meet here, separating Harwich and Felixstowe with an expanse of water about a mile wide. This produces a natural harbour. Harwich still maintains its olde-worlde, dignified charm, whereas Felixstowe has become something of a candyfloss paradise. Also, Felixstowe harbour is becoming one of the most advanced in the world, as it is dredged to accommodate enormous container vessels. Given the prevailing westerly winds, this area offers tremendous boat-fishing possibilities, especially through the winter. Winter fishing can take place less than a mile offshore on well-known marks such as the Outer Ridge, and Felixstowe or Wadgate ledges. Expect whiting from September, and codling to move in the following month. There are also good bass hanging around throughout the autumn period.

Every year, towards the end of November, the Shotley Cod Competition is held slap-bang in the middle of this productive area. No matter how rough the conditions may be, boats go out and fish are caught. You can expect to find codling of between three and six pounds, and double-figure fish do show up as well. As yet, there are no official charter boats working the area, but it's possible to launch your own craft at either the Suffolk Yacht Harbour or the Shotley Marina, which is well-designed and offers every possible facility, or you might hire a boat.

Boat Safety

If you fancy getting afloat, remember that safety is absolutely paramount. Plan every trip in a professional sort of way, take a real personal pride in your boat and ensure that it's in tiptop condition.

- *If your engine dies, drop anchor and stabilise the situation. Make sure that you have sufficient anchor chain and rope to hold bottom.*
- *Keep calm. A breakdown is a mind-numbing experience but gather your composure as quickly as possible and start asking for help.*
- *Don't rely on a mobile phone for talking to lifeboats or rescue helicopters. You need a properly installed VHF to get you through to the emergency services or neighbouring boats.*
- *Don't be afraid to admit that you've got a problem. As soon as you sense danger, make that call. Act swiftly and don't let a crisis develop.*
- *Make sure you carry spares and know how to use them. Familiarise yourself with your boat and its engine.*
- *Listen to the regular weather bulletins put out by your local coastguard every few hours. If there's a sudden change in the weather, head for shore.*
- *There's always a chance you might have to wait for help, so always take life-jackets, warm clothing, food, water and flasks with you.*
- *Make sure that you have flares on board with you, particularly at night.*
- *Always tell somebody where you are going. If you change your plans, phone through the information.*
- *No matter how good the fishing is, don't leave it too late to return to port as this can be very worrying for those on shore.*
- *Always try to give the coastguard your exact position.*
- *Make sure you and everyone on your boat is wearing a life-jacket.*
- *Drinking alcohol is unacceptable out at sea – especially if you're the skipper. Keep a clear head at all times and make sure anybody fishing with you does the same.*
- *It's a good idea to have alternative means of propulsion. Stick an old engine, for example, somewhere down in the boat's hold. Even a pair of oars can make a difference.*
- *Charts are useful, and always have a compass with you.*
- *If you're a novice boat owner, join your local club for some expert advice and tuition.*
- *If you're fishing with a group of friends, for example, make sure they all know the ins and outs of your boat and what they would have to do in an emergency.*

Accommodation – contact the Tourist Information Offices in Aldeburgh on 01728 453637, Felixstowe on 01394 276770 or Harwich on 01255 506139.

Tackle shops – visit Aldeburgh Tackle at 30 Crabbe Street, or phone 01728 454030.

Boat hire – for boats, contact Barton's Marina on 01255 503552 or Vick Caunter on 01255 552855 in Harwich.

Walton on the Naze and Clacton-on-Sea

Walton on the Naze is another major sea-fishing centre offering cod, skate, mullet and dab. Concentrate on the pier and, slightly further south, on Frinton Wall and Frinton sea front.

There's more good summer fishing down at Clacton-on-Sea from the beach, the pier and the many commercial boats. You'll find dabs, plaice, bass, eels, thornbacks, tope and dogfish.

Accommodation – contact Clacton-on-Sea Tourist Information Centre on 01255 423400.

Tackle shops – quite the best tackle shop in the area is John Metcalfe's, to be found at 15 Newgate Street, Walton on the Naze on 01255 675680. You can also contact Brian Dean's Tackle Shop on 01255 425992 for details on baits and permits and for general information.

Boat hire – contact Mr S. Murphy on 01255 674274.

The River Crouch

The River Crouch is a fascinating and little-known river that joins the Thames estuary. It's sandwiched between the Thames and the Blackwater. If you're a shore angler, you'll find mullet, bass, flounder and eels through the summer. There's a well-known area called the Hole, which you'll find half a mile or so from the Essex Marina, based at Wallasea. You can fish here along an accessible stretch of sea wall. Night is generally the best time, especially in the summer when the water is warm, and you might be lucky enough to see the mullet finning or the bass actually hunting. There is also some bank space at Burnham-on-Crouch. Peeler crabs are a preferred bait for the bass, while rag and lug are good for flounder and eel. Also, expect to pick up whiting on the worm. Obviously, you can use normal beach casting gear here but I really recommend light spinning tackle for the bass if you're going to get the best out of your sport.

The boat angler is also well catered for on the Crouch. Essex Marina is the centre for all boat traffic here, and it has just undergone a major refurbishment. There's a brand new boat hoist, new boat shed and electric and water points around the hard-standing areas. A new bar and restaurant complex has been planned and is probably already in operation. You'll find toilets, showers and free parking. There's a slipway and constant water, so it's a perfect place for anglers who wish to bring their own boats. There is a charge, though, for using the facility.

It's very easy to charter a boat in this area. The Crouch is a small river and is sheltered, so the boats hardly ever have to cancel a trip. There are plenty of fish available, too, and this is pretty much a year-round venue. In the spring, you'll find good thornbacks only twenty minutes or so from the marina, along with codling, smooth-hound and bass. Indeed, the Thames estuary has been famous for years for all these species, including tope and even angler fish.

Up-tiding is the most common method, although down-tiding is also used. The water tends to be quite murky, so artificial lures are rarely tried. Favourite baits are worms, squid and peeler crabs. The nearest tackle shops are to be found at Southend-on-Sea, but the skippers all supply bait and tackle so you won't run short.

Accommodation – the Tourist Information Centre in Southend-on-Sea on 01702 215120 can advise on accommodation available in the area.

Tackle shops – see below for tackle shops in Southend-on-Sea.

Boat hire – highly recommended skippers include Dave Godwin on 01702 308043, Andy Hide on 01268 451891, Andy Lambert on 01702 218932 and Steve Smith on 07831 363629.

Southend-on-Sea

Southend-on-Sea is another town offering fantastic pier fishing, especially for flounders and school bass. Mullet are common in the summer, along with mackerel, scad and garfish. Plaice are also a target species, with cod, codling and large flounders in the winter. The pier also fishes well for whiting until late December. A small charge is levied for day permits.

Accommodation – the Tourist Information Centre in Southend-on-Sea on 01702 215120 can advise on accommodation available in the area.

Tackle shops – try either Jetty Anglers in Southend-on-Sea on 01702 611826 or the Southend Angling Centre on 01702 603303 for up-to-the-minute advice.

Boat hire – Southend has a thriving charter-boat fleet. Try the *Skerry Belle* on 01702 390842, Dave Godwin's *Creditor* on 01702 308043, the *Dawn Breaker* on 01702 469114 or the *Nitricia* on 01268 272179.

Sea-fishing Sites in South-East England

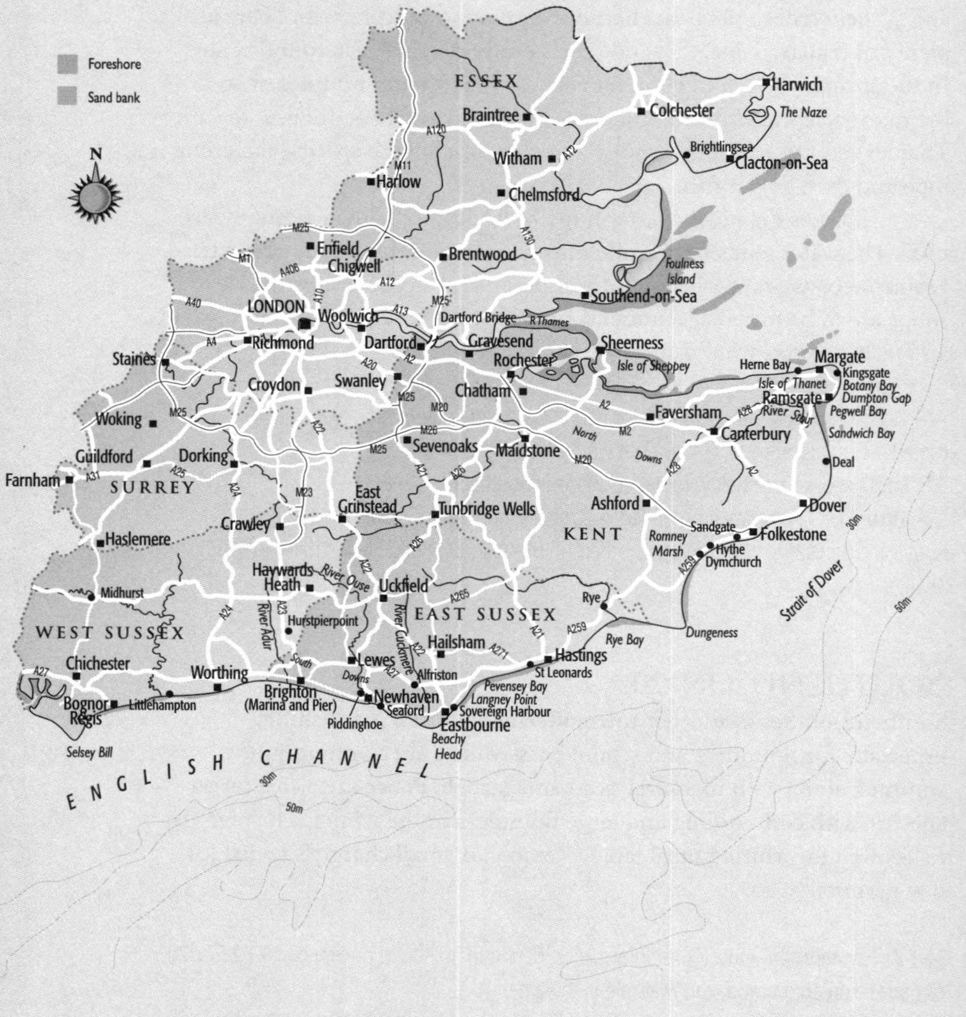

I've fished pretty well all my life out of Pevensey Bay and I've never once become dissatisfied or wished for something more dramatic. The area, as far as I can see, has got everything for the sea angler. There's some terrific beach fishing around. There are piers, if that's what you fancy, as well as marinas, rocky headlands and some tremendous boat fishing. The bass fishing in the summer is hard to beat, and I've seen some great winter codding through the course of my fishing career. This is also a really good area for the dinghy enthusiast, but launch sites are limited along the coast. Having your own craft really does make you that little bit more independent and, especially during the warmer months, can get you out to the best marks where there's little competition for places. This is also a great area for the match man, with comprehensive lists of shore and boat matches throughout the year. There are great tackle shops, lots of holiday resorts and it's all very scenic. In short, it's as good for the holidaying angler as it is for the resident.

JIM WHIPPY, EDITOR OF *BOAT FISHING* MAGAZINE

I'd like to emphasise the point that Jim makes about the holiday potential for the angler along this area of coastline. Some of the resorts that we're looking at here – Brighton and Eastbourne, for example – really do offer the entire holiday package. I caught my first mullet down here many years ago when I was a student in London. I got totally fed up with the park ponds in the capital and decided to head south to the coast. The gear that I had been using for small carp and tench proved absolutely ideal for the mullet – and believe me, they fought twice as hard! And, being a student, I was quite pleased to have something to take back for the kitchen. Not that I would do that now, even though mullet numbers aren't really threatened. For me, the biggest thrill of all is to see a fish swim away wild and free.

Sheerness

Situated on the north coast of the Isle of Sheppey, Sheerness is a famous area for cod and whiting from the autumn onwards. This has been the long-time venue of the British Open, which is held towards the end of the year when the cod have, hopefully, arrived.

Some of the famous marks include Barton's Point, East Church Gap and New Sea Wall. The Isle of Sheppey is easily reached from the M2 by turning off north at junction 5.

Accommodation – phone the Tourist Information Centre in Sheerness on 01795 668061.

Tackle shops – Island Bait and Tackle Shop on 01795 668506 is the hub of the area, selling fresh bait and dispensing up-to-the-minute information.

Herne Bay

Moving east, we come to the charming Kentish town of Herne Bay, which offers the sea angler some really good spring fishing. You can expect flounders and some of the earliest bass around the British shores. Peeler crab is one of the favourite baits, and can be bought locally. As the season progresses, the bass become more common and move up into the shallow warm water where they can be caught very close to the beach. Lugworm begins to come into its own, but spinning is even more exciting. If the sea looks reasonably clear, try anything that catches the light. Silver and gold spoons are particularly effective. However, if the water is calm, you can even catch bass in shallow water on surface-working lures – brilliantly exciting.

Remember that long casting isn't always essential and you will quite often find bass working very close inshore looking for food. When the bass are in close, you will soon discover that stealth is much more important than brawn. In fact, when you're bass fishing near to the beach like this, it's important to take a leaf out of our freshwater-fishing cousins' book and avoid crunching on the shingle.

As the summer progresses, the bass remain plentiful, but you will also find plenty of black bream, dogfish and even some stingray that can be caught from the beaches. As the autumn progresses, you can expect an influx of whiting.

Accommodation – phone the Tourist Information Centre in Herne Bay on 01227 361911.

Tackle shops – Herne Bay Angling on 01227 362127 or Ron Edwards Tackle on 01227 372517.

MARGATE

This well-known holiday centre features some tremendous fishing. One of Margate's great advantages is the wide variety of fishing on offer. It's suitable for all levels of angling ability – from the expert angler down to the novice who just wants a few hours with the children in the middle of a summer Bank Holiday. Margate is particularly noted for its very good bass fishing, which you can do either from the shore or, preferably, from a boat using spinning gear. Keep on the move until you find the fish, and also scan the waters for any surface disturbance through binoculars. Expect to see small fish breaking the surface, or a cluster of gulls gathering as bass force prey fish upwards.

Come the winter, Margate's pier is excellent for cod and whiting – certainly from November through to April or May. There's also some excellent rock fishing at nearby Botany Bay, Dumpton Gap and Kingsgate. You'll also find that there are opportunities to do a little bit of tope fishing by boat. The shallow, warm water off Margate is perfect for these hard-fighting species. Don't over-gun yourself or you won't get the best out of your fishing. In fact, heavy carp gear is just about right. Don't go too low on line strength, however – the last thing you want to do is leave fish with hooks in them.

ACCOMMODATION – phone the Tourist Information Centre in Margate on 01843 230203.
TACKLE SHOPS – contact Kingfisheries on 01843 223866.

RAMSGATE

Another top traditional holidaying area in the south east, Ramsgate can – like its neighbour Margate – become very busy in the summer, when the beaches are probably best fished early or late. However, Ramsgate offers both harbour and pier fishing and the area comes very much into its own when the tourists leave and the cod arrive!

Once again, expect some really good bass fishing, along with excellent flatfish and some thornbacks. Ramsgate's attractive little harbour is home to a vibrant little fishing fleet so, providing the weather is clement, you will be able to get offshore most days of the year. Goodwin Sands is one of the traditional hotspots, producing tope, flatfish, skate and bass.

ACCOMMODATION – Ramsgate has a wide range of accommodation and the Tourist Information Centre on 01843 583333/4 will be able to supply you with details.
TACKLE SHOPS – contact Fisherman's Corner Tackle Shop on 01843 582174.
BOAT HIRE – contact Mr Spencer, skipper of *Any Chance*, on 01843 835353.

THE STOUR ESTUARY

Sandwich Bay and the River Stour offer some very interesting fishing indeed. Entrance to the bay is by a private toll road that takes you to a wonderful, unspoilt area. There's some very good beach fishing, but one of the main delights, come the summer, is the grey mullet that run up the river. Mind you, these mullet can be fiendishly difficult to catch and they are totally unpredictable.

Mullet fishing is an art all to itself. Sometimes you'll find that they're truly switched on and you can catch them on almost any bait going. Most of the time, however, they'll have you absolutely tearing your hair out in frustration and wondering where on earth you're going wrong. Hook one, however, and the fun really begins. In fact, pound for pound, they're probably the hardest fighting fish in saltwater – on reasonably light gear, that is.

ACCOMMODATION – phone the Tourist Information Centre in Sandwich on 01304 613565.
TACKLE SHOPS – for all your bait and tackle needs, try the Sandwich Bait and Tackle shop on 01304 613752.

DEAL AND DOVER

You'll find some very interesting possibilities around Deal – Admiralty Pier is a good mark and available for a small daily fee – but Dover is, perhaps, the main attraction of this particular area, offering excellent boat and beach fishing. Some tremendous cod are taken from nearby wrecks, and there's excellent shore fishing from Shakespeare Beach. The Prince of Wales Pier is also a magnet and a perfect place for novices, offering the possibility of big mixed bags.

ACCOMMODATION – phone the Tourist Information Centre in Deal on 01304 369576 or that in Dover on 01304 205108.
TACKLE SHOPS – Channel Angling on 01304 373104 will provide bait, tackle and information On the Deal area. In Dover, phone Bill's Bait and Tackle on 01304 201457.

FOLKESTONE

Folkestone is often overshadowed by Dover, its big neighbour, but this shouldn't be the case because it really has got the lot – boat, beach and pier fishing. It is also more and more in the public eye as the gateway to Europe, standing as it does at the English end of the Channel Tunnel.

The Warren, which leads away under the cliffs on the east side of Folkestone, has some good summer fishing from May and June onwards, with bass coming on the early tides, and soles and pouting appearing near the top as darkness approaches. You'll start to find whiting and codling as winter moves in. Access to the fishing can be tricky and the best spots, as always, involve a good walk.

Next we come to Folkestone Sands, which run from Copt Point to the pier. The bottom is snag free, so it's easy fishing and it offers up small flatfish and school bass. Rotunda Beach shelves steeply and runs from the west side of the pier. Depth means that long casting isn't essential, and bass, cod and flatfish can be caught close in.

Lower Sandgate Road, which runs from Metropol Rocks to Mermaid Point, is very rocky and offers some good summer fishing from its two big concrete groynes.

The pier runs a good 400 yards out from Rotunda Beach and is accessible for a small fee. Tickets can be bought from the local tackle shops. Most locals make for the end section of the pier where there are fewer snags and where it fishes well over low water. The pier has a history of some big fish and offers a very comfortable fishing platform. It's also a good spot for conger and has produced fish over forty pounds in weight. The locals are convinced, however, that there are much bigger conger in the huge snags at the base of the pier wall. July to October seems to be the best time – try fresh mackerel as bait.

Bass fishing is an important feature of the Folkestone scene. These fish drift around all year long, although the traditional season is May until autumn. Float fishing and light spinning make headway in the shoals of school bass, and you'll also pick up garfish. Generally, the bigger bass come later on in the year, and as autumn approaches you can expect these larger fish to come in close, especially at night. Early bass seem to prefer peeler crab and ragworm, but later in the year, small live baits will do the trick. Also, try spinning with large spoons whenever the sea is reasonably clear.

There's a lively boat-fishing scene, most of which is done over the famous Varne Bank or the Ridge and the French Holes. Expect to pick up turbot, plaice and thornbacks. Pirking for cod is also a favourite. There are also some productive wrecks and the inshore cod fishing is excellent in the winter.

ACCOMMODATION – Folkestone Tourist Information Centre on 01303 358594 will give you all the advice you need on accommodation.

TACKLE SHOPS – Folkestone Angling on 01303 253881 or Harbour Tackle on 01303 220763 will advise on skippers, bait, conditions and general fishing hotspots.

BOAT HIRE – boats include the *Enterprise* on 01303 252513, *Folkestone Angler* on 01303 893264, *Pathfinder* on 01322 669159 and *Virginia Warrior* on 01622 207134.

Hotspot – The Thames Estuary

And how about old Father Thames himself – the river of comebacks? You're even getting cod there again these days, right up as far as Dartford Bridge. This is very muddy water, so you don't have to worry too much about having to fish at night. Most of the fish are comparatively small, but some are very decent indeed, with the odd double-figure specimen.

Shorn Mede lighthouse at Gravesend is a particular hotspot. It's not the easiest place to get to and it is a good long walk – some of it over thick mud. You do need to get out so that you can fish in the drop-off on the edge of the shipping lanes. The tide run here can be quite fierce, but four or five ounces of weight should do, providing you cast uptide and let a belly of line develop. Bites are generally straightforward slack liners. You don't want too strong a tide – around six yards is about right. Add to that a wind from the south or south west and you're really in – a strong wind will help you cast out even further. Lugworm seems to be a great bait, whilst a lug and squid combination tends to attract whiting.

If fishing the bank isn't quite what you're after, think about going afloat. Lee Bollingbroke on 01255 432871 is running a charter boat out of Brightlingsea, the port on the north side of the Thames estuary. His parties take good bags of cod throughout the winter and there's some tremendous bass and smooth-hound fishing through the summer; expect some thornbacks as well. A great day out.

There are plenty of good tackle shops in the area that can give advice – try Strood Angling on 01634 721300, Maidstone Angling on 01622 677326, Medway Tackle on 01634 570740 and the Dartford Angling Centre on 01322 228532.

The Romney Coast

Sandgate, Hythe and Dungeness all offer some good fishing possibilities from both beach and boats. Expect bass, codling, whiting and conger. Hythe is also well-known for its army ranges. You can't fish here all the time because it's still actively used by the army and there's a list of firing times on display at either end of the range. When the army is actually present and carrying out operations, access is guarded by sentries. The range is on the A259 between Hythe and Dymchurch and you'll find some parking spaces on the verge of the road. One of the best times to approach the range is over Christmas when there's a week or so without any activity

and it's safe to fish. Happily, this coincides with the arrival of some very good cod in decent numbers. For a number of years, there has been an annual match held during this period. The fact that the number of anglers just seems to keep going up must be a testament to the standard of the fishing. You can't take your car past the access point, so you're faced with a long walk to get to some of the best marks – travel light. You'll find that the range is basically a mix of shingle and sand, with groynes at intervals.

Locals favour the mark known as the Broken Tower, an old Martello tower that has been a gunnery target for a long time. You'll find this about a mile from the Dymchurch end of the range. It's also good as there is deep water close to a sandbar and you don't have to cast too far out.

The range fishes particularly well after a good wind, at rising and high water and up to a couple of hours down. Night is also a time favoured by the locals. Then you will pick up cod, codling, flatfish and some whiting in the winter months. Earlier in the year, you will also find bass about. All the usual baits are used with success here, including lug and squid. Cocktails are also a proven favourite.

Before leaving this area, let's have a look at Dymchurch promenade, which you will find joining on virtually from the southern end of the Hythe range. This is a sea wall that runs along the Dymchurch road. There are two particular areas favoured by the locals, especially in the winter when it's considered one of the top marks of the area. About midway along the promenade, you will come to Willop sluice. This is a culvert that channels out water overflowing from Romney Marsh that needs to get into the sea. The other place the locals favour is called the Redoubt, which you will find right at the end of the Hythe range itself. Here, once again, there's deep water close in and long casting isn't considered necessary.

The fishing is generally quite easy, but you should watch out for the remains of old groynes, which can prove to be major snags, especially if there is a heavy wind or strong tidal currents. In these conditions, you should also beware of the concrete wall itself, because the foothold can be precarious when it's drenched.

Most of the locals think the area is best attacked from half-tide up to half-tide down. However, in rough weather – which means a south-westerly wind – even low tide can be worth trying. This is obviously a very convenient spot for summer bass and flatfish but it fishes particularly well after dark, around high water for codling and, especially, whiting, which are numerous. For bass, a top tip is to get out very early in the morning, especially when the sea is calm, and watch carefully for fish hunting close in. A pair of binoculars can be a useful aid. Peeler crab can be good, but why not try light spinning gear for maximum mobility and sport? Use an eight- to nine-foot rod, fixed spool reel loaded with eight-pound line for maximum casting range, and take an assortment of silver spoons and spinners.

As a last thought, do take care where you park, and keep away from the various access roads and holiday camp entrances.

ACCOMMODATION – for details of accommodation in the area, phone the Tourist Information Centre in Hythe on 01303 267799.

TACKLE SHOPS – contact Romney Tackle on 01797 363990, Marsh Tackle in Dymchurch on 01303 873020 or try Mick Sullivan of Mick's Tackle Shop in Hythe. Mick is also involved in the organisation of any matches held in this area; he can be contacted on 01303 266334.

RYE, HASTINGS AND ST LEONARDS

Rye harbour is another place where you can expect mullet during the summer months. Moving west, Hastings offers some top sea fishing from its pier and boats – it's a centre for tope, bass, conger, flatfish and codling and whiting, especially later in the year. Hastings also hosts an international sea-angling festival in October.

New Church at St Leonards is just down the A259 from Hastings. The name New Church is actually the local nickname for St Leonards' Church itself, the building right on the sea front.

This is a very productive beach mark that has the additional advantage of good car parking! There's a car-park opposite the church itself. Moreover, the beach here is shingle and sand between groynes – an easy place to fish for all levels of ability. Locals consider the best time to fish to be early on the ebb tide, though the beginning of the flood can also be productive.

New Church comes into its own during the autumn and the winter. Expect good bags of codling, whiting and flatfish. Spring and summer, however, also offer tremendous possibilities for the visiting angler.

At times, there are some very good bass about, and once again the tip is to get out early and late and see what is feeding. Mobility is often the key. Also, in the summer, expect mackerel and plenty of eels, along with the occasional smooth-hound.

All the usual baits work here, but if you can't get anything more exotic than lugworm, don't worry, as this is arguably the favourite.

ACCOMMODATION – there is plenty of accommodation in the area, from hotels to bed-and-breakfasts. The Tourist Information Centre in Rye on 01797 226696, or that in Hastings on 01424 781111, can advise.

TACKLE SHOPS – try the Hastings Angling Centre on 01424 432178, Steve's Tackle Shop on 01424 433404 and Amber Dolphin on 01424 427005 – all in Hastings.

Pevensey Bay

Pevensey Bay is one of the main attractions along this part of the south coast, and there's a great deal of match angling going on due to its relatively sheltered position and consistent sport. Pevensey Bay itself is a pleasant village, not far from Eastbourne, so another good bet for the holidaying angler. What's more, the beach produces fish year round with few dull periods. The beach is some two miles in length overall, a mix of shingle and sand, with groynes at regular intervals. There are also Martello towers scattered along the shoreline.

So what do you get at Pevensey? Winter throws up great numbers of whiting, along with some codling and flatfish. Spring is productive, though mostly for small fish in great numbers, whilst the summer species include smooth-hound, dogfish, bass and plaice. There are garfish and mackerel about, but these are generally further offshore. Come autumn, the codling will move in. There will also be sole until the late autumn.

Hotspots? Well, the whole beach at Pevensey produces good numbers of fish, so virtually everywhere is worth trying. However, the Pevensey Bay Aqua Club, in the middle of the beach, is considered one of the better marks, and a lot of locals head towards the bungalows that can be found near the eastern end of the beach. Most local advice suggests that the most productive state of the tide would be the first two hours of the flood and the first two of the ebb. Go for all the usual baits, including lugworm, ragworm, squid, peeler crab and various forms of fish. Lug can be dug or pumped at low tide.

Let's just focus briefly on the bass fishing. There are some very good bass around, with fish over double figures a distinct possibility. These can come along at any time, to any method, but past history seems to suggest that a large fish bait is perhaps the best of all. Try half a mackerel or perhaps a smelt. If you hook up one of these semi-frozen, you'll find that you will be able to cast it a good long distance, especially if you tie it to the line with an elastic band. The same goes for another excellent, smelly, oily bait – sardine.

Look for some feature to cast to. For example, there are pipes running into the sea at various intervals and these often attract fish. Alternatively, keep on the move and work the bait a little bit. Be prepared for a big bite from a big fish. There are also plenty of small bass in the two- to four-pound bracket, especially throughout the summer. Lug are perfectly sufficient for fish of this size. Probably your best time is on a flood tide, very early in the morning before the holidaymakers begin to swarm in numbers. It's a really good idea to put these small bass – indeed all bass come to that – back alive. Perhaps keep one for the table but no more. That way we can all rely on sport to come.

ACCOMMODATION – the Tourist Information Centre in Hastings on 01424 781111 can advise on accommodation.

TACKLE SHOPS – for more detailed information and all the gear you're likely to need, phone the Anglers' Den in Pevensey Bay on 01323 460441.

EASTBOURNE

Eastbourne is really one of the jewels of South-East England, and caters very much for the more discerning holidaymaker. It nestles snugly under the cliffs of Beachy Head and is a world away from the razzamatazz that you'll find in many resorts. In fact, its sheltered position has led to the nickname 'suntrap of the south'. The Sovereign Harbour draws in yachts and cruisers from both England and the Continent.

If the town itself offers a haven to the tourist, then the sea gives bounty to the angler. Shore fishing ranges from heavy ground through to shingle beaches, and this means a good variety of fish is waiting to be caught. One popular mark is White Horses, accessible from the Pevensey Bay side of Langney Point. Aim for the Bay View caravan site and you'll find parking along part of the road. It's a great spot for the summer angler because at high tide the water is deep enough for the mackerel shoals to come inshore, where they can be caught on spinners. At night, you'll find sole feeding, and during the earlier part of the year, you'll pick up plenty of dab. It's a good autumn area for whiting, bass and codling.

Langney Point itself is also a good mark, and links up with the west arm of Sovereign Harbour. Here, you'll find massive boulders that were brought in from Norway to provide a good, firm shelter. You'll find garfish and mackerel in the summer, along with sole, dab and bass. There's a good run of whiting and codling in the winter.

Splash Point is a very central, convenient mark, very close to the World War II tank on the sea front. It's part of the promenade and gives much better access than the beach, so it's a handy place to fish.

Between Splash Point and the pier is a favourite local mark called Cambridge Road. There are good catches of flatfish and whiting, with quality cod and bass showing up occasionally; try lugworm and white rag. At low tide, you'll see the lugworm diggers in action.

The pier is particularly vibrant and offers very good general fishing for bass, pollack, flatfish, pouting and garfish. There are also some good mackerel to be caught throughout the summer. It's a fine spot for cod and whiting in the winter.

If it's bass that you fancy, try the Wish Tower. It's not a heavily fished mark, and perhaps that's its secret. However, cast a crab or a lugworm

Fishing for Mullet

Mullet are one of our most interesting species. They are often called the grey ghosts for their enigmatic behaviour, difficulty in catching and ability to disappear. Generally, however, mullet provide great sport for the sea angler. To make the most of your mullet fishing, try the following tips:

- *In most cases, all you will need is freshwater fishing gear. A typical match float rod or quiver tip rod is the ideal, paired with a medium-sized fixed-spool reel. A selection of floats, swim feeders, five- to six-pound line and hooks between size ten and fourteen will complete the job.*
- *Harbours are one of the most reliable places to look for mullet. They get used to feeding on scraps thrown to them by tourists or slivers of fish and guts from the trawlers. Try them with bread or fish titbits.*
- *Sewage outfalls – not necessarily pleasant places to fish – are also very productive. Try float fished maggot or worm.*
- *Mullet will also travel quite a way into freshwater up the estuary. Try ground baiting quite heavily with maggots and casters. Sometimes, floating bread will be taken from the surface.*
- *Explore rocky headlands and bays, especially where the water is relatively shallow and the feeding is rich. Mullet will also travel up creeks once the tide floods in.*
- *Always wear Polaroids, especially if the water is clear, so that you can see fish and gauge how deep they are feeding. Most mullet will take somewhere between the surface and mid-water, but there are times when legering or swim feeding will pick them up off the bottom.*
- *I've found warm, sunny weather to be particularly productive, although overcast days will also work if they are calm.*
- *The peak of the season is from May to October, although you'll find some fish early and late.*
- *If nothing works, try small, silver spinners, perhaps with the hook points tipped with ragworm. Failing that – if you've got the gear – small gold head nymphs fished on fly gear can be spectacularly successful.*
- *Mullet are very easily scared so your approach is vital, especially when they are not used to human activity.*
- *Mullet are spreading; reports suggest that there is barely any coastline from St Ives to the Scottish Isles that aren't visited.*
- *Despite their increasing numbers, return all mullet that are not destined for your cooking pot!*

SECOND-HAND ENGINES

You'll very often give yourself just that extra chance if you can go afloat – not necessarily right out into the ocean but inshore, perhaps exploiting the estuary mouth or harbour. But your boat will need an engine,and sometimes it's a good idea to buy a second-hand one rather than lashing out a lot of money – especially if times are tight or you're not quite sure whether boat fishing isyou. The trouble is, how do you sort out a good deal from a disastrous one?

• Just looking at the engine overall gives a good idea of whether it's been looked after. Is it battered or scratched, for example? Most important, look at the propeller and skeg for any obvious signs of a bad knock.

• Next, you've got to take off the engine cover itself and look for any obvious signs of repair. New gaskets are a giveaway, as are the sighting of any nuts that have recently been unscrewed – look out for chipped paint around them.

• With the engine securely off, grip the flywheel and try to move it backwards and forwards. There should be no movement at all; if there is, the upper crankshaft bearings are probably worn.

• It's very important to run the engine in a tank of water so that you can see it actually working.

• Once the engine is running, put it into gear to make sure it runs smoothly under pressure.

• While it's in the tank, check that both the forward and reverse gears are working well. Don't rev up or you'll spill the water.

• While the engine is running there should be a good flow of water to indicate the water pump is working. After the engine has run for a while, feel the temperature: it will be warm but it shouldn't be hot.

• Ask for any receipts of work done; these should be professional.

• Check that the tilt and lock mechanism is working – a point that's easily overlooked.

• Hold the leg of the engine and move it backwards and forwards. If there is any play, it indicates that the rubber support bushes are worn.

• With the engine off, put the gear lever in the forward position, then try to turn the propeller. If the propeller turns, it could be that the rubber shock absorber is stripped or very badly worn.

• If at all possible, use the engine for a proper session's fishing. The above checks are all important, but you can't actually beat getting the engine out on a boat, especially if there's a bit of a tide or a breeze about.

into the gullies and you may be lucky enough to get a fish of between two and seven pounds.

To get to Beachy Head, you need to walk quite a way along the path from the school (look out for access down to the rocks). It will take you a good fifteen to twenty minutes. Always make sure that you keep your eye on the tide if you're fishing the ledge here. Give yourself plenty of time to escape the rising water and make sure your exit point is well marked. The flood tide is particularly productive for bass, which stream in looking for crabs and prawns amongst the rocks.

There's some great charter-boat fishing out of Eastbourne, as there are plenty of wrecks within easy sailing. This is largely because during the war U-boats used to lie in wait as convoys passed by Beachy Head. In fact, some of the sixty-seven local wrecks are situated only seven miles from the town itself. Expect pollack, cod and conger. Good, close-in boat marks include the Chicken Run, Beachy Head Ledge, the Light Open, the Light Tower and Greenlands. Always be aware that there are some strong tides in this area, off Beachy Head in particular, and very long traces of up to twenty feet will often out-fish the standard six-foot trace.

ACCOMMODATION – Eastbourne is a major holiday centre so there's a wide range of accommodation; phone the Tourist Information Centre on 01323 411400.

TACKLE SHOPS – Eastbourne has some excellent tackle shops; phone Tony's Tackle Shop on 01323 731388 or Eastbourne Pier Bait and Tackle on 01323 648322, or try The Angler's Den in Pevensey Bay on 01323 460441

BOAT HIRE – for charter boats, phone Phil Batt on 01424 212602, Roger Wilson on 01323 766076, Nigel Snelling on 01342 712881 or Brian Kent on 01323 762439. My good friend Jim Whippy, editor of the excellent magazine *Boat Fishing,* lives in nearby Pevensey Bay and comments on the wide variety of fish that you can expect to find out from Eastbourne with any one of these skippers. Conger of seventy pounds are not unusual. Also expect some very good thornback. Bream, gurnard, dogfish and bull huss also proliferate and, of course, there are plenty of cod around the wrecks.

Seaford and Newhaven

Seaford and Newhaven have good possibilities, and the latter is a centre for deep-sea fishing. This area offers something just a little bit different – and I'm thinking here of the lighter, more intimate style of sea fishing that you can find in the river estuaries. First of all, let's have a look at the tidal River Cuckmere. You'll find the Cuckmere running towards the sea from the village of Alfriston, which is buried in the pleasant Sussex countryside. Perhaps the best access, however, is to take the A25 a mile

out of Seaford heading towards Eastbourne. The river runs under the road itself and you can park by the road bridge. The Golden Galleon pub is nearby with a large car-park, but do avoid busy times for the pub and, as a thank you, always use it afterwards for refreshments!

The river isn't wide – less than fifty yards – so you don't need traditional sturdy sea gear and, in fact, normal freshwater tackle is probably a better bet all round. What can you expect? Well, perhaps the best period of all is from May to early October. During this period you can expect eels, flounder and, most excitingly, bass and mullet. Approaches? Well, for the eels and plaice, why not try float fishing as something different? Of course, light beach gear will also do the trick. For bass, you can spin or try peeler crab, a very popular bait here and

Overcoming Seasickness

It could well be that you're looking at your first trip offshore – perhaps just drifting feathers for mackerel, spinning for bass or going a way out to do some codding. Seasickness is always a potential problem, but don't panic. There are ways round it.

- *Until you get your sea legs, don't think about going out on really rough days. Get used to boat fishing in calmer conditions.*
- *Be careful about what you have to drink the night before. It sounds obvious, but if you're feeling queasy to start with, then boat fishing is hardly going to help you.*
- *Watch what you have for breakfast. I always go for a bit of cereal and fruit. Don't overdo the fry-ups; better still, ignore them altogether.*
- *There are all manner of pills, potions and wristbands on the market designed to combat seasickness. Perhaps they work, perhaps they don't, but if they give you confidence, then go for it. A lot of seasickness is undoubtedly psychological!*
- *Don't sit next to the engine – the smell and the noise can prove a problem. Equally, if in doubt, move away from any potential grim spots, such as where the rubby-dubby is being prepared.*
- *Keep yourself occupied – talk to the skipper or take binoculars so that you can watch out for seabirds and other sea life.*
- *If you think you're going to be in trouble, concentrate on the horizon for a while – this gives you a point of reference.*
- *Try never to look down when you're tying knots or undoing tangles. This is especially important in a swell.*

everywhere. You'll probably find that the first couple of hours of both the flood and the ebb suit the bass well, and always look out for any signs of feeding fish.

Now to the mullet. These really do swarm in huge numbers up the Cuckmere, and there are some big fish. You can often find them at low water, when the flow is at its lowest and the fish congregate in the deeper pools. However, when the water is rising, expect to see them following the water line, feeding very close in, hungry for food. The problem here, as everywhere, is that the mullet's natural diet is almost impossible to imitate. Therefore, you've got to wean them onto something that you can put on a hook. Bread is very much a favoured bait and the mullet here have seen enough of it to know what it is. However, you would be very wise to ground bait with it liberally and not simply use a piece on the hook. Mix a loaf or two into a bucket with plenty of water so that it's good and sloppy, but don't make it too soft – you need to throw it out ten yards or so. You can also put in some flavourings – especially fish oils – to throw off a good scent.

There's no doubt that float fishing is by far the best method of approach for these fish. Use a twelve- or thirteen-foot freshwater float rod with an Avon-type float capable of carrying enough lead for you to cast to where the fish are. A single SSG will often do. For the hook bait, it's best to experiment. Sometimes the mullet will like a big piece of flake on a number six hook. At other times, they'll want just a shred of bread on a size fourteen. You're best fishing light – a four- or five-pound line is quite enough – and use it straight through to the hook. Don't try to stop the mullet in its first run but be prepared to give it line – you shouldn't find too many snags about.

To find the second venue in this area, the River Ouse, carry on down the A259 into Newhaven. In the centre, turn north on the Kingston road and look for the signpost to Piddinghoe. You'll find the village after about a mile and a half, and there's plenty of parking available. The river at this point is some way from the open sea and you'll find the same range of species as in the Cuckmere, but with one extra attraction – there is always the chance of sea trout between May and September. This is one of our most glamorous fish species and, although they're not plentiful, it's always worth taking a spinning rod. If you see any surface activity, it's a good idea to investigate it with a little silver spoon. Every year, some very good specimens are taken.

Sea fishing isn't always about big open beaches, rocky headlands or charter-boat wreck fishing – some of the most exciting stuff round our shores can be as intimate as the sport offered on the Ouse and Cuckmere.

The Elusive Trigger Fish

If you catch a dramatic looking fish that's as deep as it is long, and rather looks like a dinner plate with fins, then the chances are you've picked up a trigger fish. Once they were very rare, but over the last ten years or so warmer conditions have seen a good increase in their numbers.

- *They tend to stick to the south and south-west coasts.*
- *You'll be surprised how well they fight given their shape. Don't expect a tireless battle but be prepared for short, aggressive runs.*
- *They aren't particularly large fish – be pleased with a two-pounder and be very proud of anything over three.*
- *They are almost exclusively a warm-water fish, so you needn't bother looking for them before August or after October.*
- *Look for them well out of the force of strong currents. They prefer slack water and tend to shelter away from a fast flow.*
- *They have a small mouth, but one that's full of tiny, sharp teeth. Their jaws are very powerful, for crushing the shellfish that form the major part of their diet.*
- *Take care of that sharp dorsal fin when you're handling a trigger fish. To depress it, simply press the second spine of the fin and you'll find that that dagger-like first fin folds neatly down. In fact, you are actually 'triggering' the action!*
- *Trigger fish tend to move in quite large shoals, so if you catch one, there are often more following on behind.*
- *For bait, try mackerel strips, ragworm tipped with squid, or peeler crab.*

ACCOMMODATION – contact the Seaford Tourist Information Centre on 01323 897426 or the Newhaven Tourist Information Centre on 01273 483448.

TACKLE SHOPS – try the Newhaven Angler on 01273 512186.

Brighton

Brighton is the next major centre and boasts a tremendous marina for the angler. It is clean and safe, and offers up wonderful catches. The Marina Village is situated at the eastern end of the seafront and offers plentiful parking. Both arms of the marina are run by Dave Grinham, who operates to the highest possible standard. The toilets are immaculately cared for and the place is safe for children and novices alike. Day tickets are cheap and plenty of thought has been put into the whole operation.

It is the spectacular bass that makes the fishing so special in the area. There have been lots of double-figure fish landed in recent years, including one of seventeen and a half pounds. There are also plenty of mackerel and garfish for youngsters throughout the summer months, and you'll also find mullet, pollack and wrasse. There are plenty of flatfish and, in autumn, big catches of whiting and codling are taken on the night tides.

ACCOMMODATION – phone the Tourist Board in Brighton on 09067 112255 for details of accommodation in the area.

TACKLE SHOPS – Brighton Marina boasts an excellent tackle shop, The Tackle Box on 01273 696477.

WORTHING AND LITTLEHAMPTON

Worthing offers excellent beach and pier fishing and there's some good mixed catches from boats. The River Adur is also worth checking out for flounders and mullet in the summer months.

Finally, we come to the port of Littlehampton, once known as the capital of black bream fishing. Although it passed into the wilderness for a while, the bream are now returning. There is a far-sighted and enlightened policy of catch and release, so the stocks are protected and flourishing.

But there's far more to Littlehampton than bream. It offers very varied fishing indeed – everything from tope and conger through to plaice and ray. One species that is becoming increasingly common is the undulate ray, and some cracking specimens are being located. Another bonus is that Littlehampton enjoys the protection afforded by Selsey Bill to the west. In fact, conditions for the shore and boat angler only really become impossible when the wind goes round to the south east. There is plenty for the shore angler to enjoy in the area, and the upper reaches of the estuary produce great bass and mullet fishing, with plenty of flounder available. Throughout the summer, there is good mackerel and garfish, along with flatfish and bass. Selsey Bill, itself, is a prime mark for smooth-hound during the summer.

ACCOMMODATION – phone the Tourist Information Centre in Worthing on 01903 210022 or Littlehampton on 01903 713480.

TACKLE SHOPS – in Worthing, phone Ken Dunman on 01903 239802 and Prime Angling on 01903 821594. The top tackle shop in Littlehampton is the Tropicana on 01903 715190.

BOAT HIRE – phone M. Pratt on 01798 342370 or S. Hipgrave on 01903 691697. The full list can be obtained from the Harbour Master on 01903 721215.

Sea-fishing Sites in Hampshire & Dorset

'This is a great boat-fishing area, especially around the Solent. I just tend to work the west, often very close to the Needles, but working offshore during the summer. There's a huge variety of fish to be caught and something for everybody, no matter what the season. The cod, of course, are something special – the biggest I've ever had on my boat is forty-two pounds, but twenty- and thirty-pounders aren't at all uncommon. I run a competition every year for the biggest cod to come onto my boat. I put up £200, and it's invariably a big fish that takes the money. It just adds a little bit of spice to everybody's day I guess, and is regarded as a bit of fun. It does show the stamp of the fishing that we have on offer here, however.'

DAVE STEPHENSON, A SKIPPER OFF YARMOUTH

Dave is a man of huge experience in this area and he quite obviously loves what is on offer. The black bream fishing is absolutely superb, especially during the spring and summer months. Dave suggests using a ten-pound line for these game and very attractive fish. After all, what's the point of using tackle so heavy that you don't feel the true excitement of the fight? My very first taste of sea fishing came at Mudeford, years and years back. I was fishing for flatties in Christchurch Bay. They were only up to a pound or so, but provided great sport on the light gear I was using. However, I couldn't come to grips with the vast shoals of grey mullet that I saw. They were simply beyond me, far too cunning, far too finicky. Mind you, forty years on, I'm not sure that I still have any hard and fast recipes for success! Southampton Water offers some very intriguing estuary fishing, and flounders are very common. However, in the summer, mullet, mackerel, bass and all manner of other species abound. The Solent is also a very interesting site for tope. In short, this portion of the English south coast is a tremendous area offering some superb possibilities.

The Solent

For the best opportunities, get yourself afloat in the Solent. There are all manner of marks, and the relative shelter afforded by the mainland and the Isle of Wight means that it is rare for trips to be cancelled. There's sport all the year round and endless species to be targeted. Historically, the Solent offers some very big cod, especially from the late autumn onwards. Expect fish of twenty or even thirty pounds. Get them on big baits – squid is a favourite and so, too, is pirking. There are cod in the summer, and you'll probably find them close to the wrecks. Expect big pollack, too, along with conger and ling.

In summer, the Solent is an absolute treasure trove for those interested in smaller sporting species such as bass and black bream. Fish for these comparatively light and you are in for a really magnificent time. The tope fishing can be tremendous and you will also find several species of ray, as well as smooth-hound. Selsey Bill, at the eastern end of the Solent, is particularly noted for tope and smooth-hound.

The Nab and the Needles are two of the top marks – you'll find Lymington boats fishing the Needles, and the Langstone fleet heading for the Nab. There's some controversy amongst local anglers as to which is the better area – the Needles to the west or the Nab to the east. Both areas are quite fabulous and offer superb possibilities – especially for winter codding, which is perhaps the prime fishing of all.

There isn't a huge amount of interesting ground around the Needles. In fact, the top marks to the south east are comparatively featureless. The bottom is certainly very flat, with only infrequent rough patches to break it up. There are some very shallow gullies where the cod are known to feed, but you will need a skilful skipper to locate these. You don't catch great numbers of cod off the Needles, but there are plenty for everybody and they are of a very good size – certainly more big fish come from the Needles than the Nab.

The Nab, however, does have an enthusiastic following and it's not hard to understand why. The Nab area is environmentally more exciting to fish and there is a real range and variety of sport there. Nevertheless, perhaps because the cod are more grouped, blanks are arguably more common than they are around the Needles. However, both areas offer great sport, which can be accessed with skippers of huge experience.

There are all sorts of bonuses in the summer. I've already mentioned the black bream fishing, but you will also come across some great conger fishing. There are plenty of fish in the fifty-pound mark and a lot of these are free swimming, so you can enjoy the fight and not worry about lugging them away from the wrecks.

Accommodation – for accommodation in the Solent area, phone the Southampton Tourist Information Centre on 02380 221106.

Tackle shops – Paiges Fishing Tackle, Hayling Island on 02392 463500 is a mine of information on the best skippers, best tackle and best methods in the area.

Boat hire – if you want to try fishing the Needles, contact the skipper of *Challenger* on 01425 619358. Ron Bundy on 01425 629776 offers wreck and reef fishing, along with shark and other exotica! Tuition is also available. Dave Stephenson, out of Yarmouth on the Isle of Wight, on 01983 821225, also has a great reputation. The Lymington fleet is extensive, but try Arthur Savage on 02380 897111 for starters.

The Isle of Wight

My limited trips to the Isle of Wight have all proved hugely successful. There's just so much sea fishing around that great experience isn't necessary, especially as there are so many good skippers and tackle shops willing to give advice for the newcomer.

One of my own favourite spots is Ventnor, situated on the south of the island. The western end of the beach there often proves a favourite, with some good bass, skate and conger about.

I don't know what it is about feathering for mackerel, but I'm invariably beaten by everyone around me, no matter how inexperienced they are. This can be an extremely humiliating experience, but you've got to wear it with good grace! What it does show is that mackerel fishing really offers good sport for everyone and I can't think of a better way of getting kids, especially, interested.

If you're not after a great number of fish, my own tip is to sally out with really light gear and perhaps a single feather. If you're using an ultra-light spinning rod, a mackerel of a couple of pounds will give you exhilarating sport. Far better than just winching them in on tackle fit for a tope.

Close by, just to the east, is the tiny village of Bonchurch with its excellent rock marks. Conger and bass feature heavily here.

Moving west from Ventnor, you come to the long, western stretch from Blackgang to Freshwater Bay – an intriguing area for all manner of species. Ray, conger and bass are the target species here throughout the summer and into the autumn. Top marks feature the Brighstone end of Atherfield, somewhere between the holiday camp and Dutchman's Point. Expect conger and bass – the former often going to forty pounds or so. Great sport.

The area around St Catherine's Point, just to the east of Blackgang, offers a whole complex of ledges and gullies generally best looked at when the water is low and plans can be formulated. Always be aware of rising tides, however, and make sure you've got a good exit in mind.

The piers of the island at Yarmouth, Ryde and Sandown all fish extremely well. Sandown is particularly notable for good painted ray, and you will find cod putting in an appearance as autumn draws on. Yarmouth can also produce some surprise species – for example, you may find the occasional good stingray.

Cowes is a long-time favourite for flounder fishermen, all along the River Medina that runs from Newport down to Cowes Harbour. You'll probably find the best sport in the early autumn – October would be my choice. Some local knowledge is well worth seeking out as the shoals do move around according to the season and the state of the tide.

Fish are of a good average size, however, and you'll also see plenty of mullet on the move, along with school bass. It's an area that you can target successfully with freshwater gear. How about float fishing with small worms and lines of around five to six pounds breaking strain? You'll also pick up small silver eels to boot. As for Cowes Harbour, expect to see some staggering mullet. Once again, you can expect flatfish (including sole), along with some decent bass.

My old fishing partner, John Nunn, began his teaching career down in the Isle of Wight and his tales of the splendours of Bembridge inspired me to make the occasional visit. I'm glad I did. The number of species to be caught there is endless – conger, ling, bream, turbot, bass, brill, skate, ray, pollack... and that's not mentioning the countless sizeable mullet that drift around the harbour.

There's shark fishing available, too, during the high summer months, along with tremendous mackerel fishing for the more fainthearted! Top areas include the shore from White Cliff to Bembridge, which combines rock and shingle – perfect for both bass and conger. Near the Crab and Lobster Inn there's a sand gully that can be accessed from nearby rocks.

If you can get out to the Bembridge Ledge early in the year, you can expect good bream, along with the mackerel. And those mullet in Bembridge Harbour are big enough to make your eyes water. Mind you, they're very canny and exceptionally wary of heavy gear.

I'm very aware that I've only scraped the surface of the tremendous fishing that the Isle of Wight has to offer, but I hope I've given a sample of the sport that the visitor can hope to expect. As a holiday venue for the whole family, it is unsurpassed.

Accommodation – the island is very attractive, easily accessed by ferry, and offers the visitor a wide range of accommodation. Contact the Tourist Information Centres at Ventnor, Shanklin, Sandown, Cowes and Ryde for details. All have the same telephone number: 01983 813818.

Fishing for Cod

All along the south coast, big cod continue to come inshore during the autumn and winter. However, despite the gloomy forecasts of the fishery scientists, good cod are there to be caught throughout the summer, especially if you take a charter boat out to the more distant offshore wrecks. These will be situated at least twenty miles out, with most of the really good marks being found at thirty-plus miles. Cod can generally be caught from the end of April right through to August, but it's best to contact an experienced skipper who is aware of their comings and goings. Cod are very mobile fish indeed, and you've got to keep a tag on their movements. The following tips may help:

- *A good fish finder is absolutely essential for pinpointing the shoals. Don't expect them to be present at the same point day after day. Look for clumps of fish showing close to the bottom.*
- *Pirks are generally considered the most 'killing' method. However, in recent years, modern, plastic lures have become more and more popular. The main reason for this is that they can be fished with leadheads to get them down deep and direct to the bottom. Their fluid, fluttering movement can also prove absolutely irresistible.*
- *The Twin Tail is a particular 'killer' – go for it in electric shades of red and orange.*
- *Be prepared to change both the size of the Twin Tail and the amount of lead needed according to the state of the tide. You want to get the Twin Tail down deep as quickly as possible, but you don't want such a heavy lead that the action is masked.*
- *Work the Twin Tail with a jigging-type action once it hits the bottom.*
- *Over very rough ground, or in heavy tides, it pays to wind the lure rather than jig it – you lose fewer rigs and have better control.*
- *Smaller Twin Tails often work well for bass and other bonus species. For bass, let the lure flutter around in the tide. Use as light a leadhead as you can get away with.*
- *Twin Tails aren't the only plastic lures available. The originals were Redgills and they can still prove a real winner if fished properly. Also, try different coloured shads and jellyworms.*
- *Contact Fishtek on 01647 441020 for all the latest in plastic lures. The Harris Angling Company also offers a huge selection; you can contact them on 01692 581208 for all the latest advice on some tremendous products.*

TACKLE SHOPS – with such great fishing, there are tackle shops aplenty: Stuart's Bait and Tackle in Shanklin on 01983 868100 and in East Cowes on 01983 280985, Scotties in Newport on 01983 522115 and in Sandown on 01983 404555, The Screaming Reel in Ryde on 01983 568745, and the Tacklebox at Totland Bay on 01983 752260.

BOAT HIRE – contact Chris Solomon in Bembridge on 01892 874100, or Dave Stephenson, skipper of the *Becky M*, in Yarmouth on 01983 821225.

LYMINGTON AND BEAULIEU

Lymington offers some exotic fishing for tope, stingray and big bass. However, I personally have had most of my fun at Beaulieu, a little way up the estuary. This is a mark with a great deal of history about it, situated as it is so close to the great house of Beaulieu. It's a tremendous area for a family holiday – Beaulieu itself offers everything children need for a couple of days, and there are always the ponies of the New Forest.

There are plenty of flatfish about, but what particularly attracts me to the area is the tremendous mullet fishing. You can expect some bass as well, but the mullet really flock here. And what mullet they are – shoals and shoals of really good fish.

As always with this enigmatic species, catching them can be another matter altogether. I've done particularly well on one or two occasions with maggots and then failed with them completely just a day or two later. Tiny worms – either portions of rag or even small redworms – have also done well from time to time. I've caught the odd fish on tiny silver spinners with the hooks tipped with pieces of worm, too. What I've always tried to do is get the mullet going on mashed bread. This has happened for me once or twice around the countryside, but never, so far, at Bucklers Hard.

It's fascinating fishing when you can achieve a breakthrough – just watching the shoals of three- to five-pound fish ploughing into the bread, slurping it from the surface before the gulls can get it. Float fish a piece of flake some eighteen inches down along with the current through the area. Bites are rapid, and, it's got to be said, frequently difficult to hit.

All in all, this is a terrific place for some summer fishing and plenty of fun for all the family.

ACCOMMODATION – accommodation is abundant. Phone the Southampton Tourist Information Centre on 02380 221106.

TACKLE SHOPS – contact Forest Sports, Milford on Sea, Lymington, on 01590 643366.

TICKETS – tickets for Beaulieu can be obtained from the Harbour Master, Bucklers Hard, on 01590 616200 or from the Estate Office, Beaulieu, on 01590 612345.

BOAT HIRE – contact Ted Entwistle in Beaulieu on 02380 845272.

Poole

Poole offers a huge amount for the holidaying angler. It's a top tourist destination with plenty of activities to keep the non-fishing members of the family interested. There's good beach and quay fishing in the huge natural harbour. However, the place has really taken off when it comes to charter fishing. You don't have to go too far out to find some terrific opportunities and the inshore marks fish very well indeed – especially with a light line approach.

The reefs off Poole are home to a wide variety of species and there are plenty of black bream and pollack during the summer. The sandbanks and ridges are also excellent for members of the ray family and you can have good sport with small-eyed, blonde and undulate if the conditions are kind. Old Harry Rocks is a well-known mark, and if your skipper knows his stuff, he'll be able to point you in the right direction for some very good bass fishing. It's also a top area for tope.

Holes Bay Road in Poole is one of the top shore marks, and is easily accessible for the visiting angler. This is a real hotspot for flounder, from October right through to the later part of the winter. You'll also pick up mullet and bass during the summer. The area is muddy at low tide, but it fishes particularly well on the flood. If possible, try and get there in the evening. The area is skirted by a dual carriageway that offers no parking, so you will have to park in the centre and walk. It will take you fifteen to twenty minutes, but it's well worth the effort.

Accommodation – contact the Tourist Information Centre in Poole on 01202 253253.

Tackle shops – for good local advice, contact Poole Sea Angling Centre on 01202 676597, A C Angling on 01202 734451, Castaways on 01202 739202 or Dick's on 01202 679622.

Boat hire – contact skipper Mike Taylor on 01202 687200 to arrange a trip on his boat, the *Just Mary*. Poole Sea Angling Centre on 01202 676597 organises a great deal of charter fishing. Or, try Sea Fishing Limited on 01202 679666 for bass trips and deep-sea expeditions.

Weymouth

Weymouth is a quaint coastal town and very much a top holiday area in the south of England. So, once again, this is a perfect venue for the sea angler setting out with the family. But, above all, Weymouth is really becoming well-known for its exceptional charter fleet. It offers Channel Island trips and wrecking, reef and bank fishing for groups or individuals. The Weymouth Conger Festival is also something that has

THE GOOD SKIPPER

What makes a good charter-boat skipper? If you're new to an area or on holiday, what are the things to look out for once you're afloat? After all, a skipper can absolutely make or break your day.

- *Generally, a really good skipper will have been, or is, an angler himself. Only then can he really understand what an angler actually wants.*
- *The good skipper makes you welcome. He's not surly or secretive but open and fun. You know instinctively that it will be good to spend the day with him. After all, you are his guests and you deserve the best.*
- *A good skipper will go that extra mile and really put himself out in every way just to make sure that his guests have a really splendid day.*
- *A good boat will often have a really good crewman – the sort of person who's always there to sort out tangles with the net or offer a cup of tea.*
- *A good skipper won't simply rest on his laurels if a fish or two is caught. If sport dries up, he'll up-anchor three or even four times a day in a constant effort to find the fish that his clients want.*
- *The modern skipper will be good with electronics, able to read his screens and know exactly where to put the boat.*
- *But there is more than simple electronic gadgets to a good skipper's armoury. He'll have that real, solid bank of experience so that he knows exactly where to put a boat to fish a wreck. A GPS screen can only show you so much.*
- *Conservation will be a vital issue to the good, modern skipper. He won't dream of killing any fish unnecessarily and he certainly wouldn't gaff congers, for example. Rather, he would use a T-bar to make unhooking easy. Around Hayling, for example, skippers will never kill a smooth-hound – something common only a few years back. The best skippers have very large landing nets, virtually always home-made, that are capable of taking a forty-pound tope or a fifty-pound conger. That way, they can be taken from the sea safely, weighed, unhooked and put back without any damage being done to their internal organs.*
- *A good skipper will have a sound reputation around the harbour or in the tackle shops.*
- *The good skipper will be the one who has survived and has a long history. It's good to check, if you can, just how long he's been in the job.*
- *You can't do better than buy* Boat Fishing *monthly. This is a tremendous magazine and really pinpoints some of the best skippers around our shores. An excellent starting point.*

become a major talking point among anglers. The first Weymouth Open Conger Competition took place in 1994 and it's now an important date in the diary of any angler who seeks big eels.

The whole concept of the festival is encouraging. First of all, it's run over three days, so luck plays very little part indeed. Competitors also fish with the skipper of their choice – this is a great idea, for it means the skipper becomes an integral part of what's going on. Teamwork becomes more and more important, and catches certainly benefit.

What I like the most about the competition, though, is the huge amount of thought that goes into conserving the eels. For example, the skippers keep in constant contact with each other over the radio so that only the very biggest eels, the potential winners, have to go through the ordeal of being weighed. For the rest, the skippers make their own assessment and keep score. This means that the vast majority of eels can be brought to the boat and unhooked with very little risk of harm. For example, the 2001 competition saw 802 conger caught with 790 being returned alive – that's a huge percentage, one that would have been inconceivable just a few years ago.

As I've said, it's the skippers that really run the competition. It's up to them to find the bait – generally mackerel. Then they've got to make the right choice over the target wreck. This isn't always easy, especially with the amount of commercial fishing in the area. The state of the tide has got to be taken into account, as you need to anchor up to fish successfully for eels. Any drifting and you're in trouble. The logistics take some working out – for example, the tides, the wrecks, steaming time, fishing time – so the competition is really organised like a military campaign. In short, it's a good job that the skippers have a very good grasp of what this type of fishing is all about. There are many good people to contact (see overleaf).

If you're serious about conger fishing then it's a good idea to consider joining the British Conger Club (BCC). They have a lively AGM, an annual conger festival, a yearbook and three newsletters a year. Best of all, you will be a part of a group of like-minded individuals and be able to swap information on tackle, baits, methods and the best places to find your favourite fish.

To get into the club, you have to catch either a conger of twenty-five pounds plus from the shore, over thirty pounds from a reef or over forty pounds if you're wreck fishing. You don't have to kill the fish, you just need the signatures of two independent witnesses. There are over 1,500 members of the club. The BCC is a very right-minded organisation and is passionately committed to the conservation of these fascinating fish. They do a lot of tagging, which gives valuable insights into the movements of conger.

ACCOMMODATION – phone the Tourist Information Centre on 01305 785747.

TACKLE SHOPS – contact the Anglers Tackle Store on 01305 782624, Weymouth Angling Centre on 01305 777771 or Reels and Deals on 01305 787848.

BOAT HIRE – the conger competition was first devised by Pat Carlin and Chris Caines, and their boats *Channel Chieftain* and *Tiger Lily* are well worth investigating; contact them on 01305 787155 and 01305 821177 respectively. Another top name is Paul Whittall; his boat, *Off Shore Rebel IV*, saw the capture of the winning conger for 2001 – a magnificent ninety-pound specimen; contact Paul on 01305 783739. There are fourteen skippers in all making up the charter fleet, so go along and really get into those big eels.

CHESIL BEACH

Moving further westwards, we come to the rightly famous Chesil Beach that leads out to the isle of Portland. Chesil runs for seventeen miles from West Bay, near Bridport, right out to Portland, and the pebbles steadily increase in size as you move from west to east. It is incredibly scenic and offers a huge range of opportunities. For holidaymakers, a base at Abbotsbury can hardly be bettered. It is central for Chesil Beach and offers some great shore fishing. The village and environs are incredibly picturesque, with perfect Dorset thatched cottages. You'll find a large car-park on the road signed 'To the beach' and a wooden walkway will take you right up to the top of the shingle. There's a café and toilets to cater for your every need. To get here, take the road out of Weymouth and follow the signs for Portland. It generally pays to walk some distance from the crowds. Keep on the move for fifteen to twenty minutes and you'll usually be pretty much on your own. The area is fairly featureless, but the water is deep close in and the abundance of species makes for exciting fishing.

Where do you begin... trigger fish, pout, mackerel, dogfish, whiting, bull huss, cod and dab, smooth-hound, plaice, garfish, mullet, gurnard and the odd conger eel – they're all there.

Many of the locals like float fishing here, especially for garfish, bass and mackerel – the latter can be very, very prolific. You'll pick up plenty of high-quality plaice and dab on the bottom, along with trigger fish, which are a brilliant species. If you haven't tangled with them yet, it's well worth making the effort (see page 42). They seem to go for crab or ragworm, with squid also proving popular.

Calm sunny weather is generally favoured in the summer, especially for the mackerel. Autumn is a good time. After the school holidays, the whole area quietens down and whiting begin to appear in numbers. If you walk eastwards towards Portland from the beach, you will come to the Dragon's Teeth – generally considered one of the top marks for cod. These are, in fact, a series of concrete slabs created as tank traps during the war.

At any time of the year be careful of strong south-westerlies, as the undertow makes the shingle very unstable indeed.

Let's now move to the extreme western end of Chesil Beach, to the picturesque town of West Bay with its idyllic, little Dorset harbour. This, again, is a perfect holiday area, but do be aware that it can get very busy during the summer as there are several caravan parks and campsites around. Shore fishing abounds – the promenade and harbour wall are generally favoured, from the summer right through to October. Mackerel, garfish, scad and wrasse are all plentiful. You'll also pick up dogfish and bass in good conditions. Mullet fishing around the harbour can be brilliant, with both thin-and thick-lipped mullet around. Four-pounders are quite common and you will see fish of six pounds or, occasionally, above. This is one place where you really can get them going on bread.

The East Beach is also a top shore mark and is found on the Portland side of the harbour. It's really a steep shingle bank with lots of rubble on the bottom. There's an offshore reef, which can just be reached by long casting. There are some very big plaice around – certainly two-pounders – and after dark you stand a chance of catching bass up to that magical ten-pound mark. Lug and rag both work well, especially tipped with a piece of sand eel or mackerel. Midway along the beach, you will come to Port Coombe, which is the local name for the very obvious cliff. You'll pick up all the species already mentioned. In the winter, the area also produces some half-decent cod fishing. The best results come at the top of the tide, especially around the half-light, either morning or evening.

West Bay also offers some really good boat-fishing opportunities. There are half a dozen or so charter boats working out of the town during the summer months, of which a couple fish the wrecks for cod, ling, pollack and conger. You'll also meet up with some really good bass fishing. There's even a limited amount of shark fishing on request. Reef fishing is the other option, particularly for the excellent bream fishing from midsummer onwards. You will find conger and pollack, along with bull huss, wrasse, dogfish and ray.

Overall, the whole area of Chesil Beach is a magnet for sea anglers, whatever their favourite species. It's a great place for the family holiday, but be aware that it's always a busy area during the summer. Providing you don't mind this too much, get yourself there as quickly as possible.

Accommodation – there's a wide range of accommodation – phone the Bridport Tourist Information Centre on 01308 424901.

Tackle shops – the West Bay Angling Centre on 01308 421800 and the Tackle Shop on 01308 423475 offer information, bait, tackle and access to the charter boats.

Boat hire – contact Geoff Clarke 01308 425494 or Chris Reeks on 01460 242678.

Float Fishing

Float fishing has long been popular along the rocky coastline of the West Country and around the Channel Islands. It's an attractive form of fishing and provides lots of advantages over traditional legering methods. To get the most out of float fishing, follow these tips:

- *You can only use floats under certain conditions and at certain times of the year. There would be little point, for example, trying to cast out a float eighty yards on a winter's night into a raging surf!*
- *Top species to pursue with a float include garfish, mackerel, wrasse, mullet, flounder, bass and sometimes pollack. Obviously, floats are of little use for big, deep-living species such as conger.*
- *A basic float technique is to use a small pike float sliding up and down the main line with the depth set by a stop-knot. Make sure you put on a drilled bullet big enough to cock the float. Use it with a light carp rod and eight- to ten-pound line so that you can cast the rig a decent way.*
- *Set the float to around about four feet to begin with. You can readjust it during the course of the day.*
- *Bait up with fish strips, prawn, crab or ragworm.*
- *It will help if you can ground bait around the float. Or attach a swim-feeder onto the line under the float and fill it with oil, pieces of fish or anything that has a good odour. An oil-soaked rag is also a good idea. It's a good method for fairly calm conditions from jetties or beaches. It's also excellent employed from a boat.*
- *Simply let the float drift around, and strike as soon as it goes under.*
- *You can also spin using a float – simply put a float on the line above your spinner. This is particularly useful when you're targeting fish, such as mullet, that swim mid-water or just under the surface.*
- *Light floats are particularly excellent for estuaries.*
- *Use floats such as traditional Avons and Wagglers with six-pound line.*
- *Pay some attention to your shotting patterns. Put most of your shot around midway between float and hook with another shot near the hook if you find you're tangling during the cast.*
- *Visibility can be a problem. Red and orange are favourite colours, but you'll also find black stands out very well under many conditions.*
- *Perhaps you fancy night fishing with a float. Go to your tackle shop and ask for a Drennan-type float with a starlight isotope to put into the insert at the top. Depending on the power of the isotope, you can see a float anything up to twenty-five yards away under most conditions.*

ST HELIER, JERSEY

The Channel Islands, which can easily be reached by ferry from Poole, offer some superb sea fishing, really sport-defying superlatives. For those unsure where to target, St Helier, the capital of Jersey, is a must. For a holiday, it is ideal – the family have plenty to entertain them, while the angler can creep away and enjoy him- or herself totally. You can go afloat or you can fish from the harbour walls or the adjacent beaches. Don't forget the duty-free shopping and the lovely weather either. Who can resist the call of the islands when you throw in record ballan wrasse and rays caught from the shore?

The beach fishing is best done either very early or late on, for obvious reasons, but the rewards can be tremendous. The best fishing, right in front of what is called the Gunsight Café, can be mind-blowing. The harbour at St Helier provides a good amount of wall space, and if you're into mullet I doubt whether you will find better fishing anywhere in the world. Mackerel, garfish and bass are also there to be caught. You'll also find wrasse where rocks make up the bottom. Try a sliding float or small spinners. Elizabeth Castle, a sixteenth-century fortress, also provides tremendous sport, with wrasse, pollack, mackerel and garfish, and you'll find some very big eel close in, hiding almost in the foundations. You can expect fish up to fifty pounds!

Most of the locals have their own boats, so there is only a handful of charter boats operating, all based at St Helier. There's wreck, reef and bank fishing and some superb tope on offer. The area is littered with wrecks that produce fantastic cod and pollack. The reefs are well-known for their conger, and black bream are something of a speciality here. The banks offer ray, turbot, bass and brill.

Always take care with the tides at Jersey – they are amongst the biggest in the entire world. This is very important if you should happen to be out in a small boat or fishing from rocks. Also, beware of the sun – you might feel you are in England but, believe me, the rays are much more penetrative.

ACCOMMODATION – tourism is what Jersey is all about; contact Jersey Tourism on 01534 500777.

TACKLE SHOPS – contact PJN Fishing Tackle on 01534 874875, JFS Sport on 01534 58195 and I S Marine on 01534 877755.

BOAT HIRE – for charter boats, contact Tony Hurt on 01534 863507 or David Nuth on 01534 858046.

Sea-fishing Sites in South-West England

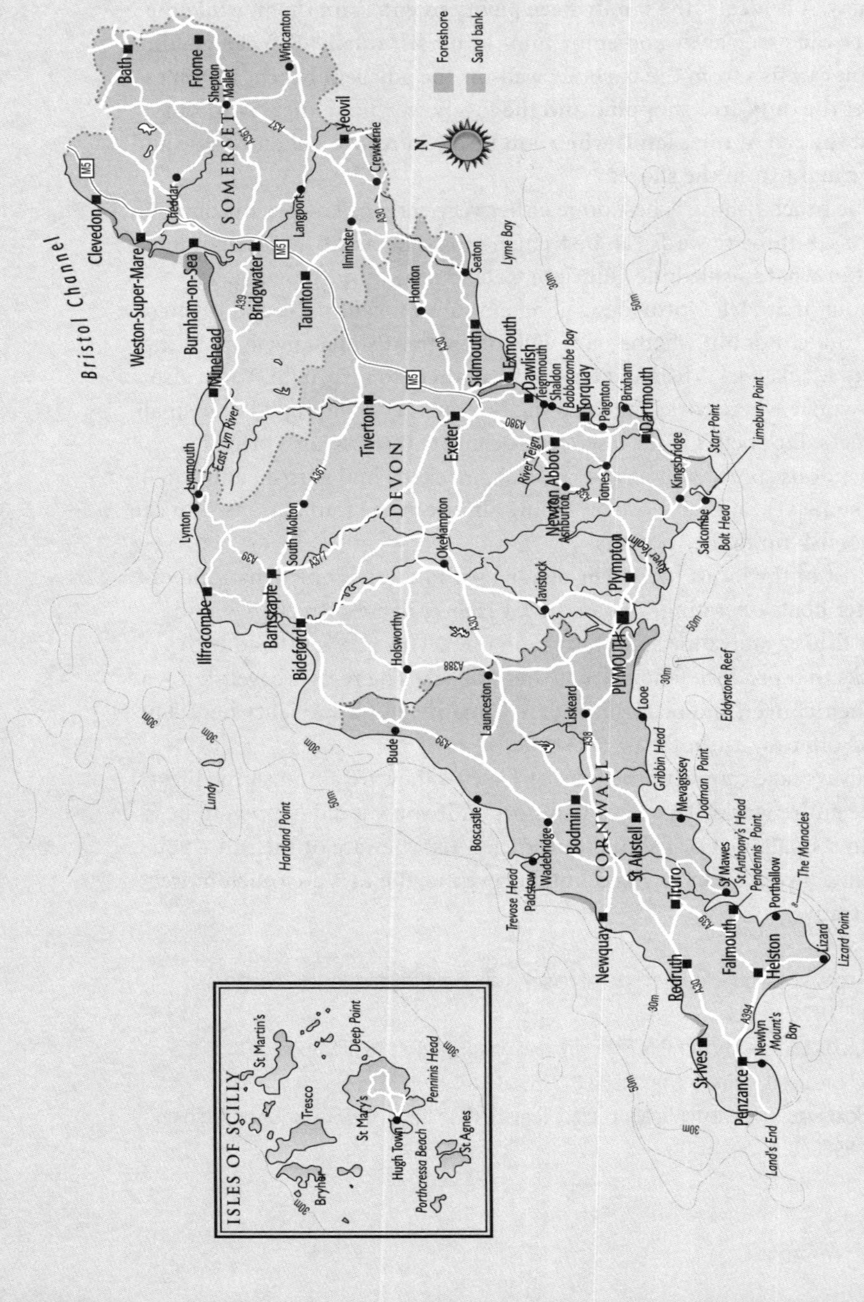

'The sea fishing down here in Devon and Cornwall is, without any shadow of doubt, the best in the country as far as I'm concerned. We've got the best boat fishing by far, and we've got the best shoreline. We've got the best fly rodding; we've got every sea fish that swims, from cod to porbeagle; and there's masses of sheltered water of every description. We've also got Plymouth, a really bustling port with some of the best-developed deep-sea wreck and reef fishing in the country. Take Plymouth Sound, for example – it's not unusual to go out there in a small boat and get amongst twelve different species in a day. It's just incredible. If you ask me, it's an area that's been generally under-publicised for years. Really, if the rest of the world knew what we've got here, we'd be inundated. Add to that some really beautiful coastline, stunning cliffs, great pubs, fantastic accommodation, and you've got a bit of Paradise.'

ROBIN ARMSTRONG, ARTIST, WRITER, FISHERMAN

Robin really is quite correct. There's arguably no other section in this book that offers the quality, quantity and variety that's to be found in the south west. One interesting fact is that a large number of normally freshwater-only anglers turn to the sea when they come down to this area. There are just so many possibilities that every angler wants to try some intimate, hands-on sea fishing – casting heavy weights to the horizon is not the only key to success.

You also have to think about the glorious countryside and coastline when it comes to assessing the fishing in this part of the world. Think of the south Devon coast – the bays, pretty little beaches and snug villages with cosy olde-worlde pubs. Add to that the generally clement weather, and you can see why it's such a popular holiday destination. Stick in your fishing tackle – slightly up-graded freshwater gear is often all you'll need – and join in the fun.

TEIGNMOUTH

The River Teign enters Babbacombe Bay just below Newton Abbot, where it becomes wide and shallow and perfect for summer fishing. It's a haven for sand eels and that means one thing – bass. However, the real draw of Teignmouth is the flounder fishing, which is absolutely legendary. It's traditional winter fishing, but this shouldn't mean the kiss of death for the summer tourist. During the warmer months, mullet, garfish, bass and mackerel are all available. Do remember, though, the rules regarding bass fishing around here – it's designated a nursery area, so boat fishing is not allowed in many areas.

Try Fish Quay at Teignmouth for mullet, though you will need a drop net because of the long haul up from the water. You will find fish around four or five pounds. Mashed mackerel is a favourite ground bait and try a shard of flesh on a small hook under a float. Freshwater hooks tend to be slimmer than sea hooks but still with the requisite power. A size six to twelve is about right. If the fish are very scary, you can go even smaller.

The top end of the estuary is always worth a look. If you press a long way past the road bridge, you will come to the site of a former power station. This is called Newton Quay and it's a favourite place for mullet and flounder in the summer time. Mackerel are also great roamers and will often push a good way upstream – cast small spinners well out into the channel.

Summer flounders are well worth considering. Although they might not be there in the same numbers or size as fish you'll pick up in the winter, you could be in for a real treat towards the end of the summer. You'll pick them up from the well-known winter marks such as Red Rock, Flow Point, Coombe Cellars and Shaldon beach.

ACCOMMODATION – phone Teignmouth Tourist Information Centre on 01626 215666.
TACKLE SHOPS – get your bait and information from McGeary Newsagents, Northumberland Place, Teignmouth on 01626 7723380.

BRIXHAM BREAKWATER

The fishing continues abundantly as we travel south along Babbacombe Bay through Torquay, Paignton and Brixham. Brixham Breakwater, in particular, is a great summer spot, especially for the tourist. It protects the old fishing port of Brixham from easterly gales and runs about half a mile out into Tor Bay. In the summer, you'll find float fishing works really well for mackerel and garfish. Also, expect a few pollack. It pays to walk at least midway up the breakwater and fish on the outside. The best spot is right at the end at the lighthouse, but watch out for boat traffic. Legering

can turn up wrasse and flatfish and, on the inside, in the calm water, you'll find some good mullet, fish up to four or five pounds in weight. If you're up for an early or late session, you can fish for bass or even hope for the odd conger or two. Sand eel is one of the top bass baits here.

One of the nice things about the breakwater is that tides are no real problem. Even the winds are unlikely to trouble you, especially in the summer. However, a very strong easterly will give you problems if you're trying to fish light gear, a float for example, and don't think of going out in an easterly gale. Probably the best time, the locals say, is from two hours before to two hours after high water.

So, this is a perfect place to bring your light, freshwater gear to enjoy some really good fishing with wrasse, mullet, bass and mackerel. Oh, and I'd better warn you – you might see some divers, so beware.

ACCOMMODATION – contact the Tourist Centre in Brixham on 0906 680 1268 (this is a premium rate number).

TACKLE SHOPS – there are two angling shops – the Quay Stores on 01803 853390 and the Angling Centre on 01803 858199. Both shops sell bait and are open year round, including Sundays.

DARTMOUTH

Dartmouth is an area that I have known and enjoyed since childhood. All the usual species are to be found around the river – tremendous mullet and bass, but also some serious conger, along with thornback ray.

However, it is perhaps the boat fishing that people most enthuse about when they talk about Dartmouth. Plaice are to be found in good numbers and size early in the year, with larger ones appearing as the months go past. Try chartering a boat to take you out to the famous Skerries Bank. A knowledgeable skipper is a must to get the best out of the Skerries. It's wrong to think of the flatties being spread around like currants in a cake – they have set lies known only to those who fish regularly.

ACCOMMODATION – Dartmouth Tourist Information Centre on 0906 680 1268 (this is a premium rate number) will advise on accommodation.

TACKLE SHOPS – for further information on fishing in the area, contact Sport 'n' Fish at 16 Fairfax Place, Dartmouth or phone them on 01803 833509.

BOAT HIRE – Steve Parker is one of the leading skippers hereabouts and he takes parties out to the famous Skerries Bank. Steve is a real expert at locating plaice, not least because he was an angler before becoming a skipper, so he has his priorities well worked out. He can be contacted on 01803 329414.

Salcombe

The south west just doesn't come prettier than this. Salcombe is an idyllic, picturesque, bustling little town with a world-famous estuary. In fact, the outer and inner estuaries are possibly the most important small boat angling areas in Britain.

Almost every species is available to be caught in this area. However, once again, note that there is a nursery area for bass: the species may not be targeted upstream from a line between Splat Point and Limebury Point between April 30th and January 1st.

The estuary is particularly noted for turbot and plaice. Between Bolt Head and Mewstone Rock, you will find a very rocky, weedy area that is heavily frequented by wrasse. Five-pounders are common and fish have been landed to seven pounds plus. Don't go too light – this is quick water and it flows over snaggy ground.

You will also find wrasse around the Wharf Rock reef. This is marked by a green buoy and nearby are two patches of rough ground marked by striped navigation pylons.

Plaice and dab abound in the River Salcombe, which is generally held as part of the inner estuary. Once the warm weather arrives, you will find thornback ray and huge numbers of mullet. There's wide availability for hiring your own small boat to whip around the estuary. Alternatively, you may like to join up with one of the charter organisations for some excellent wreck fishing.

Moving further west, we come to the estuary of the River Yealm. This is a truly stunning area, often overlooked by anglers but offering some superb fishing. The estuary is home to good flounder, bass and mullet and you can fish either off the rocks or from beaches.

You'll find that flounder are around throughout the year, but the recognised season runs from early autumn through to the middle of winter. There are also some wrasse, especially around the Old Cellars beach, and they, like the bass and the mullet, are at their most prolific during the summer months.

Access is not difficult and a lot of useful information will be gleaned from the friendly local tackle shops.

Accommodation – for details of accommodation in the area, contact the Tourist Information Centre in Salcombe on 01722 334956.

Tackle shops – for all your tackle and bait needs contact Whitestrand Boat Hire on 01548 843818 or Tucker's Boat Hire, Victoria Quay on 01548 842840.

Boat hire – contact Whitestrand Boat Hire or Tucker's Boat Hire on the above telephone numbers.

Eddystone Reef

You'll find Eddystone Reef some fourteen miles or so out of Plymouth. This location has been justly famous for its sea fishing for a century or more and is an all-round brilliant venue. Once upon a time, the Eddystone Lighthouse was manned and the lighthouse keepers who worked there used to tell anglers where the fishing would be at its best. Unfortunately, that's not the case today and you've got to do all the hard work yourself! Experience and skill are necessary to locate the shoals of fish, which – like the lighthouse keepers – are nowadays considerably fewer in number!

So what does this famous mark have to offer? Well, the pollack are legendary, with double-figure fish to be expected at the right time of year – certainly between late spring and the autumn. And if it's not pollack that you're after, the reef still produces some extraordinary bass. Of course, you can winch both species in on any gear you like, but I personally would recommend using sporting gear. Choose either twelve- or sixteen-pound class tackle to get the very best out of pollack. These fish really fight like crazy if you give them half a chance – they are big, beautiful fish and it doesn't do to rush the experience. You'll probably need traces of between fifteen and twenty pounds – say eight feet long in slack water or fifteen feet in full flow. Leads will be around six to eight ounces, but with a weak link – the reef is full of tackle-grabbing snags.

One or two tips – sand eel live bait really do the trick for both bass and pollack. Try catching them on small shrimp-type feathers. Work them on a slow retrieve but don't be in a hurry to strike when you get a take. Continue winding and with any luck the fish will hook itself.

Spring tides are the very best for both pollack and bass at Eddystone.

Accommodation – the Mount Batten Centre has become the mecca for sea anglers in this part of the world. It offers superb, economically-priced bed and breakfast with a choice of rooms with shared facilities and en suite rooms. There's a brilliant drying room for when you come in all wet and smelly from the sea, freezers for bait and a secure lock-away for all your tackle. The car-park is free and the centre's pontoon is right by the front door so you can tumble onto your charter boat still half asleep. There's a bar, restaurant and good shore fishing all around. Highly recommended for any discerning sea fisherman! For information, phone 01752 404567.

Tackle shops – the following are all to be found in Plymouth: Clive's Tackle and Bait on 01752 228940, DK Sports on 01752 662361, Manadon Angling Supplies on 01752 795060, Osborne and Cragg on 01752 223141, The Fishermen's Friend on 01752 606300, The Tackle and Bait Shop on 01752 361294.

Boat hire – a highly recommended skipper in the area is Rob Street, boss of the *Vagabond*. Contact him on 01752 768892 or on his mobile 07770 225160.

Fishing for Blue Shark

What of the blue shark? The body is streamlined, long and very graceful. The back is blue, merging almost to black, the flanks are paler and the stomach is white. The tail is a main feature, with the upper lobe much longer than the lower one. The fish has two dorsal fins and long, curved pectorals. With this fin arrangement, the blue shark has huge mobility. The teeth are small but, beware, they are strong and ferociously sharp. Given the power of the jaws, the mouth is a formidable killing machine. The skin is rough to the touch and made up of innumerable tiny scales. Shark can look like killers – the 'Jaws of the Deep' – but, like most creatures, the truth belies the fiction. Shark, like all fish, can easily be harmed. Nowadays, nearly all shark are returned, so the days of hauling them over the side of the boat and damaging their internal organs are long gone. To be returned, a shark has to be lifted clear of the water and unhooked without any damage or pressure inflicted on its delicate internal structure.

There are not the numbers of blues left that there once were. Go back to the 1950s and 1960s and you'll be sickened by the old photographs of quayside corpses. The growth rate of blues is slow – around ten pounds a year – so conservation is absolutely essential. Also, remember that the big female you catch is very probably carrying young that will be born in the late spring and early summer. Some females produce twenty or more young. Now that conservation is the watchword, stocks are likely to build up and, who knows, before long multiple catches may occur again.

Tagging is a rewarding conclusion to your fishing. Perhaps that blue has been tagged before and you know someone else has had the pleasure and satisfaction of catching it. By releasing your own blue, this trend will continue. It's also fascinating to see how far round the globe our Cornish blues can wander. It's not unusual for them to turn up in the West Indies!

The blue is a large, hard-fighting species, but don't go over the top with heavy gear or you won't really appreciate the fight. Use sporting tackle for these fish, as you would everything else in the sea. A seven-foot rod in the thirty- to eighty-pound class is about right. You will need a multiplier that can cope with some 400 yards of fifty-pound mono or braid. Pack a butt pad to give you extra leverage and to avoid severe bruising in the abdominal area. It's vital that once a blue is hooked all other anglers reel in and watch the fun. If they don't, the chance of line tangles and a lost fish is immense. Keep mobile around the boat. You'll often have to follow a fish from one side to the other as the blue nears the boat and shows its agility. Be careful of going near the bow when the boat has a cabin, especially if there's a brisk wind and a big swell. Many skippers won't allow this anyway.

The hook will be large – 10/0s are favoured. The trace will be wire, 200-pound test is not too much, and make sure that it is long. Five or even six yards is not excessive, as the shark will begin to twist as it comes close to the boat. Remember those sandpaper-like scales I talked about earlier – they cut through nylon like a knife.

As for bait, mackerel or herring – providing they are fresh – are hard to beat. Pilchard can also take fish, as can quite sizeable pollack. The blue shark will pick up the bait and run with it, rather like a pike in freshwater. Don't strike at this moment, but once the second run begins, click the multiplier into gear and strike hard and firm. Some skippers recommend multiple strikes to set the hook in the hard mouth.

It's usual to fish something between four and six baits from a shark boat and these are set at different depths, usually supported by balloon floats. These are easily seen in even rough weather and burst when pulled under so the taking shark feels no resistance. The baits are set anything from ten yards or more beneath the surface.

The skill of the skipper is absolutely essential if really good fishing is to be located. The day's fishing depends on how successful the drift is once the ground has been reached and the engine cut off. It's possible to fish ten or more miles during the day, following the tide. It's up to the skipper to know exactly the best areas for fish and, also, to start up a successful rubby-dubby trail. This is the crunch time for the fisherman. What has often seemed a perfect day can turn into a nightmare if you're at all unsure about your sea legs. The best rubby-dubbies really do smell absolutely foul. They're often never really changed throughout the season – the skippers simply top them up with all manner of disgusting fish insides, blood, bran, pilchards and the devil knows what.

The rubby-dubby trail is absolutely essential to draw the hunting shark in towards the bait. You'll see it slicking out over the surface of the sea, almost to the horizon. It's vital that the boat follows this trail and the baits work within it – all down to the skill of the skipper. Shark hunt very much by smell, moving up-water towards the rubby-dubby trail and the baits. Generally, it takes anything up to an hour before the first shark homes in and the action begins. It's exciting stuff when that balloon begins to race across the surface.

Looe and Mevagissey

Travelling westwards along the south coast of Cornwall, we reach the towns of Looe and Mevagissey, centres famous back in my youth for the first real shark fishing available for the tourist. It was a revelation – the idea that a lad like me could travel down from the north, stay in an idyllic Cornish town and then get out to sea and catch shark, fish bigger than I'd ever clapped eyes on before, or even dreamed possible! Sadly, back in the 1960s, conservation was not an issue, and tremendous harm was done to the stocks. Now, thankfully, a lot more consideration is shown.

Looe's reputation, in particular, is built upon the broad backs of the fabulous blue shark that have inhabited the lower part of the English Channel for so long (see pages 64–5). We have the Atlantic Gulf Stream to thank for their presence here in such great numbers. The first blues begin to arrive early in May, but they're a long way offshore and it's not really until June that the fishing starts in earnest. At this time, you'll find them just twenty or so miles off the Cornish coastline and they're beginning to feed.

Of course, this area has a lot more to offer than just shark, but Looe remains the headquarters of the Shark Angling Club of Great Britain (for details, see below), which was founded way back in 1953. Conservation is now their watchword. Any fish now caught are not hauled onto the boat to be weighed but are instead judged by their length and their girth. Once upon a time, a prospective member of the club had to bring a body back to shore for his or her membership to be accepted. Thankfully, this is no longer the case, and the skipper's decision that the fish weighs a minimum of seventy-five pounds is enough to gain membership.

The shark club has a whole list of recommended skippers, men who really know how to contact the shark and, importantly, how to look after them once they've been hooked.

Accommodation – for details of accommodation in the area, contact the Tourist Information Centre in Looe on 01503 262072.

Tackle shops – contact Fishing Shark, Fish Market Quay on 0800 0743554, or the following at The Quay, West Looe: Jack Bray on 01503 262504, Looe Angling Club on 01503 263337 and The Tackle Shop on 01503 262189. In Mevagissey, try Mevagissey Shark Angling, West Wharf on 01726 843430 and Tackle Box, 4 Market Street on 01726 843513.

Boat hire – you can contact the office of the Shark Angling Club of Great Britain on Looe East Quay anytime between 10:00am and 1:00pm daily. Phone 01503 262646 for a list of the main boats and also general angling information. Just as a rough guide, expect to pay something between £30 and £40 for a day's shark fishing; good value indeed on clean, well-run, safe craft. You can also contact Harry Barnett on 01503 263218 for all information on deep-sea boats. In Mevagissey, skippers can be contacted via Tackle Box on 01726 843513.

Bass on the Rocks

One of the main reasons that bass come in close to feed around rocks is the peeler crab, the soft crab that is shedding its old shell. Crabs begin to peel once water temperatures average 11°C (52°F). Crabs peel on and off from the spring right through towards the autumn.

- *Bass love to forage amongst big rocks looking for peeler crabs.*
- *The rougher the ground, the better. Look for beaches that are mostly rock and boulder with comparatively little sand or gravel.*
- *Fissured rocks, large boulders, crevices, weed and all similar features are attractive to both crab and bass alike.*
- *Try putting a crab bait on a piece of sand between rocky areas. The bass will pick it up as they move from one hunting ground to another.*
- *Look for areas that will hold passing food items. Make a note of pools still full of water at low tide – excellent places. Note the position of weed beds and big boulders lying amongst smaller ones; both are good places.*
- *Look for deep gullies amongst the rocks and boulders. Bass use these gullies as highways from one feeding area to the next.*
- *Don't worry too much about depth – the bass will be happy anywhere between three and twelve feet.*
- *Ask local advice as to the best time to fish because there are simply no hard and fast rules. You might find the best time is one hour before low water and two hours after. Two hours before high water again seems to be good in many areas, but it pays to experiment.*
- *A good onshore wind tends to increase the number of fish moving in to feed. Don't be afraid of fishing into a good swell, but always ensure your personal safety and don't risk being cut off by a tide.*
- *Try to use as light a lead as you can get away with. A heavier lead will often snag the bait or pull it down into places the bass can't reach.*
- *Long casting is often not necessary. A lot depends on how deep the water is in close. If it's over two yards, expect them almost under your rod tip. In shallow water, be prepared to cast fifty to sixty yards.*
- *For a big bass, use a big hook like a 4/0 or a 5/0 and use the halves from two or three crabs pushed up the shank to make a bait some five or six inches long.*
- *One of the best methods is a sliding Paternoster.*
- *Use heavier line than you would think necessary. Twenty-pound breaking strain is a good compromise in really rocky surroundings that can chafe tackle unbelievably.*

The Tip of Cornwall

There are many excellent fishing locations in the most westerly part of Cornwall. Falmouth, for example, is a terrific area for both holidays and fishing. There's pier and shore fishing, as well as some great boat opportunities. The Manacle's, Pendennis Point, St Anthony's Head, Porthallow and Lizard are all legendary marks.

Penzance just has to be one of my own favourite areas – beautiful countryside, a pleasant town and some excellent boat, pier and shore fishing. Boat trips can be arranged from the Shell Shop (see below) and you will also find some opportunity for shark fishing.

Why not get away from the bustle a little bit and try Newlyn harbour, just a little south of the main town. Access it on the B3315, just off the A30. Newlyn has a long north pier, where the local trawlers dock, and a shorter south pier, which has a lighthouse. You will find the pier heads are busy during the summer months, but as the light fades, the crowds disperse and the fishing improves. True darkness can give you a good chance of a conger or two. Between May and October, the harbour itself often swarms with mullet. Fish for them light and generally under a float. You will get a lot of information from the Penzance tackle shops (see below).

If it's a fishing and family holiday combined that you're looking for, then it's hard to beat St Ives on the tip of the north Cornish coast. The bay, like the town, is quite wonderful and there's a whole array of fishing possibilities.

Accommodation – contact the Tourist Information Centre in Falmouth on 01326 312300.

Tackle shops – contact the Tackle Box in Falmouth on 01326 315849 for advice on tackle, baits and methods. Or, try Symons in St Ives on 01736 796200. In Penzance, contact Jim's Discount Tackle on 01736 360160, John Wing on 01736 363397 or West Cornwall Angling on 01736 362363.

Boat hire – in Falmouth, contact *Blue Minstrel* on 01326 250352, *Gamgy Lady* on 01326 375458 or Frank Vinnicombe on 01326 372775. In Penzance, boat trips can be arranged from the Shell Shop on 01736 68565. In St Ives, phone the Harbour Master on 01736 795081 or try Symons in the Market Place (see above).

The Isles of Scilly

The Isles of Scilly, just twenty-eight miles off the coast of Land's End, offer one of the most unexplored areas of fishing around our shores. In fact, to be honest with you, I've never fished there myself. However, the tales that come out of the place are sensational. You've got deep water close inshore and pretty well unexploited fishing. There are four main inhabited islands here and you can get holiday accommodation quite easily. St Mary's is the

largest island and possibly offers the most opportunities. There are charter boats available and blue shark are a real speciality here, along with some very big conger. Mind you, there are bound to be endless surprises for anybody who takes the time to explore the area.

Because of the Gulf Stream, spring comes very early indeed and, if the commercial fishermen are to be believed, some big porbeagles move into the area. Rumour has it that there are wrasse everywhere for the shore fisherman, along with conger, dogfish, pollack and mackerel. Areas to concentrate on are Porthcressa beach, Penninis Head and Deep Point. Take my advice – go and explore!

ACCOMMODATION – the possibilities for holiday accommodation are endless. The Isles of Scilly Tourist Information Centre on 01720 22536 is a mine of information; phone them for brochures and up-to-the-minute advice.

TACKLE SHOPS – contact Sports Mode, The Parade, St Mary's, on 01720 422293.

BOSCASTLE AND BUDE

Boscastle in north Cornwall is an absolute dream, the perfect place for the sea angler on holiday. The village is picturesque, the coastline gorgeous and the tiny harbour as cute as anything you'll find anywhere in the world. In short, it's the perfect venue for a holiday in this part of the world. Boscastle is primarily a summer venue too – the Atlantic swells in the winter mean that boat traffic is pretty well nil, so it's the warm months for this super little place.

Boscastle is really the jewel of the north Cornwall coastline, sheltering as it does behind the giant Meachard rock stack that guards the narrow entrance to the harbour. In fact, it's almost fjord-like here, the blue sea twisting and turning amidst high crags. You could almost think that you were in Norway.

There are two main options to pursue when you take a boat out of Boscastle. You can head south past Tintagel Head and along the coast in the direction of Padstow and search out the excellent bass fishing. Alternatively, steam north past Cambeak and Dizzard Point into Bude Bay, where you'll find rough ground, reefs and a whole variety of fish including tope, pollack, black bream, bull huss and, for the guys gunning for the real biggies, even some porbeagles.

Bude Bay really does offer a bit of everything for everybody. You're not fishing far out – just three miles or so from Bude's sandy beaches themselves, but it's a different world out there and you never know what's likely to turn up. A whole variety of baits work – obviously mackerel is

Big Eels

It's arguable that the south west produces the best conger anywhere around the shores of Britain. The big ports for the enthusiast are Plymouth, Dartmouth, Salcombe and Brixham – all areas where you can pick up really experienced charter-boat captains. As a general rule, you'll be fishing over mid-channel wrecks, often in the shipping lanes.

Conditions are important, and you really need a tide that allows the skipper to anchor his boat just off the wreck so that you can fish a static bait. Conger take their time to pick up food and you won't catch them on the drift. The plan is to put the bait – as often as not a mackerel flapper – on an 8/0, or even a 10/0, as close to the wreck as possible without actually being inside it. Wait for the eel to scent the succulent bait, sidle out and engulf it, and then hit and hold before it gets back to sanctuary. To do this, you're going to need thirty-pound plus tackle. You'll need a 200-pound wire trace – mono-filament will do if it's really, really thick.

Very often, the bigger the conger the more gentle the bite, so be alert. Once you know you've got conger interested, hit it and then the battle really begins. Very often it's tempting to think that you've actually lost the fish and that it's got back into the wreck. But don't give up – a really big eel does feel like a doomed, sunken boat. Suddenly, you'll feel it come off the bottom and your heart, as well as the fish, will begin to lift. Now the battle begins in earnest. You'll need a butt pad, strength and plenty of determination. Eels can swim backwards, and this gives them an added trick up their sleeves. Once you have an eel off the bottom, make sure it doesn't get back there, and keep pumping. Lift the rod as high and as gently as you can, and then wind in furiously as you lower it again towards the sea's surface. Keep repeating this process and, little by little, the giant will come towards the sunlight.

Happily, in these more enlightened days, conservation is the key word. Gone are the days when dead and discoloured conger would litter the quays of Brixham and Plymouth. Ninety-nine per cent of fish, whenever humanly possible, are now returned alive to fight another day. The key is to bring the conger, as quietly as possible, to the boat side. A pair of long-handled pliers are clamped to the hook shank and then twisted until the hook comes free. Carry out the operation as carefully as you can.

For real, full-blooded, absolute power there's hardly anything in the sea to beat a big brute of a conger. It's an experience that every sea angler should go through. But, be warned, it can become addictive!

best for the tope. Squid also works well, as do cocktails of ragworm and squid. Try jellyworms, too, especially for pollack when the tide is easing. That is the real beauty of fishing in Bude Bay – you can run through a whole range of baits and methods and pick up anything from black bream to really serious tope.

Boscastle is a great venue once you're back on shore – cafés, restaurants and good pubs with plentiful accommodation. The National Trust actually owns the area and that means that it is always maintained in tiptop condition. Have fun!

ACCOMMODATION – phone the Boscastle Information Centre for all your accommodation requirements on 01840 250010.

TACKLE SHOPS – try Bude Angling Supplies, 6 Queen St, Bude on 01288 353396.

BOAT HIRE – a highly recommended skipper is Ken Cave, boss of the *Peganina*. He can be contacted on 01288 353565. Fred Siford is the Harbour Master at Boscastle and can arrange launching for your own boat; phone him on 01840 250453.

LYNMOUTH

Lynmouth is a typical north Devon coastal town – very picturesque, perfect for a holiday and with all manner of attractions for the family. It has good harbour possibilities and some cracking summer mackerel fishing. Trips run from the harbour in the centre of the town and are very scenic. Mind you, most times I've been out, I've been shown up badly… most recently being out-fished by a rather loud-mouthed American girl aged no more than six!

The harbour arm can be prolific at times, with tremendous possibilities for both bass and grey mullet – typical of the north Cornwall and Devon coast in fact. This is where the freshwater fisherman on holiday can really win out – simply pack your standard float and spinning gear and you can get some tremendous sport. Do, however, remember to rinse off any salt after the trip or you'll have problems with rust once you get home and autumn draws on.

And can I make a suggestion here? If you're in the area and you have either freshwater tackle with you or reasonably light sea gear, then make enquiries at the Tourist Centre as to whether there are any salmon up the East Lyn River.

Salmon generally run late in the summer but any high water can push them up much earlier than that. Indeed, anything can have an effect. For example, back in 2001, some porpoises came into the bay and began hunting the salmon that had gathered there preparing to run the river later in the year. Rather than face the onslaught from the porpoises, though, the fish began to run much earlier, following each and every tide over a couple of days or so. The result was that the river, for at least two to two and a half miles, was full of salmon between four and perhaps ten pounds – quite brilliant sport.

Get your day or week ticket from the Tourist Information Centre and make sure you have your Environment Agency freshwater licence to boot. The rest is up to you. I would advise getting a good supply of lobworm, a bait that is allowed on the river at certain times – check your ticket for up-to-date information. If you have fly gear with you, so be it, but I realise this is unlikely to be the case if you're a hard and fast sea angler!

Travel light – this is important. You want to seek out as many of the pools as you possibly can from the town right up into the moor.

Wear Polaroid glasses. This is essential so that you can watch the water in front of you – especially when the water is clear. With any luck at all, you should be able to see salmon moving in and out of the shallows and deeper runs.

Let's say you get to a pool and you can see a couple of salmon on the fin, perhaps in mid-water – you're in with a real chance. First of all, don't scare the fish. They will be very wary. Remember they have just come in from the sea, so they are constantly on the lookout for predators. Make use of every bit of cover that's available while you try to get close to the fish.

Two or three lobworms on a size six hook should suffice as bait. The big question is how much weight you're going to need. Use too much and the splash may well scare the fish. Also, you want to try and present the worms at the level they're swimming, so it pays to start light. Perhaps one or two SSG shot are all you're going to need. Try to work out the strength of the current and consider carefully where you are going to cast your bait. I'd advise putting it in two or three yards upstream of the fish so it gives them plenty of time to see it as it closes towards them. Remember, if you use a reasonably light line, your casting distance and accuracy will be greatly increased. I'd recommend something between eight and ten pounds.

Your worms are drifting towards the salmon. A fish of about seven pounds suddenly moves purposefully through the current and seizes it. You have a decision to make… delay the strike, as old-fashioned salmon anglers used to do, and you'll end up with a deep-hooked fish that will almost certainly have to be killed. Strike almost immediately and the fish will either get off or it will be hooked in the lip so that you can return it. The decision is, to some degree, yours and the ticket says that some fish may be retained for the table. However, can I make a plea with you and beg that the fish are returned. I know it's asking a lot, and a bright fresh-run salmon is a mouth-watering prospect, but do think about the good of the river in the future and the all-important question of the angler's image. Let's say it is summer. Let's say that the weather is decent. If it is, then there will inevitably be a whole procession of tourists walking along the riverside path up to the Watersmeet Centre. If these tourists see a fisherman bashing a fresh silver salmon to death with the nearest rock then, once again, the popularity of our sport takes a nose-dive. If, on the other hand, they see the angler keep the fish in the water, gently unhook it and watch it swim away, then our reputation is enhanced.

Perhaps salmon fishing isn't true sea fishing, but you are talking about a fish that spends the majority of its life in the sea. Moreover, you've got the sound and smell of the sea in your nostrils when you're fishing this lower stretch of river. Above all, this is an intriguing way to spend a day and that should be all that matters. In my book, it doesn't really matter whether you're going for big-beach midwinter cod, wrasse from a rock pool, tench from an estate lake or pike from a Scottish loch… it's the fact that we're all fishing that matters!

One piece of advice. If you can get out on the river with your ticket either very early or late – before or after the tourists have descended that is – you'll probably find that your chances are greatly enhanced.

If you do hook a fish, try to keep it in the pool. If you let it get out through the tail, then you'll be involved in a long scramble down perilous, rocky ground, which could prove bad for the fish and is potentially dangerous for you! Playing a fish hard is by far the best method on rivers such as this.

Don't be in too much of a hurry to leave behind the pools in the towns themselves. These frequently hold fish that are just in from the sea and these are often quite willing to make an open mouth at a passing worm.

Do take care of your lobworms, especially on a warm summer's day, because you'll find they're every bit as vulnerable to high temperatures as lugs and rags. Keep them in a damp tub, perhaps under moist newspaper or moss. Don't go too small on bait. Two, three, four or even five big lobs are what a salmon is looking for. But ring the changes. If you don't get any reaction with a big bait, then it doesn't do any harm to give it a cast or two with a small one.

Accommodation – for accommodation try the Exmoor National Park Visitor Centre on 01598 752509 – they are extremely helpful.

Tackle shops – sadly, I have to report that tackle is pretty well impossible to buy in either Lynmouth or Lynton – a good business opportunity for someone perhaps?

Boat hire – for fishing trips, contact Matthew Oxenham on 01598 753207.

Fly Rodding in the South West

Fly rodding around the Devon and Cornish coastlines has been long established. Men such as Robin Armstrong and Ewan Clarkson helped pioneer the method decades ago. Today, experts such as Russ Symonds are taking the technique ever further.

First of all, what sort of species are really obtainable or pursuable on the fly? Well, certainly mackerel and, most glamorously, bass. You can also pick up mullet when they're really in a frenzy, packed together and feeding hard. Other fish will take a fly – notably pollack – but it's these three species that attract the bulk of fly-rodding attention.

And the tackle? Some of the guys use straightforward bonefish outfits. These, after all, are absolutely designed for the job and perfect for working through a light surf. Don't despair, though, if you've only got typical freshwater fly-fishing tackle. A floating line is probably what you're going to need and a general seven or eight weight outfit.

Flies? We're really talking lure fishing here… it's not dry fly fishing a chalk stream or nymphing for grayling! The generic term for what the bass and so on are feeding on is elvers – perhaps small eels, but just as commonly tiny fish of all species that tend to migrate together through the summer months. Therefore, you're using a fly that looks like anything small, silvery and edible. You can take it a bit further – one of the peak ways of taking bonefish in the warmer seas is on an imitation crab; these work brilliantly for bass.

Whereabouts? All these fish will come in very close indeed, and it's very much a stop, search and find type of method. Keep your eyes open – this is vital. On many occasions you'll see the ocean actually boiling as mackerel or bass are hammering into the prey shoals. Keep on the move. Keep your eyes open. Have binoculars with you and you'll see a whole sight more. You can pick all these species up off rocks, off the beaches, up estuaries – really anywhere that fish are coming in to forage.

The best times? Well, you don't want a big wind. This makes fly fishing difficult physically, and you don't want to run the risk of getting tangled up or, worse, doing yourself injury. Furthermore, a big wind can stir up the sand and make the water cloudy. Much better are temperate conditions – not too much wind and a reasonably clear sea. Obviously, if you can get out early or stay out late, then you are probably going to do best. In many places, it doesn't depend too much on the state of the tide. Even in low water, for example when fish get caught up estuaries, they will swim around not doing much in particular but willing to make a mouth at a tasty-looking fly.

And the technique? Remember that you don't have to strain massively to reach huge distances. Very often you will pick up bass just a few yards out actually in the surf. It's better to cast short distances and approach gently rather than splash around and scare the fish. You don't really need to work the fly much at all in a strong tide, the sea will do it for you. If, however, there's little flow – say you're up a low-water estuary – then it pays to give the fly some good old tweaks and keep it on the move, simulating a fleeing fish.

Whatever species you're after – mackerel and bass especially – expect a good, solid thump. They don't mess about when they're hitting into a prey fish and it's just the same when they're after your fly.

Of course, fly rodding doesn't necessarily mean that you're going to catch the most or the biggest bass, but what the heck? Believe me, a three- or four-pound school fish fights stupendously on fly kit and I'd rather catch half a dozen like that than fifty on feathers. And don't overlook the mackerel… in fact, a one-and-a-half-pound mackerel fights at least as well as a four-pound bass and that's saying a lot. The mullet, too, are something special on a fly rod. Oh, and one more thing if you're after mullet: don't overlook a very sparsely dressed nymph pattern – perhaps with a gold head bead to give a bit of weight and a bit of flash. Expect takes from mullet to be just a little less vigorous than those you pick up from bass or mackerel.

Above all, this is very much a pioneering method from which you can take some satisfaction. If you have a fly rod and you are heading for the south west, pack it. Ask the locals for advice – they're almost certain to prove helpful. Keep your eyes open and if you see surface feeding activity, get that rod out and you'll soon hear that reel screaming.

Sea-fishing Sites in Wales

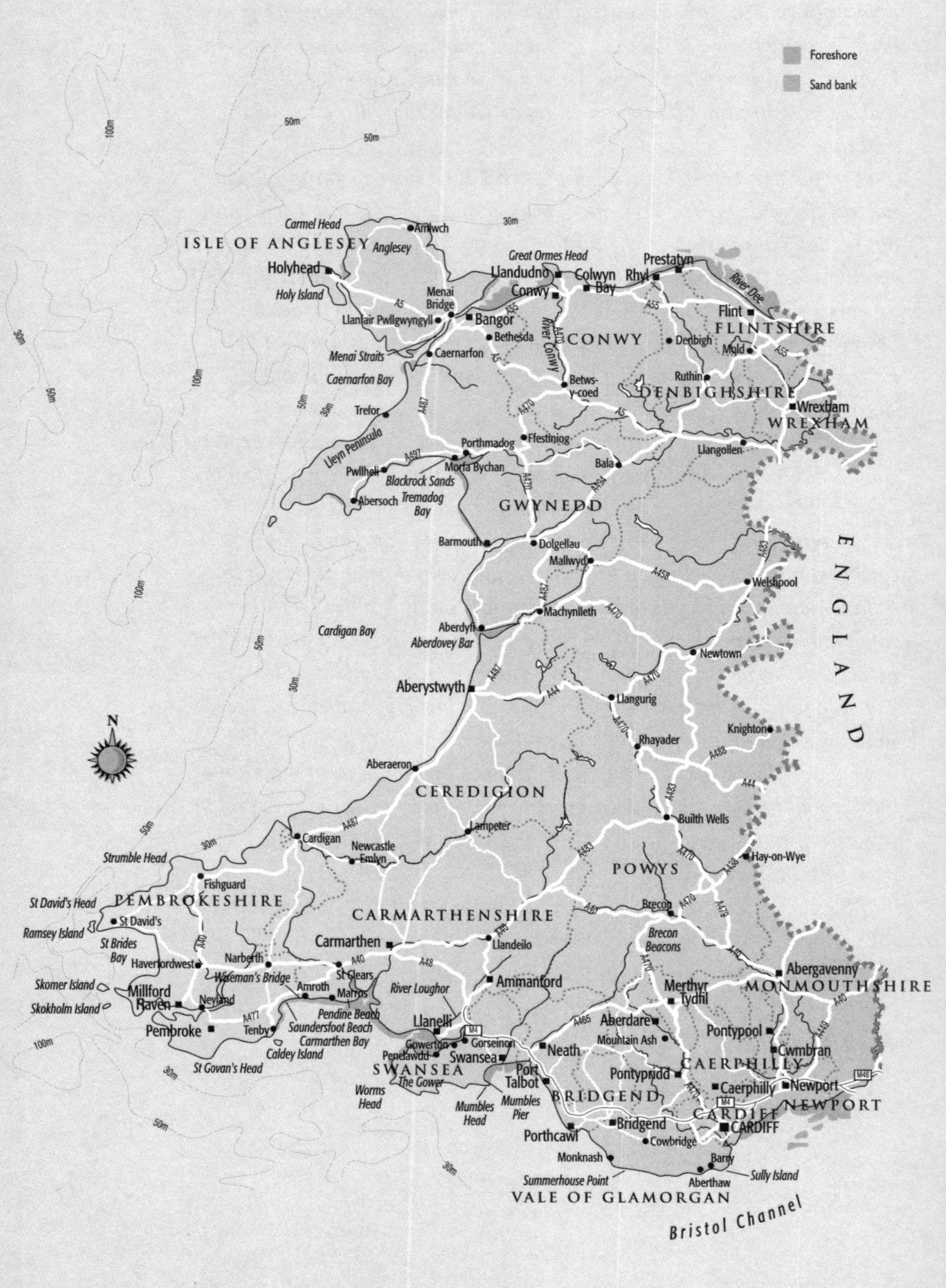

‘Although I came to Wales for the quality of the freshwater fishing, it wasn't long before I realised the outstanding sea fishing available in the principality. Personally, I tend to be quite selective about what I do when it comes to my saltwater outings and Wales really offers some tremendous treats. The bass fishing is superb and there are some very interesting mullet possibilities. The sea trout are virtually everywhere and the tope fishing can be fantastic. And if it's cod you fancy, there's plenty of good sport around Newport, Cardiff and Swansea. Try Fishguard, Conwy and the Menai Straits too. One of the best things, from my point of view, is that if you get out of the towns, just a little way, you'll find plenty of deserted beaches and headlands. I'm used to solitude when it comes to my freshwater fishing and, believe me, with the huge expanse of coastline that Wales has to offer, solitude is one thing you can easily find.’

PETER SMITH, HOTELIER AND WRITER

The coastline of Wales really does offer another world of sea fishing. Some of it is stunningly beautiful and much of it very remote. You really can get away from the madding crowds in many parts of the principality. Ask local advice to give you a starting point, but then strike out on your own and do a bit of exploring. Wales is another prime holiday area and it's possible to please both the family and the fisherman in many locations. Moreover, after the foot and mouth epidemic of 2001, the tourist industry everywhere is eager to welcome people back into the countryside, and what could be better than going there with a sea rod to hand. Peter makes a point about the sea-trout fishing in Wales – well, it's virtually the capital of sea-trout fishing in the UK, and, if you get the chance, watch the Welsh boys at work. Believe me, they are wizards and their skills might even inspire you to do a little night fly fishing yourself.

NEWPORT

The south coast of Wales has long been a mecca for sea angling. Newport has a lot to offer, situated as it is at the throat of the Bristol Channel. A pal of mine has his own boat there that he launches to fish this area and, in the summer, he takes a bewildering number of species. He tells me the skate and ray fishing are unexpectedly good.

ACCOMMODATION – for details of accommodation in the area, contact the Tourist Information Centre in Newport on 01633 842962.

TACKLE SHOPS – phone Dave Richard's Angling Shop on 01633 254910 or the Pill Angling Centre on 01633 267211 for advice on fishing in the area.

CARDIFF

Cardiff has a lot going for it, too. Perhaps the first place to mention is the beach fishing at West Aberthaw, which you will find by heading towards Cardiff airport and continuing west along the B4265. Find the petrol station in Aberthaw itself and turn left down to a large car-park on the west side of the power station. You'll find the hot water outfalls to your left. The renowned Summerhouse Point is the rock headland on the right. This is a large bay – very rocky and weedy – so it's a real tackle-grabber. The cod fishing, especially in the winter, is something pretty special. It fishes best, the locals say, a couple of hours either side of low water. It looks good at high water, but results plummet quickly. As the ground is so rough, visit at low water to get some idea of the terrain. As a tip, try to fish from the highest ground you can find into deep water close in.

Favourite baits include lug, razor fish, squid and fresh peeler crab. As you can guess, this venue is very exposed to strong southerlies, so avoid these if there's a big swell on. Be very careful about establishing your exit route, particularly at night. If in doubt, ask the advice of locals.

We've concentrated on the cod, which are a really magnificent winter bonus, but there are other species on offer too. During the winter, you will come across pouting and whiting and there are some big conger about in the autumn and early part of the winter. In the summer, expect a lot of smooth-hound and bass, along with a few wrasse and, I'm told, even the odd trigger fish. And, once again, this is a perfect venue for my personal favourite style of sea fishing… using freshwater gear and a float for the plentiful mullet that love to feed amongst the weed and rocks. A great place all round.

It would be quite wrong to leave the Cardiff area without some mention of Sully Island, which is directly south of the city. For winter cod, this is a mark that's hard to beat. It's a small tidal island and you'll find it at the eastern end of Sully Bay. It's accessible for around two hours either side of low water. But do, do, do be warned – don't cross the tidal causeway connecting the island to the mainland, even if you think it's safe to do so. If you're in any doubt, ask the locals or enquire at the nearest tackle dealers.

Come winter, there are plenty of codling about, but it's the double-figure cod that really prove the attraction. Low water generally produces most of the cod, and top marks are Monkey Pole, a post on the island's eastern end, where forty- or fifty-yard casts are all you need out onto clean ground where the big cod feed. Green Island, to the south of Sully, offers rough ground but plenty of big cod as well. Top baits for the island include lug tipped with squid, ragworm and peeler crab. Look out for a gentle south-westerly, but as this is a very exposed area, too much wind can bring its own problems.

ACCOMMODATION – contact the Tourist Board in Cardiff on 029 2022 7281.

TACKLE SHOPS – contact Aspinall's Angling Supplies on 01446 742645 or Barry Angling Centre on 01446 747638.

MONKNASH

There are all manner of lanes leading to the sea from the B4265 road that runs westward from Barry. However, one of the favourite locations is at Monknash, a tiny little village beyond Llantwit Major that is very easy to miss. Get yourself to the pub, The Plough and Harrow, and turn down the lane for about half a mile towards the sea. Soon the road turns right and becomes a rough single-track. Park here and walk. Take the left fork, across the stile and through a wood. Allow twenty minutes for the walk. You'll find yourself on a wonderful beach that offers superlative ray fishing, probably the best in the area.

Thornbacks arrive as early as March, but the sport really heats up from mid-April right through to the autumn. Small-eyed ray abound and there are some good double-figure fish. There's some rough ground about, which attracts bass, conger and codling, but if you head for the large sandy area on your right and walk a good way into it, you should be able to fish over a clean bottom. This is very much a place to fish on the low tide. Approach it two or three hours down and the same up. Sand eel is rated by the locals as a top bait here. You'll find most of the bigger fish are pregnant females, so it makes sense for all future sport to put back the rays that you catch.

ACCOMMODATION – contact the Tourist Board in Bridgend on 01656 664906.

TACKLE SHOPS – there are two excellent contacts in the area – Ewenny Angling Supplies in Bridgend on 01656 662691 and the Barry Angling Centre in Barry on 01446 747638.

Hotspot – Penclawdd

I'm always looking out for intimate sea-fishing adventures, and there are few better places than Penclawdd, west of Swansea on the north Gower coast. Here, where the Loughor estuary meets the sea, you will find some close-in flounder-fishing of the highest quality. Penclawdd is probably at its peak from September right through to December, though you may well catch the bigger specimens in the early spring. The summer months here can also be really interesting, with some tremendous mullet and bass fishing.

It can be a bit of a hike through the marshes and mud, so waders, perhaps even chest waders, are advisable. Nonetheless, the scramble is well worthwhile. Indeed, the fish come so close in that some locals are even beginning to catch them on a freshwater pole set-up. You can, of course, leger for the fish – mullet, bass or flounder – with traditional gear, but they will come so close in that float fishing is always a really good option. A simple freshwater float rod can offer tremendous possibilities in these conditions.

The area does fish well, as you'd expect, on the flood tide. Neap tides are the ones to go for – the problem with the high tides is that they will fill up the dykes behind you and even come over the marsh itself. So, do be very careful and make sure that you check out the state of the water before you set out.

Harbour ragworm appear to be one of the top baits here – put a good few on the hook so that you've got an obvious, unmissable bait.

This really is an area that offers a great deal. You can often catch fish as close as twenty yards or less. Consider fishing light, so you can keep your bait on the move, and take seriously the idea of using freshwater float-fishing gear – you'll enjoy your sport even more. Imagine a good bass or mullet in such a situation…

Enjoy your surroundings, too – this is a pretty, wide-open place, which is a joy to fish, particularly when the sun is out and there's a light breeze on the in-coming tide.

You find it by following the M4 to junction 47 and exit at the signs for Gower. Make your way to Gowerton and then head west on the B4295 until you reach Penclawdd. If you just drive out of the village towards the west, you'll find the car-park. From here, you can walk to the channel. I repeat, it is a bit of a slog, so travel light and make sure that your footwear is up to the job.

SWANSEA

Moving westwards we come to Swansea, the city by the sea, set in a lovely bay midway along the coast. It's a busy port and has the second highest tidal range in the world! These facts alone give a lot of scope for the angler. One of the top shore marks is the East Pier and breakwater. To get there, follow the A483 from junction 42 on the M4 and motor on to Swansea Docks. Look out for the Queen's Dock and the breakwater. The Associated British Ports (ABP) allow anglers to fish the weirs but you must get a permit beforehand. Apply to the Port Manager, Harbour Office, Lockhead, Kings Dock, Swansea, SA1 1QR. The permit costs just over £20. There are some really good cod and whiting fishing, especially in the winter. Summer catches are generally made up of ray, smooth-hound, conger and bass.

If you continue along the A483, you will eventually come to the West Pier. This long pier offers some tremendous fishing and is very popular with the locals. The summer produces bass, mullet, dogfish and flounder, along with some plaice. Expect whiting and codling during the autumn and winter. It's a good place to float fish for mackerel in the summer and, if your gear is fine enough, you'll probably pick up a mullet or two on a small rag or even a pinch of breadflake.

The beach offers great opportunities and you can follow it westwards along the A4067, the Oystermouth Road. Eventually, you will reach the town of Mumbles. There are many access points and you'll find predominantly sand and mud as you approach the west. There's some rougher ground with some deep gullies. Expect to catch good bass, flounder, dab and dogfish through the summer. Winter again provides cod and whiting.

It's worth talking about Mumbles Pier. Some angling is permitted at a charge of £3 per rod but you must be off around dusk. The fishing is extraordinarily good and you will generally find plenty of space. Double-figure cod often show up in the winter and in the summer expect all the usual species with some tremendous bass fishing. Take a drop net with you – a double-figure bass is always on the cards.

From the pier, you can see the famous Mumbles Head and its lighthouse. This is a tidal island, noted for great bass fishing. The ground there is very rough, and do take care not to get cut off by an incoming tide. The Head is accessible for a couple of hours either side of low tide. The gullies between the islands are very productive and you'll find the current goes through at a fair lick. Try spinning in the summer and float-fished live prawn.

Before leaving the Swansea area altogether, we ought to look at an area popular with the locals – the River Loughor, situated just east of Llanelli. To get there, leave the M4 at junction 47 and head through the town of Gorseinon. You will see the river quite soon and access is possible at several places near railway and road bridges. This is a good spot for a visiting angler, especially one who likes a bit of light line-fishing and hasn't got too much time to spend. It's regarded as one of the top flounder rivers in the area, especially in the early months of the year. Mind you, it's also good in the summer for silver eels, mullet and bass. In fact, the mullet-fishing on light gear can be exceptional. For the flatfish, a standard flowing trace is generally used but many of the locals add beads to the hook bait as an added attractor. Start at low water and fish right the way up. Watch for the mullet coming in very close, feeding hard in shallow water. Put down some bread-mash ground bait and you will stand some chance of holding them.

ACCOMMODATION – phone the Swansea Tourist Information Centre on 01792 468321 or the Mumbles Tourist Information Centre on 01792 361302. The latter is particularly good on accommodation for the Gower Peninsula.

TACKLE SHOPS – for local advice, contact Roger's Tackle on 01792 469999, Mainwarings on 01792 202245, Hook, Line and Sinker on 01792 701190, Baits and Bites on 01792 480490 or Country Angling in Gowerton on 01792 875050.

BOAT HIRE – try *Blue Thunder Mark* on 01403 797974, *Lady Gail* on 08850 718572, *Susan Jane* on 01792 648033, *Sarah Louise* on 01792 798180 or the *Enterprise* on 01443 450602.

CARMARTHEN BAY AND PEMBROKESHIRE

Moving further west, we come to Carmarthen Bay – a succession of wild beaches that are paradise for the bass and flounder fishermen. These golden beaches include the well-known Pendine and Saundersfoot beaches. A little-known area is Amroth, a picturesque, small coastal village lying between Llanteg and Wiseman's Bridge. The beach faces south east and lies behind some high cliffs, so it's well sheltered from severe westerlies. You'll catch flounders, whiting, dogfish and rockling throughout the winter, with occasional bass showing up in mild conditions. There are lots of bass and flounder in the spring. In the summer, mackerel and dab show up. Ragworm is the top bait, along with razor fish and lugworm for the bass.

Amroth is a clean beach apart from a large area of rocks right in front of the village itself. These are visible at low water. The right-hand side of the beach offers deeper water. Fishing for bass is ideal after a good onshore surf, and you'll find night conditions particularly successful. Long-range casting isn't a big deal here and you rarely need to go further than eighty yards.

It's simple to get to Amroth: just follow the A40 west from Carmarthen to St Clears. Take the A477 signposted towards Tenby. Amroth is eventually signposted on the left. The Amroth Arms offers a welcoming haven after a windy and wet night session!

ACCOMMODATION – for information on accommodation in the area, contact the Tourist Board in Carmarthen on 01267 221901 or the Tourist Board in Tenby on 01834 842402.

TACKLE SHOPS – depending on where in the bay you find yourself, contact the following: Morris Bros Ltd, Troy House, St Julian St, Tenby on 01834 844789; Bay Fishing Tackle, High St, Saundersfoot on 01834 813115; The Fishfinder, 51 King St, Carmarthen on 01267 220226; Anglers Corner, 80 Station Road, Llanelli on 01554 773981.

CARDIGAN BAY

The west coast offers legendary bass fishing. There is both excellent surf fishing and spinning from the many rocky headlands. As we move north, we come to Cardigan Bay. This is really top tope country – as is much of the Welsh coast. However, here on the west, Aberdyfi, Aberystwyth and Pwllheli offer some great opportunities. You'll find tope in shallower water, hence the attraction of Cardigan Bay. You can sometimes pick them up off the beach, but more often you're going to have to hire a boat.

Tackle will usually be a reasonably heavy uptide rod and a 7000-sized multiplier. If you're fishing a slack tide and the boat isn't crowded, then you can get away with heavy carp gear, but you've got to know what you are doing because you don't want the fight to go on overlong and the fish to become overstressed. Keep your rig simple. A running leger is the norm, with a six- to eight-foot trace of 200-pound mono, and a size 6/0 or 8/0 tied and crimped to the end. It's a straightforward rig, but you'll have to change it after catching a couple of fish. Don't use stainless steel hooks, in case you have to leave a hook in a fish – you will want it to rust away and drop out.

Best baits are live eels and mackerel, but squid and dab have also been used with success. Tope prefer fresh bait to stale – they're not scavengers. Think about rubby-dubby – fresh minced mackerel is good but so are older blood and guts. Try to be after your tope when there's a reasonable tide running – the moving water carries the smell of the bait to hunting fish. May to October is the prime period for this part of the coastline.

A typical bite will be a couple of bangs on the rod tip followed by a screaming run, so it's vital to have your reel set correctly. Don't clamp down the clutch too tight or all you will see of the rod is a fast-disappearing handle. Tope will immediately drop a bait if they feel too much resistance, so you've got to get the drag set just right. Once that run starts, give it a second or two, then tighten up and strike. It was once common practice to delay the strike, even until the second run. This, however, resulted in a lot of deep-hooked and dead fish. Today, tope should always be released. To do this successfully, you need a good quality disgorger to hand. If the fish is hooked deeply, the kindest thing to do is to cut the trace as near to the fish's mouth as possible.

Looking After Your Tackle

It's very tempting to come back from a trip, dump your tackle either in the back of a van or in a shed and forget all about it. Don't. The seawater is bound to do it harm, sometimes irreparably.

• Always wipe down your rods with a damp cloth and pay special attention to the eyes. Make sure all salt spray is wiped off.

• Wipe down the reel seats especially carefully and, from time to time, use a little light oil on them.

• A good strong rod holdall is good for carrying your rods along the beach, but is especially important if you are transporting them. It's all too easy to snap off a tip or an eye.

• After a session, wash your reels gently under a tap for a couple of seconds. Then wipe dry with a soft cloth. Let the reel dry out totally before putting it back in its bag. Don't blast your reel with water and don't immerse it. A gentle drizzle is enough.

• Your waders – especially neoprenes – are expensive, so look after them. Don't allow them to fester crumpled in a corner. If they remain damp, cracks will begin to appear. Rather, hang them upside down from a hanger. This will allow air to circulate and for them to dry off naturally and keep their shape.

• Your lamps are also important, so spray them with fresh water and wipe off. Wash any dirt off the glass globe. If you've got a headlight with rechargeable batteries, top them up at once. If they become exhausted, batteries don't recharge successfully.

• Dry off your rigs, your leads and especially your hooks. Your hook is everything, so wash it off in fresh water to prevent rusting.

• It is also vital to pay close attention to the state of your line, especially if it's been subjected to harsh conditions or been used over rocky ground. If you're in any doubt about whether the line has been frayed or weakened, remove it and refill your spool.

• Look after your catch, too. If you can, gut and clean it on the beach or on the boat, or at the very least as soon as you get home. Don't leave this job – all you will end up doing is wasting the bounty of the sea.

• Always ensure that you dispose of unwanted tackle and litter in a responsible fashion. Don't, under any circumstances, just shove it all under a big boulder hoping that it will never see the light of day. Disposal of nylon line is particularly crucial – any left on the beach could mean the death of a seabird.

ACCOMMODATION – contact the Tourist Board in Aberystwyth on 01970 612125.
TACKLE SHOPS – try Aberystwyth Fishing Tackle Shop on 01970 611200.
BOAT HIRE – in Aberystwyth, contact the *Spindrift* skippered by Jean Roche on 01544 388492; in Aberdyfi, contact *Isle de Nord* skippered by Dave Saddler on 01970 828844

BARMOUTH

Lying between a mountain range and the sea on the mouth of the River Mawddach is the beautiful old town of Barmouth. It is a good fishing area to concentrate on. The harbour provides really good fishing, especially for beginners. Walk along the breakwater and fish off the shingle bank back into the harbour. You will find the seabed is very clean, although the inside edge near to the breakwater is rougher.

You can get away with spinning rods and twelve-pound line, especially for the bass, flatfish and eels. A two-ounce weight should be quite enough. Long casting is not necessary and try to keep within the thirty- to fifty-yard mark. This is also a top area for mullet – try a tiny bar spoon tipped with ragworm. Light float-fishing with tiny strips of mackerel can also produce fish. You might also pick up garfish. Dab fishing is excellent from spring right through to autumn, when the whiting move in. Mullet and bass throng the area through the summer.

This is an easy spot to find: enter Barmouth on the A496 and take the Promenade Road. You will soon find the car-park on the beach front. Head for the boats at the eastern end of the car-park and pick up the footpath along the breakwater. Where the concrete breakwater starts and the sand dunes end, you will find a shingle beach. Fish facing the harbour.

ACCOMMODATION – contact the Tourist Board in Barmouth on 01341 280787.
TACKLE SHOPS – for up-to-the-minute advice contact the Seafarer Fishing Tackle Shop, Church Street, Barmouth on 01341 280978.

BLACKROCK SANDS AND PORTHMADOG

Carrying on further north, we come to a favourite mark called Blackrock Sands, near Porthmadog. To get there, find Woolworth's in Porthmadog itself and take the road signposted Morfa Bychan and Blackrock Sands. Take the road through Morfa Bychan until you come to the beach. This does get quite busy in summer, so early and late are best. Blackrock itself is the name given to the northern stretch of the beach. The name comes from the small rocky headland that dominates the fishing.

The beach itself doesn't have many features, so it pays to get close to the rocks themselves. Summer fishing is absolutely excellent for bass. They arrive some time in May and generally stay around until October or so. Also, in the summer you will come across dab and flounder. Early and late in the year, you find that some of the thornbacks move just within casting distance. A lot of the locals favour the mark in the autumn when huge numbers of whiting come in – these arrive during September, but thin out in December. During the summer, there are massive shoals of mackerel and garfish that come in close to feed on sprats and small fish – great for the kids in the family. This is great sport on very light spinning gear. Take one or two for the pan and you'll appreciate just how good they taste fresh from the sea.

ACCOMMODATION – contact the Tourist Board in Porthmadog on 01766 512981.
TACKLE SHOPS – contact the Fisherman, Central Buildings, High Street, Porthmadog on 01766 512464.

NORTH WALES

Next, we come to the small port of Trefor, on the north Welsh coast, just south of Anglesey. This really is a place best fished from your own boat, and launching is moderately charged at just over £6. The port used to be famous for smooth-hound, and the latest information is that these appealing fish are very much on the return. Look for them west of the harbour during the early part of the summer. They are generally found over sandy, clean ground. Peeler crabs are a great bait and pick up other species such as bull huss and thornbacks. Failing crab, try strips of mackerel or squid. To get the very best out of the fishing, don't go too heavy. In fact, stepped-up pike tackle is probably all you need. Go for a rod with, say, a three-pound test curve and load up with ten- or fifteen-pound line. This way, those smooth-hounds, with those great big pectoral fins of theirs, will really give a good account of themselves.

If you have a boat, you'll really like Trefor. The locals couldn't be more friendly and there's a really nice atmosphere to the place. There are plenty of fish around – especially now that most are being put back.

The north Welsh coast begins in earnest at Bangor, centre for the Menai Straits and Anglesey. This is a top area in very scenic conditions. Further east, the Conwy estuary is particularly good for flatfish. You'll also find bass and mullet running up in the summer months. Winter produces larger whiting and codling, although the rougher ground around Llandudno offers the best chance for codling and coalfish.

Still further to the east lies the attractive holiday resort of Rhyl. This offers a whole range of fishing year round. There's plenty of both shore and charter-boat opportunities available.

BAIT TIPS

Fish aren't ravenous all the time and on occasion they need to be encouraged, especially when your time is tight. Adding something to the bait in terms of visuals and flavour can sometimes do the necessary trick.

- *It often pays to attach a spoon some six inches or so up the trace from your bait. This gives a visual signal as well as sending out vibrations. It could be that bigger fish think a small flatty is trying to make off with the bait.*
- *Putting beads on the trace above the hook has long been part of the sea-angling scene. The newer booby beads are especially good as the metallic rattle attracts fish. Use a combination of colours.*
- *It's important to catch your quarry's eye – try a strip of squid or mackerel, on or above the hook.*
- *Cocktails can really work a miracle and stimulate a tired appetite. Mind you, just simply loading different baits onto a hook isn't necessarily the answer and it needs thought. Try lug and cockles, or rag and strips of mackerel belly. Peeler crab and sand eel strips work well, as do lug and pieces of squid.*
- *Pilchard oil really draws fish in. Apply it from a plastic squeezy bottle; it's expensive but worthwhile. Cod liver oil is cheaper and can work, while there are those that swear by WD40!*
- *Try putting a big swim feeder, such as coarse fishermen use, twelve inches or so up the trace. Pack this with a pilchard oil-soaked rag and/or bits of left-over bait.*
- *There is also a host of shop-bought additives that you can try. A lot of them work well on the fish.*
- *If you're float fishing, for example, close in off rocks or even from a boat, it can pay to ground bait the area. Make a mini rubby-dubby out of fish, worm or whatever, and feed it so that it falls slowly through the water. This is particularly attractive to wrasse and bass.*
- *There are times when fish want a bait presented to them in a different manner. Flounder, for example, will frequently take a bait that's fished above the bottom and on the move, whereas they will refuse one that's static and legered.*
- *If you're fishing the estuaries, try maggots bought from the local tackle shop. These can be especially effective for mullet and it's worth trying a big bunch for flatfish.*

ACCOMMODATION – details of accommodation can be obtained from the Tourist Information Centres in Llandudno on 01492 876413 and Colwyn Bay on 01492 530478.

TACKLE SHOPS – contact Happy Valley Angling, Llandudno Pier, North Parade, Llandudno, on 01492 877678. In Colwyn Bay, contact Rhos-on-Sea Fishing on 01492 544829 and the Victoria Angling Centre, Victoria Pier, on 01492 530663.

BOAT HIRE – contact Bangor Angling Supplies on 01248 355518. In Rhyl, try Blue Shark Fishing Trips on 01745 350267.

ANGLESEY

Let's now have a look at the island of Anglesey, beginning at Holyhead on the north of the island. The big feature here is the Holyhead breakwater, well over a mile long and renowned for both summer and winter fishing. Inside the breakwater the fishing is easier as there are fewer snags, but it's outside, over rough ground, that the best of the sport is to be had. Sometimes you can drive your car along the breakwater, but at other times it is closed and you have to walk. There are good spots right along and it's useful to ask local advice. Take note of that rough ground: make your tackle simple and always with a rotten bottom in case you have to pull for a break. Top baits are lug, rag, crab and squid. Another problem with the breakwater, apart from the rough ground, is the high wall. You need a drop net and, ideally, a good mate. Not a venue for juniors or elderly people.

In the summer, you can expect wrasse, dogfish, pollock; later on, smooth-hound, conger and ray. In the winter, look out for whiting, codling and coalfish. Boat fishing is also good – expect tope and thornback.

Moving clockwise round the island we come to Amlwch, which has a really good reputation for skate, conger and tope from the boats. There's also some good herring and mackerel fishing in the summer.

Beaumaris, on the south-east tip of the island, is renowned for boat fishing. From here, charter boats fish the Menai Strait, which is sheltered from prevailing south-westerly winds. Even if the winds are coming from the north or east, it is still possible to move down the Strait towards Caernarfon Bay. Caernarfon Bay is a real favourite – rays into double figures, tope to fifty pounds and big bull huss, along with mackerel and dogfish. There are also a few sandbanks that hold good numbers of bass and even the odd turbot.

ACCOMMODATION – contact the Tourist Information Centre at Llanfair PG on 01248 713177, or in Holyhead on 01407 762622.

TACKLE SHOPS – try the the Pilot Store and Fishing Tackle on 01407 831771.

BOAT HIRE – Stan Zalot runs Starida Sea Services, contact him on 01248 810250 for details of the extensive boat fishing available. Other contacts are Dave Jones, Beaumaris Marine Services on 01248 810746, and Anglesey Boat Company on 01248 810359.

LOOKING AFTER THE FISH

Fifty years ago, it was normal to slaughter everything caught either on the beach or from a boat. Today, this is no longer the case. Stocks of fish are much lower and have to be preserved. Also, we need to think about our image. Times have moved on and we need to be much more considerate, caring and conservation-minded, for our own good as well as for the good of the sea.

- *Only ever take home fish that you plan to eat. Underestimate, rather than overestimate, your needs.*
- *Naturally, return all under-sized fish at once.*
- *If at all possible, hold your fish in the water until they are strong enough to swim off, and don't allow them to drift away with the tide.*
- *Don't drop fish off piers or high-sided boats.*
- *Weigh fish (if you must) in slings and not from the gill.*
- *Keep shark species in the water. If you take them out, then without the buoyancy of the water to keep them in shape, their guts will drop under their own weight; this can easily lead to the rupturing of small blood vessels. Also, remember that all big fish thrash around on a boat or on the beach and can do themselves harm.*
- *Chat to your boat skipper before booking him up and ask him to return any fish that aren't required or which are inedible; conger are one of the best examples.*
- *It's the same with bait – don't dig or take more than you're going to need. Try to preserve any left over carefully for your next trip.*
- *When bass fishing from the shore, try not to take the fish from the water at all. You can simply play the fish out, lead it into the shallows and there slip the hook free with a pair of forceps. It's taking the fish out of its own environment that does the most harm.*
- *To avoid deep-hooking fish, strike as soon as is practical and avoid giving a fish the time to swallow the bait down deep.*
- *If you do hook a fish down deep that is bleeding from the gills, you are advised to kill it immediately. Once the fish is losing any amount of blood in that way, its chances of survival are minimal.*

Sea-fishing Sites in North-West England

North-West England

The Lake District is much underrated when it comes to sea fishing. There's very little commercial activity, and the whole area is pretty well unexploited. For many years, I had a boat based in Ravenglass and the tope fishing was excellent. Very often I'd get anything up to a dozen fish in a day, including some big ones. The best I caught was fifty-seven pounds but I actually saw a monster of seventy-four pounds. There's also good pollack fishing, cod to double figures and great spur dog. The skippers in Whitehouse and Workington have located wrecks and you can also get out of St Bees. If you go twenty miles, you'll come across more wrecks, which give up pollack, cod and ling. I haven't even mentioned the bass fishing in the Esk estuary. There are some big mussel beds and some big fish come in. The Ravenglass estuary is also very good. Look for the rocks and punch a bait out. There really are some hot possibilities.

ANDY NICHOLSON, WRITER AND TV PRESENTER

My experiences off the coast of north-west England go back to 1961, a club outing out of Fleetwood into the storm-tossed waters of Morecambe Bay. I was initially put to shame by the beery anticipation of the adult members of the club who felt that a crate each was a prerequisite for the day. However, a short way out, my modest provisions of a flask and plain sandwiches began to look more sensible. Within half an hour of arriving at our chosen mark, I was the only one out of thirty people still with a rod in my hand. Sickness I'd obviously seen before that day, but never to this grotesque gothic level. The skipper maintained the torture for some three and a half hours, by which time the boat was beginning to look as though it had been struck by bubonic plague. The fact that I'd caught two dabs and an eel made me unpopular with the rest of the club members, but that I was capable of eating my lunch confirmed that I was to be loathed for the rest of that season.

Merseyside

Historically, the waters around Merseyside have been regarded as little more than open sewers. However, the Environmental Agency has put a lot of the wrongs of the past decades to right with brave and pioneering work. New sewage treatment plants have played a major part and now next to no crude sewage is being pumped into the river. In short, the Mersey estuary is now proving a revelation. Over thirty species of fish have been recorded, with coarse fish colonising the top of the water and more and more species pushing upwards. Even sea trout have been reported. There's talk, too, of salmon not being far off.

Dinghy fishing is possibly the best way to fish in the Mersey. Boats tend to go outside the river in the summer and stay inside during the winter. This isn't something forced upon them by the weather but more a trend induced by the habits of the fish. During the summer months, the river is good for plaice and flounder and you can expect the odd bass or two. Make sure that you have a chart, or, preferably, go out with a skipper or someone who knows the area. You really do need to head for the top marks. For example, Dukes Buoy is highly regarded as a cod area, whereas The Dee and Hilbre Island are good places for early summer tope. Jordan Spit can offer tope, rays, gurnards and some good mackerel fishing. There are plenty of shallow-water wrecks in the Mersey estuary and some of them produce conger. In winter, boats head well up-river and you'll see them dotted around the Liver Buildings and off Cammel Lairds, too.

Weather isn't too much of an issue as the Mersey is well-sheltered from the common south-westerly and westerly winds, but avoid north-westerlies or south-easterlies. You don't need to be far out, as most of the fish are close in to the edges. This is a help in strong winds and it does keep you out of the main shipping lanes. If you want to get out on the water and it's too far to bring your dinghy, charter boats are available to get you to the wrecks, although overfishing has depleted cod stocks in particular. Expect pollack and conger with the odd huss, spur dog, tope and ray.

There's a lot on offer for the shore fisherman. There are plenty of fish year round and well within casting range. You can expect fish from the river mouth as far up as Otterspool. The problem for the shore angler is that a lot of the river is made up of docks and steep walls that you just can't access. However, there is good beach fishing around New Brighton and it is possible to fish from some of the best dockside on the Liverpool side of the river. Alexandra Dock, Gladstone Dock and the Seaforth Rocks can be fished by permit holders. Permits are available from the North West Association of Sea Anglers on 0151 5260197. You will catch some cod and whiting in the winter, with flatfish, eels and some bass in the summer. In the winter, the river really does flow muddy, so fish hunt very much by scent rather than sight. For that reason it is very important to keep your bait freshened up – big, black lug is a favourite hereabouts.

Accommodation – contact the Tourist Information Centre in Liverpool on 0906 680 6886.
Tackle shops – contact Star Angling on 01744 738605, The Tackle Shed on 01744 810805, Fisherman on 0151 6534070 or J. E. Robinson on 01744 534136.
Boat hire – contact Liam McElroy on 0151 2807445.

Frozen Baits

Anglers don't always have the luxury of fresh baits, especially if they are travelling. For example, it's generally not possible to carry worms or crabs long distances in the car, especially in sunny weather. Also, you might well be visiting an area that is just too far from a top-quality tackle shop. And how about those impromptu sessions where you just fancy the odd quick cast? Well, frozen baits can help you out to some degree, especially if you've got the facility to move them from one freezer to the next.

- *You'll probably need a cool box and ice packs. These will prolong the life of your bait considerably. Take bait from just one packet at a time to avoid waste.*
- *When you do open a packet of bait, cover it with a rag soaked in saltwater to prevent a fast thaw in the sun.*
- *Try to buy frozen baits from a big shop with a fast turnover. The bait is more likely to be fresh that way. Watch out for giveaway signs such as ice crystals in the bag – a sure sign of poor freezing or long past shelf date.*
- *Sprats are often better as bait when they are blast-frozen, as they're not so soft and can be cast a greater distance – especially if they're tied on with thread.*
- *Peeler crab are excellent frozen. Keep all the bits and pieces that fall off them to tip off your worm baits in the winter.*
- *Shellfish and calamari squid freeze well. Buy squid in bulk for economy. Put the frozen block in the microwave at thaw setting. Break away individual pieces for refreezing in trip-sized packs.*
- *When freezing at home, try to ensure the bait is as dry as possible. Kitchen tissue soaks up moisture well. Also try to ensure that all the air is forced out of the bag to avoid freezer burn or dehydration.*

New Brighton

Before leaving Merseyside completely, let's look at one very famous mark – Perch Rock Beach at New Brighton. The beach on the east side of the Perch Rock is very much a low-water venue. At high water, the currents are often too strong for reasonable fishing. This mark is a godsend for locals and visitors alike, as it does fish pretty much year round.

The spring sees some good flatfish – both flounder and plaice. The summer sees good numbers of small bass, with the occasional bigger one putting in an appearance. September and October really see things hotting up, with whiting and codling moving into the Mersey in increased numbers. You'll find them hanging on throughout the winter months and it's probably only February and March when the area is really in the doldrums. We're not talking big fish here. The whiting are probably not much more than a pound. You can expect codling of a couple of pounds or so, though the odd big fish does show up occasionally.

Crabs appear to be the most popular bait during the summer months for the school bass, whereas cocktails go down well for the codling. Try lug tipped with mackerel or mussel.

To get there from Liverpool, use the Kingsway Mersey tunnel and then look for signs for New Brighton. Get on to the King's Parade (the A554). You will see the Fort at Perch Rock before reaching New Brighton – turn off the main road towards it.

Accommodation – there is accommodation available but don't expect to find it on top of the fishing – this is an industrial rather than a tourist area. Phone the Tourist Information Centre in Liverpool on 0906 680 6886.

Tackle shops – there's a wealth of tackle shops in the area, all of which can give excellent, up-to-the-minute advice. Contact Ken Watson on 0151 6384505, Ken Hopkins on 0151 6778092, Winnicott Tackle on 0151 4282718, Anfield Tackle on 0151 2608223, Champs Tackle on 0151 4943029, Sharps Fishing Tackle on 0151 9282626, Johnson's Angling Centre on 0151 5255574 and Tasker's Angling Centre on 0151 2606015. Try also John's Bait and Tackle in Wallasey on 0151 6391069 or Parkes Angling in Birkenhead on 0151 6520606.

Blackpool and Morecambe

Blackpool and Morecambe remain two very popular holiday centres in the north west and although the fishing might not be of the highest quality, both areas offer quite enough to make it worth packing the tackle if you're off on holiday. Fleetwood, between the two, is where I began my fishing career, and it is also worth a visit. At Blackpool, there are seven miles of beach fishing available, as well as sport from the North Pier.

The problem is that Blackpool's beaches do get very busy in the hot summer periods. Early and late in the day offer the best opportunities. In fact, it is probably better to get afloat. At Morecambe there is plenty of beach and jetty fishing yielding flatfish, bass and eels during the summer months. Expect some codling and whiting in the winter. Heysham harbour and North Wall offer good opportunities for a wide range of species year round. You can pick up anything from conger to mullet during the summer.

ACCOMMODATION – contact the Tourist Information Centre in Blackpool on 01253 403223 or in Morecambe on 01524 582808.

TACKLE SHOPS – contact Morecambe Angling Centre on 01524 832332 and Charlton and Bagnall, 3–5 Damside Street, Lancaster on 01524 63043. In Fleetwood, contact Langhorne's on 01253 872653 for information and some good fresh bait.

BOAT HIRE – contact P. Atkinson on 01253 825217 for charter possibilities. In Fleetwood, C. B. Bird offers charter hire on 01253 873494 or contact the *Viking Princess*, a favourite boat of the area, on 01253 873045.

ARNSIDE AND BARROW-IN-FURNESS

Moving into Cumbria, Arnside is a quaint little village situated on the south side of the River Kent estuary. The place is gaining a reputation as one of the best flounder marks in this part of the country. Throughout the year, the fish average a pound, but something three times this size is always possible, especially in the winter. You can fish the mark when the tide is out and the fish are concentrated into the channels that remain. You'll find these are deeper just seawards of the village's small pier. However, they're closer to the shore upstream near the viaduct. This means that casting is easier and you can get away with lighter gear. By and large, the bottom is comparatively snag-free, though you'll see the odd rock outcrop amongst the sand and mud.

Fish the mark a couple of hours either side of low water for the best results. But, be warned – there can be a strong tidal bore here and sometimes this can reach two feet in height and catch you out if you're unaware. Ask advice from the locals and, most importantly, if you hear the warning siren, gather up your belongings and move very quickly away from the bank. This is a top spot, but do take all precautions.

Tackle rather depends on where you are fishing. If you're going for one of the further channels, then you might need to cast anything up to eighty yards or so, which calls for standard beach tackle. If, however, you look for one of the closer in marks, lighter gear will do. The locals swear by harbour ragworm, and it can work even better with a piece of mackerel hooked up as a cocktail. Lugworm can also take fish. Don't go for small baits – flounders are greedy creatures and, in murky conditions, home in on a big, smelly bait.

The fishing is easy to find. Leave the M6 at junction 36, follow the A65 and turn off for Crooklands. Once in Crooklands, turn left onto the B5282 and this will take you into Arnside. Park near the viaduct.

Moving round to the west of Morecambe Bay, Barrow-in-Furness offers some good boat and shore fishing, especially for tope and bass in the summer months. Expect some codling and whiting in the winter.

ACCOMMODATION – contact the Tourist Information Centre in Barrow-in-Furness on 01229 894784.

TACKLE SHOPS – for further details on the sport in this region, contact Charlton and Bagnall in Lancaster on 01524 63043, Fawcett's (also in Lancaster) on 01524 32033, Gerry's of Morecambe on 01524 422146 and the Morecambe Angling Centre on 01524 823332.

BOAT HIRE – contact Stewart McCoy, skipper of the *Revenge*, on 01229 826160.

WORKINGTON

Travelling north, Workington offers some good possibilities. The harbour, for example, is well worth looking at. Here, at the mouth of the River Derwent, there's some good sport, with eels, flounder, occasional plaice and bass throughout the summer months. As the year wears on, you begin to find whiting and codling. What's good about the area is that the channel itself is protected on all sides – to the south by the breakwater and to the north by a jetty. This means that you can fish here in comfort through most conditions, even high winds.

Another good thing about Workington is that the bottom is not too rough and you don't have to fish any great distance – certainly thirty to forty yards is quite sufficient for most occasions. This means that you can use light gear and really make the most of the generally small-sized fish on offer.

You'll find the sport here begins in the spring, with the eels and flatfish. The bass, if they're going to appear, will follow on soon afterwards. The codling and whiting fishing is at its best from October onwards. An onshore wind is particularly good, packing the codling, especially, into the estuary. The mark fishes at most stages of the tide. Finding the mark is easy – simply follow the A597 into Workington and keep to the south side of the river. You'll find plenty of parking along the harbour wall.

ACCOMMODATION – contact the Tourist Information Centre in Workington on 01900 606699.

TACKLE SHOPS – contact Graham's Gun and Tackle on 01900 605093.

HAVE YOU CAUGHT YOURSELF A RECORD?

It's the dream of every angler to catch a fish that will immortalise him or her with a place in the record books. Line class records are taken very seriously in the world of sea fishing, but what do you do if you think you've won the lottery and landed that whopper?

- *First of all, it's essential to fill in a claim form. This needs to be completed and sent off within sixty days of the capture of the fish.*
- *You will need a clear photograph of the catch, so there's no doubt as to its identity. Also photograph any notable distinguishing marks.*
- *Keep a long sample of the reel line that you were using when you caught the fish.*
- *Get a scale certificate to say that the scales upon which the fish was weighed have been checked by an independent assessor.*
- *The claim will be acknowledged and you will be told what records you are being considered for.*
- *All information can be obtained from David Wood, The Light Tackle Club, 78 Beech Road, Horsham, West Sussex, RH12 4TX. Phone him on 01403 217884.*
- *If accepted, you will get a certificate, a badge and your place in the record books! But remember, fame isn't everything. Only put a fish through the stress of being weighed if you're sure you've got a whopper.*

MARYPORT

Just a few miles further north in Cumbria, Maryport is building up a good reputation for sea fishing. The port boasts a flourishing fishing fleet, along with a maritime museum and, of special interest to anglers, the Lake District Coast Aquarium. If you want to see how your favourite species actually look in the water, this is the place to go to. It is easily accessed via the A66 and A594 from the M6.

There is good shore fishing, which makes it attractive to the casual visitor. The promenade, especially, offers easy access, but there are some very productive rocky outcrops to the south of the town. Look around here for Black Banks, a couple of miles from the centre. Access is close to Siddick village. Excellent fishing, but do be careful of the quickly rising tide. Both piers at the town are open to fishing and the best of the sport is about two hours each side of high tide. Forget low water.

Maryport is really the flatfish centre of the north west and you can expect some really good-sized plaice over the two-pound mark. Flounders are also of an impressive size. You'll also see some mullet and bass during the summer months. Codling and whiting begin to show up during the early winter. The best of the sport is generally after dark. All the usual baits work well – lug, white ragworm and peeler crab being local favourites. You can buy most baits locally or dig them yourself.

Before leaving Maryport, let's have a look at another local mark, Grasslot Beach. You'll find this south of the Harbour Arms in Maryport and it's very much a favourite amongst locals from the late summer onwards. In fact, September to December is the peak period when large numbers of codling in the two- to three-pound bracket move close inshore. You'll also pick up some whiting and perhaps even a few dogfish. Fish the beach on larger, flowing tides, especially at night. You'll find a south-westerly wind also pushes fish closer inshore. Whilst most of the locals favour the autumn and early winter, this is also a good place for the visitor during the summer, with large bags of plaice and flounder to be caught. Lugworm works well throughout the year and some of the larger flatfish also come to peeler crab.

Just north of Maryport, you will find Allonby, an area principally of mud and sand where you will catch plenty of flounder to two pounds and plaice up to four pounds. Halfway between Allonby and Silloth, you'll come to Dubmill Point, which again is excellent for flatfish but does involve a long walk at low tide. Do avoid the racing flood tide as you can get caught out. Watch what the locals are doing and retreat in safety.

Accommodation – phone the Tourist Information Centre in Maryport on 01900 813738.

Tackle shops – there's no tackle shop anymore in Maryport, the last one closing down a short while ago. However, contact Graham's Gun and Tackle in nearby Workington on 01900 605093 or the Tackle Shack in Whitehaven on 01946 693233. These shops will not only sell you all the tackle and bait you need but will advise on the numerous competitions held throughout the year.

Boat hire – Peter Hewitt on 01900 817926 can arrange charter-boat hire from the town.

Silloth to Bowness-on-Solway

Moving up the Solway Firth to the north-west tip of Cumbria, you come to the town of Silloth, very much a Victorian relic with its wide, cobbled streets and impressive promenade. From here you get awe-inspiring views across the Solway Firth towards the imposing Scottish Borders. This is a great area for the holidaying angler and his family. Nice scenery, pleasant and relaxing, with lots to do and plenty of accommodation.

In Silloth itself, Tommy Legs is very popular and you'll find it close to the entrance of the dock. There's some slightly deeper water here and flounder and plaice are again the main species. There's the odd codling or two as well, although not particularly big ones, and even an occasional thornback. The promenade stretches eastward from the town and offers hugely accessible fishing. Like Maryport, Silloth offers some amazingly good flatfish possibilities during the summer months. This means you won't need particularly heavy gear, although a standard beach caster will do fine. Your main line can be around the ten- to fifteen-pound mark and bait can either be bought or dug locally. Silloth is very much a shore-fishing area, both east and west of the town. You'll find a good range of ground from rocky scars to clean, sandy beaches. Access is easy as the road runs alongside the coastline. Long hikes, therefore, aren't generally necessary.

Skinburness is just a little further up the coast, and offers shallow water over a sandy beach. Flatfish are again numerous, but there are plenty of school bass in the summer months. Not large fish, but they give great sport at around a couple of pounds in weight.

Finally, try Bowness-on-Solway, the legendary end of Hadrian's Wall. This is a top mark and you can often expect a really good bag of flatfish. Most anglers fish just in front of the village, a real beauty spot. Remember that anglers are very much on show here to the general public, so make it a constant rule to tidy up not only your own rubbish but anything else you might find in your vicinity. There are no charter boats available in the area, but if you bring your own dinghy, you can launch it from the public slipway at the lifeboat station situated on the promenade. Getting out that little bit further is bound to give you a head start, but it's not essential.

ACCOMMODATION – for accommodation phone the Tourist Information Centre in Silloth on 01697 331944.

TACKLE SHOPS – see the entry for Maryport for details of tackle shops in the area.

The Isle of Man

Perhaps the cream of all the fishing in the north west can be enjoyed on the Isle of Man. The island, though small, offers huge variety. To the north, you're looking at typical surf beaches. To the south, the coastline is more rocky. Moreover, the Isle of Man is a great holiday destination and once again you're looking at a place that can be enjoyed by the whole family, as well as the angler. To some degree, the sea fishing on the Isle of Man has not been largely exploited, and you'll do well to go there expecting a certain amount of adventure.

Douglas offers a great deal – expect to catch flatfish, especially large sole, pollack, dogfish, coleys, pouting and a few codling from both the

Using Squid as Bait

Squid is a cracking bait and you should always try to have some with you. It's a staple foodstuff for virtually every fish, and can turn a blank day into a really hum-dinging one. It's relatively cheap and it's almost universally available from supermarkets, fishmongers or tackle shops.

• Most anglers use a whole squid, especially for big fish such as cod, conger or tope. This will require a pennel rig – two hooks on the same hook snood. There are all manner of variations that you can use but one of the most common is to slide a 3/0 onto the trace line. You then tie on a 6/0 to the end. Put the point of the big hook through the squid's body so the point is buried inside. Push the rest of the hook inside the body. Using a pair of forceps, work the hook down through the squid and pull it out of the opening by the head. Now pass the point of that hook through the eyes. Pull the second hook down so that the point sits just above the end of the body. Wrap the trace line round the hook three times and simply pass the point through the tail of the squid. Take hold of the large hook and slowly pull the trace line above the second hook to tighten everything.

• For smaller species – especially sole – you'll need much smaller strips that have been cut from the main body of the squid. Cut off the head, then cut through one side of the body. Open the squid out, remove all the innards, and cut strips about three inches long and around half an inch wide. To hook up, simply put the hook through one end of these strips.

• For species such as rays, a half squid is a preferred compromise. Simply cut the squid in half and use either the head or the tail section.

• Strips of squid with rag and lugworm make excellent cocktails. The squid makes a superb visual attractor and also helps a soft worm stay on the hook during casting.

• Some anglers stuff the body of squid with enticing titbits such as pieces of peeler crab or mashed up mackerel. Once the body is filled, you whip it with thread or elastic and hook it in the normal fashion. It's best to make these squid parcels at home and then freeze them.

• If you're using frozen squid, make sure you give it time to thaw out naturally. Putting the frozen squid into water simply dissipates the smell and makes them less effective. Any unused, defrosted squid should be thrown away at the end of the trip. It won't refreeze naturally.

• Don't be in too much of a hurry to throw away the head of a squid if you're making strips. It can prove a top bait for smaller fish with its smell and succulence; even mullet may be tempted.

Victoria and Battery piers. Douglas Head is a popular mark for whiting and coleys, especially in the winter. The Loch is popular after heavy winds for dogfish, flatfish and codling. Boat fishing can also be successful. There are some tope, along with good skate and conger.

On the south coast, Port St Mary offers some tremendous and varied sport. For the visitor, you can concentrate on the wrasse from the rocks and the pier. You should also be in luck with flatfish and some mackerel – all accessible from the pier itself. The boat fishing, too, is first rate, with tope, cod, conger and skate. Port St Mary is generally considered the hotspot for sea angling on the island and it fishes well into the winter, with plenty of coalfish down by the front wall. Fish light for the best results.

On the west side of the island, Peel offers another hotspot. It fishes well during the holiday season, from both the beach and the breakwater. Expect mackerel and all manner of flatfish, along with some dogfish. There is rock fishing available and this offers good pollack fishing. In the winter, the breakwater also yields plenty of coalfish and the promenade is good after a spell of north-westerly winds, again for coalfish and a few flounder. These can be of good size.

Situated near the northern tip of the island is the famous Manx match. To find this, take the A10 from Ramsey to Bride and turn right at the roundabout close to the church. Move onto the A16 and head for the Point of Ayr. Look for the landfill tip and you will find a track that leads down to the car-park. This is generally regarded as the best match venue on the Isle of Man, especially in the summer months. It is popular for locals and visitors alike. Dogfish are one of the main target species here. It's rumoured that you're going to have to expect at least five fish an hour to be in with a chance of winning! The best fishing is at low water and this avoids struggling with the strong tides that move round the Point of Ayr itself. During the summer, especially early on, the fisherman can also expect a few bull huss. These are rare, but reach double figures when you find them.

Accommodation – contact the Isle of Man Tourist Department on 01624 686766 for more details on the wide variety of accommodation.

Tackle shops – tackle shops will provide bait and information on the best skippers. Contact Hobby Time on 01624 625720, Intersport on 01624 674444 and the Tackle Box on 01624 836343 at Foxdale. Phone the Ramsey Warehouse on 01624 813092 for information on competitions and up-to-the-minute advice on bait and methods.

Sea-fishing Sites in Scotland

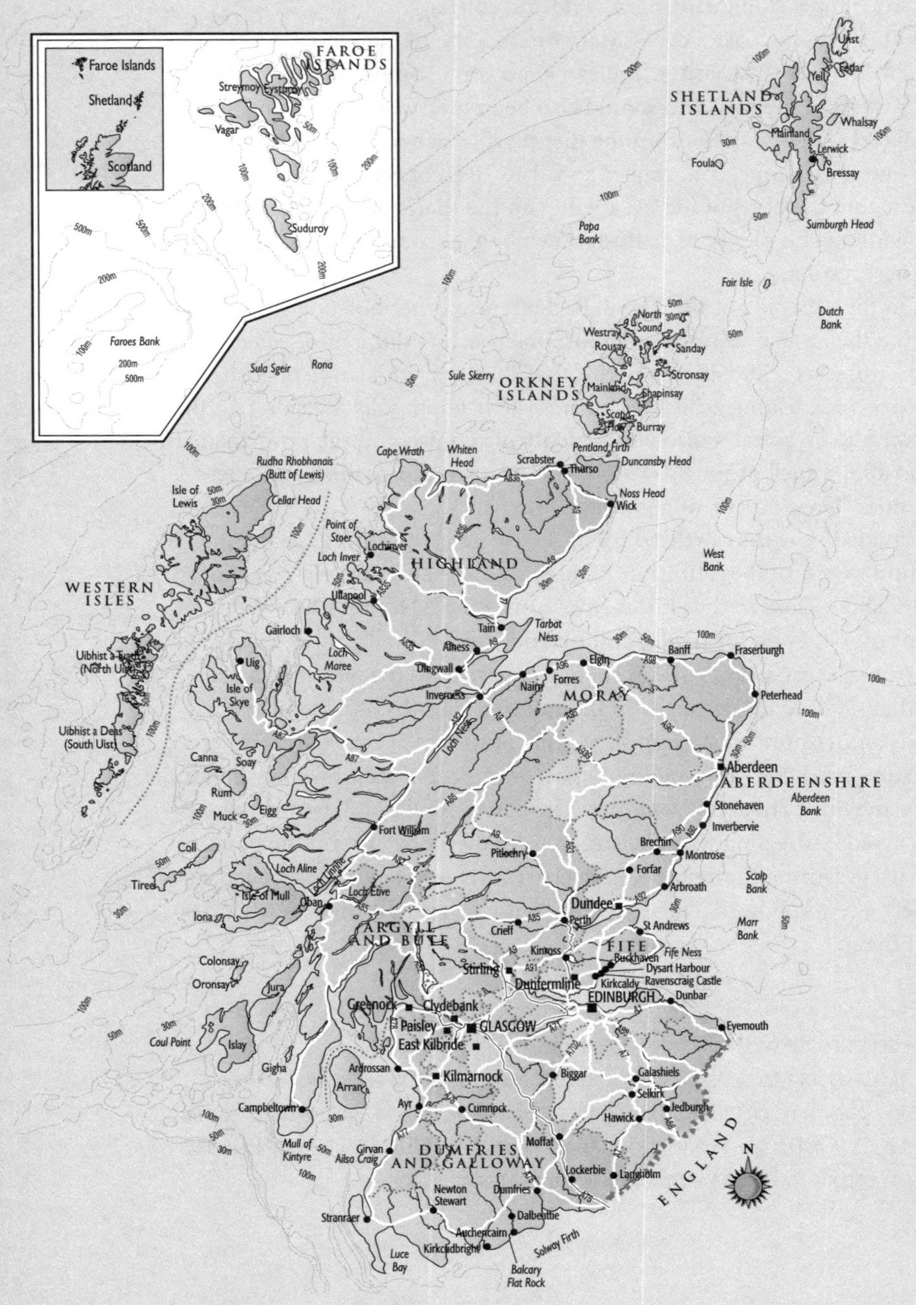

"I never realised before moving up here twenty or so years ago how immense the Scottish sea-fishing scene actually is. You've got a huge, heavily indented coastline with a never-ending number of bays, rocky headlands, sea lochs, wrecks, islands, sandy beaches, fertile worm beds – just about everything imaginable. Add to that the warm waters of the Gulf Stream and the very cold depths of the far north and it really does have an almost frightening amount on offer. To my mind, there are all sorts of sea fishing that you can target. First of all, there's all the general sort of angling available – great cod, pollack and haddock. After that you've got the truly magnificent fish – the fish of your dreams perhaps. For example, huge skate from places such as Loch Aline, giant porbeagles off the north coast and there is even a rumour of blue-fin tuna coming back along the shores of the north west. These are big fish that can barely be matched anywhere else in the world."

CHRISTOPHER WEST, EX-FISHERY SCIENTIST, NORTH UIST

I couldn't agree more with Christopher but, in my own experience, there is another aspect of sea fishing round Scotland that he hasn't covered – light-line fishing. You can fish for bass and sea trout in innumerable rocky coves, both on the mainland and out on the islands themselves. You will also find wrasse amongst the kelp and the rocks. There are even large shoals of mullet that patrol many areas throughout the summer. These can be very big fish indeed, even this far north, and, like the bass and the sea trout, demand a specialised, thoughtful approach. So, you can catch mackerel off a summertime pier, stalk bass in crystal-clear sea pools or set out on a serious boat in the depths of winter for a porbeagle shark, weighing anything in excess of 500 pounds. When it comes to sea fishing, Scotland really does have the lot.

Balcary Flat Rock

Let's start with a look at the well-known Balcary Flat Rock, near Auchencairn on the west coast. This is a great area for the visiting angler, and the village of Auchencairn is a timeless little place that is loved by visitors. It's a typical old fishing village that was once a centre for serious smuggling activities. Nowadays the money of the village comes from bed and breakfast rather than imported rum.

To find Balcary Flat Rock, take the Solway coast road (the A711) out of Dalbeattie. In a few miles, you will come to the coastal village of Auchencairn. Turn left at the War Memorial and follow the signs for the Balcary Bay Hotel. Go down a single-track road until you come to the hotel car-park. From here, go right and you will see a signpost for Balcary Point and Rascarrel. It is a fifteen–twenty minute walk from there to the mark, through fields and countryside. You will then see the Flat Rock itself, with its wooden monument. The pathway down to the Rock isn't too difficult and you will find comfortable fishing into deep water and over clear ground. The easiest fishing is at slack water – during the ebb and flow strong currents can prove a problem. Locals fish this area in the winter, often during tough weather, for cod, but, as a visitor, I'd suggest great caution. This is very much a place for the summer angler to enjoy some stunning scenery.

The winter cod can really be something special – double-figure fish are not uncommon – but let's forget these for the moment and bear the visitor in mind. Spring sees some thornback rays but, as the weather warms, anything can take the bait. You can expect flatfish (including flounder, plaice and dab), bull huss and dogfish. There are also some very good conger around. Big bunches of lobworm are an obvious favourite for the winter cod. In the summer, smaller worm baits will pick up the flatfish. Mackerel is a good bait for the conger and the thornback.

The Rock is the prime mark in the area but there are other rocky points about that all demand a bit of investigation.

Accommodation – contact the Tourist Information Centre in Dumfries on 01387 253862.

Tackle shops – the local tackle shops are McCowan's in Dalbeattie on 01556 610270 and Mitchell's in Kirkcudbright on 01557 330426. There's also a sea-angling club in Kirkcudbright; contact Stewart Ross on 01557 330845.

Oban

Let's now look at a real jewel, the Argyllshire town of Oban. This is a fabulous town set amongst stunning scenery. It's a world of glens,

forests, lochs and streams, and, of course, amazing sea fishing. Oban buzzes with charter-boat traffic. It's an area of hugely deep water and many, many islands. The Sound of Mull, the Firth of Lorne, Innish, Back Islands – legendary places. The common skate hereabouts grow to 200 pounds or more, making Oban the skate centre of Europe. Mind you, there's an awful lot more on offer – thornback, ling, doggies, spur dog, conger, cod, tope, even a few hake. Get out to the islands and drift close to the rocks and you'll even start picking up some tremendous ballan wrasse. Expect pollack in deeper water and, throughout the high summer months, big runs of mackerel.

But let's have a look at what makes Oban truly great – the skate. Most of the skate fishing takes place over very deep water – expect to be fishing a hundred yards plus. There is water going down to more than double that and that's sometimes where the very biggest fish live. So you'll have a real fight on your hands.

March, April and May seem to be the best months for the really huge fish, which show up on neap tides. But it's all in the lap of the gods. You can charter a boat for a week and get nowhere near fish, especially if you're looking at south-westerly or north-easterly winds.

You'll need a fifty-pound plus rod – some people prefer eighty pounds – and a serious multiplier. Most skippers swear by star drag, as opposed to lever drag, over such deep water. One thing you'll definitely need is a butt pad. A shoulder harness is also advisable. Think in terms of a 250-pound six- or eight-foot mono trace and a 10/0 hook. Two pounds of lead is the norm, but you can double that in a strong tide.

Bait? Some people swear by pollack, but probably all you'll need are a few mackerel. Whole fish are best. Bites are signalled by a prolonged bouncing of the rod tip. Reel in, tighten up and you are about to embark on a gruelling fight. Andy Nicholson has compared it to bringing up a cement mixer! Certainly, it can be heartbreaking to winch a big fish close to the surface, only to have it dive unstoppably back to the depths once again. It's not a task to be undertaken lightly.

Conservation is now a big issue all round Scotland. Photograph your fish certainly, but then make sure it goes back alive. Under no circumstances are these skate to be killed. They might seem thick on the ground, but this is a very specialised and comparatively small environment and the tagging programme seems to suggest that there are not as many fish as one might have originally thought.

ACCOMMODATION – there's a huge amount of accommodation in the Oban area, but two places that are very welcoming to anglers are the Strathnaver Guesthouse on 01631 563305 and the Arbour Bed and Breakfast on 01631 563393. For further information on accommodation, skippers and everything to do with this fabulous area, contact the Tourist Information Board on 01631 563122.

TACKLE SHOPS – try the Anglers' Corner in Oban on 01631 566374.

LOCH ETIVE

Before leaving Oban, let's look at just one more ace up the town's sleeve. The worst wind for the Oban charter boats comes from the north east. This can cause problems as heavy weather begins to hit Loch Linnhe from the direction of Fort William. There is, however, a way round this and local skipper Ronnie Campbell has the answer. He takes his boat up from Oban and heads into the sheltered Loch Etive. This is quite an operation and involves a hair-raising journey over the reef beneath the Connel Bridge. The water can really race out here, so timing is absolutely critical.

Loch Etive is quite a place – a bit of a conundrum for the traditional sea angler. A large part of the loch holds fresh water and, indeed, rainbow trout are actually farmed there. However, as freshwater is less dense, it tends to float on top of the seawater that lies beneath. So, you have a typical Scottish freshwater loch on the surface, but look deeper and you'll find some fantastic sea fishing. Spur dog exist in large numbers, especially in the deeper parts. There are some huge conger, good thornback, cod and pollack. Interestingly, there are hake present as well – not very many, but some very good fish.

Most of those in the know fish quite heavy, generally using braid rather than nylon. This obviously gives greater bite sensitivity and also helps get a fish up from the bottom more quickly. This can be important. The fish population of Loch Etive is a delicately balanced one and Ronnie insists on the vast majority of any catch going back very quickly. The sooner any fish is allowed to return to the depths, the greater its chance of survival.

ACCOMMODATION – see the entry for Oban.

TACKLE SHOPS – contact the Angler's Corner in Oban on 01631 566374.

BOAT HIRE – for charter boats, contact Ronnie Campbell and Donald McClean on 01631 750213 or Adrian Louder on 01631 720262.

GAIRLOCH

Gairloch is a wondrous place, very close to the magical Loch Maree. This is a marvellous area for a family holiday and the fishing, too, is

good. There's plenty of sheltered water close in, offering cod, haddock, mackerel in the summer, pollack and even thornback. There's great fishing to be had further out.

ACCOMMODATION – the Tourist Information Office on 01445 712130 can advise on accommodation in the area.

TACKLE SHOPS – contact West Highland Marine Boats on 01445 712458.

BOAT HIRE – contact West Highland Marine Boats (see above).

ULLAPOOL

Now we move on up to Ullapool. This, again, is a remote and challenging area, with some extraordinary possibilities. In fact, prominent members of the Angling Writer's Association recently set out from Ullapool on one of the most remarkable of fishing quests. They had information that very big broad bill and great white shark had been seen by commercial net men, some sixty to seventy miles offshore. Great whites are not too concerned about water temperature, as food is the key to their lifestyle. And for food, read seals, especially in the pupping season. The trip, however, was not a success. Any quest like this is heavily dependent on the weather conditions and the winds just blew and blew. Mind you, every great challenge like this takes time and the information they came back with was certainly promising. There is a feeling that white shark are out there to be caught.

For an adventure such as this, you will obviously need the right boat for the job, a skipper with the requisite amount of knowledge and, importantly, the right window in the weather.

ACCOMMODATION – contact the local Tourist Board on 01854 612135.

TACKLE SHOPS – contact Ardmair Point Boat Centre on 01854 612054.

BOAT HIRE – contact Ardmair Point Boat Centre (see above).

LOCHINVER

Moving up the coast, we come to the busy coastal fishing village of Lochinver. This picturesque little village is perched on the edge of some of the most remarkable scenery of the northern Highlands. The port itself is an absolute hive of activity as boats come and go with their precious cargoes. The fish market really is a sight to behold.

Looking out to sea from Lochinver, you will see Loch Inver in the foreground, which provides a sheltered location for the angler. Lochinver is a spectacular two-hour drive from Inverness.

ACCOMMODATION – contact the Lochinver Tourist Board on 01571 844330.
TACKLE SHOPS – try the Loch Inver Fish Selling Company on 01571 844228
BOAT HIRE – contact the Loch Inver Fish Selling Company (see above).

THURSO

Let's move now onto the north coast and Thurso. Thurso is situated on the north shore of Pentland Firth, and boasts excellent visitor services for the whole family.

Most boat activity goes out of Scrabster and it was from here that my good friend, Chris Bennett, made history back in the 1990s. Chris is of the old school of sportsmen – a man with huge imagination, colossal dedication and absolutely no fear. Chris talked constantly to the commercial fishermen of the area and began to realise with greater and greater conviction that the Gulf Stream was bringing huge porbeagle along the north coast of Scotland at certain times of the year. His dedication to the job in hand was enormous. Trip after trip was thwarted by appalling weather conditions but Chris persevered, putting up with the six-hour round journey each day back to his home in the great glen.

At last, Chris was successful and after an extraordinary fight of over three hours boated a porbeagle of over 500 pounds. See what I mean about the dramatic side of Scottish sea fishing!

ACCOMMODATION – contact the Thurso Tourist Board on 01847 892371.
TACKLE SHOPS – visit Harper's Tackle Shop in the High Street, on 01847 893179.
BOAT HIRE – Harper's Tackle Shop (see above) can advise on boat hire.

ORKNEYS, FAROES AND THE WESTERN ISLES

All the islands offer sea fishing of tremendous quality and Orkney, especially, is famous for its huge skate and halibut. And if we want to go even more into the wilds how about the Faroes? These islands were once part of Denmark, but now they are self-governing. They have their own fishery policy and that means a 200-mile limit.

The islands have also got something called the Faroes Bank, one of the most famous cod marks in the entire world. There's no commercial fishing allowed on it, just long-lining and jigging, and even then it gets rested for long intervals. The result – some extraordinary sport with cod of a size unknown in the United Kingdom.

A couple of years ago Bob Brownless mounted his first trip to the Faroes Bank. His team flew from Aberdeen to the islands in the first week of May and then boarded a restored wooden-hold fishing smack, over a

WHITING TIPS

Although other parts of the UK probably enjoy greater numbers of whiting, there are parts of Scotland that see some very good specimens caught – though not often in huge numbers.

• Possibly the best bait is lugworm, tipped off with squid. Alternatively, try a strip of mackerel doused in pilchard oil.

• Whiting and frost are often linked together. This is probably because frost coincides with calm weather – favourite whiting conditions.

• Whiting are nocturnal feeders and come close inshore with the onset of darkness.

• Whiting are bottom feeders, so make sure that you get your bait down deep. This is very important.

• Autumn and early winter often see a major migration of shrimp along the UK shoreline. At this time, shrimp is a great bait for whiting.

• Watch the tiny, needle-sharp teeth of the whiting. Use a disgorger or you'll find yourself with many small, painful cuts.

• The best period for whiting is probably between October and January – they're certainly at their fittest then.

• Whiting don't put up much of a fight on heavy gear simply because of their size. If you can, pursue them with carp gear, or even coarse float-fishing tackle from a boat.

• Whiting may appear numerous but we can dent the stocks if we take away unreasonable amounts. Leave the bin liners at home and only take what you can reasonably eat at a sitting.

• If there are a lot of whiting around, it often pays to go for a multi-hook one-up-one-down rig. It's not a bad idea to use a strong hook, however, in case you're fortunate enough to hit into a cod.

• If you're getting lots of small bites, which are typical of the whiting, leave the rod alone and let the bite develop into a positive pull. If you're using two hooks, you'll often get two fish at a time.

• If you're worried about hitting the bites, use lighter tackle. A light bass rod will really show the bites up with startling clarity.

• If you catch a two-pound whiting from the shore, you can be a proud angler. A four-pounder from a boat is really something to tell the world about and if you get anything approaching seven pounds, then it's worth checking the record books!

• Whiting are very widespread and are caught from Norway as far south as Gibraltar.

hundred years' old, complete with refitted diesel engine and two masts.

It's about six hours sailing to the Faroes Bank and the lads weren't disappointed. The cod came out in endless numbers and to a really serious size. Many fish of over thirty pounds were taken, although the general feeling was that they had left it just a little bit too late in the year. Probably prime time is February, when the huge females gather on the Faroes Bank to spawn. Bob and his group were predominantly catching males – but of an amazing size. Certainly, in February and March, cod of fifty and even sixty pounds are well on the cards. Fifty-pound outfits are recommended for creatures like this, set up with conventional perch rigs. Big reels are advised – especially over the deeper areas that can go down a hundred yards or more.

There are many other species available on the Faroes Bank – Bob tells me that they landed twenty-three in that one trip alone! Halibut, too, are the thing. Monstrous creatures reaching well over 300 pounds!

The weather, of course, is the key. Bob's initial outing was brought to a swift end by the appearance of a force eleven cyclone! They simply upped and left and spent a very uncomfortable six hours getting back to land. Was it worth it? No-one who has ever been out to the Faroes Bank can ever doubt that, and Bob is more than willing to keep putting groups together to sample what is possibly the best boat fishing anywhere in Europe. I'd give it a go!

But not all the fishing on the islands is done with eighty-pound gear and shoulder harnesses. One of my own favourite destinations is the island of North Uist, easily accessed by car ferry from Oban or Skye or even more quickly by plane from Glasgow.

Uist has a wonderful feel to it – it's like going back to a land forgotten. It's generally low-lying, but there are impressive hills and the inland trout fishing is spectacular.

It is for the bass that you ought to think about Uist. One of the real beauties of the place is that hardly anyone ever fishes for them. One or two locals are in on the secret but, by and large, you'll have this island and its amazing complex of creeks and tidal pools to yourself. Of course, you've got to check out the fishing rights – this is prime sea trout and salmon territory and not all the waters are open. The hotels will be able to advise you.

The bass aren't always large, but they are prolific and they can be taken easily on the fly – very exciting. It's wild, untamed stuff and you really feel like a pioneer. There are also plenty of wrasse found close to the shore in amongst the kelp beds.

ACCOMMODATION – contact the Orkney Tourist Board in Kirkwall on 01856 872856 for further details on accommodation and boat hire in the Northern Isles. In North Uist, try the Loch Maddie Hotel on 01876 500331 or the Langass Lodge Hotel on 01876 580285.

TACKLE SHOPS – contact the Orkney Tourist Board (above) or the Western Isles Tourist Centre in North Uist on 01876 500321.

BOAT HIRE – for trips to the Faroe Islands, contact Bob Brownless at Bobsport on 01313 326607.

ABERDEENSHIRE

Moving south towards Aberdeen you will meet with a stern, unremitting coastline that, in truth, doesn't do a great deal for the visiting summer tourist. This is more a land of strenuous cod fishing during the winter months. The area demands a really positive approach – and that's putting it mildly – especially when north-easterly winds thrash the shoreline.

Stonehaven, which has several boats covering good rough ground, produces cod, plaice, haddock and ling. There are also some wrecks that can produce very good cod fishing.

Further south, one of the best places to look at is Inverbervie, which is one of the really notorious cod marks on the Aberdeenshire coast. It's got a lot going for it. The beach is only about a quarter of a mile long, but it's an end-to-end hotspot, with some good, deep water very close in. Moreover, there are no problems with accessibility. The beach is very close to the main street and you can almost fish from the car itself – something that makes it popular with visitors and locals alike, especially in tough weather, which is frequent. Big gales obviously dislodge a lot of food and attract good cod – often into double figures – in close. However, you've got to be wary of your own safety and look out for heavy swells or dislodged shingle. Really heavy water can cause a problem with uprooted weed as well. Perhaps it is best – for fishing and for safety – to concentrate on the back end of bad weather.

The cod season starts in early November generally and runs through to February, with the mid-period usually considered the best. Of course, it's all weather-dependent and you do need rough weather to get those fish moving and feeding close in. Don't worry too much about night fishing – daytime can also be good, especially on the last three hours of the flood and an hour over the top. Go for big baits and tackle suited for a very tough job indeed.

ACCOMMODATION – contact Tourist Information in Stonehaven on 01569 762806.

TACKLE SHOPS – contact Fraser's Fishing Tackle in Aberdeen on 01224 590211.

BOAT HIRE – contact A. Troup on 01569 62892, A. Mackenzie on 01569 63511, W. Lawson on 01569 63565 and J. Lobban on 01569 65323.

Searching out the Bass

In Scotland, you may well find yourself on your own when it comes to fishing for bass. All that shoreline, with hardly any anglers, should be a delight – but where on earth do you start?

• Bass feed on prawns, shrimps, sand eels, crabs, worms, small fish and so on, so look for areas where foodstuff is likely to live.

• Favourite areas are big rock outcrops. These give cover and protection for the foodstuffs we're talking about.

• Look also for weed patches on large boulders – very good starting points.

• Big rock pools hold all the foodstuffs we've just mentioned when they are stranded by the falling tide. Bass will look for these areas as the water begins to seep in again.

• Look for seemingly insignificant inlets between steep-sided cliffs. These are important collecting points for food items. The cliffs themselves provide cover for the bass.

• Look for areas of shallow, muddy or sandy water where worms thrive. Bass like warm water and shallows heat up quickly.

• Watch for areas where the tide's current is at the strongest and the waves are more turbulent – this is where bass will find their food.

• You'll need to do most of your searching at low tide. Take a pencil and pad with you so you can make a quick map of all the promising points that you find.

• Always check the tide table before going out to look for new marks. Leave for high ground the very moment the tide starts to come in and make sure that it doesn't cut you off.

• Don't go out if it's wet. Weeds and boulders can turn to glass under moisture. Watch out for dangerous holes and crevices.

• Avoid steep cliffs. Look for a safe way down or forget them altogether.

• Try not to go out alone – it's important to have a friend with you for safety's sake.

• Try to get out on dawn or dusk tides when the weather is calm. You sometimes see bass hunting on the surface.

• Take a pair of binoculars with you at such times so that you can scan large areas of coastline.

• Take as little gear as possible when fishing. That way you are very mobile and can search out as much new territory as possible.

• If you can find local advice, use that as a starting point and add your own experiences to it as you go.

FIFESHIRE

Let's move down the coast now to Fife, an area that offers really good sea- fishing opportunities, especially to those holidaying in Edinburgh. The capital, of course, is a stunning city, with plenty of restaurants, shopping, and places of historical interest.

North of Edinburgh, but well within driving distance, we come to Dysart Harbour. This is an appealing place and has the advantage of the piers that surround the harbour, an area that gives good access. For the visitor, you'll find some quite good mackerel fishing through July and August. It's not a long season, but the fish can be prolific. There are also some good flounder available, although the very big fish tend to show up from September onwards. This, however, is a popular mark for locals in the winter when the codling fishing can be excellent, along with a better class of flounder. For the mackerel, try lightish spinning tackle first. You might need quite a heavy lure to cast a decent distance. The fish often do hang further out. For flounder in the summer, try to get crabs if you can – very much a favourite here. You'll find plenty of parking available around the harbour.

Ravenscraig Castle is also a good centre on the Fife coast and just south of there you'll find Kirkcaldy. As on much of the Fife coastline, you'll find a lot of broken ground here, with some rough patches. These are the marks where the locals target cod throughout the autumn and winter. You'll run up against some bass and quite a number of flounder in the summer. So watch out for snags and use a rotten bottom to avoid constant, complete break-offs.

ACCOMMODATION – contact the Tourist Information Centre in Kirkcaldy on 01592 267775.

TACKLE SHOPS – in Kirkcaldy, try We're Game on 01592 654301 and Spike's Plaice on 01592 597231, and in Buckhaven, try Intersport on 01592 712480.

Sea-fishing Sites in North-East England

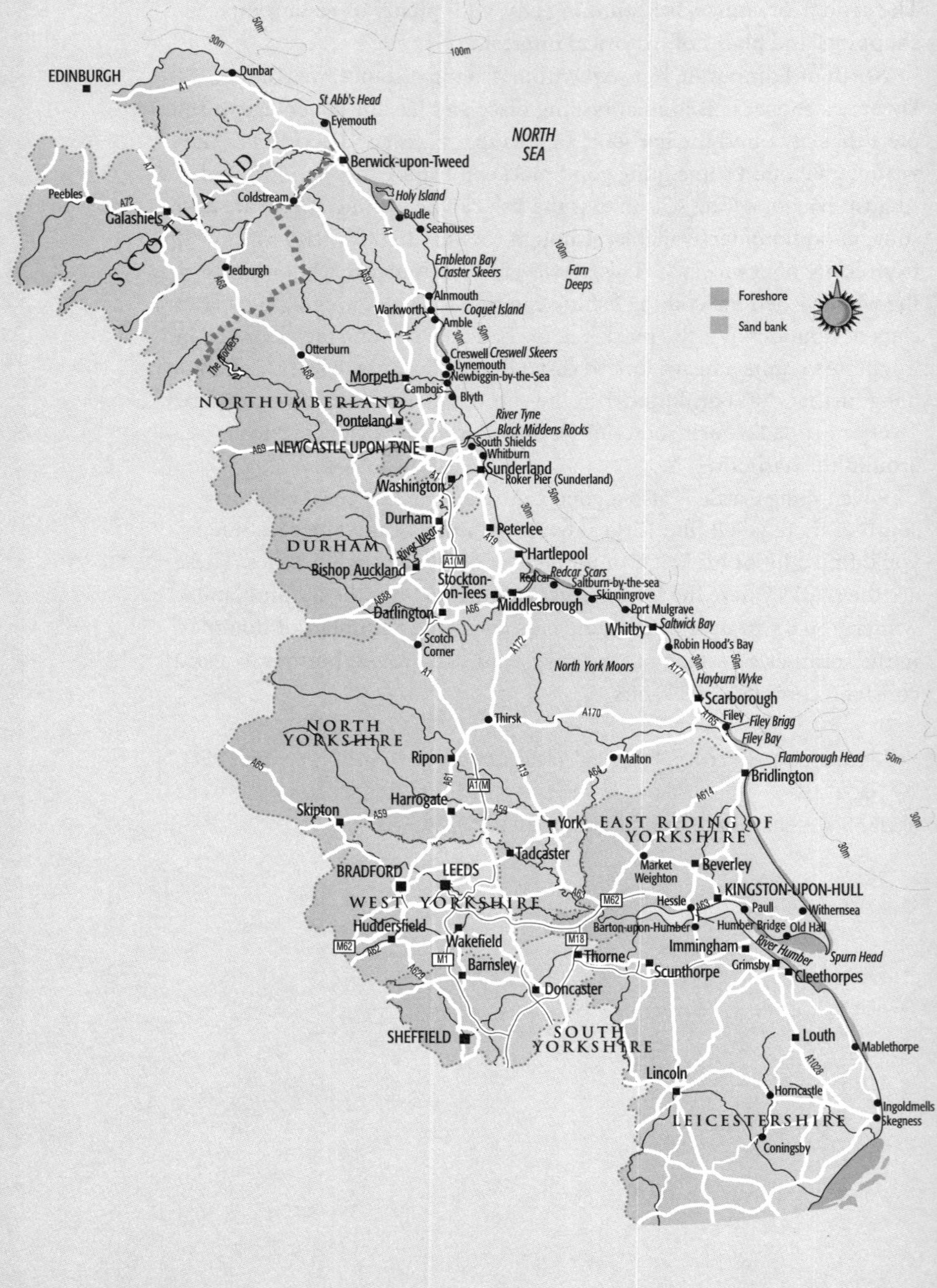

"The future up here is really buoyant for both shore and charter fishing. We're going through a real boom time and seem to be doing a lot better than many, if not most, places. We hardly ever experience total blanks. There are times when we absolutely bag up with codling, along with some coleys and pollack. The winter shore fishing, too, is magnificent. If you get the slightest bit of wind, this coast is second to none. All the beaches fish with a sea on. You can catch off sandy beaches with anything like a wind, otherwise look out for the rock ends amongst the kelp beds. Expect fish between two and eight pounds, with the bigger fish coming off the shore with the sea running. I recently went out with a friend and we caught ten fish of between two and a half and nine pounds, all on cocktails of white worm, lug and crab. I ought to add that the summer fishing is increasingly good. However, this seems to be a sport reserved for the visitors – historically, fishermen up here aren't sport anglers, but simply fish for the pot. I guess they need a bit of education as to what total sea fishing is all about."

BOB WHITE, AMBLE SKIPPER AND TACKLE SHOP OWNER

The north east has traditionally been a coast for hard men, guys who work long hours and who feel they can justify their sport if they take home some fresh fish for the table. Fine, but history can be re-written and, as Bob says, the summer sport along this coastline is coming along in leaps and bounds. There used to be the odd bass or two, but now there are plenty between two and even five or six pounds. You can get them on float-fished or legered ragworm. A lot come from the beaches on bait intended for flatfish. There are even mullet now as well. In fact, commercial net men say they get as many mullet as salmon and sea trout. So, whether it's winter codling or summer bass and mullet that you want to target, this is a real up-and-coming area.

Berwick-upon-Tweed

The area from Berwick-upon-Tweed to St Abbs Head is well known for codling. You'll also pick up great bags of cod, pollack, ling and wrasse off shore. Berwick-upon-Tweed itself is a great town for holidaying, full of romance, history and natural beauty. It sits just south of the Scottish border, proudly and defiantly offering a whole lot to the sea angler.

If you go out of the town towards the north, you will find high cliffs and rugged rocks everywhere. Moving south, you will find some rock and also plenty of sandy beaches. If you're thinking of shore fishing, the rocks offer some very good wrasse and, at times, you will find both bass and mullet.

If you can bring your own boat up, then you'll be in for some great sport offshore. Contact the Harbour Master, Captain Peter Blanche, on 01289 307404 for details of the local slipway, which is on the southern side of the Tweed close to the lifeboat station.

Accommodation – contact the local Tourist Board in Berwick-upon-Tweed on 01289 330733.

Tackle shops – contact Gamefare on 01289 305119.

Boat hire – contact David Thompson, skipper of *On A Promise*, on 01289 302749.

North Northumbria

The extreme north east, south of Berwick, is fertile ground for cod, flatfish and coleys. Holy Island, Budle and Seahouses all offer some great fishing. Embleton Bay produces cod, flounder and pollack. Try evening tides in particular. Try Warkworth for flatfish on rag, lug and strips of fish. Night fishing on the beach is especially productive for cod and codling.

However, Amble, one of the jewels of the Northumberland coast, is particularly worth a try. Amble has a commercial history and the harbour was built back in early Victorian times to convey coal from the local mines. The port was closed in the 1960s as the coal industry declined, but later years have seen a great deal of development. A marina and an active boatyard all give the impression of a bustling town that is going places.

Amble has a reputation for boat fishing and large catches of cod. One of the great bonuses of the place is that you don't have to steam for hours to find the fishing grounds. The cod come in close, indeed you can find them on the doorstep. Expect big catches of cod at good times of the year, especially if the season is half kind. It's not unusual for a boat to take over a hundred fish.

You'll also be catching coalfish, pouting, wrasse, ling and, possibly, some mackerel. So you can expect a good mixed bag and some good close-in fishing. The best-known local marks are Cresswell Skeers, Craster Skeers, Coquet Island and North and South Bay.

Amble is also a centre for some tremendous bass fishing. North-East England isn't renowned for the species but Amble is a great place to start for this most desirable of fish. You probably won't be getting super-big specimens, but, with a good number of fish between three and four pounds, this is hardly an issue. Look for them north of the town, all the way to Alnmouth. You can fish for them from the shore, and try fishing at low tide with ragworm. You'll also pick up flounder, turbot and dab, which are prolific in the area. The exposed South Pier at Amble also produces smaller fish, especially in rougher weather – if you can take the exposure! Cliff House and the paddling pool promenade behind the pier also give plenty of bass, especially during the summer time. Try crab for the best results.

Amble is also one of the best areas for mackerel fishing along the north east. The South Pier has always been a focus for mackerel, and though results aren't anything like what they used to be in the past, it is still well worth the effort. Look for the flattest possible seas and an early morning or evening high tide. Try using float-fished mackerel strips, feathers or just single spinners. If there are a lot of fish and you don't want to take that many, snip off a couple of the hook points to make return much easier. Be conservation-minded, and make sure that all fish that aren't required for eating or bait are returned at once and as gently as possible. Stocks are on the way back, so let's not deplete them.

Amble is also a major centre for open competitions. The big one, the Amble Open, takes place early in the year and has in the past attracted up to a 1000 competitors. However, there are many club matches fished around Amble during the summer months, which always prove an additional attraction for the visitor.

Perhaps Amble rings a bell with you… Well, it was in the national news back in the late 1990s with Freddie the dolphin – an enchanting creature that made its way to the area, liked what it saw and decided to stay for a while. He soon became something of a local celebrity and the local boatmen, always with an eye to a profit, began taking tourists out for a viewing. I suppose the fact that Freddie stuck around speaks volumes about the amount of fish available in the area.

Moving south, Druridge Bay fishes well for flatfish, codling and the odd bass. Cresswell, Lynemouth, Newbiggin and Cambois are all worth visits. Expect several species, notably the occasional big cod.

Accommodation – there's a wide variety in the area – phone the Tourist Information Centre in Amble on 01665 712313.

TACKLE SHOPS – Amble Angling Centre, 4 Newburgh Street, Amble on 01665 711200 is a mine of information, with excellent tackle and bait available. Boat trips can also be arranged from the shop.

BOAT HIRE – try Bob White on 01665 711200, Micky Potts on 01665 575731, Jim Kelly on 01665 711008, Dave Builth on 01665 712561 or Andy Toward on 0191 2863848. If you're in the area on holiday, it might be worth contacting David Grey on 01665 712313 – he takes trips to the Cockett Island Bird Reserve every day. The island is famous for its puffins, eider duck and flocks of terns.

BLYTH

Blyth is our next port of call – a once thriving port and still a major centre for sea fishing. The Blyth estuary and river are both very heavily fished throughout the summer and winter alike – a good area for experienced anglers and beginners. The port itself is protected from the north-east side by the Cambois Pier, now out of bounds for anglers but still offering protection from severe north-easterlies. The South Pier, however, is open to anglers and is a good fishing area, both in daylight and darkness. It has wooden piles and you can catch by either dropping down or distance casting. You get to the pier through the south harbour – just a five-minute walk. Expect cod and coalfish in the winter, with some good plaice during May and June. You will find it very busy in July and August when the schools break up and the mackerel arrive in even greater numbers than the children! You'll pick mackerel up between one and two pounds, on either light spinning tackle or float fishing with a smidgen of fish strip for bait. Expect good sport at high water, dawn and dusk.

Peeping Tom's Rocks, just inside the mouth of the Blyth estuary, is a favourite area. It is only accessible two and a half hours either side of low water by means of the small beach. Make sure you get your timings right. When you're casting from the rocks, the bait will go straight into the river's main channel. The fish feed well when the water is on the move, especially from dusk into darkness. Expect large shoals of coalfish through the autumn and winter, with a few codling.

The Blyth Quayside is located very near the centre of Blyth itself and you can actually drive to the area, making it popular with the casual fisherman and just about everyone else when the river is foul.

Bate's Jetty, actually composed of a series of wooden jetties, is also a favourite area and makes casting into the main channel easy. You will find the area down a small dirt track behind the Golden Fleece pub. You've only got to cast fifteen yards or so and you'll be in the main channel, once again amongst big numbers of codling and coalfish.

It's also worth looking at the area between the marina up to Black Bridge. This constitutes the upper reaches of the Blyth, which, at low water, is a network of mudflats and channels. It's best fished in the summer for flounder and eels. High water is the best time. The fish that live in the inaccessible channels now fan out over the mudflats feeding hard. Fish light with worm or peeler crab to get the best of the sport.

ACCOMMODATION – contact the Tourist Information Office in Newcastle on 0191 26?0610.

TACKLE SHOPS – contact Sport and Leisure in Blyth on 01670 365980.

THE RIVER TYNE

On our southward journey, we inevitably come to Newcastle and the River Tyne. Newcastle is a hotbed of enthusiasm – for culture, music, soccer and sea fishing. The town is centre to a major sea-fishing brotherhood and local competitions are phenomenally well attended. The Tyne offers a huge amount of fishing possibilities. The shore fishing at the mouth of the river is made extra special by the two piers that jut out, giving shelter to the inner harbour.

The pier at South Shields is a real favourite, open all year round, apart from during severe weather conditions. It fishes particularly well during the winter, with terrific catches of cod and coalfish. In fact, it's probably the hottest mark in the north east. In summer, the pier is equally popular with youngsters and visitors who catch good numbers of mackerel and launce sand eels. Depending on the weather, these flock the river from July through to the middle of August. Access to the North Pier is much more restricted and is generally only allowed to local clubs for pre-arranged matches. But, if you can get there, expect some very good cod, coalfish and flatfish.

Sticking with the shore fishing, see if you can get to Black Middens Rocks. These constitute a notorious shipping hazard, but at low water they are massively productive for the fisherman. Expect good bags of cod and coalfish, along with some really top quality flounder. For bait, try peeler crab or lugworm.

The lower estuary absolutely bristles with jetties and fishing possibilities. However, as Newcastle's prosperity expands and development marches forwards, the number of jetties open to the angler is necessarily declining. This is, obviously, a great shame, but it does mean that pressure on stocks is more limited. On the north bank of the estuary, the prime area for anglers is the open Fish Quay between the Fish Market and the Ice Store. Look next at the old Smith Docks or the Bergen Quay. You'll pick up the usual bags of cod, coalfish and flounder, along with eels at certain times of the year. This is good fishing, but long casting out into the main channel generally gives the best results. On the south side of the lower estuary, try the Groyne, Mill Dam and the Velva Liquids Jetty.

Don't ignore the upper estuary either. This is particularly productive during the summer for flounder and eels. Newcastle Quayside has been renovated with anglers in mind and there is a mass of fishing opportunities. The Walker Riverside Park is also a hot area – watch out for abandoned shopping trolleys, however!

For those wishing to go afloat, Newcastle-upon-Tyne is a real haven. The port is home to any number of experienced charter skippers who have been working the inshore waters and the offshore wrecks for their entire lives. You'll generally be offered an inshore trip, going some twelve miles out. Alternatively, you may like to try a trip to the Graveyard, which is three times the distance. The skippers know which is best at any one particular time, so be guided by them. There's a proliferation of wrecks out there. Be warned though – they're all home to monster fish.

Moving further south, Whitburn is a delightful small village situated between Newcastle and Sunderland, but still maintaining a pleasant, rural feel to it. The fishing can also be good, especially for codling and the odd bigger cod.

Accommodation – accommodation is widespread, as you'd expect in such a large area. The nearest Tourist Information Office can be contacted on 0191 2610610.

Tackle shops – try Billy's on 0191 2596262, ID Fishing on 0191 2763041, John's Fishing Tackle on 0191 2343412, Reelsports on 0191 4300247, Steve's Tackle on 0191 2579999, Walker Tackle Shop on 0191 2764774, Two Jacks Fishing Tackle on 0191 2345640 and the Country House on 0191 2616669. Apart from selling bait, tackle, clothing and all the necessities, these shops will also advise on local charter skippers.

Boat hire – for direct contacts, try Jim Rutherford on 0191 4832745, George Skinner on 0191 2657288 and Alan Skinner on 0191 2764863.

The River Wear

Inevitably, we now come to Sunderland and the River Wear. There are plenty of piers in the area – four alone around the mouth of the River Wear – and they all offer distinct possibilities. Of them all, perhaps Roker Pier, the most northerly one, is the favourite simply because it offers tremendous sport summer and winter alike. It's a popular venue throughout the season, but is especially patronised during the autumn and winter codding. But, for the summer tourist, there's plenty of activity with dab, plaice and flounder, especially when you cast into

the harbour side of the breakwater. Summer also sees mackerel shoals coming in – great fun on light spinners or feathers. If you really enjoy mackerel fishing – and who doesn't – try float fishing for them on coarse gear with perhaps just a sliver of fish as bait. Use four-pound line or so and you will certainly have a fight to remember.

In the winter, lugworm is the top bait for the cod, but peeler crab works well throughout the year – if you can get it that is! Another local tip is to fish for the prolific whiting with lugworm that has been tipped with a trace of squid or mackerel.

Just a word of caution: towards the end of the pier you will come across quite a few snags so it's wise to fish with a rotten bottom so you can pull easily for a break. There's also a difficult area halfway along called the Barrier. However, this area of rock and weed produces some of the best fish! Isn't that always the case?

The pier offers free fishing but it is closed during severe weather conditions, generally in winter. You will find a free car-park close by, along with a pub and café serving refreshments.

ACCOMMODATION – accommodation isn't quite as prolific as you'll find further up on the Tyne, but there's still a good spread. Phone the Sunderland Tourist Information Office on 0191 5532000/1.

TACKLE SHOPS – the local tackle shop is Rutherford's and they keep a good supply of fresh bait. Contact them on 0191 5654183.

HARTLEPOOL TO SALTBURN-BY-THE-SEA

Moving south again, Hartlepool is another favourite area, especially for codling. Redcar Scaurs is always worth a try for codling, particularly when the weather is rough. Saltburn-by-the-Sea is one of the major centres of this particular area. This is a serene and small seaside town that really comes to the fore during the winter. It's a major area for both winter cod and, especially, whiting, which come in huge numbers during the autumn. The best spot, by far, is the end of the town's pier. It's not unusual to see catches exceed twenty fish, with some of them being in the two-pound bracket. You'll also pick up the odd flatfish and bass, with mackerel shoaling during the summer.

About a quarter of a mile to the right of the pier, just by the cliffs, you'll come across a patch of rough ground and a deep gully called Penny Hole. This is another top winter mark renowned for holding large cod – some into double figures. Night fishing, as so often, pays dividends, especially at low water when you can get a bait right into the Hole. It's

Rock Fishing

Although the north east is not quite as blessed with rocks as say Devon and Cornwall, there are still good rocky areas, notably Filey Brigg. Rock fishing, however, is a skill all of its own.

• Safety must always govern your choice of venue. Pay particular attention to weather conditions and the state of the tide. If you are a stranger to the area, ALWAYS check with the locals on matters of safety. At best, you might have to sit marooned on a rock for a few hours while the tide recedes. The worst doesn't bear thinking about.

• It's always good to wear flotation aids. In winter, these can help retain body warmth, as well as perhaps saving your life if you should slip.

• Conger eels inhabit rocky areas and you can often catch them close in, especially when the water is coloured after a blow. If your fishing is restricted to daylight hours, go for cloudy days when there's a good wind.

• Calm settled weather is good for wrasse.

• Wrasse are a great rock species – full of fight and startling to look at. You can fish for them with any tough coarse-fishing gear, but a good bass rod often provides extra length and power. Even a three-pound fish takes some subduing. Don't tackle them with less than a twelve-pound line.

• If you're fishing in the rocks for big fish species, don't consider going light. A big multiplier such as the Abu 9000, with two-speed gearing and a tough drag, is the sort of reel you're looking at; thirty-pound line is an absolute minimum. Rods must match – go for powerful tournament casters, not beach rods as these won't give you that added spine.

• Back to safety: make sure that your fishing platform is way above the range of any rogue swell that could come along. Make sure that you can land a fish easily and without danger. Always check that your emergency exit is easily found and accessible – especially in the dark.

• Wherever possible, study your rocks carefully, especially at low water, which gives you a better idea of the ground you're fishing over.

• For the holidaying angler, daylight fishing is the most likely option. This is where wrasse come into their own. Try float fishing for them as this drifts the bait in and out of crevices that legering can't reach. If you're going to fish a static bait on the lead, try touch legering. Bites are generally very bold.

• Wrasse are also very obliging for the holiday angler – they start appearing around most of our shoreline in the late spring and are present throughout the summer. For bait, try either crab or lugworm.

good to watch where the locals are going at this particular time because it's not always easy to locate the gully. Also, ask advice about the tides as it's easy to get cut off. Close to Penny Hole is the Ship pub – an excellent area for bass in the two- to four-pound mark.

To the left of the pier, you will find shallow, sandy flats, which look absolutely featureless but, surprisingly, can pay dividends through the winter. The secret is the sandbank that is located about a hundred yards out, running parallel to the beach. If you can get a bait the other side of this feature you'll hit straight into codling. Expect also some bass – schoolies primarily during the summer, but some big fish through the winter and into early spring. Ten-pounders are not that uncommon.

ACCOMMODATION – contact the Hartlepool Tourist Information Centre on 01429 869706.
TACKLE SHOPS – contact Cairns Angling in Hartlepool on 01429 272581.

SKINNINGROVE

Moving into North Yorkshire, we come to the old industrial town of Skinningrove. This town has a pier built about a hundred years ago at the behest of the local iron and steel industry. Over the years, heavy seas and neglect have destroyed a good part of the pier, and walkers and fishermen can no longer use its entire length. There is still, however, a good amount remaining, and the area around the Gate – the cut-off point – is renowned for flounder, whiting and some big cod. There is year-round sport of the highest quality.

The beach at Skinningrove is also top quality. Flounder and whiting are caught year round on light tackle. Long casting isn't necessary and you'll pick up codling in the late winter and early spring. Lugworm is the killing bait, especially tipped with mussel, squid or mackerel.

Moving further along, you'll come to an area of rocky coastline and the first important mark, Hummersea Steps. This is a well-known area for cod, with some big fish, along with pouting and plenty of rockling.

As a general rule, try to fish the pier in darkness. A spring tide is particularly productive. A north-east or north-west swell also helps matters. Hummersea Steps is a high-water venue, especially in rough conditions when there's a north-westerly blowing.

ACCOMMODATION – contact the Hartlepool Tourist Information Centre on 01429 869706.
TACKLE SHOPS – the local tackle shop, Keith's Sports on 01287 624296, will provide all the information that you're likely to need. It's also worth contacting the Skinningrove Angling Club on 01287 639572 for further information and possible membership.

Port Mulgrave

Just a little way down the coast from Skinningrove, we come to Port Mulgrave, another really fabulous mark. An old and now disused stone jetty is central to the fishing at Port Mulgrave. The jetty is surrounded by rocky outcrops and slate ledges. The whole area is a mass of gullies and heavy weed growth – ideal shelter for fish, crab and all the foodstuffs that make up the diet of cod.

Port Mulgrave fishes best at high water from the jetty or low water from the outcrops themselves. Both attacks are successful. You're not going to find a great depth of water around here, and this is one of the reasons most of the locals try to get there by night.

To get down to the sea, you need to go along a winding path that descends the cliff face. It's quite a walk on the way back up, so try to travel as light as you can. Although this is rocky ground, you won't lose too much gear, so don't over-burden yourself.

I've mentioned cod here but you're also likely to pick up eels and coalfish. Peeler crab, mussel and worm are all top baits.

This is a romantic, remote sort of place to fish and it's a good place to get away from the hurly-burly of the bigger cities. And you're in with a chance of catching a double-figure cod to boot.

Accommodation – details of accommodation available in the area can be obtained from the Tourist Information Centre in Whitby on 01947 602674.

Tackle shops – for more information on the fishing in this area, contact Keith's Sports on 01287 624296 and Whitby Angling Supplies on 01947 603855. The Whitby Angling Club also organises matches here during the winter, mostly in the evenings. They can be contacted on 01947 895429.

Whitby

Whitby is the next major mark as we proceed south. For many years now, Whitby has been a popular wrecking centre, with charter boats travelling upwards of thirty miles out into the North Sea. There have been some huge catches here – including cod to over fifty pounds, along with haddock, whiting, flatfish, ling and mackerel.

The West Pier is a favourite for locals in the winter and holidaymakers in the summer. There are plenty of flatfish and mackerel for the holiday angler, but you'll find a greater number of codling off the East Pier frequenting the rocky bottom.

Saltwick Bay is another cracking area, found just south of Whitby itself. It fishes particularly well in the winter and has easy access, especially after nightfall when the fishing really picks up. The area generally fishes best when a good sea is running. Apart from cod you'll also pick up flounder and the occasional coalfish.

ACCOMMODATION – contact the Tourist Information Centre in Whitby on 01947 602674.
TACKLE SHOPS – Whitby Angling Supplies on 01947 603855 will provide a host of information on this very popular venue.
BOAT HIRE – contact John Brennan on 01947 820320. Whitby Charter Skippers Association is also worth contacting for further information. The telephone number is 01609 780412.

HAYBURN WYKE

The next port of call is Hayburn Wyke. This really is a jewel of a place, remote and largely unfished, except by locals. No wonder it was once notorious as a smugglers' cove. It's in the North York Moors National Park and this makes it a particularly serene area. Hayburn Wyke fishes well throughout the year, but, like so many of these coastal venues, it really comes alive in the winter.

The fishing peaks between December and February, as the truly large cod begin to move in. Real monsters – fish of over twenty pounds – have been taken in the past, but the general run is of plentiful smaller fish of four to six pounds.

Locals use cocktails – any combination of worms, crabs or mussels. A long rock rod, a 7000-sized reel and thirty- to forty-pound line will suffice. Don't worry too much about long casting unless the sea is heavy and you've got to get beyond the surf.

Locals swear by a strong south-easterly, and high water is generally considered the top period. However, the covered conditions mean that you can catch fish either day or night. In fact, make sure that you fish the venue during the hours of light at least for your first two or three visits, so that you can familiarise yourself with the surroundings. Never go to a new area for the first time in the darkness.

Hayburn, which is five miles north of Scarborough, takes just a little bit of finding. Find your way to the Hayburn Wyke Hotel and then look for the pathway to the left. This will takes you through the woods and down to the shoreline.

ACCOMMODATION – contact the Tourist Information Centre in Scarborough on 01723 373333.
TACKLE SHOPS – try Buckley's Angling Supplies in Scarborough on 01723 363202.

SCARBOROUGH

Scarborough is another one of the jewels of the Yorkshire coastline, long famous as a major holiday resort, but also offering intriguing possibilities to the sea angler. Most of the year round, the sea fishing is good and can be undertaken from either a charter boat or from the harbour piers.

The West Pier stands on sandy ground, whereas the East Pier, over rock, generally offers the chance of bigger fish, especially cod and codling. The codling usually come in from August onwards – look for numbers of these on the marks north of the town, especially Robin Hood's Bay. The charter boats hereabouts specialise in great catches of cod, especially as the colder months draw on. There are some big fish around.

ACCOMMODATION – as Scarborough is such an important tourist town, there's a great deal of accommodation available. Contact the Tourist Information Centre on 01723 373333.

TACKLE SHOPS – for further information, contact Buckley's Angling Supplies on 01723 363202.

BOAT HIRE – charter boats on offer include the *Valhalla* on 01723 632083, the *Wandering Star* on 01723 374885 and the *Sea Fisher* on 01723 364640.

FILEY AND BRIDLINGTON

Filey has long been a Mecca for sea anglers, especially the famous Filey Brigg, a ridge of rocks running out into deep water and fishable during most tide and weather conditions. This rocky headland offers natural protection to Filey Bay on the south side of the point. Fish the area at night, especially when there's a good northern wind – you'll find that fish are moving onto the worm bed. Flounders are particularly prevalent.

There's a whole host of marks along Filey Brigg – Ben Storeys, Black Hole Corner, High Nab, Green Rock and so on. Ask the locals for advice. Crab is the top summer bait and cocktails take over in the winter. Codling go very well on ragworm and mussel, especially around Christmas time. Make no mistake, Filey really is a prize on this stretch of coastline.

Just south of Filey, you will find Bridlington. The South Pier is a real favourite with holiday anglers. It is free and offers all the usual summer species to keep the irregular sea angler totally involved. The North Pier is only open in the winter when you'll pick up good codling.

Just a word before we leave this very productive area of the Yorkshire coastline. It does produce some tremendous cod fishing throughout the winter months but there is, as ever, a right and a wrong way to go about approaching it. Talk to the locals. Look at their rigs if you can and see what bait they are using. And keep on the move. If you're not getting fish,

Ragworm

The king ragworm is the most commonly used type of rag in the United Kingdom and attracts just about every fish species that swims. Keeping your rag in perfect condition is quite straightforward. You will usually buy them either in peat or in fine sand. Keep them just slightly damp – a spray bottle filled with seawater is ideal. Wrap them lightly in newspaper and keep them cool – not cold – in the fridge. If that's not possible, then a cold stone floor such as in a garage will serve the same purpose.

- *Most rags sold to the angler are between six and eight inches in length – the ideal length.*
- *Smaller worms will work perfectly in cocktails with crab, shellfish and squid strips.*
- *Really big worms can be cut into sections.*
- *If you've got a really big worm, it is best to hook it in the head and fish it on the drift for bass.*
- *Beads and spoons on the snood above rag help attract flatfish.*
- *Ragworm are much tougher than lug, and generally prove quite resistant to crabs. However, if you do have any problems, put a few turns of fine elastic thread up and down your baited worm. This will give it extra strength.*
- *The best hooks are long shank fine or medium wire patterns.*
- *If you use ragworms extensively, you will find the acidic juices from their bodies will begin to make the flesh on your fingertips sore. To help with any soreness, soak your hands in a bowl of hot water into which you've dissolved half a cupful of salt.*
- *Harbour ragworm – often called muddies – are a smaller member of the family. They are very good for flounder and mullet. They are also perfect for cocktails with most other baits.*
- *White ragworms are a vital part of the match-fishing scene, as they seem to catch fish under the most impossible of circumstances. These valuable worms are best stored in clean sea-water in a fridge.*
- *Small whites are best fished in a bunch – perfect for bass and flounder.*
- *Big whites – snake whites – are the ideal bait for codling after the Christmas period. Don't go without them!*
- *Always remember that ragworm have a nasty pair of pincers and can give you a good old nip. Beware!*

have another battle plan in mind. This means travelling light – a rucksack and perhaps just one rod, a bait bucket and, if you must, a rod rest. During daylight, visit all the areas you might fancy fishing , especially at low water, and look for fish-holding features. The best sea anglers will always have a really good grasp of where they're fishing and what they're doing. Okay, flukes do happen, but for sustained success it's essential to put the time and effort in.

Accommodation – contact the Tourist Information Centre in Filey on 01723 518000.
Tackle shops – if you're planning a visit, it makes sense to pick up top quality information from either Filey Fishing Tackle on 01723 513732 or GB Angling in Scarborough on 01723 374017. Filey Brigg Angling Club also is helpful with advice – contact them on 01723 515981.
Boat hire – from Bridlington, many of the boats go out to Flamborough Head or to the wrecks offshore. Contact I. Taylor on 01262 679434 or J. Jarvis on 01262 604750.

Spurn Head and the Humber Estuary

Spurn Head is a four-mile spit of land that has been created over the years by coastal erosion. It is the last outpost of Yorkshire, curving into the Humber estuary across the water from Cleethorpes. Spurn Head is a major nature reserve and you'll find a great number of birdwatchers in the area, but there's also some brilliant sea fishing.

It can be fished in most conditions for cod, bass, flounder, along with the odd ray and plaice. There is a toll to get onto Spurn, so take change with you. Also, as the area is heavily frequented by tourists, walkers and birdwatchers, especially on summer weekends, do remember to portray our noble sport to the best of your ability.

It's also worth looking further up the estuary from Spurn Head towards Kingston-upon-Hull itself. The area just downstream of the Humber Bridge isn't the prettiest in the world, and the water itself is all stirred up by passing boat traffic and the influx of major rivers, the Trent especially. The fact the water here never runs clear does at least mean the fish feed well both day and night. Concentrate on the Hessle area – almost in the shadow of the bridge itself. Light gear for flounder and eels is a winner, especially during the summer.

Follow the Clive Sullivan Way eastwards and come off where you see a large Cash and Carry – the Makro mark. This is a favourite area for cod, even though it is snaggy and there's a big drop down to the water.

Moving on down the estuary, Bellway Homes, Paull and Old Hall all have their devotees. All produce good fish, winter and summer alike, though the

Hook Choice

A lot of attention is paid to rods, reels, lines and so on, but it's the hook that makes the first contact with the fish and is probably the item of tackle most likely to let you down. Don't be afraid to ask an experienced skipper for advice. He will welcome that much more than lost fish.

- *Sharp, fine wire hooks will penetrate more easily than thick wired hooks. However, fine wire hooks bend under pressure, so you need to think about your target species and your bait. Match anglers are more likely to go for fine wire hooks. Most boat anglers use either medium wire or, occasionally, extra strong, heavy wire hooks. A lot depends on conditions and location.*
- *You can target a big fish in reasonably shallow, snag-free, calm water on a medium wire hook. Hook that same fish over snags or in deep, turbulent water and you'll have to go for heavy wire.*
- *Balance the hook to the bait. You need a hook big enough to hold the bait comfortably, but you don't want the hook hidden up by the bait so that it can't penetrate.*
- *When using large baits, it's a good idea to use bait elastic to tie them to the shank and eye of the hook. This will hold the bait in the position you want it and stop it sliding down towards the point and masking a strike.*
- *A lugworm on a size 4/0 hook is about right. You could thread four or five lugworms, however, on a 4/0 or 5/0.*
- *Always keep your hooks dry and corrosion-free.*

latter two in particular can take a bit of finding. For Paull, take the signs for Withernsea, look for the signpost, turn right and take the small road until you reach the lighthouse. Note that if you're fishing Old Hall, it's quite a walk. You can't drive down the farmer's tracks to the water, so travel light.

Grimsby has long been a commercial fishing centre, but it also offers excellent possibilities along both the Humber and the foreshore. All the usual species are available, with some good codling, especially in the colder months.

Accommodation – contact the Tourist Information Centre in Cleethorpes on 01472 323222.

Tackle shops – for further information, call East Coast Tackle on 01964 535064, Top Sport Angling on 01964 612340, Fred's Fishing Tackle on 01472 352922 or Tight Lines in Cleethorpes on 01472 200400.

Sea-fishing Sites in Ireland

As you know, John, I'm primarily a freshwater fisherman for anything that swims over here in Ireland – pike, trout, rudd, even bream and tench, and you'll find me there. But, like many Irishmen, I can't just ignore the quality of the sea fishing that's on offer. It's simply mind-blowing. What's more, you can enjoy a great deal of it using your normal freshwater gear, so you don't have to be involved in a vast amount of expense if you don't want to specialise too much. Mind you, if it's blue-fin tuna that you're thinking of pursuing, that's a different matter altogether! You're not going to land a creature of a 1,000 pounds – and they do grow that big – with freshwater gear are you? And another thing – the coasts of Ireland are simply stunning. You won't see more glorious scenery anywhere in Europe, or the world come to that. See you there!

RICHIE JOHNSTON, IRISH ANGLER AND AUTHOR

Richie has been very much my guide when it comes to Irish sea fishing and, like all the Irish, he and his friends have proved an absolute fund of detailed knowledge. But that's what you find wherever you travel in Ireland – hosts of the most genuine hospitality and courteousness. I've been travelling to Ireland since the1960s and, believe me, I've never experienced anything but warmth and welcome. Ireland is the perfect destination for any family looking for unspoilt countryside, peace and relaxation away from the stress of modern rat-race life. For the sea angler, the coastline is awesome. It boasts endless variety and limitless potential. You'll find quaint little villages with welcoming olde-worlde pubs and guesthouses. Just a word about transport. Once, getting to Ireland was something of a haul. Now, numerous low-cost flights and relatively inexpensive car hire make journeys easy and cheap. If you wish to take your own car, the high-speed ferries are highly recommended, especially if you're taking children.

DUBLIN

There are many possibilities around Dublin itself, especially with pollack and wrasse. You can try Dalke Island, which is only fifteen minutes by train from the centre of Dublin. Another possibility is the port of Dun Laoghaire, which offers good pollack and bass opportunities. It also provides pier fishing, with dabs and conger in the summer months. You'll find whiting, codling and coalfish coming in during the winter.

Moving a little way down the coast, you come to Greystones in County Wicklow. To get there, just take the N11 south out of Dublin. There's a little harbour in the village, but if you turn right you'll come to the beach. This used to be one of the centres of Irish cod fishing, but catches have faltered in recent years. The great thing about Greystones – and the reason why it is such a centre for competitions – is the huge amount and variety of fish in the area. You can fish it almost year round, with just a quiet period at the end of the winter. In the summer, codling, bass, coleys, pollack and sea trout all show well. Coleys and codling feature from autumn throughout the winter. All the usual baits succeed – peeler crab, lug, rag, mussels and sand eels. However, don't neglect spinning, especially when the sea is relatively clear. It's a cracking method for sea trout and bass, especially.

Sea trout can be fished all along the south coast, as well as huge shoals of mullet. These seek out any estuary or trickle of fresh water and sometimes you'll find vast shoals, but, as ever, they can be difficult to tempt.

ACCOMMODATION – phone the Tourist Board in Dublin on 00 353 (0)1 6057700.

TACKLE SHOPS – contact Patrick Cleere in Dublin on 00 353 (0)1 6772351.

BOAT HIRE – there are plenty of charter boats available in the area; for details, phone 00 353 (0)404 68751.

CORK AND KINSALE

Cork City itself offers some great sport, both inside and outside the harbour. Kinsale, a little to the west, boasts a fine natural harbour and has been a famous Irish angling centre for many decades. Kinsale is a lovely town with a long-standing fishing history, offering five hotels, at least thirty guest houses and, apparently, over forty pubs and restaurants! So, although the town is small, it has a friendly atmosphere and there's a great deal for everyone to do. The Castle Park Marina fleet is extremely modern. High-speed boats (with a forty-mile offshore licence) mean that anglers can try out several different hot marks in a single day. There's deep water close into the town – twenty minutes or so – so huge amounts of time are not lost in travelling. There are big reefs and plenty of wrecks,

including the *Lusitania*. The area offers just about every fish that swims the sea, including some very good blue shark fishing.

A little further west you come to the delightful village of Courtmacsherry, which has all the sea angler could want – along with a beautiful setting to boot. The reef fishing is superb, with some huge common skate in residence – fish to nearly 200 pounds have been caught. You can pick up conger from the pier, and mullet and tremendous bass and flounder off the beaches. It's a great place for the whole family – there's lots of exploring to be done and you can always have a bash at the mullet that throng the area around the pier. Try very small pieces of mackerel on a size ten, for example. You can actually watch the meat going down amongst them and free-line. Or you could use a small float. It's the sort of fishing that children adore.

ACCOMMODATION – try the Cork Tourist Information Centre on 00 353 (0)21 4273251.
TACKLE SHOPS – contact the Cobh Angling Centre in Cork on 00 353 (0)21 1813417 for tackle and for advice and contacts in the Cork area.
BOAT HIRE – ring the Cobh Angling Centre (see above). For information on blue shark fishing, contact the Castle Park Marina Centre on 00 353 (0)21 774959. Also try Mark Gannon in Courtmacsherry on 00 353 (0)23 46427; Mark is very much one of the local experts and offers both accommodation, charter-boat hire and unparalleled knowledge of the area.

CAHERSIVEEN

The south west is where everything really begins to take off. How about the little village of Cahersiveen in south-west Kerry? It's just north of the enchanting town of Waterville and is set in really beautiful countryside on the famous Ring of Kerry. It's an all-round sea-angling holiday destination. It's close to Valentia Island, but there is a myriad of small islands, rocks, jetties, harbours – perfect for shore fishing and boat fishing alike.

The boat fishing here is very well organised and productive. And there are lots of pollack to be caught close in. Cuckoo and ballan wrasse proliferate, along with plenty of mackerel. You'll find coley, ling, bull huss, haddock, cod, plaice and even skate and shark in the deeper water. What more could you possibly ask for? And if it's conger you fancy, try the pier after dark.

Shore fishing is brilliant. Fishing from the pier is great, but also try the road bridge and the old stone fort. Coonanna Harbour also offers a tremendous amount of opportunity for pollack, wrasse and dogfish. Check out the mullet and the very big bass. You will also find a lot of the shore fishing blissfully unexploited, as most of the locals tend to go out in boats. Be prepared to do a bit of exploring.

ACCOMMODATION – contact the Irish Tourist Board on 00 353 (0)20 74933201; they have an exhaustive list of accommodation in the area. Highly recommended is the Reenard House Bed and Breakfast on 00 353 (0)66 9472752 – a lovely place with great views.

TACKLE SHOPS AND BOAT HIRE – as far as the fishing goes, the Anchor Bar is the centre for everything that goes on – bar, tackle shop, meeting place and charter-boat hire centre! Hugh Maguire on 00 353 (0)66 9472049 can help with boat arrangements.

DINGLE AND TRALEE

Beautiful Dingle Bay can be found just to the north of Cahersiveen. One of the most popular places to fish from the shore here is Clogher Head, on the north side of the bay. To get there, follow the road out of Dingle for Smerwick Harbour. Drive through the village of Ballyferriter and carry on for a couple of miles. The cove is signposted. There's a headland about a mile away with a car-park overlooking the small beach. It's a really good rock-fishing venue, and the sandy cove itself can produce good sport at times. You'll pick up specimen wrasse and pollack from the rocks. There are also huss and conger eels. The sandy beach throws up flounder, dab, dogfish and plaice. It's a beautiful area, best fished from April through to October – fitting in nicely with the holiday season. Do take great care when you are fishing the rocks, and don't think of going down there if there's an onshore wind or a big swell – it could prove dangerous.

Moving up the coast again, we come to the popular Tralee Bay and the famous little fishing village of Fenit. Fenit is well sheltered, in common with many of the little ports in this fascinating part of the world. The boat fishing is spectacular. June to September is tremendous for skate and the shallow water inside Tralee Bay offers marvellous fishing for both tope and monkfish. May and June are peak times. It's common to use a rubby bag and a mackerel flapper as bait. If the wind is kind, you can travel far out, but if it's stormy, you can just tuck into the bay itself and enjoy some cracking sport there. The shore fishing is also superb. Monkfish are possible and the bass fishing is excellent. You can even, if you're lucky, pick up common skate from the pier! So if boat fishing isn't for you, there are other possibilities!

ACCOMMODATION – in Dingle, contact the Tourist Information Centre on 00 353 (0)62 61333 or try the Pax House on 00 353 (0)66 9151518. In Tralee, contact the Tourist Information Centre on 00 353 (0)66 21288 or try the Rosedale Lodge on 00 353 (0)66 7125320. In Fenit, Godley's Hotel is the centre for everything – you can contact them on 00 353 (0)66 36108.

TACKLE SHOPS – tackle can be bought at the Dingle Marina (see below).

BOAT HIRE – contact the Dingle Marina on 00 353 (0)66 59947.

KILRUSH

The Shannon estuary has some great possibilities, and the town of Kilrush is particularly popular. There's some superb pier fishing offering conger, flounder and dogfish. However, the shark-fishing possibilities are enormous and so it pays to consider getting afloat.

Kilrush certainly merits the support of sea anglers everywhere. Several million pounds have been spent on creating a lock system to trap the flow of the Shannon and to give access from the spanking new marina out onto the sea. What you have now at Kilrush is a safe base – even in the winter – on the exposed west coast of Ireland, along with the security and the facilities of a purpose-built marina.

The fishing is absolutely superb. There are plenty of tope, which provide great sport on lighter gear. Thornbacks proliferate, along with bull huss, common skate, conger and blue shark. There are endless well-known marks such as Scattery Island and Carrigaholt Bay. Excellent stuff.

ACCOMMODATION – Shannon Angling on 00 353 (0)65 52031 offers both boat charter and accommodation.

TACKLE SHOPS – contact Michael O'Sullivan on 00 353 (0)65 51071 or Michael Clancy on 00 353 (0)65 51107.

BOAT HIRE – try Atlantic Adventures on 00 353 (0)65 52133 or Shannon Angling (as above). The Kilrush Creek Marina on 00 353 (0)65 52072 is the hub of everything.

CONNEMARA

Moving up to Connemara, you can't do better than the town of Clifden – really picturesque, great bars, great scenery and some great fishing. There are really good possibilities for deep-sea shark fishing. Another excellent place is Westport, in the south-east corner of the famous Clew Bay. Clew Bay is sheltered by the wonderful Achill and Clare Islands. This is a huge bay dotted with some 300 tiny islands, so there's always shelter for those wanting to take a boat out.

The fishing is quite magnificent. Inside Clew Bay, you'll find ray, tope, skate and turbot. Move a little out of the bay and you'll come into the grounds of cod, pollack, coalfish and the occasional John Dory. You've got to go heavy for the skate hereabouts because they really grow large – it's wise to use fifty- to eighty-pound plus gear, with perhaps 8/0 hooks. Remember that it's illegal to kill skate and all must be tagged and returned. You can go a bit lighter for the tope fishing – thirty-pound class should suffice, with 6/0 hooks. You'll need a wire trace and a long leader of very heavy nylon. If tope begin to twist, then lighter lines can go with a vengeance.

Fishing for Tope

Tope are a free-running species, so you will get a tremendous all-action fight from them. Ireland is one of the really hot areas for tope fishing.

• When you are fishing over a rugged reef or a place where there are snags or very strong currents, thirty- or even fifty-pound class tackle is advisable.

• If the water is shallow and sandy without big tidal pushes, very heavy freshwater gear will mostly suffice. Use heavy carp or pike rods, along with fifteen- or twenty-pound line.

• Mono is generally considered preferable to braid for tope fishing. The elasticity of mono, often considered a drawback in many forms of sea fishing, is actually good when you're pursuing very fast-swimming tope. Line stretch is often a blessing, especially for the inexperienced angler.

• Rigs: you needn't use more than twelve to eighteen inches of wire to cope with a tope's teeth. A few feet of heavy-duty nylon – sixty to 100 pounds – make up the leader. Hooks should be 6/0 or 8/0, depending on bait.

• Bait: a whole dead mackerel can produce big fish, but also use strips of the fish and try and leave the guts exposed. Cut off the tail of any dead fish to stop it twisting in the tide, looking suspicious and kinking the line. Calamari squid provide a really good alternative bait.

• Timing the strike: tope have often been thought of much like pike – they run, stop, turn the bait and then take it in. For this reason, tope angling in the past was often built around the longest delayed strike. This resulted in deep hooking and dead fish. Far better to hit a fish soon after the run develops. Timing is largely down to experience. Strike early with the first run and, if you miss, just delay a few seconds for the next and so on. A lost fish is better than a deeply hooked dead one.

• Play the fish calmly and with determination. Don't let the tope dominate the fight or it will simply tire itself out.

• Once in the boat, don't let a tope thrash about on the bottom. A carp-style unhooking mat is a very good idea here for the fish's welfare. Try to kneel over the fish so that it's between your legs – it's head, obviously, pointing away from you. A T-bar disgorger is necessary to get beyond the teeth and to have enough grip to get the hook from the tough skin. Try to have somebody else keeping control of the tail.

• If you must take a photograph, make sure that you support the weight of its body cavity with your arm to avoid damaging the fish internally.

• Above all, get that fish back as quickly as possible. Tope are coming back big time; only our care for them will see this promising trend continue.

Check out Tramore Bay, not a particularly well-marked place, but one that offers fantastic tope fishing, especially around Claggan Island. Tramore is attractive to tope because of the huge numbers of flatfish it contains. There are also mussel beds to the west, home to giant monkfish. Multiple catches of tope around Claggan Island are not unusual, with some big fish amongst them. The Central Fisheries Board has had a tagging operation in place for some time now, and catch and release is certainly the way forward.

This is excellent sport – the water is shallow and often clear with endless inlets and bays to explore. And in such skinny water, don't the fish go! Expect long runs and breathtaking fights, especially on light gear.

This part of Eire is now easily accessible. Of course, you can still do the mammoth drive across England, ferry cross the Irish Sea and then drive the breadth of Ireland. Alternatively, you can fly into Knock Airport in no time at all.

Accommodation – for angler-friendly accommodation, contact Josephine and Mattie Geraghty on 00 353 (0)97 85741.

Boat hire – the area is well set up with enterprising skippers. Try Micky Lavelle on 00 353 (0)97 85669. For deep-sea shark fishing, contact J. Brittain on 00 353 (0)95 21073 or J. Ryan on 00 353 (0)95 21069.

Donegal

Let's move north even further, up to the splendid county of Donegal. Downings is really beginning to make a reputation for itself, just inland from the famous Tory Island. There's tremendous shore fishing around here, with piers, rocks, estuaries and beaches. The pier offers conger, especially on a mackerel head at night. You'll also find flounder, plaice and dab. If you move westwards from the pier, you'll come across several rock marks. Expect thornback, ray, flatfish, pollack and mackerel – superb spinning opportunities during the summer months.

Close by is the wonderful beach of Tra Na Rossan. This offers brilliant September and early October opportunities with bass. Try to the left of the beach, tight to the rocks – especially on the early flood tide. You'll pick up flatfish all the year, with plaice quite common from June through to October. Also expect thornback and spotted ray and a few turbot in the early autumn. Huss come close into those rocks at night.

Going back to Downings, it would be totally wrong not to mention the most exciting development of all, one that has all tongues wagging – the return of the blue-fin tuna, the so called 'tunny' that dominated the big game-fishing psyche back in the 1930s and 1940s. In those days, most of the fishing took place on the east coast of England, but the overfishing of mackerel shoals drove these monstrous, beautiful creatures away. Nowadays, however, there are signs that the coast of Donegal could be the new stamping ground for people wishing to test themselves against these spectacular fish.

Much of this has to do with the North Atlantic drift, which warms the coastal waters as it brushes the west coast of Ireland on its way to Scotland. The big fish follow their prey and come close in to the coast of Donegal. Mid-August is, arguably, the best time of all but the season does run much earlier and later. You're talking about big fish – certainly 300- and 400-pounders, but tuna of 500 to 1,000 pounds are always possible. For this reason, you must use heavy-duty gear. We're talking a 130-pound test with 16/0 hooks allied with 300- or even 400-pound traces. These fish battle brutally: they'll pick up your mackerel bait with a screaming run and then give a wonderful fight. They run long and hard, always pushing deeper. Okay, you won't see them tail-walking, but that doesn't take anything from the wonder of the fight. These are fish that just never give in.

What you don't really want – for your comfort as much as anything else – is stormy weather. You will often find these massive fish pretty close in, certainly within four or five miles of the shore. The mackerel are the key to finding them, being the major prey of the tuna shoals. Of course, you're never quite sure at what level the mackerel are running and where the fish will be feeding, though on some blessed occasions you will actually see the tuna hit into shoals of mackerel on the surface. Could there be a more exciting sight on the seas?

It's most common to use balloons as floats and set your baits – live mackerel – at differing depths. For example, work some on the surface, others at mid-water and others down deep, just off the bottom, in fact. A preferred method is to use a live mackerel and troll it very slowly behind the boat. Be warned, you'll be in no doubt when a tuna is on – prepare for absolute fireworks.

Derek Noble is really the expert on tuna fishing in Ireland. He reckons that late August through to October is the very best time for these amazing fish. They probably hang on later than that, but weather, of course, is a major problem. It's taken Derek quite a long time to get to grips with the fish and, even though he was seeing them, it was a while before he began to experience hook-ups. Live mackerel are good, but artificials also can work well when, like Derek, you know what you're doing.

There's certainly no shortage of fish. Some of the groups are only five or six strong, but thirty to forty is probably more common. And, just occasionally, you will see hundreds, with areas of water twice the size of a football pitch just erupting with these big fish – and I mean big. The average size of the tuna that Derek is taking at the moment is something over 300 pounds – and that's nothing! In September 2001, he saw a colossal fish come out of the water about seventy yards away from his boat – a fish well over 400 pounds. This is really thrilling stuff and you don't necessarily have to hook into a fish to appreciate the day if you see one as close as this. As Derek says, to watch the sea-birds shear off the surface as these colossal fish plough through the waves is a sight never to be forgotten.

One thing that Derek stresses is a catch-and-release policy. It's important to be seen to be doing our bit for the future and although tuna can be valuable, it has to be taken in and iced as quickly as possible – not something you want to do if you're intent on enjoying a day's sport. So, put the monetary side right out of your mind and just enjoy one of the most incredible sport-fishing experiences in the world today. And it's virtually on our doorstep!

ACCOMMODATION – contact the Tourist Information Office on 00 353 (0)7161201.

TACKLE SHOPS – try Erinn Tackle in nearby Ramelton on 00 353 (0)87639 3933 for all the latest information.

BOAT HIRE – contact E. O'Callaghan on 00 353 (0)7331288, Brian McGilloway on 00 353 (0)7331144 or Antony Doherty on 00 353 (0)7331079.

PORTRUSH AND RATHLIN ISLAND

The availability of sea fishing in Northern Ireland has been promoted on a huge scale over the last few years. The Northern Irish Tourist Board has recognised that angling is a very important part of tourism in Ireland and has worked diligently to promote it. With excellent results, too, – both on the fresh- and sea-water fronts. Southern Ireland often grabs the attention when it comes to all manner of fishing, but the north shouldn't be forgotten – certainly for sea fish. It boasts hundreds of miles of staggeringly beautiful coastline, unpolluted and unexploited. There are well over twenty species of sea fish regularly caught, including all the favourites such as bass, tope, shark and skate.

Portrush is a favourite area near the mouth of Lough Foyle and the River Bann. The town offers good pier and beach fishing and there are conger in the harbour itself.

Moving round the coast, we come to the magical Rathlin Island, situated a little way off the coast opposite the town of Ballycastle. This offers really good wreck fishing in Church Bay and some tremendous sport with just about everything.

BRAID

As technology moves on, braid becomes ever more efficient, offering an alternative to nylon. It is perfect for signalling bites... the slightest tap bucks the rod over. With its reduced diameter it's excellent for holding deep water in strong tides with a minimum of lead. It's also limp and doesn't spook the fish, but there can be problems.

• Knots and braid haven't always gone well together, so obey any knotting instructions that come with the line. Use a doubled length of line for all knots. Dab superglue on the knots for added strength.

• Put the backing on the reel as tight as it will go to avoid bedding-in. Load the braid itself under pressure and not just from a free spool. This will probably require a friend to help out.

• Casting is easy with a fixed-spool reel, but not as straightforward with a multiplier. Presuming you are using a multiplier, don't go too fine or the spool's braking will cause a problem. If this is proving difficult consider using the new forms of coated braid, which can help.

• Start your cast with maximum braking force – for example, two big brake locks and the use of thick oil. Make sure your cast is smooth and not snatched.

• Use a longer shock leader than usual – say ten or twelve turns round the spool, at least.

• Braid comes into its own particularly when spinning or float fishing with a delicate rod and fixed-spool reel. Casting is enhanced, and there is less chance of breaking up on fine lines.

• Always check your braid very carefully for any evidence of wear and tear. It might seem indestructible, and often proves to be so when you're pulling for a break, however, when you go to unhook that elusive monster conger it can snap like cotton! If you're in any doubt, and you fear that the line may be fraying, then, expensive though it may be, re-spool and start again.

• My own opinion? I'm going to be controversial here: experience in many different types of water all over the world leads me to say that if you are fishing over particularly rocky and punishing ground then you are possibly better off considering ordinary nylon. In my experience, nylon is that little bit more resistant to the chafing that harsh ground gives it and is less likely to snap unexpectedly. Braid does have many advantages, but the measure of unpredictability in tough environments casts doubt over it in my mind.

ACCOMMODATION – contact the Tourist Information Centre in Portrush on 028 7082 3333.
TACKLE SHOPS – Joe Mullan is a mine of information; contact him at his tackle shop at 74 Main Street, Portrush.
BOAT HIRE – Geoff Farrow in Portstewart (close to Portrush) offers boats for hire – contact him on 01265 836622. Contact C. McCaughan on 01265 762074 for details about boats in the Rathlin Island area.

BANGOR AND DONAGHADEE

Just over ten miles from Belfast city itself, you'll find the town of Bangor situated on Belfast Lough. This lough offers some really sheltered, prolific fishing. You can dig your own lugworm and expect to catch good flatfish, along with codling and whiting in season. There are even some turbot.

Just south of Bangor, you will come to Donaghadee, which offers pier and rock fishing for pollack and codling and huge numbers of mackerel in the summer months. The Rigg sandbar is a good mark off shore, offering mixed sport.

ACCOMMODATION – contact the Tourist Information Centre in Bangor on 028 9127 0069.
TACKLE SHOPS – try Trap and Tackle on 01247 458515.
BOAT HIRE – contact Mr Nelson on 01247 883403 for wreck and reef fishing.

STRANGFORD LOUGH

Strangford Lough offers some superb boat fishing and is sheltered from all but the very worst of the winds. There's excellent skate and tope fishing, but note that both fish are protected and must be returned alive. There's some very good wrasse around the entrance to the lough where the water is deep.

One of the beauties of sea fishing in Northern Ireland is that, to some extent, you are still, even in the 21st century, something of a pioneer. Okay, the locals and some visitors in the know are well aware of the possibilities but even today the vast majority of visiting anglers still head for the south. This can be a mistake when you consider the big opportunities and the warm welcome that the north extends.

ACCOMMODATION – contact the Tourist Information Centre in Bangor on 028 9127 0069.
TACKLE SHOPS – contact Country Sports at nearby Newtownards on 01247 812585.
BOAT HIRE – charter boats are available in the nearby town of Portaferry – contact Mr Rogers on 01247 728297 for details.

Author's Acknowledgements

Thank you to Carol Selwyn for her unstinting efforts during the research, typing and checking stages. Thank you also to Daniela and Anne for checking the fine detail.

My heartfelt thanks also go to Robin Armstrong, Bernard Bishop, Bob Church, Christopher and Maddie, David Cooper, Leslie Crawford, Bernard Double, Keith Elliott, Clive Gammon, Ross Gardner, Frank Guttfield, Steve Harper, Matt Hayes, Gordon Heath, Bob James, Martin James, Charles Jardine, Richie Johnston, David Judge, Martin Locke, Robert and Stephanie Maloney, Eric Marsh, Bob Moss, Andy Nicholson, all at the Northern Irish Tourist Board, John Nunn, the late Arthur Ogilsby, David Overy, Dave Plummer, Charles Plunkett, Jan Porter, Joe Reed, Michael Robins, Reel-screamer Row, Paul Seaman, Carol Selwyn, Mike Shortt, Mike Smith, Peter Smith, Charlie Stuart, Peter Suckling, Mike Taylor, Terry Thomas, Chris Turnbull, Anne Vossbark, Christopher West, Jim Whippy, 'Woody', Roger Wyndham Barnes and the late Dermott Wilson.